IN THE SHADOW OF THE VIRGIN

JEWS, CHRISTIANS, AND MUSLIMS

FROM THE ANCIENT TO THE MODERN WORLD

Series Editors
R. STEPHEN HUMPHREYS, WILLIAM CHESTER JORDAN, AND PETER SCHÄFER

IN THE SHADOW
OF THE VIRGIN

INQUISITORS, FRIARS, AND *CONVERSOS*
IN GUADALUPE, SPAIN

Gretchen D. Starr-LeBeau

PRINCETON UNIVERSITY PRESS

PRINCETON AND OXFORD

Library of Congress Cataloging-in-Publication Data

Starr-LeBeau, Gretchen D.
In the shadow of the Virgin : inquisitors, friars, and conversos in Guadalupe, Spain /
Gretchen D. Starr-LeBeau.
p.   cm — (Jews, Christians, and Muslims from the ancient to the modern world)
Includes bibliographical references and index.
ISBN 0-691-09683-X (alk. paper)
1. Jews—Spain—Guadalupe—History.   2. Marranos—Spain—Guadalupe—
History.   3. Jewish Christians—Spain—Guadalupe—History.   4. Jews—
Persecutions—Spain—Guadalupe.   5. Inquisition—Spain—Guadalupe—
History.   6. Guadalupe (Spain)—Ethnic relations.   I. Title.   II. Series.

DS135.S7 S72 2002
946'.28—dc21   2002025292

British Library Cataloging-in-Publication Data is available

This book has been composed in Dante Typefaces

Printed on acid-free paper. ∞

www.pupress.princeton.edu

Printed in the United States of America

1   3   5   7   9   10   8   6   4   2

CONTENTS

MAPS AND ILLUSTRATIONS

MAPS

ILLUSTRATIONS

ACKNOWLEDGMENTS

AT MANY POINTS while writing this book, historical work seemed intensely solitary, and so it is; yet this project, like all histories, could not have been completed without the assistance, guidance, and support of very many people, both here and abroad. Sabine MacCormack was present from the very beginning of this project, suggesting Guadalupe as a site to investigate and supervising the earlier incarnation of this project as a dissertation. Her advice was, and is, both sage and eminently practical, and she has taught me to be a better researcher and a better writer. Diane Hughes provided helpful comments throughout my graduate career, and Miriam Bodian has continued to offer useful advice. A number of institutions provided the financial support necessary to carry out the research for this project, and I would like to acknowledge my gratitude to the University of Michigan, the Andrew Mellon Foundation, the Fulbright/Hays and Spanish government program, the National Endowment for the Humanities, and the University of Kentucky Office for Research and Graduate Studies.

I am grateful, too, for the opportunity to contemplate before revising. A number of people contributed to this process by reading and commenting on various revisions and drafts. William B. Taylor read closely through the entire dissertation and made invaluable comments. Peter Laipson recorded comments made at the dissertation defense; this record, as well as his own comments, were an important starting point in the revision process. Dan Gargola, Elka Klein, and Karen Petrone all read and commented on various chapters. Elka also fielded several questions on details of Jewish observance. Mary E. Giles has not read any of this book, but working with her closely on another project helped me to improve my prose style (such as it is) immensely. Holly Grout and Keri Manning watched my infant daughter during a critical phase of the revisions, allowing me the opportunity to contemplate at all. Several women in the History Department at the University of Kentucky read and commented on what is now the introduction to this book, helping me clarify what I was trying to say. Without their help, writing this book would have been much more difficult. Judy Fugate at the W. T. Young Library at the University of Kentucky helped me get books I needed, as did the long-suffering Interlibrary Loan office. Dick Gilbreath produced the maps, the Guadalupe map being a particular challenge. Joe Jones read through the penultimate version of the entire manuscript, giving me a number of suggestions and saving me from many awkward or inaccurate translations, and Sherry Velasco and Aníbal Biglieri helped me with my translation of the trial at the end of this book. Of course, final responsibility for all translations is mine. Ray LeBeau also read through the entire manuscript. As always, his advice was cogent, kind, and on the mark. Mary Elizabeth Perry and Teófilo Ruiz generously gave of their time to make detailed and helpful comments about the manuscript; I have not always followed their advice, but this book is definitely the better for their criticisms. At Princeton University Press, Brigitta van Rheinberg and Carol Hagan have been most helpful, and William C. Jordan has been equally encouraging.

The number of people I have to thank in Spain is legion. Archivists at the Archivo Histórico Nacional and at the Raros y Manuscritos room at the Biblioteca Nacional, both in Madrid; at El Escorial; and at the Real Monasterio de Nuestra Señora de Guadalupe in Guadalupe (Extremadura) all provided material assistance. Father Sebastián García, OFM, and Antonio Ramiro Chico in Guadalupe were especially important to the completion of this project. Without Fr. García's willingness to let me see a number of sensitive materials, I could never have written this book. My friends from Guadalupe know who they are, and there is no way I could list them all. I can only thank them, once again, for their graciousness and generosity in welcoming me into their homes and their lives. In Madrid, Dña. Beatriz Fernández de Bobadilla González de Aguilar and her son, Miguel Hernández Fernández de Bobadilla, were my first contacts and first friends in Spain, almost ten years ago now, but I still treasure their friendship. Jerónimo Iñiguez was another early friend who continues to make me feel welcome whenever I am in town.

Closer to home, my family has helped shape me and this book into our present forms. My grandparents, with their love of history and of family, particularly my grandfather, William L. Starr, who early shared his love of reading and writing with me; my parents, Bill and Karen Starr, who helped me learn to read; my sister, Heather; and my children have all made my life the richer. My affection for, and my debt to, my husband Ray beggar description; this book, with whatever merits it may possess, is for him.

IN THE SHADOW OF THE VIRGIN

INTRODUCTION

On June 11, 1485, at the pilgrimage town of Guadalupe in western Spain, the Holy Office of the Inquisition executed Alonso de Paredes as a heretic. Paredes was one of the first people tried in Guadalupe, in one of Fernando and Isabel's first ad hoc inquisitorial courts. His case, however, was unusual. The Holy Office of the Inquisition was established by the crown to root out apostasy among Jewish converts and their descendants (known as New Christians, or *conversos*), but the summary of Paredes's trial mentions no Jewish practices whatsoever, simply stating that he had been found to be a heretic and apostate. Unlike in other trial summaries, Alonso de Paredes (a New Christian) was not accused of leading Jewish services in his home, or of praying "in a Jewish fashion," or of failing to observe Christian dietary rules. Rather, Paredes almost certainly attracted the attention of the inquisitors for another reason: the economic and political threat he posed to the friars who both ran the town and helped manage the inquisitorial trials. Paredes was a wealthy cloth merchant and a force to be reckoned with. Only a few years before, he and several other converso merchants had tried to establish a monopoly in town; once, he had attacked the Jeronymite friars' tax collector; and the evidence suggests that he was involved in an attempt to bribe the friars to elect a prior more sympathetic to his concerns.

Alonso's life and death at the hands of the inquisitors is revealing of more than his own tribulations, however. His history, and the history of Guadalupe, shed much light on Spain's transformation from the late medieval to the early modern period. A close study of the town of Guadalupe reveals two interrelated points: first, that the Inquisition's investigation of conversos reshaped religious and ethnic identity; and second, that this refashioned identity transformed local political conflicts, thus altering the exercise of local and royal authority. By demonstrating the contingent nature of religious identity in fifteenth-century Spain, we can demystify the sources of inquisitorial power by locating them in the ability of the Holy Office to construct oppositions—and thus potential sites of power—out of ambiguities. That this ability could be employed by local as well as royal officials, and even to some extent by other residents of the community, meant that the Inquisition could, from its earliest appearance as an arm of the emerging Spanish state, be used to establish and extend royal and local political authority. Thus, religious identity and political authority were contemporaneously and mutually constructed—each emerged out of engagement with the other.

This book's argument develops in three parts: first, it examines in close detail the complex range of practices of New Christians in the context of Old Christian communities. Second, it connects Christians' contested religious identity with the nascent and malleable power of the Inquisition. And third, it traces exactly how local and royal officials deployed inquisitorial power for their own ends. In the process, the work moves from traditional microhistory to the interrelation of local and proto-national concerns. In this history, the Virgin's shrine in Guadalupe emerges as a crucial site—a prominent element in the propaganda of Fernando and Isabel, and the stage on which the transformative conflicts among the crown, local officials, the church, and conversos like Alonso de Paredes were played out.

The first part of this argument—that religious identity in late-medieval and early modern Spain was negotiated, rather than emerging from simple either/or categories—is best seen at the local level, in a town like Guadalupe. Guadalupe was admittedly unique; the cult of the Virgin of Guadalupe, located there, transfigured the religious landscape of the community and the peninsula.[1] When Isabel and Fernando's key Jewish tax-farmer and advisor, Don Abraham Seneor, converted to Christianity on June 15, 1492, he traveled to Guadalupe with his king and queen to do it. A few years later, on July 29, 1496, Christopher Columbus brought two Taíno Indians from the Caribbean to the Virgin of Guadalupe to have them baptized as Christians, and to thank the Virgin for her protection on his voyages. Columbus was not alone in his pilgrimage to the Virgin's shrine. Pilgrims of all social ranks traveled to her shrine from throughout the Iberian peninsula and beyond, making it the most popular pilgrimage site in fifteenth-century Spain. Many presumably stayed on, contributing to the town's rapid growth and somewhat fluid social hierarchies during the fifteenth century. And the presence of over 120 friars certainly colored local devotional practices, like lay religious brotherhoods and processions, in ways unfamiliar to many Iberians of the period. Religiously, economically, socially, even politically, Guadalupe was a "company town" in the service and shadow of the Virgin of Guadalupe.

Still, in many ways, Guadalupe was typical of late-medieval and early modern Iberian towns. As in so many late-medieval towns, residents

---

[1] This is a different advocation of the Virgin from the better-known Virgin of Guadalupe of Mexico. The latter Guadalupe was named by conquistadors from Extremadura.

and local lords—in this case the friars—entered into sharp debate over local governance. Townspeople struggled for more independent governing authority, while the friars attempted to consolidate their power. Local uprisings were a fact of life in Guadalupe in the later Middle Ages, as they were in so many towns. Religiously, too, Guadalupe shared characteristics with other Castilian towns of the period. As elsewhere in the peninsula, religious rites, processions, and other rituals marked out the year. Lay brotherhoods or confraternities tended to the poor and to the spiritual needs of their own members, encouraging lay devotional practices similar to those practiced across Spain. The devout rubbed shoulders with the profane, the curious with the uninterested. Discussions and debates about what practices and attitudes signified a devout Christian identity were common among the heterogeneous community of merchants, pilgrims, travelers, and locals. Furthermore, Guadalupe had a significant minority population of conversos—about 5 percent. This was not unlike other towns in Spain, whose Jewish populations had declined, but whose descendants remained behind.

It is these conversos who highlight the negotiated quality of religious identity in fifteenth-century Spain. Following a series of riots and anti-Jewish preaching in the peninsula in 1391, vast numbers of Jews converted to Christianity. Many of these conversions were forced, though as time went on others converted somewhat more freely. The social status and economic privileges of Christians appealed to some Jews, while anxiety about the future of Jews in Iberia influenced others. Whatever the reason, Iberian kingdoms were increasingly faced with a large and growing number of converted Jews with questionable loyalty to their new faith. The social, cultural, and political problems generated by friction between some so-called Old Christians and this new, partially assimilated but distinct population would plague Iberians for generations.

Not surprisingly, the religiosity of Jewish converts to Christianity and their descendants has attracted the sustained attention of scholars for many years. In part, this is because of inherent human interest in "secret lives" or double identity. But this research also has origins in a more specifically Jewish interest in conversos as an example of Jewish oppression, assimilation, and maintenance of cultural distinctiveness— all issues of great concern in the modern world. Many scholars, most notably Yitzhak Baer and his student Haim Beinart, have argued that New Christians were Christian in name only—that profound links to Jews and Judaism persisted for generations, and that those executed on orders of the Inquisition "went as martyrs to the stake."[2] More recently,

---

[2] Haim Beinart, *Conversos on Trial: The Inquisition in Ciudad Real* (Jerusalem: Magnes Press, 1981), 285; see also Yitzhak Baer, *A History of the Jews in Christian Spain*, vol. 2

David Gitlitz and Renée Levine Melammed have developed more complex depictions of conversos in their work, though they, too, seem at times to envision a coherent ideology and community, and heroic crypto-Jews.[3]

Other scholars, particularly Benzion Netanyahu, Norman Roth, and more recently Henry Kamen, have argued that New Christians were entirely assimilated until Christians hostile to Jews used the Inquisition to fabricate converso devotion to Judaism. Netanyahu has argued that the Inquisition was the product of a fundamentally racist society, and that Jews were innocent of the spurious charges brought against them.[4] Kamen, in a similar but slightly different vein, argues that descendants from the first generation of conversos—those converted after 1391—became, by the end of the fifteenth century, genuine if not devout Christians. Only after 1492 and the expulsion of the Jews from Spain (and the conversion of many) did real Judaizing emerge.[5] Norman Roth, though he disagrees with Netanyahu in many respects, echoes the argument that conversos "were no longer to be considered part of the Jewish people in any way."[6]

Between these extremes of genuine and feigned assimilation, other scholars, including I. S. Révah and, more recently, Mark Meyerson, Pilar Huerga Criado, and Yirmiyahu Yovel, have begun to consider alternatives to these stark models. As early as the 1950s, Révah was exploring the range of practices among New Christians, while Meyerson and Huerga Criado have both contributed to a new historiography that neither glorifies conversos nor demonizes Old Christians.[7] David Niren-

---

(Philadelphia: Jewish Publication Society, 1966, repr. 1992), 424–425. The passage begins, "*Conversos* and Jews were one people. . . ."

[3] See David Gitlitz, *Secrecy and Deceit: The Religion of the Crypto-Jews* (Philadelphia: Jewish Publication Society, 1996), and Renée Levine Melammed, *Heretics or Daughters of Israel? The Crypto-Jewish Women of Castile* (Oxford: Oxford University Press, 1999). The term "crypto-Jew" seems problematic to me, since it implies a coherent religious ideology and clear-cut distinction between those observing Jewish law and assimilated New Christians.

[4] These arguments are presented in *The Marranos of Spain: From the Late Fourteenth to the Early Sixteenth Century According to Contemporary Hebrew Sources*, 3d ed. (Ithaca: Cornell University Press, 1999); and *The Origins of the Inquisition in Fifteenth Century Spain* (New York: Random House, 1995).

[5] Henry Kamen, *The Spanish Inquisition: A Historical Revision* (New Haven: Yale University Press, 1997), especially chap. 3.

[6] Norman Roth, *Conversos, Inquisition, and the Expulsion of the Jews from Spain* (Madison: University of Wisconsin Press, 1995), xii.

[7] See I. S. Révah, *Spinoza et le Dr. Juan de Prado* (Paris: Mouton, 1959); Mark Meyerson, "Aragonese and Catalan Jewish Converts at the Time of the Expulsion," *Jewish History* 1–2 (1992), 131–149; and Pilar Huerga Criado, *En la raya de Portugal. Solidaridad y tensiones en la comunidad judeoconversa* (Salamanca: University of Salamanca Press,

berg, in parallel work on relations among Christians, Jews, and Muslims in the medieval world, has made a similar point about interreligious contact: namely, that claims about religious difference were subject to a constant process of barter and negotiation, rather than being part of an unself-conscious persecuting discourse.[8] Most recently, Yovel has fundamentally reoriented the debate through his important work on the duality of converso identity.[9] This book builds on the work of these scholars by arguing that conversos—both individually and collectively—engaged in a range of Christian and Jewish practices. Those devotional practices might vary over time within the broader community, within a single family, or even within one individual's lifespan. By juxtaposing inquisitorial records with secular records from Guadalupe, I demonstrate that what it meant to convert, or to be the descendant of a convert, was not nearly as transparent as many contemporaries desired.

The lives of Old Christians in Guadalupe were apparently more straightforward than those of their new coreligionists, but they, too, exhibited a spectrum of religious practices and attitudes toward the church. Of course, the range of that spectrum was somewhat narrower than that of so-called New Christians. In the ritual activities of the Christian calendar one could witness a breadth of commitment, from the faithful confraternity member, to the man who frequented the tavern instead of attending mass on Sunday. The fact that both Old and New Christians engaged in Christianity in a variety of ways meant that the distinction between them was to an extent artificial. Both, for example, might complain about the attitudes of friars in the confessional, or disparage the Virgin Birth. Both might question the intent and purpose of the inquisitors. Yet the inquisitors (as well as later historians of New Christians) struggled to discern, from such noncanonical or heretical practices, distinct beliefs. This study of religious life in Guadalupe shows how counterproductive such a search must inevitably be; while I do not deny that distinct beliefs may have motivated similar actions, the effective boundaries between theoretically distinct groups of people were quite permeable.

The religious identities of the friars were equally complex. A significant minority of the friars—as many as 15 percent—were conversos.

1993). Angus MacKay, in his article "The Hispano-*Converso* Predicament," *Transactions of the Royal Historical Society*, Fifth Series, London, 35 (1985), 159–179, makes a similar argument, as does, to an extent, José Faur, "Four Classes of *Conversos*: A Typological Study," *Revue des Etudes Juives* 149 (1990), 113–124.

[8] David Nirenberg, *Communities of Violence: Persecution of Minorities in the Middle Ages* (Princeton: Princeton University Press, 1996), 6.

[9] Yirmiyahu Yovel, "The New Otherness: Marrano Dualities in the First Generation," Swig Lecture, Swig Judaic Studies Program, (University of San Francisco, 1999).

Several of these friars were suspected of observing Judaism in secret, while other friars, both Old and New Christian, overtly or covertly supported converso factions in town. Still others expressed great devotion to the Virgin of Guadalupe, and the miracles they witnessed and repeated to one another sustained their Christian faith. Once again, simple binary oppositions, such as New Christian/Old Christian, replicate historical, quasi-racialist categories, while obscuring mutable distinctions of religious practices, political sympathies, and personal beliefs.

It is out of the contested religious identities of friars and residents in Guadalupe, as well as the friars' blending of political and religious concerns, that we move to the second part of my argument, namely, that the power of the Inquisition came from its ability to construct difference out of ambiguity. In their pursuit of intention, as well as act, the inquisitors in Guadalupe and elsewhere created clearly defined categories of innocence and guilt, Old and New Christian. Yet this power of definition was not limited to the inquisitors themselves. All residents of Guadalupe were expected to come before the inquisitors to accuse, and thus define, their neighbors, rivals, and family. Of course, some voices carried more weight before the inquisitors: the friars, for example, held more influence than lay residents of Guadalupe, and some witnesses—adults, men, those with property, those who appeared more religious—were considered more reliable than others—children, women, those without property, those who appeared only casually religious. Yet the potential power given to anyone willing to speak before the inquisitors was not lost on Guadalupenses themselves. This is what I mean by "demystifying" the sources of power of the Holy Office of the Inquisition. As is becoming increasingly clear to scholars of the Inquisition, the Holy Office was not an oppressive state court, imposed upon a helpless populace from without. Indeed, it could not have succeeded without the opportunistic support of locals, who often willingly participated with the inquisitors in order to gain their own ends, be they casting suspicion on a neighbor, exacting vengeance on a former employer, or undermining a business rival. Others went so far as to criticize particular friars, with devastating effects within the friary. In Guadalupe, a close examination of civil and inquisitorial records and the citizens involved in them makes clear the political and social context of this widespread popular participation in the activity of the Inquisition.

The political implications of the power of definition bring us to the third and final element of my thesis. From the very beginning of the Inquisition's status as an arm of the Spanish state, local residents and local officials, as well as royal officials, made use of the Holy Office to further their own political ends. In Guadalupe, this is evident even in how the Inquisition arrived at the shrine site in the first place. In 1483 a small group of friars and lay conversos (possibly including Alonso de

Paredes) attempted to influence through bribery the outcome of the prior's election. The election of a new prior was of political importance to all Guadalupe's residents, since the friars governed the town, but the bribe was a failure. The candidate of this small group lost, and the newly elected prior, apparently aware of the political maneuvering that preceded his election, requested that the Inquisition come to Guadalupe soon after. In return, the Crown named him chief inquisitor.

As an arm of the state, the Inquisition represented a new, usually unwelcome intrusion of royal political authority into municipal government. In Guadalupe, though, the inquisitors, working in conjunction with the friars, actually bolstered the influence of the local friary through a wholesale redefinition of Guadalupe's residents as primarily New or Old Christian, devout or heretic. While pursuing the stated purpose of the Inquisition by trying those conversos suspected of practicing Judaism, the chief inquisitor also targeted converso opponents of his election as prior. This silenced opposition to the friars' authority, permitting the friars to gain the kind of control over the town that they had always desired. At the same time, the Crown used the popularity of the shrine to spread knowledge of the new institution of the Inquisition, which moved from its successful prosecution of conversos in Guadalupe to more permanent bases in other cities in Spain. In those cities, too, the inquisitorial courts became quickly embroiled in local and royal political concerns. The presence of the Inquisition in Guadalupe had profound political repercussions that all residents were aware of, and that many residents, more or less successfully, attempted to turn toward their own ends. Ultimately, though, those most successful at utilizing the power inherent in the Inquisition were the friars who had brought it to Guadalupe.[10]

Despite fears of local officials elsewhere when first confronted by the Inquisition, Guadalupe proved that the Holy Office provided another field for fighting local battles, rather than merely subjugating local officials to a new royal bureaucracy. Local and royal attempts to garner power were not necessarily operating at counterpurposes, particularly

[10] This argument both engages and enriches the recent historiography of the Inquisition. Scholars including Carlo Ginzburg, *The Night Battles: Witchcraft and Agrarian Cults in the Sixteenth and Seventeenth Centuries* (Baltimore: Johns Hopkins University Press, 1983), and Emmanuel LeRoy Ladurie, *Montaillou: The Promised Land of Error*, tr. Barbara Bray (New York: Vintage, 1978), have used inquisitorial records to build an impressive understanding of medieval and early modern culture, while Spanish historians such as Jaime Contreras, *Sotos contra Riquelmes: Regidores, inquisidores y criptojudíos* (Madrid: Anaya and Mario Muchnik, 1992), have begun to address the role of the Inquisition in local and national political conflicts in the sixteenth century and beyond. My analysis complements the work of these scholars by focusing on how opportunities for local authorities and townspeople to employ the Inquisition for their own specific political and social ends were present from the first establishment of the Holy Office.

when religion created a common bond among allies and a common enemy against which to rally. Helen Nader has argued cogently for the interdependence of local municipalities and the absolutist Hapsburg state, but I wish to return attention to the local conflicts that could help cement that alliance. In Guadalupe, the friars welcomed the introduction of Fernando and Isabel's Inquisition. Guadalupense friars early learned what later became apparent elsewhere as well: that local as well as royal officials could employ the Holy Office to bolster their authority in their respective domains.

The political repercussions of the presence of the Holy Office extended long past the departure of the inquisitors. Here again, a close study of Guadalupe reveals the intersecting interests of local and royal authorities. For the friars who governed the town of Guadalupe, the Inquisition became only the first element of their attempt to exert more thorough control over the community. The inquisitorial trials enabled them to eliminate many of their wealthiest and most powerful rivals in town, and the authority this demonstrated, backed by the implicit support of the Crown, allowed them to cow other residents as well. Perhaps even more importantly, the friars were more united among themselves than they had been previously. New Christian friars, and those sympathetic to New Christians, had been reprimanded, imprisoned, or in one case executed; as a result, discord within the ecclesiastical community diminished.[11] With their newfound unity of purpose and evident support from the Crown, the friars finally defeated residents' attempts to gain an independent town council. The failure of Guadalupe's Old Christians to gain more independent authority for themselves, despite repeated attempts during the sixteenth century, reveals that the interests of church and Crown, when working in parallel for common ends, could derail the general tendency for decentralization in Hapsburg Spain. But the long-term importance of the Inquisition was not limited to local sites like Guadalupe. Just as the friars strengthened their secular authority through association with the Crown, so too did the Crown strengthen and sacralize its authority through association with the cult of the Virgin of Guadalupe and the Holy Office of the Inquisition. The aura of the sacred continued to surround royal activity for decades to come.

The first chapter of this book introduces the Virgin of Guadalupe, her friars, and the town that grew up around her shrine as her cult grew in

---

[11] A copy of the witnesses' statements from the first set of inquisitorial trials against the friars in 1485 is housed at the Archivo del Monasterio de Guadalupe (AMG), unnumbered, internal Inquisition.

popularity in the fourteenth and fifteenth centuries. Early histories of the shrine and the friars, as well as evidence about the construction of the town, provide a means of surveying the physical, social, and spiritual landscape of the community. This descriptive, narrative chapter reveals the tensions present from the establishment of the town. From the first arrival of the friars, citizens of Guadalupe resented the authority granted to the clerics by the Crown and the archbishop of Toledo, and civic unrest was common. Furthermore, the prominence of New Christians as lay officials for the friars engendered political and religious suspicions among Old Christians in town. The religious significance of Guadalupe was undeniably unique, but the religious, social, and political tensions that plagued the town were common throughout Castile at the end of the Middle Ages.

Chapter 2 demonstrates how religious identities were constructed by examining how Christians, both Old and New, defined their religiosity in a town that was explicitly Christian but not uniformly devout. Remaining civic records, confraternity documents, local ordinances, and inquisitorial records reveal much about religious practices in Guadalupe from the fourteenth to sixteenth centuries and clarify the range of acceptable Christian practices for those living in the shadow of the Virgin of Guadalupe. A "thick description" or interpretive description of life rituals, weekly worship, and religiously oriented communities demonstrates the broad range of acceptable practices, the interactions of so-called Old and New Christians, and the limits of what was tolerated at the shrine site.[12]

Chapter 3 moves from the thick description of practices to a closer analysis of those forced most explicitly to negotiate an ambiguous religious identity, namely, conversos. New Christians were not a community apart from other Guadalupenses, nor were they uncomplicated devout Christians or unreconstructed Judaizers. Rather, they were fully integrated into Guadalupe's social, political, and religious life. The sometimes plaintive record of inquisitorial documents and civil papers reveals that individual conversos can be placed across a continuum of Jewish and Christian practices, their own activities changing over time and in response to the demands of family, friends, and the community as a whole. It is this contingent, mutable self-understanding of religious identity that has so challenged historians of New Christians in the past.

Given this analysis of social and religious identity in Guadalupe, we can then re-examine the purpose and impact of the Holy Office of the Inquisition. This begins in chapter 4 with a close study of the events

---

[12] On the concept "thick description," see Clifford Geertz, *The Interpretation of Cultures* (New York: Harper, 1973), chap. 1.

leading up to the introduction of the Inquisition in Guadalupe. Social conflict in Guadalupe was on the rise in the second half of the fifteenth century. Arbitrary lordship, in the person of the prior, Diego de París, exacerbated tensions both within the community of friars and in the town of Guadalupe as well. Suspicion of the conversos who helped govern the town as lay functionaries grew, though Old and New Christians united in their hostility toward the friars who permitted little of the self-governance typical of Castilian communities. Even the friars were at odds with one another and the town. What Guadalupe's residents found to be heavy-handed government seemed in the eyes of the friars barely controlled anarchy, and the friars were divided among themselves about what, if anything, needed to be done. All that changed with the prior's election of 1483. When that small group of friars and conversos attempted—without success—to bribe the friars to elect "their" candidate to the priorate, the new prior wasted little time in requesting that the Inquisition be brought to Guadalupe.

In chapter 5 we can begin to see how the inquisitors' vision of those they tried changed the status and even the identity of New Christians in Guadalupe. The chapter traces the actions of the Holy Office over the course of the year 1485, from their first arrival in town to the final sentencing at the last *auto de fe*. The structure of the trials, and the haunting experiences of those who lived through them, paint a stark picture of the effects of the Inquisition on those pursued by it. At the same time, careful, comparative examination of inquisitorial records and contemporary civil records reveals how many residents of Guadalupe made use of the Holy Office to pursue their own ends.

However, New Christians on trial before the Inquisition were not without options, as chapter 6 makes clear. Many of Guadalupe's residents made use of the legal structures of the Holy Office for their own ends, and New Christians, while less successful, were no different. Even within the walls of the inquisitorial prison, the accused were able to manipulate, to some extent, their collective fate at the hands of the inquisitors. The inquisitors were largely unchallenged in their activities in Guadalupe, but this chapter shows that there were limits to their ability to remold religious and political realities in town.

Chapter 7 turns attention to yet another aspect of the politically transformative power of the Inquisition—namely, the importance of the Holy Office in ending the internal struggles among Guadalupe's friars. Out of extant documents from the friary, as well as the voluminous inquisitorial testimony of the friars against one another, we can see the deep fissures that separated the friars on political and religious questions. Indeed, the friary serves as a microcosm of divisions within Guadalupe itself. The friars, like Guadalupe's residents, exhibited a range of

Christian and Jewish practices—a fact even more astounding for occurring within the walls of the friary. As on the outside of the friars' community, inquisitorial trials revealed these divisions, delineated them in clear categories, and allowed "devout" friars to exert control over their "heretical" brethren, whether that heresy entailed primarily religious acts or political maneuvering. This internal reorganization of the friars' community in Guadalupe marked a turning point in their relations with the town as a whole.

Finally, the continuing repercussions of the Inquisition after its departure are made clear in chapter 8. Here the arguments about the intersections of local and royal authority are brought to a close. Once again, the comparison of civil documents from the town of Guadalupe with inquisitorial records reveals that, in unexpected ways, the Inquisition continued to affect life in Guadalupe long after it had left. Despite the Inquisition's apparent focus on heretical acts, for example, Judaizing New Christians quickly returned to Guadalupe from their sentences of "perpetual" exile. In addition, those conversos who had supported the friars' governing received solicitous attention from the friars for years to come. But in other ways the Inquisition's presence radically transformed life in Guadalupe. New Christians may not have disappeared, but resistance to the friars' overlordship was severely undercut. Using their increased authority, based in part on a new internal solidarity and on the secular support of the Crown, the friars handily defeated Old Christian protests against ecclesiastical government in Guadalupe. At the same time, the Crown took advantage of the sacred approval of the friars and, by extension, the Virgin of Guadalupe, to emphasize a spiritual underpinning for their regime. The sacrality of the early modern Spanish state, which appears in its first outlines here, would come to have increasing importance in the reign of Philip II and beyond.

ONE

BEFORE THE INQUISITION:
GUADALUPE, THE VIRGIN, AND THE
ORDER OF SAINT JEROME

THE Virgin of Guadalupe, the friary dedicated to her cult, and the town that sprang up around them came into their own in the fourteenth and fifteenth centuries. With the support of prelates from Toledo and the ascendant Trastámara dynasty, the regional cult of the Virgin of Guadalupe increased in spiritual significance and economic strength, becoming an international shrine with royal backing. As Guadalupe secured its place in the temporal and spiritual landscape, the town grew in population and importance. Pilgrims flocked to the image of the Virgin as markets located in the town drew merchants from throughout the region. In 1389 the Order of Saint Jerome, an Iberian order with close ties to the Castilian crown, assumed control of the shrine. With their friary in Guadalupe the Jeronymite friars secured their own place in Iberian religious life and affirmed their links to the Castilian court. The friars insured their spiritual significance to contemporaries as guardians of the increasingly important cult of the Virgin of Guadalupe. By the mid-fifteenth century Guadalupe was the center of a well-maintained temporal dominion that reached into the most profitable lands in Extremadura. In town, the friars worked, often with little success, to consolidate their grasp on Guadalupense political and economic matters; out of town, they attempted to maintain neutrality in the political conflicts of late-medieval Castile. Thanks to the Virgin, Guadalupe was a town whose nature reflected and affected broader Iberian society. Thus, before examining the details of relations between Guadalupenses, the friars, and the Crown, we need to situate Guadalupe in the physical, political, and spiritual landscape of late-medieval Iberia.

THE LANDSCAPE AND THE VIRGIN

Traveling to Guadalupe, the modern pilgrim passes through a striking landscape that has changed little in five hundred years. Going south from Madrid, or north from Seville or Badajoz, one eventually leaves behind the plains for the cluster of small mountain ranges that stretch roughly north to south, separating modern Spain from Portugal. The western face of the mountains directs rainfall from the Atlantic to Portugal and leaves much of Extremadura arid. As one nears Guadalupe, the changing climate of the upper elevations is evident as pines, olive groves, chestnuts, and vineyards replace the dry grasses of the Toledan plains. Rocky outcroppings covered with lichen attest to centuries of erosion caused by springs hidden throughout the Sierra of Guadalupe. The uneven, picturesque landscape of the Villuercas Mountains immediately surrounding the town preserves microclimates that have supported wildflowers and beekeepers for thousands of years. From almost any spot in Guadalupe, vineyards and olive groves can be seen scattered on the hills that spread out to the horizon.

A newly paved highway has made Guadalupe more accessible in recent years, but the town remains almost as isolated as it was at its founding. Several old Roman cities, such as Mérida, Talavera, and Trujillo, were still linked by the road that had run across the ancient Roman province of Baetica; but that road ran some 50 kilometers to the west over rough terrain. The Silver Road, used to guide the Spanish Reconquest, lay even farther west. Similarly, the influential sheep-farmers' guild known as the Mesta drove the newly introduced Merino sheep across Extremadura during its semi-annual migrations, but their established routes also bypassed the site of the future shrine.[1] While the land supported some agricultural products, much of Extremadura was notoriously poor; from its earliest days the town imported grain, and since time immemorial the land has supported only small numbers of seasonal laborers. Through most of the thirteenth century Extremadura was the site of battles among Castilian, Portuguese, and Muslim fighters, and the Villuercas and Extremadura as a whole remained lightly populated. Cañamero, a fortified town built as part of the Castilian king's policy of repopulation, *repoblación*, following the Christian reconquest of the land, stood to the southwest; Alía, a small agricultural community, lay on the other side of Guadalupe at the eastern edge of

---

[1] The N-5, a national Spanish highway running from Madrid to Badajoz, generally follows the route of the Roman road from Talavera de la Reina to Badajoz. See Derek Lomax, *The Reconquest of Spain* (London: Longman, 1978). See also Marcelino Cardalliaguet Quirant, *Historia de Extremadura* 2d ed. (Badajoz: Universitas Editorial, 1993), 44. On the routes of the Mesta sheep guild, see Julius Klein, *The Mesta* (Cambridge: Harvard University Press, 1920). The recent study by Carla Rahn Phillips and William D. Phillips, Jr., *Spain's Golden Fleece: Wool Production and the Wool Trade from the Middle Ages to the Nineteenth Century* (Baltimore: Johns Hopkins University Press, 1997), is an essential companion to Klein.

the mountains. It was onto this landscape that the Virgin of Guadalupe first projected her influence during the thirteenth century (map 1).

The legend of the appearance of the Virgin and the founding of the town has been often told.[2] One day a cow herder from Cáceres, who according to later versions was named Gil Cordero, was tracking a missing animal in the mountains. When he found the cow it was dead, so immediately he began to slaughter the animal, cutting a cross into its chest. At that moment the Virgin appeared. She told the herdsman that where he knelt an image of her had been buried; priests from Seville had buried it there to protect her after the Muslim invasion of 710.[3] The Virgin ordered Cordero to bring the bishop of Cáceres to recover her image and organize a shrine. On this site, she prophesied, a great town would be founded.[4] As the Virgin disappeared, Cordero's cow revived, bearing a cross-shaped scar on its chest, and Cordero and his animal hurried home to Cáceres. The bishop's disbelief vanished

[2] See Archivo Histórico Nacional (AHN) codex 48B and AHN codex 101B for two accounts of the legend. For printed sources on the legend and the history of the friary, see Diego de Ecija, OSH, *Libro de la invención de la santa imagen de Guadalupe* (Cáceres: Departamento Provincial de Seminarios de F.E.T. y de las J.O.N.S., 1953); Gabriel de Talavera, OSH, *Historia de Nuestra Señora de Guadalupe* (Toledo, 1597); José de Sigüenza, OSH, *Historia de la orden de San Jerónimo*, 2 vols. (Madrid: Nueva Biblioteca de Autores Españoles, 1908, 1912); German Rubío, OFM, *Historia de Nuestra Señora de Guadalupe* (Barcelona: Industrias gráficas Thomas, 1926); Arturo Alvarez, OFM, *Guadalupe* (Madrid: Ediciones Studium, 1964); Sebastián García, OFM, and Felipe Trenado, OFM, eds., *Guadalupe: Historia, devoción, y arte* (Seville: Editorial Católica Española, 1978); J. Carlos Vizuete Mendoza, *Guadalupe: Un monasterio jerónimo (1389–1450)* (Madrid: Antiqua et Mediaevalia, 1988); and Sebastián García, OFM, ed. *Guadalupe: Siete siglos de fe y de cultura* (Madrid, 1994). There are also two plays that retell the history of the Virgin: Fray Diego de Ocaña, OSH, *Comedia de Nuestra Señora de Guadalupe y sus milagros*, ed. Teresa Gisbert (La Paz: Biblioteca Paceña, 1957); and Miguel de Cervantes (attributed), *Comedia de la Soberana Virgen de Guadalupe, y Sus Milagros, y Grandezas de España*, ed. José María Asensio (Seville: Sociedad de Bibliófilos Andaluces, 1868). William Christian, Jr., *Local Religion in Sixteenth-Century Spain* (Princeton: Princeton University Press, 1981), does not specifically mention the origin of the Virgin of Guadalupe, although he does mention her importance in sixteenth-century religious life. He also discusses several narratives of the discovery of saints or Virgins that share structural similarities to the history of the Virgin of Guadalupe. The most recent analysis of the various examples of the legend of the Virgin of Guadalupe is in Françoise Crémoux, "Pèlerinages et miracles à Guadalupe (Extrémadure) au XVIe siècle" (Madrid: Casa de Velázquez, 2001), 10–15.

[3] On using the date 710, rather than 711, to mark the start of the Muslim conquest of Iberia, see Roger Collins, *The Arab Conquest of Spain, 710–797* (London: Basil Blackwell, 1989).

[4] The Virgin's prophecy seems designed to explain why the image of the Virgin was not brought to Alía, the nearest town. Alía is located just across the Guadalupejo River, after which the Virgin was named. Present-day Alianos still occasionally argue that the Virgin should be theirs.

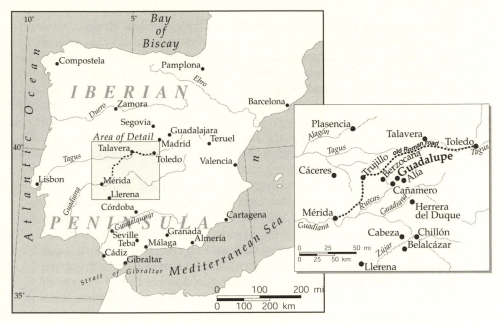

MAP 1. Iberia, circa 1500, including Guadalupe and environs.
Map by Richard Gilbreath.

after the herdsman's son was resurrected through the intercession of the Virgin, and soon a large company returned to the site of the vision in the mountains. Accounts differ on whether Cordero and the bishop found the carved cedar image of the Virgin at a spring or in a cave, but all agree that a history was found with the Virgin that linked her to Saint Leander of Seville, Pope Gregory the Great, and in some accounts the evangelist Luke himself.[5] Just as the Virgin demanded, the bishop established a shrine, and the narratives relate that Gil Cordero and his family maintained the site for the rest of their lives.

Recent art historical research dates the statue of the Virgin to the twelfth century, a period of great instability in Extremadura.[6] At the end of the eleventh century the Muslim Almoravids had seized much of the Muslim kingdoms of Batalliaws and Tolaitola, which comprised northern Portugal, Extremadura, and the area south of Toledo. The Almoravids never gained a firm control over their territory, however, and

[5] Some Guadalupenses today claim that the present church stands precisely where the Virgin was found; they state that the spring where the Virgin was found is located directly under the altar, although few are allowed there.

[6] See García and Trenado, *Guadalupe*, 23, on the history of the image.

Christian raiding parties from León, Castile, and Portugal claimed parts of Almoravid Extremadura for their own. It is possible that the image of the Virgin of Guadalupe was introduced to the region at that time. Ultimately, these Christian settlements proved temporary, and by 1172 the Almohad Berbers had swept north from Africa and claimed much of Extremadura for themselves.[7] But in 1229, in the aftermath of the spectacular Christian victory at the battle of Las Navas de Tolosa in 1212, Cáceres once more fell into Christian hands, this time permanently. The thirteenth century witnessed the slow repopulation of Extremadura.

By the early fourteenth century, Guadalupe had established itself on the spiritual, as well as physical, landscape. Peter Linehan has persuasively argued that as early as 1326 the shrine in Guadalupe was a well-organized pilgrimage site basking in the support of the *scholasticus* of Toledo, the future cardinal Pedro Gómez Barroso. This support, Linehan argues, reflected a debate between Gómez Barroso as the representative of the archiepiscopal see of Toledo, on one hand, and the see of Santiago de Compostela, on the other. Geographically Guadalupe pertained to the diocese of Plasencia in northern Extremadura, which in turn answered to the archbishop in Santiago de Compostela. By the later Middle Ages, regional civil strife and declining numbers of pilgrims had weakened the venerable shrine of Saint James; as a result, ecclesiastical authorities in Santiago and Plasencia looked to Guadalupe as a new source of revenue. Pedro Gómez Barroso, on the other hand, argued that Guadalupe fell under the ecclesiastical jurisdiction of Toledo, because this city was much closer to the Extremeñan shrine. While in Avignon in 1326, Gómez Barroso was able both to support Guadalupense interests at the papal court and to seize ecclesiastical control of the Marian shrine for Toledo. Bishops in Plasencia and Santiago protested, but with the support of the increasingly powerful Gómez Barroso, Guadalupe remained in the diocese of Toledo.[8]

Guadalupe's support from Toledo and growing popularity also brought more immediate, tangible benefits to Castile. The now-cardinal Pedro

---

[7] See Lomax, *Reconquest*, chap. 3, sec. 3, and chap. 5, sec. 1, on the process of reconquest in twelfth-century Extremadura. For the history of Muslim Extremadura and the Extremeñan reconquest, see Cardalliaguet Quirant, *Historia*, 59–96. Critical for any study of medieval Extremeñan history is the *Historia de Extremadura*, gen. ed. Angel Rodríguez Sánchez, 4 vols. (Badajoz: Universitas Editorial, 1985). This work covers the history of Extremadura through a series of essays by leading scholars in the field; it also provides sizable bibliographic essays.

[8] See Peter Linehan, "The Beginnings of Santa María de Guadalupe and the Direction of Fourteenth-Century Castile," *Journal of Ecclesiastical History* 36 (1985), 284–304. Linehan's article is an important reappraisal of early Guadalupense historiography. Guadalupe remains in the diocese of Toledo.

Gómez Barroso enjoyed the support of the regents of Alfonso XI (reigned 1312–1350), as well as that of the pope, and through him the Crown began to make use of the popular shrine for its own ends, granting it privileges and supporting it as an outpost of Castilian authority on the frontier. Ultimately, Guadalupe became the spiritual expression of a royal policy in the 1320s and 1330s that increasingly looked to the economic and political opportunities of the south and west.[9] Castile had encouraged Mesta activity, new commercial routes, and Christian resettlement in Extremadura through *repoblación* sites like Cañamero.[10] Alfonso XI further solidified Castile's links to Portugal and western Iberia by marrying the daughter of Afonso IV of Portugal. By the fourteenth century, however, the Virgin attracted more men and markets to underpopulated Extremadura than any other settlement or shrine. In so doing, the Virgin and her shrine bolstered the Crown's attempts to strengthen Castile's presence in the reconquered territories.

The first reference to Guadalupe in Castilian legal records occurs in 1337, when the adult Alfonso XI awarded the shrine site independence from the town of Talavera. Three years later Alfonso's attention returned to the shrine when he visited there to pray for the Virgin's aid before the battle of Salado. Alfonso defeated the Muslims at Salado, and in gratitude for his victory he showered the nascent community with gifts. The most important of these was a secular monastery supported by local taxes formerly owed to the king. A secular monastery held monks who did not belong to any particular order, although in most cases the monks tended to observe some form of the Augustinian Rule. The prior and monks of the Guadalupense monastery remained under the authority of the archbishop of Toledo, supported by privileges from Toledo and the Crown, as well as the broad popular interest in the cult of the Virgin of Guadalupe. By the time of the accession of Alfonso's son Pedro I to the throne in 1350, concludes Linehan, "forty years before it was entrusted to the care of the Jeronymite Order, Guadalupe enjoyed an international clientele and was securely under the aegis of the Castilian monarchy."[11]

This political and ecclesiastical support would have been incomprehensible without the Virgin and her cult. By the fifteenth century the little dark lady of the Villuercas Mountains, *la morenita de las Villuercas*, stood at the center of a powerful, popular cult, in all the senses of those words. The Virgin of Guadalupe rewarded her royal, ecclesiastical, and

[9] Ibid., 303.

[10] Julio González, *La repoblación de Castilla*, 2 vols. (Madrid: Universidad Complutense, 1975).

[11] Linehan, "Beginnings," 296.

popular defenders with her numerous miracles, which included rescuing Christians taken captive by Muslims, aiding sailors at sea, and converting Muslims to Christianity. Pilgrims visited from throughout the peninsula, particularly Extremadura, but friars from Paris, Germany, and Poland who settled in Guadalupe suggest the range of the Virgin's appeal.[12] Fray Gabriel de Talavera, prior and historian of Guadalupe in the sixteenth century, retells accounts from the miracle books of numerous pilgrims who came to thank the Virgin of Guadalupe for their deliverance from Muslim-controlled dungeons, *mazmorras*. Some prisoners, including in a later century Cervantes, offered the Virgin their chains as a sign of gratitude. These were hung on the inside walls of the church, perhaps like the chains still hanging outside the church of San Juan de los Reyes in Toledo.[13]

Physically and spiritually, Guadalupe had become a prominent feature on the Castilian landscape of the later Middle Ages. The Virgin and her monastery were a locus of spiritual power in the recently settled Extremeñan territories, one that captured the imagination of Iberians throughout the peninsula and attracted the attention of Castile's political and religious potentates. It is not surprising, then, that the shrine soon gained new masters with connections and authority in the Iberian Peninsula commensurate with the importance of the Virgin.

THE JERONYMITES

Secular monks under the authority of the archbishop of Toledo continued to maintain the shrine of the Virgin of Guadalupe for almost fifty years, but as the Virgin increased in popularity and importance, the secular monastery's relatively informal organization proved insufficient to meet the growing managerial demands placed upon it. As a result,

---

[12] These places of origin are based on the place names of Jeronymite friars alive in the later fifteenth century. For a discussion of use of place of origin rather than surname among Jeronymite friars, see below.

[13] Unfortunately, the early volumes of the church's miracle books are now lost. The Virgin's rescue of Muslim prisoners and conversion of Muslims to Christianity is examined at length in my article "'The Joyous History of Devotion and Memory of the Grandeur of Spain': The Spanish Virgin of Guadalupe and Religious and Political Memory," (*Archiv für Reformationsgeschichte / Archive for Reformation History*) 93 (2002), 238–262. On pilgrims rescued from Muslim captivity, see, for example, the miracles described in Talavera, *Historia*, 230r–235r, or Rubío, *Historia*, 214–217. On 83v–84r Talavera tells how prior Gonzalo de Madrid organized the redemption of fifty prisoners held by Muslims; these people were rescued and brought to Guadalupe. More miracles are recorded in Talavera and in Fray Diego de Montalvo, OSH, *Milagros de la Soberana Virgen de Guadalupe*, 2 vols. (Lisbon, 1631). On Cervantes in Guadalupe, see García and Trenado, *Guadalupe*, 335, 342.

the archbishop, together with King Juan I (reigned 1379–1390), began to consider giving the monastery to a more established order. For Juan I, awarding the monastery and shrine to an Iberian order in particular would serve political, as well as pragmatic, ends. A lucrative donation could strengthen an alliance between the Crown and an order as well as facilitate maintenance of the Virgin's cult. Such a donation also would continue the tradition of his father, Enrique II Trastámara (reigned 1369–1379), who secured his position after a divisive civil war by awarding the nobility elements of the royal patrimony.[14] In addition, giving Guadalupe to an established religious order would strengthen the burgeoning repopulation and economic growth of Extremadura by insuring the shrine's stability and organization. In this sense Juan was continuing a policy initiated by his grandfather Alfonso XI.

By the 1380s the king and the archbishop of Toledo had begun to search for an order to manage the shrine. Aided by Guadalupense prior Juan Serrano, they sought an order that could govern the large pilgrimage site and attendant town, assimilate the current secular friars, and complement the particular devotions of the Virgin of Guadalupe. In return, the order selected would gain political autonomy and significant financial rewards. The monks were the only temporal authority in the town; that is, the monks and town were politically autonomous under the aegis of royal support. Guadalupe's townspeople were under the spiritual as well as temporal guidance of the secular monks, but although the incoming friars would remain spiritually autonomous under the rules of their own order, the townspeople were considered part of the diocese of Toledo.[15]

By 1389 the king, primate, and prior had arranged for the friars of the newly formed Order of Saint Jerome to assume control of Guadalupe. It seems at first glance a curious choice. The order had won approval of the pope a mere sixteen years earlier, and Guadalupe would be only the sixth house for the new order. Guadalupe would have been an exceptional addition to any order's domains, but the contrast to the Jeronymites' other houses was particularly striking. The Order of Saint Jerome in Spain emphasized humility, isolation from urban centers and public life, contemplation without intellectualism or extensive study,

[14] Enrique II, half-brother to Pedro I (1350–1369), launched a civil war in 1366 that ended with Enrique's murder of Pedro. Enrique's rewards to his supporters, and his attempts to establish his position with the church and nobility through donations, earned him the name "Enrique of the favors," "Enrique de las mercedes."

[15] For this reason the town of Guadalupe was not simply a *prelatura nullius*, that is, a parish pertaining to no diocese. On this question, see García and Trenado, *Guadalupe*, 79–83.

and economic self-sufficiency that enabled the friars to focus on their spiritual lives and to devote themselves to the Mass and its music.[16]

The Jeronymites' focus on isolation and contemplation revealed the order's eremitical origins. The earliest Jeronymites in Italy, Castile, and Aragon associated themselves with the practices of Saint Jerome in the desert without following any rule or affiliating themselves with any order. In some respects, the Jeronymites' earliest activity was reminiscent of the goals and actions of the adherents of the modern devotion, *devotio moderna*, in northern Europe. Both groups shunned formal organization and formal rules, preferring a simpler, lay status. Early Jeronymites and followers of the *devotio moderna* both espoused humility and contemplation without intellectual activity or extreme asceticism.[17] In addition, both groups advocated economic self-sufficiency rather than following a rigid rule of poverty. Despite these similarities, however, the two movements developed in profoundly different ways. The Jeronymites' unconventional activities—particularly a humility that led individual Jeronymites to shun their noble ancestry—as well as the lack of formal organization or ecclesiastical status of Spanish Jeronymites earned them the suspicion of the ecclesiastical hierarchy. Ultimately, sustained persecution led a group of Castilian Jeronymites to seek permission to organize as the Order of Saint Jerome. Pope Gregory XI decreed in his 1373 bull founding the order, *Sane Petitio*, that the new

---

[16] The fundamental work on the Order of Saint Jerome (OSH) is José de Sigüenza, OSH, *Historia*, which was composed in 1600. Also useful for the early growth of the Jeronymites is Josemaría Revuelta Somalo, *Los Jerónimos. Una orden religiosa nacida en Guadalajara*. Vol. 1, *fundación y primera expansión, 1373–1410* (Guadalajara: Nueva Alcarria, 1982). A collection of articles, including surveys of some archives, is *Studia Hieronymiana*, 2 vols. (Madrid, no publisher, 1973). Eugene Rice, *Saint Jerome and the Renaissance* (Baltimore: Johns Hopkins University Press, 1985), provides important background on changing interpretations of Saint Jerome in the medieval, Renaissance, and early modern periods, and briefly discusses eremitical movements devoted to Saint Jerome in late medieval Italy and Iberia. Music was an essential element of Jeronymite devotion, particularly in their day-long celebrations of the Divine Office. In addition to references in *Studia Hieronymiana*, a survey of music at the Escorial has been completed recently by Michael Noone, *Music and Musicians in the Escorial Liturgy Under the Habsburgs, 1563–1700* (Rochester, NY: University of Rochester Press, 1998). While specific to the Escorial, a unique Jeronymite foundation, many themes addressed in his work are relevant to the history of music in the order generally.

[17] When Castilian nobleman Hernando Pecha received approval from the pope to found the Order of Saint Jerome, several other eremitical groups or informal religious communities were using the same or similar names; see Rice, *Saint Jerome*, and Revuelta Somalo, *Los Jerónimos*. An eremitical tendency runs through the early history of the Jeronymites, for example, the early history of the Valle del Hebrón community outside Barcelona. A more severely eremitic branch of the order was founded in 1428. The Jeronymites emphasized moderation rather than rigid asceticism, however. On the early history of the community at Val del Hebrón, see Sigüenza, *Historia*, 1:100–101; on fray Lope de Olmedo's more ascetic branch of the OSH, see Sigüenza, *Historia*, 1:311–329.

order would use the Rule of Saint Augustine and the Constitutions of the friary of Saint Mary of the Holy Sepulcher.[18]

Even after the organization of the Order of Saint Jerome at their first house, called San Bartolomé de Lupiana, quiet contemplation remained central to the daily activities of the friars. The Rule and Constitutions, states Vizuete Mendoza, "converted the Order of Saint Jerome . . . into a monastic institution with a contemplative tendency, that in an atmosphere of solitude, silence, prayer, and austerity attempted to bring its friars to a union with God."[19] Guadalupe did provide the economic self-sufficiency that would allow the friars to devote themselves to worship at the Divine Offices, but few would argue that the shrine allowed solitude, silence, or simple austerity. The growing number of pilgrims and the frequent noble visitors to the Virgin's shrine hardly afforded the opportunity for quiet, isolated contemplation, or freedom from worries of administration. Why had the order been offered the friary in Guadalupe, and why did they accept?

Their early and rapid success affords some clue. The Order of Saint Jerome may have existed a scant sixteen years, but their five houses suggest that they were well supported in their early years. In fact, the founders of the order included several eminent figures from the Iberian, especially Castilian, royal courts, and their emphasis on humility was in counterpoint to their own aristocratic origins.[20] The aristocratic supporters of both Guadalupe and the Jeronymites at the Trastámara court may have suggested the link; the patronage of the Order of Saint Jerome and the Virgin's shrine by noble families such as the Mendoza also may have encouraged a union of the two.[21] Furthermore, while the

---

[18] The requirements of the Rule of the Order of Saint Jerome are detailed in Sigüenza, *Historia*, and Vizuete Mendoza, *Guadalupe*, 111–136. One copy of the Rule is available in the United States at the Houghton Library at Harvard University. The possible links between the Order of Saint Jerome and *devotio moderna* have never been fully examined. Two studies that address the question are Américo Castro, *The Spaniards: An Introduction to Their History* (Berkeley: University of California Press, 1971), and Charles Fraker, "Gonçalo Martínez de Medina, the *Jerónimos*, and the *devotio moderna*," *Hispanic Review* 34 (1966), 197–217. A useful introduction to *devotio moderna* can be found in John Van Engen, *Devotio Moderna. Basic Writings* (New York: Paulist Press, 1988).

[19] Vizuete Mendoza, *Guadalupe*, 115.

[20] On early aristocratic links to the Order of Saint Jerome, see Roger Highfield, "The Jeronimites in Spain, Their Patrons and Successes," *Journal of Ecclesiastical History* 34 (1983), 513–533; Revuelta Somalo, *Los Jerónimos*; and *Studia Hieronymiana*. Jeronymite friars identified themselves by place of origin rather than surname as part of their discipline of humility. The practice held special meaning given the noble origins of many friars.

[21] Like the Jeronymites, the Mendoza were based in Guadalajara, and the Mendoza were closely linked to both the early history of the Jeronymites and the Trastámara court. A member of the Mendoza family in Medellín in the mid to late fifteenth century known as the Countess of Medellín had frequent dealings with Guadalupe. See Archivo

Extremeñan shrine may not have conformed to earlier Jeronymite institutions, it did provide its custodians with international prestige and financial independence, and it confirmed its newfound importance. Finally, Jeronymite assumption of the Guadalupense shrine institutionalized
aristocratic support of the Order of Saint Jerome through their gifts to
the Virgin of Guadalupe. The Order of Saint Jerome, the archbishop of
Toledo, the Castilian king, and the shrine all benefited from the installa-
tion of a young, dynamic order to supervise the Virgin's cult.

An earlier, abortive attempt to transfer control of the shrine suggests
additional motivations for bringing an established order to Guadalupe.
A few years before the arrival of the Order of Saint Jerome in 1389, the
secular prior, archbishop, and king invited the Mercedarian Order to
assume control of Guadalupe and its monastery. Like the Jeronymites,
the Mercedarians were an indigenous Iberian order. Like the military
orders of Alcántara, Santiago, and Calatrava, the Mercedarians emerged
during the reconquest of the Muslim south, though for the Mercedarians the goal was not battle but liberating Christians held prisoner by
Muslims. Clearly, this was a raison d'etre that suited the Virgin of Guadalupe well. However, the challenges of ministering to large numbers of
pilgrims and assimilating the secular monks proved too difficult for the
order. Few records remain from their tenure, but evidence suggests that
the Mercedarians left Guadalupe within a year after their arrival.[22]

The Jeronymites, apparently, were an Iberian order better suited to
the task of organizing and administering the town and shrine, as well as
incorporating the secular monks into their community. Fray Fernando
Yáñez, one of the order's founders, became Guadalupe's first Jeronymite
prior; under his tenure the Jeronymites began an ambitious building
program to meet the needs of the growing community of friars and the
ever-increasing numbers of pilgrims. Fray Fernando's program was not
carelessly expansive, however. The Order of Saint Jerome was careful to
build up the town in a way that reinforced the sanctity of the Virgin,
the importance of the pilgrims' approach to her, and the centrality of
the Virgin and the friars in Guadalupe's existence.[23]

---

del Monasterio de Guadalupe (AMG) codices 74 and 74bis, *Actas Capitulares*, passim. For
the Mendoza family, see Helen Nader, *The Mendoza Family in the Spanish Renaissance,
1350–1550* (New Brunswick: Rutgers University Press, 1979).

[22] On the Mercedarians in Guadalupe, see Diego de Ecija, *Historia*, 111, and Benigno
González Sologaistúa, "Los Mercedarios en Guadalupe," *El Monasterio de Guadalupe*
237–238 (1933), 187–189. These two sources are summarized in García and Trenado,
Guadalupe, 35–36. On the Mercedarians, see Bruce Taylor, *Structures of Reform: The
Mercedarian Order in the Spanish Golden Age* (Leiden: Brill, 2000).

[23] This may have parallels in other Jeronymite foundations. For example, the Jeronymite foundation of San Jerónimo in Madrid was sited at one end of an important

One historical example will help clarify the kinds of pilgrims' experiences that Jeronymite building helped to create. Six months after their victory over the Muslims of Granada, and three months after issuing their edict to expel the Jews, King Fernando of Aragon (reigned 1479–1516) and Queen Isabel of Castile (reigned 1474–1504) traveled once again to Guadalupe. As they neared the end of their journey on June 10, 1492, they climbed through the small towns and rocky landscape into the Villuercas Mountains. At a sudden turn in the road, the monarchs were treated to their first view of the Virgin's town. The entourage halted, and Fernando and Isabel knelt, thanking God for their victory over the Muslims.[24] This anecdote is still told by Guadalupenses proud of their town's links to past and present royalty. Some townspeople assert that the Humilladero, the small, "humbling" shrine where the Catholic Monarchs stopped, was built to commemorate that moment. In fact, the Humilladero was erected as part of an initial building program by the Order of Saint Jerome in the early fifteenth century, and many pilgrims had given thanks there for reaching their goal. The shrine still stands, somewhat in disrepair, as does the road, and the site still provides the best starting point for exploring the town of Guadalupe and its expansion under the Jeronymites (fig. 1).[25]

The Humilladero shrine, with its impressive view of Guadalupe, was put there with a purpose. As is true elsewhere in the town, ritual approaches were dramatized by concealing and revealing the shrine at specific points in the pilgrim's journey. This conscious concern to structure the environment was not limited to pilgrimage routes. To a degree the spatial control of residents predated the Jeronymites, but during their tenure ecclesiastical control of the physical environment achieved full expression.[26]

---

processional route in Madrid before the establishment of the capital there in 1561. Not surprisingly, San Jerónimo was an important part of premodern *madrileño* ritual activity. Further research would be required, though, to clarify if this were typical of and unique to the Order of Saint Jerome.

[24] Records of this visit, and other visits by the Catholic Kings, are recorded in García and Trenado, *Guadalupe*, 93–104; in Ecija, *Historia*; and in various articles in the friary's journal *El Monasterio de Guadalupe* (later titled *Guadalupe*); see especially Arturo Alvarez, "Visitas de los Reyes Católicos al Real Monasterio de Guadalupe," 434–436 (1952), 16–18, and Eugenio Escobar, "Visitas de los Reyes Católicos a Guadalupe" 2 (1908).

[25] Puebla de Guadalupe was the formal name of the town during this period. Today the official name of the town is La Puebla y Villa de Guadalupe. Residents occasionally referred to their town as *la Puebla*; this word should not be confused with the Spanish word *pueblo*, which means any small town.

[26] Nicholas G. Round explores the Jeronymite impact on the physical environment in his article "Fifteenth-Century Guadalupe: The Paradoxes of Paradise," in *Medieval and Renaissance Studies in Honour of Robert Brian Tate*, ed. Ian Michael and Richard Cardwell (Oxford: Dolphin Book Co., 1986), 135–150.

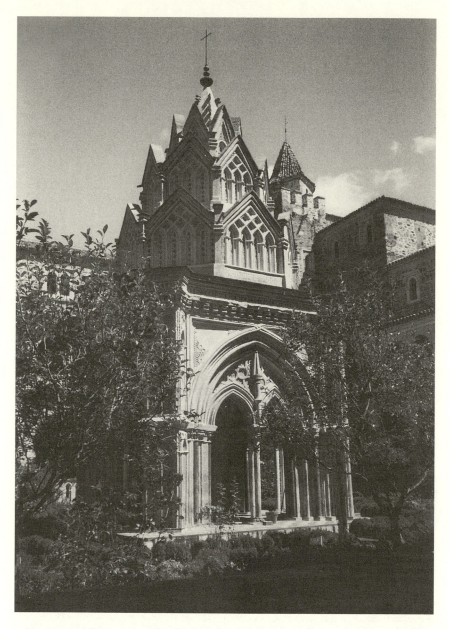

FIGURE 1. The *templete*, located at the center of the Mudejar cloister. The *Humilladero*, which is in poor repair, closely resembles the recently restored *templete*. Photo by the author.

From the vantage point of the Humilladero, the outlines of the town are clearly visible. Sprawling down a hillside, Guadalupe was centered around the friary, a large, walled complex that included a church shared by friars and townspeople, a cloister, and other outbuildings. In the century after the arrival of thirty friars of the Order of Saint Jerome in 1389, the Jeronymites ordered construction of the primary cloister, known as the Mudejar cloister, as well as a choir loft for the friars, additional fortifications, and several outbuildings and hospitals. A royal hospice tucked behind the Mudejar cloister was completed for Fernando and Isabel's 1492 visit. By the sixteenth century the friary also included an oven, a smithy, a tannery, a butcher, a shoemaker, stables, and a second, Gothic cloister used as a hospital, pharmacy, and medical school. Construction of the shrine itself had begun in the thirteenth century, with the first interest in the Virgin of Guadalupe, but the bulk of ecclesiastical construction occurred between the late fourteenth and mid-sixteenth centuries. Building continued on a lesser scale into the seventeenth century.

From the hub of the friary and main plaza, the streets curved out in two spiral arms that spread up and down the valley. These two arms formed the two neighborhoods of Guadalupe, and since at least the fifteenth century residents have referred to people and buildings as being uptown, *arriba*, or downtown, *abajo* (map 2).[27] Although there was no articulated status distinction between uptown and downtown, downtown appears to have served as a business district, housing more artisans and merchants.[28] The only evidence of commercial activity uptown is the animal market that was held on New Street, Calle Nueva, along one wall of the church. Most pilgrims entered the town downtown, winding through Eras and Seville streets. On their way they passed Guadalupe's shoemakers, dyers, and renowned copper workers. Public facilities for pilgrims, including toilets and possibly running water, were

[27] My geographical understanding of Guadalupe is based on a current map, documentary references, information from local residents, and my own observations. Further evidence is provided by drawings in Richard Kagan, *Spanish Cities of the Golden Age: The Views of Anton van den Wyngaerde* (Berkeley: University of California Press, 1989), 431–434. This information should be considered provisional since there have been no archeological surveys of the town and I have found few records of the history of non-Jeronymite construction in town. The sharp geographic distinction between uptown and downtown has been obscured by recent road building in Guadalupe, but at the end of the twentieth century older roofs still marked out the older parts of town. Even today, Guadalupenses conceptualize their town as being divided uptown and downtown around the friary.

[28] Note, however, that a processional route mandated by prior Diego de París in 1475 for the Ascension of Jesus passed uptown and downtown. AMG codex 79, *Ordenanzas Municipales*, 76r–77r.

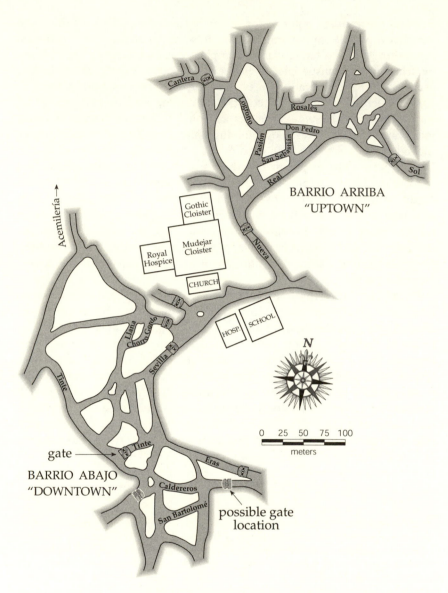

MAP 2. Guadalupe, circa 1500. Map by Richard Gilbreath.

located downtown, a short distance from the shrine. Guadalupe's two moieties did duplicate some amenities. Public fountains were scattered uptown and downtown, as was the underground supply of running water. This not only was convenient for townspeople but also may have helped ease the constant conflicts over the town's water supply and rights. A public oven was located both uptown and downtown, with a third at the exclusive disposal of the friars. Pilgrims tended to lodge near the friary and the taverns but probably stayed both uptown and downtown.[29]

The friary and the plaza in front of it have been the hub of Guadalupe for six hundred years. Into the nineteenth century, only three main roads led to the central plaza: one from uptown, and two from downtown that led pilgrims to the friary. The main road from downtown, Seville Street, obscured the friary from view until a sudden turn in the road led one's eyes through the final gate to the bronze doors of the church. In addition, one smaller road entered the plaza from downtown but appears to have led immediately out of town.[30] At the center of the plaza was a large fountain. Along the plaza covered walkways sheltered a ring of taverns, artisans' shops, and inns, *mesones*.[31] To one side stood the entrance to the friary. Located on the highest point in the plaza, a flight of steps bridged the roughly three meters between the ground level of the plaza and the entrance to the friary. A patio provided access to the parish church; until 1488 the cemetery was situated to the right side of the doors; to the left was the friary's doorkeeper, *portero*, who dispensed alms to the poor and mediated contact between the friary and the townspeople. From its monumental vantage point, the friary looked down on the plaza and the town; it was on the patio,

[29] References to craftsmen and their location occur throughout the *Actas Capitulares* (AMG codices 74 and 74bis), the *Ordenanzas Municipales* (AMG codices 75–79), and the Inquisition files (passim). The *Libro de las cañas de aguas* (1540; includes material from first ed. of 1521; AMG codices 114–116, and also available at the Ayuntamiento of Guadalupe) includes detailed information about the public water supply, including the substantial provisions for visiting pilgrims, and the elaborate system of running water (both hot and cold in the kitchen) for the friars. Conflicts over water rights are also discussed below.

[30] Alfonso Eleventh Street, which today circles around the friary through what was once the Royal Palace, did not exist until the nineteenth or early twentieth century. However, remains of an arch or gate are apparent in the wall of the friary at the road's entrance. I suspect that this led to further Jeronymite possessions or, like the *chorro gordo* arch, led out of town.

[31] The municipal ordinances, Inquisition files, and *Libro de las cañas de aguas* all include references to inns (particularly the Mesón del Rincón and the Mesón Blanco) and taverns; the municipal ordinances also refer to craftsmen in the plaza, especially pot makers, who disrupted daily high mass with their loud work.

at the edge of the cemetery, that many of the Inquisition's rites of public penance, autos de fe, were held at century's end (fig. 2).

The church, which served Jeronymites, townspeople, and pilgrims alike, physically and metaphorically linked the town and the friars. The choir, where friars sang the Divine Office for much of the day, held some of Guadalupe's richest treasures.[32] The church and shrine were used by all, and a constant round of masses, confessions, and other activities encouraged frequent interaction between the townspeople and the friars who were their spiritual leaders and temporal lords.[33] At the same time, the church served as a line of division between friar and villager. The nave runs parallel to the plaza: pilgrims and Guadalupenses entered from the right side, not from the rear of the church. The friars entered down a small set of stairs from the cloister, or from other entrances to the choir or altar.[34] When tensions flared between friars and townspeople, the church was a logical focus for that hostility. On one occasion when Guadalupenses rebelled against a new tax ordered by the prior, townspeople attacked "the church," threatening to destroy the friary and presumably their own church with it.[35]

Protection from outside invaders was accomplished by means of a double series of walls and gates that encircled the friary and town. No archeological or historical research has been done to determine the exact location or building history of the walls, and only small traces of them survive today. The gates and sections of wall that do remain, however, suggest a defensive system that could control uncooperative Guadalupenses as well as repel outside attackers.[36] An external series of walls and gates controlled access into and out of town, and a second series of gates restricted immediate access to the plaza and friary. The friars' role in protecting part of the wealth of the Castilian monarchs

---

[32] Fifteenth-century ceiling murals painted over the choir by Juan de Guas were uncovered during restoration in the second half of the twentieth century. The bronze facistol and portative organs are still present today, as are dozens of elaborate fifteenth-century illuminated manuscripts lettered with choir music for the Divine Office.

[33] Although confession was less common before the sixteenth century, frequent mention of confession by townspeople and pilgrims suggests that the practice might have been somewhat more common in Guadalupe, particularly in the fifteenth century.

[34] My thanks to Sabine MacCormack for pointing out to me the unusual arrangement of the church. In the twentieth century the level of the floor in the church was raised by several feet to make it level with the cloister floor. This facilitates contemporary processions, which pass from church to cloister and vice versa.

[35] Documents specifically state that the church was under attack. Since the friars were on the roof of the church and in the towers, it is unlikely that the townspeople were threatening merely to destroy the *portero*'s office. This event is discussed in greater detail below.

[36] My thanks to Manuel Torrejón Collado for sharing his ideas on Guadalupe's walls and architecture.

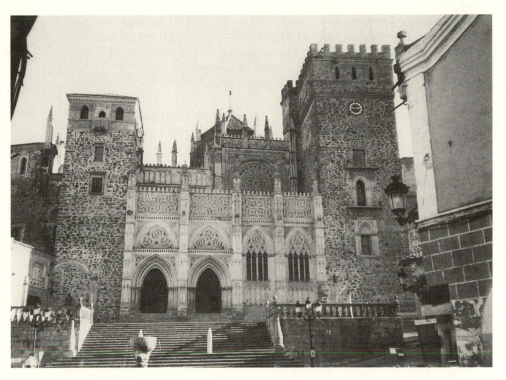

FIGURE 2. The church in Guadalupe. The friary is behind and to the sides of the church entrance; the square *portero's* door is to the left, while the cemetery was to the right. The top of the fountain is visible in front of the stairs. Photo by the author.

indicates the security these structures provided. The double series of gates and walls reinforced the geographic, economic, and political centrality of the Jeronymites. The internal set of walls also allowed the friary to regulate lay movement in the town. Access to the friary could be restricted, and if necessary uptown and downtown could be isolated from one another. The Jeronymites completed their building program in town with additional protection for themselves—a network of underground tunnels, some still existing today, which led from the friary to their barns and fields outside of town.

Physically and figuratively, the Jeronymites constructed Guadalupe. Their political connections, their popular message of humble, spiritual contemplation, and their organizational skills helped them establish the order and its presence in Guadalupe. Until the foundation of the Escorial palace-monastery by Philip II in 1565, Guadalupe was the lodestar of the Order of Saint Jerome, with more wealth and more friars than any other house in the order.[37] The friars at Guadalupe refused the honor of serving as the mother house for the Order of Saint Jerome when it was offered to them in 1414, but no one could deny the importance of the Jeronymite foundation in Guadalupe.

The Expansion of Guadalupe's Economic and Spiritual Authority

The Order of Saint Jerome may not have relished the public role demanded of them by the Marian shrine, but there can be no doubt that Guadalupe's numerous sources of income bolstered the standing and influence of the order. As temporal and spiritual authorities in Guadalupe, the friary claimed two kinds of economic privileges: tithes to the church and taxes to the friary as lord. Each year on June 24, the feast of Saint John the Baptist, townspeople gathered to bring their tithes in cash and kind to the friary. The friary theoretically did not ask residents to pay tribute, but by custom Guadalupenses collectively offered the friary a "gift" of livestock, wine, bread, and other goods worth up to eight thousand maravedís.[38] Most townspeople were also required to pay the friary rents or other fees as individuals, although the friars might demonstrate their generosity by forgiving debts owed to them by individual residents or, like lay lords of the period, by making donations for bridal dowries.[39] The friary collected fees from businesses as well. Over time, the Jeronymites used part of this income to purchase most of the land in and around Guadalupe, as well as substantial landed estates throughout Extremadura. As a result, the Order of Saint Jerome was the primary financial institution in Guadalupe and earned a comfortable income, not only from residents' donations but also from livestock and land.[40] The friary's economic resources also included royal and papal favor. A series of grants, *mercedes*, from Castilian royalty gave the friary the right to hold markets,

[37] Marie Claude Gerbert, "La Orden de San Jerónimo y la ganadería en el reino de Castilla desde su fundación a principios del siglo XVI," *Boletín de la Real Academia de la Historia* 179 (1982), 219–314; J. Carlos Vizuete Mendoza, "El patrimonio del monasterio de Santa María de Guadalupe (1340–1785)," *Hispania Sacra* 33 (1981), 593–619.

[38] Rubío, *Historia*, 331–332. Rubío states that much of this was returned to the town in the form of alms for the poor and in other social works, thereby enhancing the friary's power over the townspeople.

[39] Records of dowry gifts appear frequently in the *Actas Capitulares*, AMG codex 75.

[40] AMG codex 72, *Libro de donaçiones, testamentos*, is a 1676 compilation of records of all land transactions from the fourteenth to the seventeenth century. The records are organized by property rather than by year, making it easier to look for documentation to support the friary's claims to the land. Also useful is Vizuete Mendoza, "El patrimonio."

bringing merchants and financial benefits to the town. Grants from the pope awarded the friars in Guadalupe special indulgences for pilgrims, special permission to pardon pilgrims and administer the Eucharist, license for various activities of the order, and the right to ask alms for the Virgin throughout Castile without paying tribute to any other diocese.[41]

Guadalupe's support was not limited to its subjects and to the Crown and papacy. Together with the privileges and visits of generations of Castilian Trastámara kings and queens came thousands of pilgrims from Extremadura, Toledo, and elsewhere in Iberia. The Virgin of Guadalupe was the most popular shrine in the peninsula in the fifteenth century and welcomed more pilgrims annually than did the more venerable shrine of Santiago de Compostela. A French scholar notes that the Virgin of Guadalupe had an "international reputation for spiritual power."[42] Roads and bridges in the neighboring province of Toledo were named for the pilgrims' road to Guadalupe, an indication of the frequency with which people traveled west to visit the shrine.[43] Another measure of the shrine's appeal appears in the fact that around 1462, the friary gave 813 rations of meat to the poor daily, most of these presumably pilgrims rather than native Guadalupenses.[44] Finally, the Virgin's popularity is underscored by the success of friars who crisscrossed the peninsula asking for alms for the Virgin. So successful were they, in fact, that imposters frequently claimed association with the shrine to steal for themselves, something the friars fought bitterly.

Encouraged by the Virgin's popularity, the friars attempted to consolidate their spiritual preeminence in the region by challenging the independence of rival shrines.[45] Berzocana, a village northwest of Cañamero, is a particularly striking example of this. In 1223, during the final Re-

[41] Vizuete Mendoza, *Guadalupe*, 53–107; Rubío, *Historia*, 333–334.

[42] Cremoux, "Pélerinages," 127. Cremoux has determined that more than 90 percent of those listed in the miracle books in the sixteenth century were Iberians (123), so while Guadalupe was a more successful shrine than Compostela in these years, it was also drawing from a more limited base than Santiago de Compostela did in its heyday. William Christian, Jr., in *Local Religion* also comments in passing on the popularity of the Virgin of Guadalupe as indicated in documents from around Castile.

[43] *Relaciones topográficas de los pueblos de España*, ed. Juan Ortega Rubio (Madrid: Sociedad Española de Artes Gráficas, 1918) passim. The archbishop's bridge, *puente del arzobispo*, located in a town of the same name in Toledo, was built to accommodate pilgrimage traffic to the Virgin of Guadalupe.

[44] Enrique Llopis, "Introduction," *Guadalupe, 1752. Según las respuestas generales del catastro de Ensenada* (Madrid: Tabapress, 1990), 26, citing Perrin. Antonio Pérez y Gómez, *Dos historias, la una de la santa casa de Nuestra Señora de Guadalupe* (Valencia: Artes Gráficas, [1575] 1965).

[45] What interested them were sacred, powerful relics, not the responsibilities of organizing parishes. At one point the friars refused an offer to extend their temporal and ecclesiastical holdings to nearby Alía, for example.

conquest of the region, a number of bones were found near the village. Consensus declared them to be the relics of San Fulgencio and Santa Florentina, the two siblings of the Visigothic saints Leander and Isidore of Seville. The importance of the relics as a link to Iberia's pre-Muslim past was reminiscent of the Virgin's history, and Berzocana's fortunate location on the road to Guadalupe allowed the cult of the sibling saints to become a regional rival to Guadalupe. Perhaps not surprisingly, the friars attempted to claim the saints for their own church in Guadalupe. The Jeronymites in Guadalupe spent several centuries and untold amounts of money fighting to bring these relics to their own shrine.[46] Even the legend of Guadalupe was not immune to emendation in this quest. Saint Leander, bishop of Seville, appears in all accounts of the history of the Virgin as the man who had received the image from Saint Gregory the Great; but by the sixteenth century some copies of the legend aver that the bones of San Fulgencio were buried with the Virgin as well. At least some authors, it seems, wished to promote Guadalupe's claim to the relics in Berzocana. The issue was not decided until the reign of Philip II, when he affirmed that San Fulgencio and Santa Florentina belonged to Berzocana, where the relics remain to this day.[47] Berzocana never became an important pilgrimage site in its own right, but the size and relative grandeur of the church there suggest that it continued to serve as a way station for pilgrims coming to Guadalupe.

The Order of Saint Jerome in Guadalupe was more successful in its attempts to extend its geographic control and political influence. The land immediately surrounding Guadalupe was relatively poor, but large donations and far-sighted management of landed estates made the Jeronymites in Guadalupe lords of one of the wealthiest domains in late-medieval Castile. With the financial support of royal dynasties and noble families in Portugal and Castile during the fourteenth and fifteenth centuries, Guadalupe amassed a vast and well-organized domain including herds of cattle and sheep and profitable farm land throughout Extremadura and surrounding regions. Centuries of donations and purchases allowed the friars to turn isolated donations into large, contiguous farms and pasturage. The Jeronymites maintained thousands of

---

[46] See García and Trenado, *Guadalupe*, 21. The church in Berzocana, large given the town's current population of approximately six hundred, was built after the church in Guadalupe. The size and quality of the church probably reflects the interest of pilgrims in the site. The church's architecture follows Guadalupe's in several respects.

[47] See, for example, AHN codex 101B, whose hand has been dated to the second half of the sixteenth century. The proclamation of Philip II in favor of Berzocana still hangs on the wall of the Berzocana church.

sheep and cattle across Extremadura, and careful records noted each transaction with the noble families in the region.[48]

In conjunction with the shrine's putative spiritual power and concomitant financial security, the friary also attempted to establish its regional political dominance. Cañamero, the nearby town founded during the *repoblación* of the region, was one of the first to suffer from Guadalupe's success. After its founding as one of the first settlements in the region, Cañamero had served as a military outpost as much as a civilian settlement. The tower that dominated the town had been strategically located to protect the region as well. By the fifteenth century, though, the area was securely under Castilian control, and the fortification presented a more immediate challenge to Guadalupe's regional dominance. The friars succeeded in tearing it down by the late fifteenth century.[49] By the end of the Middle Ages, therefore, the Order of Saint Jerome in Guadalupe had succeeded in establishing its political, economic, and spiritual primacy in Extremadura. Negotiating among a host of local rivals ranging from small nearby towns to powerful noble families, the Jeronymite friars had secured their position from the hub of the town of Guadalupe to the farthest reaches of Extremadura.

Unfortunately for the friars, managing the town of Guadalupe proved more difficult than managing their herds and estates, or challenging their neighbors. The influence of the friary in Guadalupe extended from the Virgin's shrine to encompass the whole peninsula, but the relationship between the Jeronymites and the residents of Guadalupe merits particular attention. Most of the friars' temporal duties involved governing their subject town. Despite the friars' occasional remarks lamenting the burdensome task, most realized that without the town the shrine could not accommodate its many pilgrims. Similarly, townspeople might resent Jeronymite restrictions on local lay activities, but they knew that the friary helped maintain the success of the pilgrimage and the wealth it brought to town.[50]

---

[48] AMG codex 72, cited above, records this information through the mid-seventeenth century. See also Llopis, *Guadalupe*, and Vizuete Mendoza, "El patrimonio."

[49] González, *Repoblación*. Narratives of the destruction of the tower of Cañamero are common knowledge among Guadalupe's residents, and particularly among residents of neighboring communities.

[50] The friary frequently stated its desire for a simple tenure and docile residents; if Guadalupenses had not been necessary for maintaining the numerous pilgrims, stated Jeronymite officials, they would have been satisfied with a few dozen residents scattered outside the friary's walls. For more on the latter comment, see Adèle Perrin's discussion of the 1526 legal dispute between the friary and the townspeople contained in AMG codex 169 in her "Moines et villageois en Extrémadure au XVIe siècle. Un exemple: Guadaloupe" (doctoral dissertation, University of Lyons III, 1978).

When the Order of Saint Jerome arrived in 1389, they theoretically gained absolute dominion over the town, but in practice they found their authority challenged by Guadalupe's residents. As Guadalupe's earlier experience with the Mercedarians made clear, establishment of an outside order in Guadalupe was not easy. The secular monks who oversaw the monastery and town were in all likelihood from the more immediate region, rather than having the broader experience and scope common in the Order of Saint Jerome. If the secular monks more closely resembled their parishioners and pilgrims, they may also have been more sympathetic to the concerns of the townspeople.[51] Whatever the reason, though, it is clear that after 1389, friars and lay residents were frequently at odds over the extent of the friars' authority in town. That authority was embodied in the prior. He, with the assistance of the *portero*, vicar, and designated lay functionaries, settled all local issues. In 1348 Alfonso XI had awarded the monastery *mero et mixto imperio* over the town and its inhabitants. The phrase indicates the friars' range of political authority over Guadalupe's permanent male residents, *vecinos*; namely, that the friars in their collective role as lord of Guadalupe answered to no one but the king. Like the lords of other Castilians towns, they wrote and enacted their own municipal ordinances and decided on the nature and scope of local lay offices.[52]

Ecclesiastical authority in Guadalupe was more complex. The Jeronymites were an independent order under their own general when they assumed control of Guadalupe in 1389, but Guadalupe's vecinos remained in the diocese of Toledo, though under the local authority of the friars.[53] Not surprisingly, few noticed the ultimate authority of the Toledan prelate on a daily basis. The archbishop was ultimately responsible for the salvation of Guadalupenses, but it was the friars who ministered to vecinos, heard confessions, administered communion at Easter, and said mass for townspeople and pilgrims alike. For most Guadalupenses in and out of the friary, Guadalupe's prior was recognized as the ultimate spiritual authority.

[51] Sigüenza, *Historia*, 83–85, argues that the secular monks were extremely remiss in fulfilling their responsibilities, but Vizuete Mendoza, *Guadalupe*, 29–32, rightly points out that this analysis is suspect.

[52] My understanding of Guadalupe's legal status has been aided by Francisco García Rodríguez, "Ordenanzas municipales de la puebla de Guadalupe dadas por los priores del monasterio de Santa María de Guadalupe, 1415–1811" (doctoral dissertation, Universidad Nacional de Educación a Distancia, Madrid, 1986).

[53] Because of its association with Toledo, Guadalupe came under the jurisdiction of the Inquisitorial court in Toledo rather than the Extremeñan court, which only settled on a permanent capital in Llerena in 1520. While few documents survive from the Extremeñan Inquisitorial court, a substantial percentage of documents from Guadalupe remain among the many extant records of the Toledan Inquisition.

The Jeronymite prior made use of two groups of subordinates to help him govern Guadalupe: friars with an elected position inside the friary, and lay residents of Guadalupe assigned by the friary to local secular positions of authority. Of these two classes of subordinates, lay authorities were by far the less powerful. These secular officials were among the most educated of Guadalupe's residents, and the most powerful, relatively speaking, in a town where nobles were not allowed to settle.[54] Their duties primarily included implementing the friars' policies in the town. Key officials included the mayor, *alcalde*, the bailiff, *alguacil*, and the public defender, *procurador*. A slightly larger group were the members of a council that witnessed official documents, known as *fieles*. For its own needs the friary employed several scriveners or notaries, *escribanos*, *notarios*, to assist friars who also served those functions. In addition, the friars hired tradesmen such as a barber-surgeon and pharmacist, *boticario*. These men were subsidized by the friary to live in Guadalupe and provide services since local business by itself would have been insufficient to maintain them. In the mid-fifteenth century the prior decided to appoint all secular positions of authority annually, but in practice officials continued to serve for extended, open-ended terms. Local authorities who in other situations might have represented vecino interests were dependent on the friary for their position and well-being, and this dependence did not go unnoticed by Guadalupenses who felt alienated from local decision-making. Townspeople often questioned the ability of the public defender faithfully to represent their interests against the friary when the public defender himself was appointed by the friars. Residents also complained about having to support these officers financially when they were chosen by the friary and did not serve residents' interests.[55]

Jeronymite friars elected to positions of authority helped to decide and implement the Jeronymites' policies among the friars and in the town. Besides the prior, most important in communicating the friars' decisions to the town, and in responding to villager complaints, were the vicar and *portero*. The vicar ran day-to-day operations in the friary and town, heard complaints from residents, and ruled on small matters for vecinos, substituting for the prior at his request. The *portero*—much more than a humble "gatekeeper"—administered alms to the town and served as the primary intermediary for communication from the towns-

---

[54] AMG codex 79, *Ordenanzas Municipales*. The provision forbidding nobles to reside in Guadalupe dates to at least the fifteenth century and presumably was designed to eliminate potential political or economic rivals from taking up residence in town.

[55] Early examples of these complaints will be discussed below. These complaints continued into the sixteenth century, when they were recorded in a book detailing the audiences that vecinos had with the prior. See AMG codex 75.

people to the friary.[56] Confessors, though they played an explicitly spiritual role in Guadalupe, were another important means of communication between friars and Guadalupenses. The role of confessor was an
elected position in the friary and carried much of the same significance
and prestige as other explicitly administrative roles.[57] Confessors ministered to both pilgrims and townspeople, and for many residents, confession must have been one of the few sites of interaction with the friars.
Evidence from Inquisition documents suggests that both sides took advantage of those moments of contact for a variety of ends. Friars did
not hesitate to engage penitents in ad hoc question-and-answer sessions
about matters of faith. Confessors might also exhort their penitents to
adopt different attitudes to daily affairs, or to treat fellow residents re-
spectfully.[58] Guadalupenses, on the other hand, took advantage of confession to bring to the confessor not only an admission of sins, but also
complaints about neighbors or other friars.[59] Use of the confessional in
Guadalupe highlights the mingling of secular and spiritual authority in
Guadalupe. Each encounter with a friar held both spiritual and secular
significance and led to a sacralization of secular affairs, even as religious
moments such as the confessional were recast as an opportunity to
speak at length with one's temporal lord.

Any complexities of temporal or spiritual lordship that the Order of
Saint Jerome faced, though, did not hinder the town's growth. In 1408 a
census taken in Guadalupe counted 289 vecinos, or heads of household,
and therefore approximately 1,156 people—already an increase from

---

[56] These offices are described in Vizuete Mendoza, *Guadalupe*, 145–148, 151–157,
from Guadalupe's constitutions.

[57] AMG codex 74, *Libro de los actas capitulares*; see also Vizuete Mendoza, *Guadalupe*,
194–204.

[58] These encounters are described in Inquisitorial records, particularly when townspeople or friars thought that some confessors were too sympathetic or lenient in regard
to the behavior of converts from Judaism and their descendents (conversos). This is
discussed in greater detail in chapter 7. For a good introduction to some of the issues
raised by the increasingly private nature of confessional, see *Penitence in the Age of
Reformations*, ed. Katharine Jackson Lualdi and Anne T. Thayer (Aldershot, England, and
Burlington, VT: Ashgate, 2000), particularly Jodi Bilinkoff, "Confession, Gender, Life-
Writing: Some Cases (Mainly) from Spain."

[59] See, for example, AMG unnumbered, Internal Inquisition, 8. Testimony of Diego
de Ecija. Fray Diego mentions a confession made by Mari Sánchez the old weaver, who
complained about the suspicious practices of a neighbor, Francisco Arroquez, and the
lack of interest on the part of her then-confessor, Diego de Marchena. For a broader
discussion of the issues surrounding confession, see Thomas Tentler, *Sin and Confession
on the Eve of the Reformation* (Princeton: Princeton University Press, 1977). Jodi Bilinkoff
is currently conducting research on the relationship between confessor and penitent in
early modern Spain; also available is Stephen Haliczer, *Sexuality in the Confessional: A
Sacrament Profaned* (New York: Oxford University Press, 1996).

1389.[60] By 1500 that number had more than tripled, to 1,030 vecinos or approximately 4,120 people, despite a population drop at century's end. Adèle Perrin suggests a maximum population of around 4,800 inhabitants or 1,200 vecinos, which is consistent with the admittedly more impressionistic accounts of townspeople in the late fifteenth and early sixteenth century.[61] Although more specific numbers are lacking, the sharp population growth confirms Guadalupe's importance in the late medieval period and indicates the increasing numbers of merchants, pilgrims, artisans, and wanderers moving to the town. Fundamentally, therefore, this was a new town, with a certain amount of social fluidity among all its residents.

New Christians made up one part of the Puebla's growth. Jews apparently were never permitted to settle in the ecclesiastically controlled Guadalupe, but conversos were free to immigrate, and many chose to do so.[62] Beginning in 1391 a series of anti-Jewish riots swept across the peninsula, bringing with them mass forced conversions of Jews. A few years later the Valencian Dominican Saint Vincent Ferrer traveled in eastern Iberia and southern Europe, preaching to large groups of Chris-

[60] Vizuete Mendoza, *Guadalupe*, 41, from a census taken March 10, 1408 (AHN Clero Legajo 1423, expediente 17). The term vecino can be used in the Inquisition documents to refer to women, but it is likely that for purposes of the census only heads of household were counted. Several studies have examined the early history of Guadalupe, and two scholars in particular have studied demography in Guadalupe. These are María F. Cerro Herranz and Adèle Perrin, cited above. I conform to the standard, in both these works and Castilian demographic studies generally, of multiplying the number of heads of household by four to estimate total population.

[61] Rubío, *Historia*, 208; Llopis, *Guadalupe*, 28–30; Perrin, "Moines et villageois," 130. An outbreak of plague in 1488 and the expulsion of the converso population in 1500 affected Guadalupe's population significantly. The 1500 expulsion is discussed in chapter 8. The memories of "old men" like the one cited by Perrin should be approached cautiously. Cerro Herranz, in "El dominio del monasterio de Santa María de Guadalupe. Estudio de su estructura económico en el siglo XV" (doctoral dissertation, University of Extremadura, 1987), estimates a total population of 6,000 in 1485, but this should be taken as an upper limit. Her estimate is based on one man's testimony during a trial that before the plague of 1488 and the Inquisition there were 1,500 families in Guadalupe. Perrin repeats this figure of 6,000 in a summary of her dissertation, "Plenitud de Guadalupe en el siglo XVI," *Guadalupe* 715 (1992), 53–70. In a related account, an elder of the town stated that Guadalupe was founded by Jews, a claim repeated by Perrin but completely unsupported by documentary evidence. Llopis, *Guadalupe*, 29, shows that Guadalupe reached its maximum population in 1485.

[62] There was no regulation explicitly forbidding Jews to settle in Guadalupe, but during the priorate of fray Gonzalo de Illescas (1441–1444, 1450–1453) an ordinance was passed ordering all residents of the town—citizens and residents, *moradores*—over the age of eighteen years to attend mass on Sundays and feast days. This regulation would, if enforced, effectively forbid Jews from living in Guadalupe. From the remaining documents, and from the described reaction of Jews who visited the shrine, it seems almost certain that no Jews lived in Guadalupe during the fifteenth century.

tians, converting Jews, and inciting widespread violence toward those Jews who did not convert. In Seville, Ferrán Martínez de Ecija engaged in similar activity. By the early fifteenth century, increasing numbers of Jews were converting to Christianity. Not all were converted directly by force; some converted out of fear of anti-Jewish violence, while others were genuinely persuaded by the message of Christianity; still others converted to take advantage of business opportunities afforded to Christians. By the mid-fifteenth century, Castile and Aragon's Jewish population had substantially declined. In its place appeared a new category: that of New Christian, or converso. The terms describe both converts and their descendants; although baptized at birth, converso children were still held suspect by Old Christians, that is, those not descended from Jews. At the same time that Jews and New Christians were facing increasing popular hostility, widespread civil unrest and decreasing royal authority made large cities ever more unsafe for both Jews and conversos. Increasingly, both groups moved to smaller towns like Guadalupe, where local lords might provide more protection and where New Christians might, if they chose, attempt to escape their family history.[63]

Because they were for all intents and purposes Christian, conversos are notoriously difficult to distinguish from Old Christians in the documents.[64] As a result, debate continues over the total number of conversos in Guadalupe at the end of the fifteenth century.[65] As Christians, conversos were baptized and buried in the church; they took Christian names and engaged in Christian trades. Only through careful reading of Inquisition documents can conversos be distinguished from Old Christians. In her doctoral dissertation, Perrin claimed that two hundred families or eight hundred people were exiled by the Inquisitors, therefore assuming that Guadalupe included at least eight hundred conversos, but this argument seems based on a misconception. Perrin apparently assumed that only heads of households were tried. Her numbers lead to the improbable conclusions that almost 17 percent of the people in Guadalupe were conversos, but that only one-third of all conversos, or

---

[63] My thanks to Teo Ruiz for his thoughts on this.

[64] Without Inquisitorial records it would be most difficult to identify New Christians at all. New Christians were the first target of the Holy Office of the Inquisition established in Spain in 1481, and it is these records that form the basis of much, though not all, of the writing on conversos. These issues are discussed in greater detail in chapter 5.

[65] In fact, there is considerable debate over the converso population of Iberia as a whole. Netanyahu discusses this debate and defends his conclusion in *Origins*, 1095–1102. Henry Kamen, in estimating the number of Jews expelled by the Catholic Monarchs in 1492, also touches on the population numbers for conversos; see "The Mediterranean and the Expulsion of the Jews in 1492," *Past and Present*, 119 (1985), 30–55.

over two-thirds of adult conversos, reconciled.[66] A more likely estimate for the late fifteenth century is that conversos made up slightly less than 10 percent of Guadalupe's population. Approximately 230 conversos reconciled, confessing their sins before the Inquisitors at the beginning of the trials. If this number encompasses almost all adult conversos living in Guadalupe at the time of the Inquisition, that would indicate that New Christians comprised slightly less than 10 percent of the population.[67]

Like the town it governed, the friary grew during the fifteenth century, but not without some challenges. Fray Yáñez brought thirty friars with him in 1389 when he established the Jeronymite foundation at Guadalupe, where they joined the small number of secular friars already tending the friary. Conflict apparently soon followed. Some Jeronymite friars complained of Yáñez's government of the friary, insisting on more rigorous observances. Some friars even murmured darkly about fray Yáñez's competence. Fifteen years after his arrival, Yáñez threatened to return to San Bartolomé de Lupiana, and King Enrique III (reigned 1390–1406) hurriedly sent for the bishop of Segovia to pacify the house. By 1407 a number of friars left Guadalupe with Yáñez's permission to found their own, more eremitical friary.[68] But even this disruption, though serious, did not long affect the friars or the shrine. Pilgrims, friars, and new townspeople continued to pour into Guadalupe, and by 1464 some 130 friars were sitting down to eat in the refectory.[69]

During these same years, residents of the Puebla voiced their own challenge to the new friars in Guadalupe. Establishing a theme that was to continue into the sixteenth century, residents charged that the friars had unfairly rescinded vecino autonomy in town. In 1404 the vecinos

> rose up against the prior and the friars, saying that that town was not of the friary, but their own, that their parents had founded it, and the prior and friars had entered tyrannically into their own property (*haciendas*),

[66] Specifically, 70 percent of adult New Christians. See Perrin, "Moines et villageois," 290, 312–313. Perrin's error has been repeated in other studies: Enrique Llopis, a careful scholar of the economic history of Guadalupe, mistakenly accepts Perrin's statements as they stand, citing also Diego de Ecija. See *Guadalupe*, 28. Research on questions such as converso demographics continues to be difficult.

[67] Assuming again a population of 4,800 inhabitants. The friary, by comparison, had 21 of its 130 friars—about 16 percent—censured for suspicious or heretical activity. Chapter 7 includes an analysis of the charges of Judaizing made against Jeronymite friars in Guadalupe.

[68] Sigüenza, *Historia*, 1:144–145; Vizuete Mendoza, *Guadalupe*, 41–42; and Revuelta Somalo, *Los Jerónimos*.

[69] Vizuete Mendoza, *Guadalupe*, 136. Vizuete also notes that this figure approximately matches with the number of beds in the friary: 48 in the dormitory, and 78 in cells (plus 27 in the hostel and 10 in the hospital).

wrongly and unjustly turning them into vassals, and that [the friars] had installed a mayor (*alcalde mayor*) without their consent, whom they brought from outside. He would have been more lenient, if he were of the town, but the outsider did not take pity on them, or pay attention to anything other than enriching himself with his tyrannies and threats. And beyond this, [the friars] had made [the townspeople] tributaries, setting out (*echando*) a certain tax, which was called in that time *facendera*, exiling people from the town for the misdoings, and in this manner [the friars] ended up with the farms by force, or buying it at the necessary price for which they could sell. [The vecinos] also alleged that [the friars] had usurped their privileges, locked in the convent's archive, where no one could see them, or understand the reason for their justice.[70]

The complaints voiced here include themes that were to plague relations between friars and townspeople through the mid-sixteenth century. Again and again, the vecinos argued that they had the right to the kind of communal self-government not uncommon in this period and should not be placed under the authority of the friars. Indeed, in their petitions Guadalupenses referred to their town as a self-governing city, *república*. More specifically, residents complained that lay officials appointed by the friary served its interests rather than the townspeople's, and that the friary imposed unfair taxes on the town. Some Guadalupenses remembered the autonomy that had been theirs before 1340, and even more seemed to hold fond memories of life in Guadalupe before the Jeronymites arrived. Locals suspected ill-will on the part of a friary that seized the charters listing vecino privileges and locked them away in the friary. Unlike their predecessors, the Jeronymites in Guadalupe had no need for or interest in lay involvement in governance of the town, a radical shift from the pragmatic attitudes present at the pilgrimage site at the beginning of the fourteenth century.

Townspeople had long begrudged the friary its renewed authority under the Order of Saint Jerome, but broader concerns may have triggered unrest at precisely this time. In 1406 Juan II (reigned 1406–1454) ascended the throne at the age of two under control of his regent, Uncle Fernando of Antequera. Though Fernando's regency passed without incident, the political transition may have affected pilgrim travel to Guadalupe's Marian shrine. The fifteenth century had its share of famine and other natural disasters, and, as Angus MacKay has noted, these periods of hunger and economic debility were often paired with social and political unrest. An extended period of drought at the beginning of the fifteenth century and a concomitant drop in pilgrim traffic may

[70] Sigüenza, *Historia*, 1:172.

account for the increase in discontent among vecinos and friars at this time.[71]

Conflict between friars and vecinos continued sporadically through 1408, the year of the first census in the town. During this period the Jeronymites employed many methods to quiet vecino unrest, but with little success. On one occasion the prior of the Jeronymite mother house in Lupiana was called upon to render a judgment in the matter. After another uprising, some residents were tried and subjected to a mild punishment: the vecinos were gathered together to listen to a speech by the friars. In their statement, the friars argued that the arrival of the Order of Saint Jerome had improved conditions for Guadalupenses: the taxes owed to the friary were less than those owed to the king, they claimed, and could be further reduced by special petition to the prior. It is possible that the census taken at this time was used to determine tax rates for the townspeople as part of a larger agreement ending the uprising. Through either the friars' actions or the exhaustion of the townspeople, the unrest seemed to have run its course with the census: after 1408 there is no mention of widespread civil disturbances until the 1440s.[72]

Anti-Jeronymite and Anticonverso Violence in the Mid-Fifteenth Century

The intervening forty years witnessed much growth for the Puebla and the friary, but little recorded tension. The friary and town grew in population, and the Virgin of Guadalupe became fully established as one of the primary cults of fifteenth-century Iberia. King Juan II visited the shrine several times, and his first wife, María of Aragon, became particularly devoted to the Virgin of Guadalupe and her friars. María took the prior, fray Pedro de Valladolid (1432–1441), as her confessor and was buried in the friary at her death.[73] Popular devotion was also on the rise, as pilgrims flocked to Guadalupe for the Virgin's festival in September.

[71] Angus MacKay, "Popular Movements and Pogroms in Fifteenth-Century Castile," *Past and Present* 55 (1972), 33–67.

[72] Vizuete Mendoza, *Guadalupe*, 40–41.

[73] Many studies describe María's devotion to Guadalupe. In addition to the above-mentioned general studies on Guadalupe, see Round, "Fifteenth-Century Guadalupe." María was the mother of Enrique IV, who also favored the shrine and the order during his reign. María's tomb, a Gothic sculpture located at the altar, was taken down and redesigned in the seventeenth century. Enrique IV was also buried in Guadalupe, though under peculiar circumstances; a memorial to him is located opposite his mother's at the altar. For more on Enrique's death and burial, see Dr. Gregorio Marañón, *Ensayo biológico sobre Enrique IV de Castilla y su tiempo*, 2d ed. (Madrid: Espasa-Calpe, 1934).

The shrine's popularity was indicated by the continued construction of the friary, which included building some outlying buildings as well as a second Gothic cloister behind the original Mudejar cloister.

The Puebla had not forgotten its claims to autonomy, however. In 1446 a group of vecinos presented a wide-ranging list of petitions to the prior, asking for increased rights in the town and its environs.[74] On November 14, 1446, prior Juan de Zamora responded to the vecinos' petitions in the capitular hall in the presence of a crowd of "many vecinos and residents," including scribes and local lay officials, together with the vicar, confessors, *mayordomo*, *portero*, and presbyters. First among the vecinos' requests was "that [the prior] produce [a copy of] the privileges that were taken away from the town. It contains the liberties and exemptions that were given and granted by the ancient kings to the vecinos and residents of this Puebla; so that the liberty and exemption that it formerly had may be restored to the Crown."[75]

As in 1406, at least some residents maintained a knowledge of their more independent status before the arrival of the Jeronymites sixty years before. Without a written record of their ancient privileges, however, the Guadalupenses were unable to counter the friary's increasing control in legal terms, or even confirm or deny the friary's right to regulate Guadalupe as it did. Few if any residents remained who remembered life in Guadalupe before the Jeronymites, but the motivation of their descendants should not necessarily be understood as nostalgia for an earlier, quieter, autonomous past. The increased wealth and prestige of Guadalupe benefited all who lived there, including the many townspeople who had moved to Guadalupe after the arrival of the Jeronymites. Locals may have resented the tight control that the friars maintained over the town, or simply wanted the right to hunt and fish near the friary; they almost certainly were not protesting the popularity of the shrine per se. In that struggle with the friary, residents could employ the earlier rights of the *república* to file suit against the friars. The townspeople may or may not have been looking for proof of independence; at a minimum, access to a list of privileges would allow them to

---

[74] Three copies of the petition, on paper and in differing hands, are bound together in parchment with other selected documents and titled "En este cartapacio esta çiertas petiçiones y juramentos de los vezinos desta puebla de guadalupe y çiertas Rrespuestas de los priores fr. Juan de Çamora 7 fr. Gonçalo de Madrid [1446–1448]" (unfoliated), AMG legajo 82.

[75] "que mande paresçer los privilegios que fueron tomados al pueblo. [I]ten que se contienen las libertades e franquesas que por los rreyes antiguos a los vesinos e moradores desta puebla fueron dados e otorgados. para que por ellos el pueblo sea rrestituydo en la posesyon dela libertad e franquesa en que estava antes." AMG legajo 82, "En esta cartapacio . . . ," Request 1, 1v.

ascertain the limits of the rights of the Jeronymites. Prior Juan de Zamora replied that he found it "just and reasonable," *justo e rrasonable*,
that the townspeople be shown their privileges and exemptions when
they wished, although they would remain in the care of the friars.

Not all the townspeople's petitions in 1446 concerned their status
in relation to the Jeronymites; pragmatic requests predominated, but
throughout the Guadalupenses sought to identify the limits of the friars'
control and the extent of lay autonomy. Townspeople questioned the
prior on his policies concerning reasonable taxes at the mills, access to
public ovens, and pasturage, hunting, and fishing rights. Unlike later
priors, fray Juan de Zamora tended to respond generously to town
requests, but some petitions proved controversial. For example, the vecinos asked permission to elect someone from the town to keep the
república's money. The townspeople promised to distribute the money
for the common good of the Puebla, and only in accord with the prior's
wishes; but the prior refused to grant vecinos that independent authority.[76] In response to a new tax of 1,000 *maravedís* to support the bailiff,
alguacil, the vecinos stated that they considered payment of this new tax
fulfillment of their requirement to pay tithes to the friars; that is, that
the new tax—as well as the office, perhaps—was not valid. Other townspeople did not pay their share of the tax burden to support the *alguacil*,
and the rest resented the fact that they were not punished. Locals also
complained that the town suffered as a result of the *alguacil*'s activity in
town. The prior affirmed the *alguacil*'s right to carry out the duties of
his office, but added:

> furthermore, good men, well you know how up to this point the offices
> of *alcalde* and *alguacil* and of the *fieles* were given without limitation of
> time. This is not done in the greater part of the kingdom, nor is custom-
> ary in the region where we live. Toward which end I have resolved and
> want and order that from henceforth the said offices will be vacated
> every year on the first day of January, for which the prior at that time
> will give them to the persons whom he wishes and who will be capable
> to have and administer the said offices.[77]

This shift in policy, although it had not been explicitly requested by
the vecinos, was perhaps perceived to work to the townspeople's bene-

[76] Ibid., Request 11, 4v–5r.

[77] "Otrosy buenos omes bien sabedes en como fasta agora los offiçios del alcaldía e
alguasiladgo e delos fieles se dauan syn lymitaçion de tiempo. Lo qual non se fase en la
mayor parte del Regno, nin se usa en la comarca donde byvimos. Por ende yo he
acordado e quiero e ordeno que de aqui adelante los dichos offiçios vagan cada año por
el primero dia de enero; para qual prior q por tiempo fuere los dé a las personas q
quisiere e fueren sufiçientes para los tener e administrar." Ibid., Request 13, 5r.

fit: theoretically, at least, more Guadalupenses would be included in lay administration of the decisions of the friars. In other towns in Castile, where local authorities such as the *alcalde* and *alguacil* had the ability to effect change and make rulings on issues of local importance, such rotation in office was of practical import. In Guadalupe, however, the prior's announcement amounted to little more than the friars' decision to spread the financial benefits of office-holding among their most trusted vassals.[78]

Other requests provoked sharp criticism. When the townspeople asked to share rights to the Jeronymites' underground waterworks, the prior replied that "this request is not just, and even less legal and proper. For as much as it pertains to the Lord [prior] to divide the water access as he wishes and as he sees fit and assess the town to repair the piping without contributing to it. . . . However, wanting to act out of mercy in this issue, it pleases me that the friary shall pay as it has paid until now."[79] This question struck at the heart of vecino concerns about Jeronymite government at midcentury. Tax burdens under the friars continued to grow, often for officials or for Jeronymite construction projects that seemed to benefit townspeople little. Water access in Guadalupe was a particular point of conflict throughout much of the Puebla's history.[80] Springs uphill from the friary provided a generally consistent source of water, as did a number of streams below the town, but retrieving that water could be a difficult process, especially in

---

[78] It is not clear that such rotation in office was instituted in practice. In the 1470s residents complained about the lack of rotation in lay offices. See chapter 4.

[79] "petiçion no es justa; nin menos liçita e honesta. Por quanto al señor pertenesçe Rrepartyr el agua como quisiere e bien visto le fuere e echar derrama al pueblo para adobar el caño sin contribuir en el. . . . Et enpero queriendo [?] de misericordia enesta parte: a mi plase que pague el monasterio segund que fasta aqui ha pagado." Ibid., Request 7, 4r.

[80] Residents' protests over the inaccessibility of water continued into the second half of the twentieth century. The importance of this resource is suggested by the *Libro de las cañas de aguas*. The work is an explanation of the entire system from the springs uphill to all the piping in the town. The *Libro de las cañas de aguas* was composed in 1540 by the friar in charge of maintaining the pipes. He used an earlier text of 1521, written when the entire system was replaced, and like this earlier book his was written to facilitate repairs. Hot and cold running water was available in the friary kitchen through a series of cauldrons and pipes, located in the chimney, that heated the water; drains either emptied back into pipes that led to gardens and similar purposes or emptied into a drainage system. The system was generally inaccessible to townspeople, but exceptions were sometimes made. In one case, a vecino with friends in the friary was able to have water pipes laid to his garden in a private arrangement with the pipe-layer, something that greatly disturbed the prior when it was discovered. A few taverns on the plaza were also supplied with cold running water, in particular the Mesón del Rincón and the Mesón Blanco.

the summer. To remedy this, the Jeronymites greatly expanded the relatively primitive system of running water used by the secular monks. Their waterworks included a reservoir in the mountains (with built-in cellars for keeping perishable foodstuffs chilled), hot and cold running water for the friary, and limited water for pilgrims at public toilets. Vecinos, though, were largely excluded from access to piped water. When Guadalupenses were asked to help pay for the pipes from which they would receive no benefit, local frustrations with Jeronymite control grew stronger.

Violence erupted within a month of the prior's responses to the town. Armed with rocks and sticks, a large group of men and women gathered outside the church, as the friars inside were singing in the choir. The vecinos demanded an end to the tribute; a small group of townspeople attempted to seize the chest where some of the town's tribute money was kept. The prior hurriedly convened a meeting of the townspeople at the patio in front of the church, and with the assistance of a public notary they produced a document that officially ended the additional waterworks tax. The new pipes would be financed by the traditional tithes paid annually by the vecinos. A formal inquest by King Juan II found in favor of the friary's right to tax Guadalupenses as it pleased and awarded the friars the seized goods as their right, but the prior returned them, in the interest of maintaining peace in town.[81] In January the townspeople agreed to abide by the prior's responses to their petitions, and throughout the next two months some 314 adult males witnessed their agreement before a notary.[82] Over the following year, the friary and its subjects continued to meet occasionally over the issue of taxes. Having gained increased access to the prior and a voice in further plans regarding taxation, vecinos were less angry. Tensions dropped still further with the election of a new prior in May, and the additional tax was ultimately dropped. For vecinos, this was a rare, successful intervention in Jeronymite politics. The prior they so distrusted was not reelected, and a new prior, one more sympathetic to their concerns, took his place.[83]

Those vecinos whose names appear on the original petition, and who represented the town in its dealings with the friary, reveal much about social conditions in Guadalupe during the first century of Jeronymite control. On January 9, 1447, a small group of friars and vec-

[81] See Vizuete Mendoza, *Guadalupe,* 49–51.

[82] AMG legajo 82, 20r–28v. On a later list compiled by the notary, 450 vecinos appear.

[83] Ibid., 38r–43v. Documents in AMG legajo 82 suggest that decreased tensions and the change in policy were encouraged by the election of a new prior, fray Gonzalo de Madrid, to replace fray Juan de Zamora. Vizuete's account emphasizes royal input into Guadalupense issues and suggests that the reversal of policy occurred under prior Juan.

inos agreed to the prior's response to the petition of the previous November. Several vecinos were listed without any specific profession. But those whose professions were named—several cloth merchants or *traperos*, scribes, a barber-surgeon, two innkeepers, a cobbler, and a former *alguacil*—suggest that many of those present were among the relatively wealthy tradesmen in Guadalupe. In addition, a significant percentage of those listed were New Christians. At least five of the twenty-eight men listed, including notaries and cloth merchants, were tried by the Inquisition forty years later.[84] Some conversos were apparently among the wealthiest Guadalupenses, although of course not all conversos were wealthy, and not all wealthy Guadalupenses were conversos. Strikingly, New and Old Christians were listed together, with little indication of distinction being made either by the scriveners or by the vecinos themselves. Only the inquisitorial records of a later date help one identify which were conversos and which were Old Christians. At midcentury, then, Guadalupe already possessed a New Christian population that was relatively well integrated into Guadalupense society and had taken advantage of economic opportunities there.

The assimilation of New Christians into Christian society in Guadalupe, at least in opposition to action by the friars, did not mean that all divisions between New and Old Christians had disappeared. In the years leading up to 1450, as vecinos were challenging Jeronymite rule, local conversos were singled out by resident Old Christians in a popular uprising. No records of the uprising exist, and it is unclear if these attacks preceded or followed the town's actions against the friars. Since both New and Old Christians were later pardoned by the friars, it seems likely that the two were not one event, though it is believable that actions against Guadalupe's friars and against Guadalupe's conversos were related. The only extant account of the anticonverso uprising is by fray Alonso de Oropesa, general of the Order of Saint Jerome. Fray Alonso, who may himself have been a converso, professed at Guadalupe and was in residence there as a young man when the uprising occurred.[85] Fray Alonso's concern was with the spiritual and philosophical implications of the event, rather than with providing a detailed historical account; however, some indications of the tensions present in Guadalupe are apparent in his comments.

> So then, while I was in the religious life as a novice and young convert in our house of Guadalupe, which on account of its greatness and ven-

---

[84] Ibid., 20r.
[85] Netanyahu, *Origins*, 896, contends that Alonso de Oropesa was not a converso, though Francisco Márquez Villanueva argues the opposite.

erability appears before the whole world as outstanding and venerable, there arose a great schism among the faithful and the inevitable scandal: charity was wounded, peace disturbed, faith oppressed, hope confounded, the rights of Christ, the adornments of the Gospel and the bonds of the Christian religion were violated. Certain evil men, moved by envy, began to harass the Jewish converts saying that they could not receive the honors and dignities of the people of God equally with those Gentile converts (which, as it can be read, were those who principally constituted the Church); [these men also said that] neither could conversos receive ecclesiastical and secular offices and benefices. On the contrary, the conversos should be ineligible for them since they were neophytes, cited by Saint Paul, meriting suspicion in the Christian faith and not conforming to the sacraments of the Church.[86]

Without further knowledge of the event, it is difficult to explain why the uprising happened when it did, but some speculation is possible. First, events in Guadalupe followed on the heels of a well-known popular anticonverso uprising in Toledo. In 1449 residents of Toledo had launched an attack on New Christians for perceived favors they received. It was the first such attack against conversos, as opposed to Jews, and marked a turning point in attitudes toward New Christians on the peninsula. For the first time, "purity of blood" statutes were temporarily instituted, demanding Christian ancestry for four generations as a precondition to obtain lay offices. The events Fray Alonso

---

[86] "Así pues, mientras estaba en la vida religiosa como novicio y joven converso en nuestra casa de Guadalupe, que por su grandeza y veneración aparece ante todo el mundo como insigne y venerable, surgió un gran cisma entre los fieles y el inevitable escándalo: se hirió la caridad, se turbó la paz, se oprimió la fe, se confundió la esperanza, se violaron los derechos de Cristo, los atavíos del evangelio y los vínculos de la religión cristiana, cuando ciertos hombres malvados, movidos de la envidia, comenzaron a apremiar a los convertidos del judaísmo diciendo que no se los podía recibir a los honores y dignidades del pueblo de Dios en igualdad con los que se habían convertido de la gentilidad, que, como se lee, fueron los que principalmente constituyeron la Iglesia, ni tampoco a los oficios y beneficios eclesiásticos y seculares; sino que había que apartarlos de ellos por ser neófitos, citados por San Pablo, sospechosos en la fe cristiana y disconformes con los sacramentos de la Iglesia." Fray Alonso de Oropesa, OSH, *Luz para conocimiento de los gentiles*, tr. and ed. Luis Díaz y Díaz (Madrid: Universidad Pontificia de Salamanca, 1977), 62. This edition is the only published version of Fray Alonso's important work, *Lumen ad Revelationem Gentium et gloria plebis Dei Israel, de Unitate Fidei et de Concordi et Pacifica AEqualitate Fidelium* (Light for the Revelation of the Gentiles and Glory to the People of the God of Israel, Concerning the Unity of the Faith and the Concord, Peace, and Equality of the Faithful). Díaz y Díaz's opinions of Oropesa's work are also summarized in "Alonso de Oropesa y su Obra," in *Studia Hieronymiana*, 1:253–313. Fray Alonso's important place in the court of Enrique IV and his work are discussed at greater length in chapter 4.

described occurred in the aftermath of the Toledo riots.[87] Second, this attack on conversos may have been related to earlier popular unrest over the water taxes issued by the friary in 1449. No author or contemporary document mentions specific hostility to conversos as part of the vecinos' complaints, but such a link is not impossible. In later decades, challenges to the friars' authority were often linked to explicit resentment of the role of New Christians in Guadalupense society, particularly when conversos were serving as local officials at the behest of the friars. Only occasionally was this link made clear in the agreements signed by the townspeople and the Jeronymites at the end of an uprising. A connection between this event and the earlier uprising would also conform to a pattern of later decades in Guadalupe, when civil unrest tended to occur in short, intense bursts about once a generation.

Whatever the context for the uprising, it is clear that some Old Christians in Guadalupe maintained profound reservations about the rising status and visibility of some conversos in town. Fray Alonso condemned this Old Christian attitude and continued by describing his response to the heightened tensions in town. "Amazed at their audacity" and freed from the responsibility of preaching, fray Alonso went into the town, speaking to the residents, seeking out those at fault, and explaining Christian charity and the equality of all before the law.[88] Ultimately, the prior in Guadalupe "counseled, indeed even urged and ordered" fray Alonso to write a treatise on this topic for those who were absent or would join the friary later, and fray Alonso agreed. The result, *Light for the Revelation of the Gentiles*, was completed over a decade later, with the incident here described opening the dedicatory preface.

Despite its limited circulation, fray Alonso de Oropesa's work represents one of the period's most important and carefully reasoned theological statements on the status of conversos in Christendom. Due to fray Alonso's position at the court of Enrique IV, his attitudes toward New Christians were widely disseminated, even if his text was not. Fray Alonso, following Saint Paul, believed that there could be no division between those who converted to Christianity from Judaism and those who converted as Gentiles. Furthermore, no offices could be withheld from New Christians simply for their status as "neophytes" in the faith. Not surprisingly, given his own probable New Christian status, fray Alonso assumed that most conversos were good Christians and that only a minority attempted to maintain Jewish practices. The Jeronymite friar saved his most strident criticism for those who accused New Chris-

---

[87] An overview of the 1449 events in Toledo is available in Albert Sicroff, *Les controverses des statuts de "pureté de sang" en Espagne du XVe au XVIIe siècle* (Paris: Didier, 1960).

[88] Alonso de Oropesa, *Lumen*, 64.

tians of apostasy out of ill will. Rather than encourage bitterness and hostility toward conversos, fray Alonso insisted on the importance of gentle correction of faults, instruction in doctrine, and the precedence of reform over punishment. Above all, he averred, Christians were one people and ought not to allow any schism to divide them.[89]

As for the place of conversos in Guadalupe in the wake of these events, the record is silent. Until the last quarter of the fifteenth century, nothing more was said about converted Jews or their families in surviving documentation. While some Old Christians may have been suspicious of their New Christian neighbors, there is no indication of widespread or large-scale attacks on New Christians as a group. Perhaps fray Alonso's discussions had an effect, or economic prosperity eased pressures on all in town. In some cases, as for example the signatures mentioned above, there were contexts in which some conversos and Old Christians mingled without difficulty. Only later in the fifteenth century would relations between New and Old Christians be strained beyond repair.

By 1450 the outlines of late-fifteenth-century Guadalupense society had emerged. The presence of the Jeronymites since 1389 had accelerated the shrine's transformation into one of the most important religious devotions in late-medieval Iberia. The friars presided over a period of rapid growth and prosperity for both the town and the friary and forged links with the Castilian royal family that benefited both shrine and Crown. As the friars attempted to extend their control over the town, their subjects cited memories of past autonomy to press for more independence from the authority of the Jeronymites. Meanwhile, the friars slowly strengthened their claims over Guadalupe by granting vecinos small or temporary concessions that effectively reaffirmed the friary's right to grant those concessions. By 1450 Guadalupe was politically, spiritually, and economically well situated in the Iberian landscape. The townspeople thrived, despite occasional unrest, because of the economic benefits of living near the Marian shrine. But how did Guadalupenses understand their relation to the spiritual power that seemed to them to be so present in town? What were the religious practices that helped to confirm their identity to themselves and others? It is to these questions that we turn next.

[89] Ibid., 320–322.

TWO

LIVING IN THE SHADOW
OF THE VIRGIN

ALL OF Guadalupe's residents lived—metaphorically, at least—in the shadow of the Virgin of Guadalupe. All of them understood their lives in town in the context both of the Virgin's spiritual power and of the temporal power of the friars who maintained her shrine. As such, a religious overlay necessarily colored residents' understandings of themselves and the place where they lived. Yet this did not mean that sentiment for the Virgin created a unified, communal identity, or even a simple opposition of New Christian and Old Christian. Rather, life in the shadow of the Virgin involved a number of overlapping communities, organized around a variety of religious and secular identities. Out of those various communities and the standards of appropriate behavior encouraged by them, we can better understand the range of attitudes present in the town of Guadalupe on the eve of the expulsion of Spain's Jews, and to what extent those were or were not considered generally acceptable to the populace as a whole.

In attempting to determine the relationship in Guadalupe among religious identity, behavior, and belief, and then to fix in view the range of individual and communal identities that comprised the Guadalupense population, it is imperative to take advantage of all the available sources. This of necessity includes not only documents generated by the friars' governance of the town of Guadalupe, but also the inquisitorial records still extant from the voluminous documents that once existed. Evaluating inquisitorial sources, however, can be difficult. Some scholars have argued that inquisitorial investigations are largely inventions, sources so biased that they are essentially useless.[1] And it is true that an uncritical reading of inquisitorial documentation would be a grave mistake. Yet a careful reading of the sources can reveal assumptions of Old and New Christians about how residents of the town of Guadalupe could or should live. Most cautiously, it is important not to underestimate the utility of gaining a clearer understanding of the anxieties of the inquisitors themselves, and of those who leveled accusations of Judaizing behavior. These

[1] Benzion Netanyahu has articulated this view in all his writings.

anxieties did not merely exist in a vacuum but carried implications about contemporary religious, social, and political concerns.

I maintain that inquisitorial documents do more than merely reflect the concerns of the Holy Office, however. In reading and analyzing records of the Inquisition, I have made use of the following critical strategies. First, inquisitorial documents can be read "against the grain," so to speak, not for information about the explicit subject—Judaizing practices in Guadalupe—but rather for implicit assumptions about social, economic, and political relations in town. The frequent mention of collective activity among women, the gossip network among Guadalupe's servant girls, the descriptions in passing of Christian as well as Jewish observances—all these can, with some caution, be accepted as generally faithful representations of life in the shadow of the Virgin.

Second, it is essential to examine inquisitorial records as a whole, each one in relation to the others. This can be accomplished, for example, by tracing the accusations of a single person across several trials. Does that accuser consistently make the same accusations, or do the claims vary from case to case? Does the accuser appear to condemn some New Christians more fervently than others? Are the accusations all made in a short period of time, or are they spread out over the course of the year? The greater the variety of content and intensity of the accusations, the more thoughtful, and therefore plausible, those accusations become. On the other hand, a frequent witness who makes an unusually virulent accusation against one person in particular calls into question that witness's motivations. One can also examine tendencies in the trials over the course of the year. Does the execution rate change from the first group of sentences early in 1485 to the last group of sentences in November of that year? Are there any noticeable changes in defense strategies as the year wears on? What evidence is there for communication among the prisoners, and possible effects on how the accused conducted themselves? As Inga Clendinnen has shown in her work *Ambivalent Conquests*, this kind of comparative examination of large numbers of concurrent trials can shed new insights on both the accusers and the accused, as well as allow one to hazard some hypotheses about the validity of the accusations.[2]

Third, it is impossible to understand these trials fully without exploring in some depth the political, social, and economic context in which the accusations took place. As Guadalupe's political divisions and social conflicts come into focus, content and patterns of accusations take on new meaning. For example, the deep divisions already evident in the

[2] Inga Clendinnen, *Ambivalent Conquests: Maya and Spaniard in Yucatan, 1517–1570* (Cambridge: Cambridge University Press, 1987).

town in the fifteenth century cast doubt on the accusations leveled against some of its wealthy merchants, while the numerous and detailed claims of Judaizing made against deceased women may bear further scrutiny. These are, admittedly, general guidelines rather than firm rules for analysis. But they do indicate the potential that inquisitorial records, carefully read, possess.

Finally, one has to be careful not to adopt the schematization of the inquisitorial documents themselves. The categorizing power of the Holy Office of the Inquisition was profound, and it is tempting to absorb unwittingly their assumptions that there were New Christians who were in fact secret Jews, and that these "univocal, integral" (as Yovel describes them) individuals composed an equally coherent, unified community.[3] In discussing the practices of actively Judaizing conversos in Guadalupe, it is important to remember that these practices were not unitary, were not entirely distinct from New Christians' Christianity, and were not engaged in by all conversos at all times in identical ways.[4]

Two caveats specific to the documentation on Guadalupe are also in order. First, of the 226 trials for which brief summaries exist, only 37 files remain. Even if we assume that virtually all New Christians were accused (if not found guilty), this spotty collection greatly limits our knowledge of the trials. Second, although all the trials date from 1485 and therefore discuss events from midcentury to the year of the accusations, it is difficult to specify within that thirty-year period when Christian devotions or alleged Judaizing activities may have occurred. This is particularly important in the case of Jewish observances, where some scholars have posited a decline in Judaizing in the second half of the fifteenth century.[5] Whenever possible, I have tried to provide a chronological context for the practices of Guadalupe's active Judaizers, as well as for the Christian practices I describe. In general, though, it can be assumed that all Judaizing events in this chapter occurred in the mid- to late fifteenth century. Christian practices generally fall within that range as well, although evidence from the first half of the sixteenth century is also included when available.

---

[3] Yovel, "The New Otherness."

[4] Throughout this book, I have chosen to use the term "Judaizing" rather than "Judaism" or "crypto-Judaism" to describe some practices of conversos. Since I contend that even actively Judaizing conversos were deeply influenced by their exposure to Christianity, it seems misleading to use the same term to describe Jewish practices and those practices engaged in by Christians trying to observe Judaism to some degree. This does not deny the fact that some Jewish and Judaizing practices were quite similar, although of course many others were noticeably different.

[5] See Kamen, *The Spanish Inquisition*, 40.

SABBATH AND SUNDAY OBSERVANCES

We begin our examination with an exercise in "thick description," a close look at the markers of identity affirmed at the end of every week as the town prepared to observe its weekly devotional rites in the second half of the fifteenth century.[6] Of course, not all Old and New Christians engaged in all of these practices. Some New Christians were genuine converts, as evidently pious as their Old Christian neighbors; conversely, some Old Christians were so lax in their observance that some of their attitudes were difficult to distinguish from apostate New Christians. What follows, then, is a generalized description. But this phenomenological approach allows us to begin to understand the complex symbolic world of late-medieval and early modern Castile, where religious action or inaction could send multiple and sometimes conflicting messages about religious belief.

Before the inquisitorial trials of 1485, Sabbath observances began at sundown Friday. Some converts from Judaism made little attempt to observe the Sabbath, particularly men, whose ritual actions were more closely tied to the more public, and hence less feasibly covert, acts surrounding weekly worship meetings.[7] Other conversos, though, struggled to maintain some observance of Judaism. For them, the Sabbath demanded consistent weekly attention to one's distinct religious identity, required no complex astronomical calculations to know when to observe it, and provided a spiritual, emotional, and practical counterpoint to Christian observances on the following day. Several women were accused of cleaning the house on Friday afternoons in preparation for the Jewish Sabbath—sweeping floors, scrubbing, and cleaning.[8] While a good Friday afternoon housecleaning was not an un-Christian act per se, many testified to such activity before the Inquisition as evidence of hallowing the Jewish Sabbath. Ana Sánchez, daughter of Isabel Sánchez the holy woman, *beata*, "said that when she was with her mother they lived across from the house of Mari Sánchez [wife of Diego Sánchez, tanner]. And Ana saw that Mari and her daughters Catalina and Isabel left off doing anything every Friday at the hour of Vespers and swept. And they cleaned the house. And they began to rest the whole afternoon, and Saturday. And they did not spin and they ceased work as if it were a holiday [*fiesta*]."[9]

---

[6] See Geertz, *The Interpretation of Cultures*, 3–30, 412–453.

[7] See Melammed, *Heretics*, 31–32.

[8] Christian women cleaned house on Saturday for the Christian Sabbath on Sunday. AHN Inquis. legajo 154, expediente 6.

[9] Ibid., legajo 184, expediente 1, 5r. "dixo que estando con su madre bivían en frente de casa dela dicha Mari Sánchez. Dela qual e de catalina e ysabel sus fijas veya de

Some women chose to prepare food before the Sabbath and leave it in the embers of the fire to stay warm while they refrained from work. The food was prepared for Saturday and so was perhaps not bound by Christian observances of fasting from meat on Fridays—certainly some conversa women did not hesitate to include meat in those slow-cooking dishes—but servants frequently questioned the practice before the inquisitors, and other New Christians tried unsuccessfully to sidestep the issue by avoiding meat preparations for the Sabbath altogether.[10] Mari Flores, deceased mother of Andrés González de la República, was accused of cooking egg stews on Friday for Saturday. In Martín Gutiérrez's home, the family tried to obscure its intentions and fulfill Christian precepts by cooking fish stews on Friday for Saturday; however, a former maid reported the family's actions to the Holy Office. For Martín Gutiérrez and his family, it was their intentions, rather than their acts per se, that led their servant to speak before the inquisitors.[11]

By nightfall on Friday, oil lamps might be set up in one corner of the house—typically resting in a shallow tray of water, to help protect against fire spreading during the next twenty-four hours. The practice elicited comment from numerous servants, who were under strict orders not to touch the lamps; they would remain undisturbed until Saturday evening, or until they went out on their own.[12] Once the sun set, observance of the Sabbath began in earnest. It is not surprising that observance of the Sabbath was a pervasive theme in Inquisition docu-

---

continuo los viernes a ora de bísperas dexauan de fazer algo e barrían. E fregauan la casa. Y começauan de holgar toda la tarde. Y otro día sábado. Y non hilauan e se parauan como de fiesta." This Mari Sánchez, many of whose family members had fled to Málaga to return openly to Judaism, was sentenced to death. There are extant inquisitorial records for six women named Mari Sánchez, none of whom were related. I distinguish them by their husband's names. Note, too, the implication that New and Old Christians lived cheek by jowl in Guadalupe.

[10] See David M. Gitlitz and Linda Kay Davidson, *A Drizzle of Honey: The Lives and Recipes of Spain's Secret Jews* (New York: St. Martin's Press, 1999), for a discussion of Judaizing dietary practices. This work is primarily a cookbook of historically informed interpretations and reconstructions of food references in inquisitorial literature, though it also includes a thoughtful analysis of food and converso identity.

[11] For Mari Flores and the stew with eggs, *cazuelas de huevos*, see AHN Inquis. legajo 148, expediente 9. Not only were eggs considered a form of meat and therefore forbidden on Fridays, but egg-and-bean casseroles left to cook in the embers were associated with crypto-Judaism. For Martín Gutiérrez, see ibid. legajo 156, expediente 11, 6r, testimony of Catalina la Talaverana, vecina of Navalvillar.

[12] Most trials include a reference to lighting cleaned oil lamps. María, a former maid of Ruy González de la Corte and his wife, provides a typical example: "The lady lit the oil lamp in her [bed? room?] and had it so it would not go out Friday night. And some mornings this witness found it burning." "[la ama] encendía la candil en su cama (camara?) e lo tenían que non lo apagauan [friday night]. E que este testigo algunas mañanas lo fallaua ardiendo." Ibid. legajo 155, expediente 13, 9r.

ments, since it was not only one of the most important complexes of observance, but also relatively easy to know when and what (at a basic level) to do. Like all Judaizing practices, however, observance of the Sabbath varied from person to person in both the extent and intensity of practices maintained. "Observance" could mean as little as lighting oil lamps on Friday evening, a more public activity such as wearing clean clothes on Saturday, or even holding secret weekly services.[13] Most testimony indicated practices that fell somewhere between the extremes of oil lamps and secret observances. Those New Christians sufficiently bound by belief, upbringing, or pressure from family and friends to light lamps often engaged in other Judaizing practices as well; relatively fewer conversos had the resources, desire, or ability to hold weekly Sabbath services.

Witnesses testified both to a desire to preserve the Sabbath and to converso fears of being found out. Beatriz Núñez, stepmother of the innkeeper of the Mesón Blanco, commented on her limited freedom of action in observing the Sabbath, and her fear of alerting her husband and servants to her activity.[14] Martín Gutiérrez, a cloth merchant, was reputed to have interrogated visiting Jews on details of Jewish ritual practice before his death some years before. One witness, Mari Sánchez, the wife of Diego Fernández, noted "that she heard Martín Gutiérrez, while standing at his door, ask a Jew who had come to buy goods how he kept the Sabbath. And the Jew said, 'Enter in your house and I will tell you.' And Gutiérrez called his children to hear what the Jew said and his children came and the Jew said how the calf was prepared and other things that she does not remember."[15]

One of the most important elements of observing the Sabbath was

[13] Juan de Texeda unsuccessfully defended Mari Flores from the charge of wearing clean clothes for the Sabbath by claiming that her position in town made her a frequent participant in baptisms as a godparent. For this reason, he said, Mari had often dressed well on Saturdays; see ibid. legajo 148, expediente 9, 4r.

[14] While her fear of revealing her Judaizing practices to her servants seems justified, her fear of revealing those activities to her husband seems less so, since the church had censured him twenty years before. In 1485 her husband was still remembered as Fernando González the heretic, *hereje*. See the trial of Beatriz Núñez, ibid. legajo 169, expediente 2, 2r. Of course, such a comment also served to protect his reputation.

[15] Ibid. legajo 156, expediente 11, 4r. "que oyó desir a martín gutierres estando a su puerta a un judío que vino a conprar mercadería le preguntó cómo se guardaua el sábado. E que le dixo el judío entrad en vuestra casa e dezir vos le he. E que llamó a sus fijos que oyesen lo que dezía el judío e venieron sus fijos e dixo de como hera fecho el beçerro e otras cosas que non se acuerda." Note also the testimony of Diego Rodríguez the shoemaker, the barnero's son-in-law, ibid.: "dixo que vido como martin gutierres trapero metio en su casa un judío físyco que andaua con el maestre de alcántara e le fizo ciertas preguntas dela briuia e que otra vez llamo a otro judío e le pregunto asy mesmo dela briuia e llamo a sus fijos e dixo fijos parad mientes [mientras?] lo que dize este judío por que deprendays."

refraining from all labor. Ceasing work on the Sabbath is central to hallowing the Sabbath, and, as Martín Gutiérrez's story suggests, a religious day without work provided the opportunity to live and contemplate with family one's alternate theology. Observing the Sabbath was also one of the most self-evident and expected of Jewish activities and fulfilled inquisitors' expectations—hence making it an easier charge to fabricate. Because men and women engaged in different kinds of labor, claims relative to avoiding labor on the Sabbath varied according to gender. Women and their servants were primarily occupied by labor in the home, such as cooking, cleaning, and spinning; they also engaged in small-scale businesses that centered around women's labor in the home, such as bread-baking or cushion-making. Although free time was available for chatting with friends in the street or at the public ovens, women always had work waiting at home.[16] It is perhaps not surprising, then, that women were more universally charged with keeping the Sabbath than men were. Women had the opportunity to speak with their neighbors while working: activities like kneading bread, shopping, waiting at the public ovens, or spinning could all be completed while engaged in conversation. One of the most common indications that a woman was keeping the Jewish Sabbath was the testimony of neighbors that on Friday evenings and Saturdays she was observed with her hands still, not even spinning.[17]

Men could more easily hide their avoidance of work than women; when men were accused of avoiding work on the Sabbath, it was often due to change in dress. Men and male servants and apprentices worked primarily in service industries—generally shoemaking, tailoring, or pot making—or in family owned vineyards outside of town that provided a convenient Sabbath getaway. Men also do not seem to have engaged in activities equivalent to the spinning or mending that occupied women, although walking through the vines with fellow workers, or talking over the tailor's scissors, may have served a similar purpose to gossiping over spun wool. Certainly games, dice, and time spent in the tavern were seen as male rather than female activities. But men were accused of observing the Sabbath as well; several were accused of dressing well on Saturdays. Diego Sánchez, a tanner, was accused of stopping work on Saturdays and then exhausting his apprentices by working them all Saturday night, once the Jewish Sabbath was over.[18]

As Sánchez's case indicates, those New Christians who wanted to

---

[16] Spinning, in particular, is frequently referred to as a common evening activity.

[17] The accusation is made against a large percentage of conversas. Some examples include ibid. legajo 155, expediente 13, 9r; legajo 148, expediente 9; and legajo 183, expediente 20, 6r.

[18] Ibid. legajo 184, expediente 2.

observe the Sabbath occasionally demanded that their servants refrain from work as well. Most interpretations of Jewish law stated that one could not profit from work done on the Sabbath, even if done by a Gentile.[19] To adhere to this requirement as a New Christian was particularly difficult, however, since to do so required revealing heretical practices to one's Old Christian servants. The risk was not inconsiderable, and certainly more serious than trying to hide one's beliefs, since servants constituted a veritable clearinghouse of gossip and rumor. Despite the possible dangers, however, some New Christians in Guadalupe do appear to have imposed the restrictions of the Jewish Sabbath on their servants or apprentices. On more than one occasion, servant girls complained of being forced to cease work from sunset Friday to sunset Saturday, "nor were the other girls allowed to spin; rather they had to go to bed early."[20]

Some of the most active or the boldest Judaizers went so far as to hold secret Sabbath services in their homes, or to set up special sites for individual daily prayer in the home. Evidence for such activity was less common than for other, less serious examples of Judaizing and was generally restricted to members of a few families. Secret Sabbath services generally included only those most devoted to Judaism and perhaps their immediate family, or those most willing to commit to weekly Jewish services in addition to attendance at mass. Services tended to be relatively small affairs—smaller groups were harder to detect and easier to manage, and less subject to betrayal. Although one witness said that he had heard secondhand that "the conversos of this village had a synagogue," it is highly unlikely that all conversos shared one weekly worship service.[21] Disagreement among New Christians about the best way to proceed and differing levels of devotion and commitment to Judaism, as well as a well-founded caution, kept secret services small.

As with all Jewish acts performed by baptized Christians, one of the pressing concerns of those involved in secret Jewish services or individual Jewish prayer was to hide the activity from neighbors, friends, and servants.[22] Servants—usually poor, young, Old Christian girls from

---

[19] There was some disagreement over how much work Jews could ask of Christian servants on the Sabbath. The best examination of this is in Jacob Katz, *The "Shabbes Goy": A Study in Halakhic Flexibility* (Philadelphia: Jewish Publication Society, 1989).

[20] "nin dexaua hilar a las otras moças salvo que se acostasen tenprano." AHN Inquis. legajo 155, expediente 13, 9r.

[21] "tenía sinoga los *conversos* desta villa." See ibid. legajo 154, expediente 14, 5r. The witness heard this statement from someone visiting from nearby Berzocana, who said he had heard it from a Jew who had come through Guadalupe.

[22] Some conversos were accused of praying in a Jewish, rather than Christian, fashion. One Jewish prayer is recorded in the trial of Juana González, ibid. expediente 20, 10r.

nearby farming villages—were commonplace in most homes in Guadalupe. They were present in all parts of the house, and beds, like all furniture, were part of the public domain. Some houses had upstairs rooms with doors that could close off access, but opportunities to make use of such a space without attracting suspicion were rare. In some cases, therefore, conversos turned to the *bodega* as a site for individual prayer. In Spanish, a bodega could refer to any place where wine was stored, including a wine store or a wine cellar, or the hold on a ship where wine was kept.[23] Often, it also referred to a separate building, located either at the vineyard or in town. References to bodegas in the inquisitorial material included references to "doors," and in at least one case to a building attached to, but distinct from, the house. In this case the bodega was located off the *corral*—an open central space behind the home that held chickens, the outhouse, and so on.[24] Less trafficked than other parts of the home, a bodega at the back of a *corral* could serve for undisturbed private meditation, but even so, questions were raised in the minds of servants.

> Each morning they locked themselves in the bodega and closed the door and also closed the other door that opens onto the *corral* from the bodega, and they did not want anyone to enter there. And if the servants had to go to the *corral* they went [upstairs and] over, through the garret . . . [and] this witness became suspicious.[25]

> [This witness] lived with Rodrigo de la Corte and with Juana González his wife. . . . she did not see them eat pork and they cooked their stew apart without pork and she also saw them shut themselves in the bodega when they got up in the morning; and she heard them praying a prayer inside that did not mention Our Lord except that sometimes they said *Adonay* and then they would leave there and go to church.[26]

[23] Sebastián de Covarrubias Orozco, *Tesoro de la Lengua Castellana o Española [1611]*, ed. Felipe C. R. Maldonado, rev. Manuel Camarero (Madrid: Editorial Castalia, 1994).

[24] Ruth Behar's *The Presence of the Past in a Spanish Village* (Princeton: Princeton University Press, 1986), chap. 2, provides an excellent description of this type of extended structure. While the specifics of her Leonese case cannot be assumed in Guadalupe, the general concepts described in her work seem to apply to references given in the Inquisition material.

[25] AHN Inquis. legajo 155, expediente 13, 9r. Maria, criada de Ruy González de la Corte. "cada manana se encerrauan en la bodega e cceraua la puerta tras sy e asy mismo cerrauan otra puerta que sale al corral por la bodega y non querían que ninguno entrase alla. y sy los moços o moças avían de yr al corral yua[n] por encima por el sobrado . . . este testigo tomaua mala sospecha."

[26] Ibid., 8v. Isabel, servant of Rodrigo de la Corte and Juana González. The bodega could also be used to hide in on Sunday, working or avoiding Christian Sabbath observances. (AHN Inquis. legajo 156, expediente 11, 6r.) "biuió con Rodrigo de la Corte [y]

Other Judaizers were not so secretive. Martín Gutiérrez, for example, who had called visiting Jews into his home to advise him on details of observance, engaged relatively openly in Judaizing earlier in the second half of the fifteenth century, before his death. When Juan de Cabeza Aguda, vecino of Guadalupe, was living with Martín Gutiérrez, he saw Gutiérrez "pray each morning from a book, behind the door, and bowing; and although he asked him what he should do he did not respond until he had finished praying."²⁷ Despite having been raised as a Christian, Gutiérrez apparently engaged in an unusually large number of Judaizing practices. An unexpected guest provided the Holy Office with an extended description of his daily prayers.

> Eight or nine years ago this witness entered the house of Martín Gutiérrez one morning. . . . he entered and called out, and the said Martín Gutiérrez did not hear him, and he was among some chests lying face down [?] with a hood on his head and he was bowing and praying; and this witness did not understand what he prayed but it did not seem like Christian prayers; . . . And this witness left the house and banged loudly on the door, and then the said Martín Gutiérrez got up and threw off the hood that he had on his head.²⁸

Books in Spanish and Hebrew were another element of individual and collective Judaizing devotions among some New Christians. In addition to playing a key role in Judaism, books provided knowledge normally accessible through one's rabbi or learned elders. Some particularly active Judaizers like Martín Gutiérrez owned prayer books,

---

con Juana Gonçales su muger . . . non veya comer tocino e guisauan su olla aparte syn tocino e que asy mismo les veya que como se leuantauan se metían en una bodega e les oya rezar ally dentro oración e que non me[n]tauan a nuestro senor saluo que algunas vezes dezían adonay e que de que salían de allí se yuan a la yglesia." This couple not only engaged in daily Jewish prayer but also apparently attended daily masses. Note that they were apparently praying in Spanish, a practice that would accord with the ad hoc prayer book owned by Manuel González of the Mesón Blanco.

²⁷ AHN Inquis. legajo 156, expediente 11, 4v. "cada manana rezar en un libro tras la puerta, e sabadeando; a que aunque le preguntaua lo que avía de fazer non le respondía fasta que acabaua de rezar."

²⁸ Ibid., 5r, testimony of Miguel Sánchez Zohano. Note that in this case the witness did not understand the prayers. They did not sound like the Latin Pater Noster or Ave Maria, and may well have been in Hebrew. "avía ocho o nueue años que este testigo entró un día de mañana en casa de martín gutierres . . . que como entró e llamó e que el dicho martín gutierres non lo oyó e que estaua entre unas arcas echado de bençes e un capirote sobre la cabeça e que estaua sabadeando e rezando e que este testigo no entendió lo que rezaua pero que non le paresçió oraçiones de cristiano e que como avía oydo desir que tenía una mandrigala pensó que estaua de partiendo conella. E que este testigo salió de casa e dió un grand golpe en la puerta, e que entonçes el dicho martín gutierres se leuantó e arrojó el capirote que tenía en la cabeça."

possibly in Hebrew, as the above account suggests.[29] Others owned books in Spanish, including Bibles and translations of or variations on Jewish prayers. Two cases of books were seized from Guadalupense conversos and burned at one of the last autos de fe, evidence of the importance and availability of books for New Christians trying to observe Judaism. Unfortunately, the burning also left little evidence of converso reading tastes.

Inquisitorial witnesses provided evidence of how some groups of conversos might have used books. For example, they might read selections at secret Sabbath meetings. One witness described the suspicious use of Bibles in Spanish, *brivias en romançe*, rather than in the more acceptable Latin. Some families also read to commemorate important dates in the Jewish ritual year. Inés González described her family gathering together to read "in a big book—I do not know what book it was—and they did this on the evening of the fasts of the Jews, and on Saturdays."[30] Others read simply to study. Adán López testified that some years before he saw his deceased sister Mayor listen to readings of a *brivia* and of "Jewish prayers" with her mother, aunt, and grandmother.[31] This unique record of women studying Jewish scripture is striking. Given the prominent position of women in preserving Jewish beliefs and practices, though, perhaps we should not be surprised after all that, possibly as long as a generation before the inquisitorial trials of 1485, women studied and read the Hebrew Bible. The incident hints at the depth of the desire of at least a few converso men and women at midcentury to observe their ancestral faith.

The only Judaizing tract in Guadalupe to survive the Inquisition was a prayer book owned by Manuel González, innkeeper at the Mesón Blanco. The small, slim volume was included in his file and became a permanent part of his record. The partially filled pamphlet included several hands of varying quality, apparently added at different times. It is possible that Manuel used the book as a place to write down remem-

---

[29] Fray Diego de Burgos the younger, one of the friars accused of Judaizing, attracted suspicion because of his tendency to read the Old Testament (that is, Hebrew Bible) in Hebrew rather than Latin. See chapter 7.

[30] AHN Inquis. legajo 183, expediente 20, 8r. Her mother is Mari Sánchez, wife of Diego Jiménez the butcher. "en un libro grand no sabe que libro era y esto que lo hasía las bísperas delos ayunos de los judíos e los sábados."

[31] Ibid. legajo 165, expediente 4, 3v. "dixo que su hermana Mayor muger de Juan de Segovia veya que pasaua a oyr leer [marginal addition: briuya e oraçiones judaycas] con sus tias leonor e juana gonçales e con su avuela violante alonso." Although he describes them as "aunts," it seems more likely that Juana Gonçales is Mayor's mother; other documents in Mayor's file list her parents as Juana Gonçales, wife of Rodrigo Alonso. Mayor also died young; her mother and remarried husband were informed of her accusation, and her children (referred to only generally) played no role in her trial.

bered or original prayers on occasion. It is likely that he used his position as innkeeper to ask traveling Jews to write down remembered prayers as well. Except for the inclusion of the word *Adonay* for God, all prayers were in Spanish with Roman letters and appear to be either remembered prayers of penitence and petitions for aid or variations on the Psalms. The booklet not only reveals the desire for quasi- or crypto-Jewish written material—they are apparently not exact copies of Jewish prayers—but also suggests one way in which New Christians employed visiting Jews to help them maintain their practice of Judaism.[32]

Whatever form it took, observance of the Jewish Sabbath was critically important to Judaizers. Highly committed Judaizers lived in a constant state of compromise, juggling half-remembered demands of Jewish law with their status as baptized Christians. Not all New Christians engaged in all of these methods of observing the Sabbath, and some chose not to observe the Jewish Sabbath at all. But it is striking how many conversos felt sufficiently safe in the second half of the fifteenth century in Guadalupe—particularly at midcentury—to observe some elements of Jewish law in a relatively open fashion. Old Christian servants who were instructed not to work on the Jewish Sabbath, and conversos who openly engaged in some observance of the Jewish Sabbath, suggest that New Christians in Guadalupe feared neither reprisals from the ecclesiastical community nor attacks from Old Christian neighbors. Indeed, Judaizers may have felt encouraged to act by the Puebla's resistance to earlier attempts to introduce the Inquisition to Guadalupe. For those conversos interested in observing some elements of Judaism, hallowing the Jewish Sabbath provided the weekly structure around which a quasi-Jewish life could built.

Just as the Jewish Sabbath was coming to a close, preparations for the Christian Lord's Day were beginning. There are many fewer sources of information on what Old Christians were doing as part of their devotions, but some aspects of Christian worship in the fifteenth and sixteenth centuries are clear. Christian women swept and cleaned their homes and made ready their clean clothes for Sunday morning. Most locals seem to have attended Sunday mass with some regularity, although they did not honor Sundays as the friars desired. The Municipal Ordinances, for example, repeatedly stated that vecinos should not spend so much time in taverns on Sunday, particularly before the main

---

[32] Manuel González's trial (including the prayer book) is transcribed in Fidel Fita's "La Inquisición en Guadalupe," *Boletín de la Real Academia de la Historia* 23 (1893), 283–343. My thanks to Elka Klein for her thoughts on the origins of these prayers.

mass at noon.[33] Furthermore, despite the importance of Guadalupe's Marian shrine, the behavior of the townspeople inside the church was often little better than that in other churches of the period, or that outside the church for that matter. Men and women stood or sat on the floor on opposite sides of the nave.[34] Tombs lined the floor of the church, and women, in particular, were keen to stake out a spot over the remains of their family members on the side of the church known as St. Gregory's Nave, even if it meant creating a scene to remove another woman who had already arrived.[35] The friars attempted to limit this debate among their parishioners, with, one senses, little success. Several New Christian women had Old Christian witnesses testify to their proper behavior during mass, and it is apparent from their testimony that New and Old Christians were not segregated in church. New Christian men, on the other hand, congregated apart from Old Christians both during and after mass. In Andrés Alonso Trujillano's trial, for example, defense witnesses stated that Andrés had little to do with other conversos and acted as an Old Christian; he did not mingle with the other conversos, either during or after mass.[36] If church masses served as a common meeting place in Guadalupe (as they did in other communities), the segregation evident here may have had as much to do with discussions of economic and political issues as it did a purely religious or ethnic segregation, though evidence elsewhere suggests that Old and New Christian women mingled much more than did Old and New Christian men.[37]

---

[33] AMG codex 79, *Ordenanzas Municipales de Diego de París*, prepared after Nov. 20, 1481, título 37, 59r. See also codex 76 (unfoliated), 27v; codex 77, 26r; codex 78, título 33, 48r (all of the proceeding are fifteenth-century collections of municipal ordinances). The ordinances state that men should leave the tavern by the time the bells strike for the Ave Maria. On Old Christian, pre-Reformation Christian attitudes, see John Edwards, "Religious Faith and Doubt in Late Medieval Spain: Soria circa 1450–1500," *Past and Present* 120 (1988), 3–25.

[34] As was customary in the premodern period, there were no pews or seats in the church. AMG codex 79, 8r–v. Ordenanzas Municipales de Diego de París, título 3, "de las sepulturas 7 enterramientos."

[35] These were gravestones set into the floor of the church, with the tombs located below the floor of the church. (The gravestones have since been removed.) Ibid., 8v. "E por lo dezir & defender algunas personas le (se?) han seguido & podrían seguir mayormente entre las mugeres muchas discordias y disensiones & turbación de los divinales oficios sobre las dichas sepolturas & asientos de las dichas mugeres por ende muger alguna non sea osada de dezir que tiene logar suyo conosçido en la dicha yglesia nin en las dichas sepolturas nin lo defender por suyo nin dezir que tiene propiedad nin señorio en la tal sepoltura porque la compró ella o sus antesçessores porque las cosas sacras & religiosas non se pueden vender nin comprar."

[36] AHN Inquis. legajo 132, expediente 18.

[37] See chapter 3 for more on this phenomenon.

Accused New Christians were regularly asked if they participated in communion, but the court was rarely able to prove nonparticipation in the Eucharist, in part because consumption of the Host by Old and New Christians was largely limited to Easter. It seems likely, however, that some conversos might try to avoid taking the Host.[38] More important for parishioners and inquisitors was the focal point of the Mass: the elevation of the Host by the priest. Until the reforms initiated by Vatican II in the 1960s, priests who performed the Mass faced away from the congregation and toward the altar and the crucifix when they raised and consecrated the bread and the wine. This central moment of the Mass, then, was in some ways a private one. All eyes were theoretically focused on the Eucharist as an object of devotion and reverence. Curiously, the strangely private moment of the consecration of the Eucharist gave conversos a certain liberty, despite their presence at mass. Indeed, even though everyone was expected to worship the Trinitarian God in the form of the Eucharist, it was unclear what, specifically, one should do to express that devotion. Old Christians usually crossed themselves, raised their hands, and in some way "adored the Host," probably by speaking or praying aloud. Both Old and New Christians engaged in frequent discussions on the topic of how one should reverence the Host, as inquisitorial documents make clear. In the trial of Mari González Cebriana, one woman testified that "one day certain women were talking, neighbors [of Mari González Cebriana], and this witness with them, about what each one said when Our Lord was raised at mass, and then Mari González Cebriana said, 'I say nothing but "blessed be He that fathered you" when the Host and the chalice are raised.' "[39]

Mari González la Cebriana was not the only woman to respond to the Eucharist with her own quasi-Jewish prayers. Juana González, daughter of Martín Gutiérrez, was reported not to have prayed the Pater Noster or Ave Maria at mass, but instead to have prayed for her absent husband. Reportedly, Juana said in a voice loud enough for others to hear: "Give me Lord what you promised me," and "Protect me and free me

---

[38] See Miri Rubin, *Corpus Christi: The Eucharist in Late Medieval Culture* (Cambridge: Cambridge University Press, 1991), for a fuller discussion of the social and theological role of the Eucharist in late-medieval Europe.

[39] AHN Inquis. legajo 154, expediente 30, 5r, testimony of Catalina Diaz. "estando un día hablando çiertas mugeres vezinas suyas e este testigo con ellas delo que cada una dezía quando alçauan a nuestro señor dezía entonçes Mari Gonçales Çebriana 'Quanto yo non digo syno 'bendito el que te crió' quando alçan la ostia e el calis.' " Notice the tacit acceptance here of Jesus as the Son of God, and, one might argue, of the doctrine of transubstantiation as well. My thanks to Elka Klein for her thoughts on this exchange.

from this strong force."[40] Many witnesses testified that conversos did not raise their hands, cross themselves, or adore the Host, but instead turned their heads away or lowered their eyes. Martín Gutiérrez was accused of turning his head away, hiding behind a marble column, or hiding his eyes behind a cloth "so that he could not see Our Lord."[41]

Even priests were occasionally aware of the nonparticipation of some conversos. Fray Alonso de Nogales, one of the friars at Guadalupe, explained how he once checked up on those witnessing the Mass. He described how he was "officiating at a Mass in the chapel of St. Anne . . . many were in attendance . . . and as I knew that there were conversos among them, at the time that the priest raised the Lord above his head I, because of the suspicions I had of them, stood up and put my eyes on the conversos, and I saw that they had their faces toward the ground; and I was quite disturbed by this and I began to say bad things about conversos and to be much more suspicious about their acts and lives."[42]

The rest of the Lord's Day was a day of rest. Old Christians did not work on Sundays, although Christians disagreed over the appropriateness of frequenting taverns and other kinds of amusements on the Lord's Day. The behavior of some New Christians, though, was considered to be a particularly obstinate refusal to observe Sunday as a holy day. Inquisitors, accustomed to the sometimes lax practices of theoretically devout Old Christians, found converso avoidance of Christian rituals less offensive than observance of Jewish ones, and fewer people provided evidence about insufficient reverence for the Christian Sabbath. Some conversos routinely worked on Sundays and saints' days when they could arrange it, either to denigrate the Christian holy days or simply to recoup the day of work lost on Saturday. Converso labor on Sunday could take a number of forms. Several of those accused had small vineyards that provided quiet places to work while remaining safely out of the sight of Old Christian neighbors. Judging from witnesses' statements, these vineyards were fairly compact; occasionally the owner of a neighboring vineyard was called in to report on the

---

[40] Ibid., expediente 20, 7v. "amparamele & libramele señor desta fortaleza." This trial is translated in its entirety in the appendix.

[41] Ibid. legajo 156, expediente 11, 4r–5r. "non que so ver a nuestro señor."

[42] AMG unnumbered, Internal Inquisition, p. 62. This source includes all the friars' statements to the inquisitors about Judaizing practices within the friary. For more on this source, and the inquisitorial investigation of the friars, see chapter 7. "officiendo una missa en santa Ana [one of the chapels at Guadalupe] . . . [había muchos] . . . y como yo supe que eran dellos [conversos], al tiempo que el preste tenía el cuerpo del señor sobre la cabeça por la mala sospecha que dellos tenía alçéme y puse los ojos sobre ellos y ví que tenían las caras en el suelo de lo qual yo fuy mucho turbado y comencé a desir mal dellos y mucho peor sentir de sus fechos y vida."

activities of his neighbor. Conversely, New Christians might also retreat to the vineyards on Saturdays in an attempt to convince Old Christian neighbors that they were working on the Jewish Sabbath. In that way vineyards could allow conversos to maintain the appearance of both working on Saturdays and not working on Sundays.[43] Others continued with their daily labors on Sundays, albeit at a reduced rate. One baker, for example, was accused of baking and selling bread on Sundays; she defended herself by stating that she did so only at the request of Old Christians who had need of bread—a plausible excuse.[44]

When conversos made a point of not observing Sundays, they might demand the same of their servants. Some servants complained of having to do light work on Sundays. Mari Sánchez, wife of Diego Jiménez the butcher, had her servants cleaning, sifting, and husking or shelling grain on Sundays.[45] Another servant said that under Beatriz Núñez, stepmother of Manuel González of the Mesón Blanco, "they had to sift and spin Sunday evenings . . . [it was] a day of spinning."[46] Apparently, these New Christians did not recognize or take interest in the resentment caused by asking their servants to work on Sundays. In Beatriz Núñez's case, confusion about the nature of Christian holy days may have inadvertently added to the frustration of her servants. If Beatriz believed that Christians, like Jews, measured days from sunset to sunset, she may have imagined it possible to employ Old Christian servants on Sunday evenings without causing suspicion. The testimony of her servants proved otherwise.

For both Old and New Christians, what it meant to observe a weekly day of rest was a flashpoint of concern, particularly since observance of the Lord's Day on Sunday varied so greatly even among the apparently devout. What distinguished an attitude of reverence from irreverence, or irreverence from heresy? Any number of mundane activities—sweeping floors, spinning, working in the vineyards, or spending time in the

[43] It appears from passing references in the documentation that landholding in the fifteenth century in Guadalupe was not radically different from landholding there today. Currently, somewhat more prosperous residents own small, compact plots with vineyards, olive groves, beekeeping, pigs, pasturage for sheep, or a combination of the above. Of course, wealthier residents may have much larger plots of land. Vines run along the ground, rather than being tied to fences, but they are often planted among the olive trees, which would provide cover to those there.

[44] See the trial of Mari Ruiz, AHN Inquis. legajo 181, expediente 16. It is possible that Old Christians, recognizing her Jewish ancestry, insisted that she work on Sundays for them.

[45] AHN Inquis. legajo 183, expediente 20, 6r. The phrase used was *quitar cáscaras*.

[46] Ibid. legajo 169, expediente 2, 7r. "fazían çerner e filar los domingos a bísperas . . . un día de filar."

tavern—could signify devotion to Christianity or Judaism or even lack of interest in either. In the face of inquisitorial questioning, the towns-people interpreted these acts as signifiers of active religious intent, as would the inquisitors themselves. And yet the variation in participation in these communal acts suggests either that intention—that is, devotion to Christianity and Judaism—also varied greatly among the permanent residents at Guadalupe's shrine, or else that not all intentions were revealed in acts. More likely, both were true—intentions varied from person to person and were not always made evident in action. Because a weekly holy day was so central to the observance of both Christianity and Judaism, most accusations centered around behavior on Saturdays and Sundays. Yet many other mundane activities reinforced a sense of communal identity. Indeed, even the simple act of eating could create multiple senses of community, or exclusion.

CHRISTIAN AND JEWISH DIETARY REGULATIONS

Like Sabbath observances, food preparation was an important element in the construction and maintenance of a collective identity. Creating meals is necessarily an intentional act; food must be assembled and prepared as a meal according to some plan, one that will inherently reflect the situation of the person or persons preparing it. All of Gua-dalupe's residents—both Old and New Christian—read meanings into meals, just as they did into all the myriad activities of daily life. Distinc-tions in meal preparation, therefore, particularly between Old and New Christians, attracted much attention, particularly in light of inquisitorial questioning.

Most of those living near the Virgin's shrine observed Christian di-etary strictures to some degree. Christians observed frequent fasts— Fridays, Lent, and numerous other holidays—during which they ab-stained from meat, milk, eggs, and cheese. Christians also might observe additional fasts to fulfill a vow to the Virgin of Guadalupe or another advocation of the Virgin or a saint. When one woman was wrongly accused of crypto-Judaizing, she defended herself by proving that she fasted in the traditional way: in fulfillment of a promise for the health of her son, she abstained from meat, eggs, and dairy products once a week.[47] But New Christians were often accused of being less diligent in remembering to observe these numerous Christian fast-days. Many wit-nesses testified to defendants' indifference to the Christian liturgical cal-

---

[47] Trial of Catalina Fernandes, ibid. legajo 155, expediente 13, 9v.

endar.[48] One servant told the inquisitors that she had found partridge bones under the family bed—evidence of secretive meat consumption on a Christian fast day. Guadalupe's notorious Judaizing friar, fray Diego de Marchena, bragged to his fellow friars that he encouraged meat-eating on Fridays. "If you boil your chicken rather than roasting it [thus hiding the smell of cooking meat] you can eat meat on the main plaza on Good Friday and no one will know!"[49]

Jewish fasts, on the other hand, demanded a total abstinence from food and drink from sunup to sundown—and from sundown to sundown for the two major fasts of Yom Kippur and Tisha b'Av. The most notable fast on the Jewish calendar was Yom Kippur, the annual day of atonement at the beginning of the new year, and some New Christians do seem to have made an attempt to observe that fast.[50] Like Old and New Christians practicing Christianity, Judaizing New Christians also observed additional fasts as a part of special vows, or in penance, perhaps for their anxiety about living as Christians. Mondays and Thursdays were frequently observed as penitential fast-days among conversos across Iberia.[51] Juana González, the wife of Lope de Herrera and daughter of Martín Gutiérrez, had already outlived two sons when the third became ill. She turned for help to local doctors, but being a conversa she also fasted in the Jewish fashion. Finally, "when my son had been sick for four or five months, having tried all the hardships of the physicians I looked for women who might cure him for money and I did what I could with drops [?] and similar things that look like heresy or witchcraft. I did it for his health."[52] When Juana was called before the Inquisition, her Jewish fasting, and her use of heretical healers, helped to seal her fate.

In addition to observing the dates and methods of traditional Jewish fasts, converso life could also be marked by at least partial adherence to the dietary restrictions known as *kashrut*, which are set out in Leviticus and elaborated in the Talmud and later rabbinic literature. References to the restrictions of a Jewish diet were not uncommon in Christian-

---

[48] For example, Beatriz Núñez, ibid. legajo 169, expediente 2; trial of Mari Flores, ibid. legajo 148, expediente 9, and elsewhere.

[49] AMG unnumbered, p. 29, testimony of Juan de Andujar, and p. 54, testimony of Pedro de Trujillo. For a fuller discussion of fray Diego de Marchena and his activities, see chapter 7.

[50] For a more in-depth discussion of observance of Yom Kippur, see below, in the section "The Acts of Community Life."

[51] See Beinart, *Conversos on Trial*.

[52] AHN Inquis. legajo 154, expediente 20, 2r. "quando [era su] fijo quatro o çinco meses doliente prouadas todas las molestias de físicos busqué quién lo curase mugeres por oro e yo le fasía lo que podía de góticas e cosas semejantes que paresçen ser eregia o fechizería físelo por su salud." The fate of her son is not recorded.

authored literature, and it is clear that there was a generalized or ste-
reotyped understanding of the differences between Christian and Jewish
food preparation practices. Andrés Bernáldez, a contemporary chron-
icler of the period, is only one example of an Old Christian writer who
referred to kosher practices in his writings. His comments in passing
indicated not only his own knowledge, but also what he expected his
readers to recognize and understand. In a society where dietary habits
were relatively homogeneous, and where Jews were a familiar, well-
known minority, the distinct eating patterns of Jews were generally familiar to Christians, and indeed an important mechanism for distinguishing Christians and Jews.[53]

It is hardly surprising, then, that inquisitors and Old Christian witnesses paid particular attention to the eating practices of those suspected of observing Jewish law. Yet active Judaizers also acknowledged
the centrality of *kashrut* in sustaining a Jewish identity. Keeping kosher
was a key element in maintaining one's status as part of the covenant
people; as such it was a strong thread in the fabric of a Jewish life. The
ritual and spiritual centrality of keeping kosher was matched by the
practical demands of maintaining a kosher household, demands that
made *kashrut* central to the coherence of a Jewish community. The
hundreds of large and small ways in which keeping kosher affected the
running of a household meant that, for those raised in Jewish or quasi-
Jewish homes, the lessons of how to manage daily life and prepare food
were inextricably linked to kosher practices. Keeping kosher, then, held
social as well as spiritual resonances that reinforced its place in family
life. This link between *kashrut* and the home further increased the emotional, social, and spiritual weight behind keeping kosher. Since *kashrut*
was a practice centered within the home and therefore out of sight of
Old Christian neighbors, it was safer to maintain than practices that
required a more public declaration of faith.[54] Not surprisingly, converso
dietary practices—whether Christian or Judaizing—also seem to have
been a particularly female concern. This may have been due to the role
women played in overseeing food preparation, although women also
seem to have been more interested in maintaining Jewish practices
generally.[55]

Correct preparation of meat was an important principle of *kashrut*,
and some of Guadalupe's conversos followed kosher practices in this

[53] Andrés Bernáldez, *Memorias del reinado de los Reyes Católicos*, ed. Manuel Gómez-
Moreno and Juan de Mata Carriazo (Madrid: Real Academia de la Historia, 1962), 97.

[54] References to kosher eating practices in inquisitorial documents come largely from
servants and family members, and only occasionally from neighbors or unrelated friends.

[55] On the differences in assimilation between converso men and women, see Melammed, *Heretics*, 31–32, and chapter 3.

regard, beginning with the ritual slaughter of meat. The kosher slaughter of meat can be traced to Leviticus; according to Mosaic law, one is not to eat the blood of any animal.[56] As a result, Jews developed a distinctive method of slaughtering meat, slitting the animal's throat and allowing the blood to drain entirely from the animal before consuming it. Had Guadalupe had an established Jewish community, Judaizers could have bought proper kosher meat from the Jewish butcher. In Guadalupe, however, some conversos occasionally slaughtered animals themselves, rather than buy meat that was not ritually slaughtered. This practice of slitting the throat of the animal elicited much comment from servants and neighbors. Prosecution witnesses frequently stated that conversos avoided buying meat from the butcher, and that, unlike others in the Puebla, some New Christians slaughtered animals at home, often noting that they did it in the Jewish fashion, *al modo judaico*.[57]

New Christians might follow other Jewish restrictions related to the preparation of meat. Most common of these was the removal of the sciatic nerve from the haunch. This practice, not current among Old Christians, attracted the attention of some servants and others associated with the house. Conversos secretly practicing Judaism might also cut some kinds of fat from meat before using it, another element of kosher meat preparation alien to gentile habits. So common and well known was the practice that adult children who were forced to confess against their mothers often pointed simply to "defatting" as a means of avoiding more damning issues.[58] By contrast, salting meat (another element of *kashrut*) was not mentioned at all in the inquisitorial documents. This may be because both Old and New Christians salted meat to preserve it.

Some women also practiced *challah*, a symbolic donation to the Temple in Jerusalem. When preparing to cook bread in the fire at home, the woman took a small mass of dough and threw it in the fire. The apparent regularity with which this practice occurred is suggested by the frequency with which servants made this accusation. One Guadalupense woman, for example, was horrified to discover that her new servant, raised in a converso home, had been taught to maintain a Jewish home and kosher kitchen, even down to the *challah* offering

---

[56] Lev. 17:10–14.

[57] Mari Sánchez, wife of Diego Sánchez, tanner, example of a woman charged with Jewish beheading, *degollar al modo judaico*. See AHN Inquis. legajo 184, expediente 1. Melammed also discusses kosher meat consumption in *Heretics*, 22.

[58] On both these practices see, for example, Beatriz Núñez, AHN Inquis. legajo 169, expediente 2, and Andrés González de la República's testimony against his mother, Mari Flores, in ibid. legajo 148, expediente 9. Gitlitz, *Secrecy and Deceit*, 547, also discusses this practice.

thrown in the fire. Haim Beinart also mentioned the practice of *challah* in his work on Ciudad Real but suggested that there it was relatively uncommon. In his opinion only the most devout conversos in Ciudad Real practiced it.[59]

Keeping kosher required not merely correctly preparing food, but also abstaining from certain foods. This is reflected in the dietary practices claimed for New Christians, including avoiding rabbit or hare, fish without scales, and wild game (with the exception of game birds). But the food commented upon most frequently, and perhaps of greatest emotional import to conversos, was pork. Pork and pork products were seen by Jews, conversos, and Old Christians alike as particularly representative of *kashrut*, and particularly important in keeping kosher. But in Iberia at this period, pork was one of the cheapest and most abundant meat sources available. Pork was an important dietary staple, not only for its chops or loins, but also for relatively inexpensive products such as sausages and lard. Iberians of the fifteenth century used lard rather than olive oil as their primary cooking fat; it was also the fat used with stews and legumes, with each person at the meal receiving a small portion for themselves.[60] Pork and pork products were such a dietary mainstay that not using them attracted much comment.

New Christians who avoided pork for whatever reason went to great lengths to defuse Old Christian suspicions. Beinart noted that some conversos maintained a supply of pork, sausages, and lard in the house.[61] Some households in Guadalupe apparently went so far as to produce two meals: a kosher meal for the family and a nonkosher one for the servants.[62] Servants frequently complained to the inquisitors that the woman of the house would refuse to eat meals that included lard. To ensure that they were not accidentally ingesting pork, some conversas insisted on a thorough cleaning of the pots after lard had been used in them or maintained a second set of cookware used exclusively for meals not including lard. Mari Sánchez, wife of Juan Esteban, kept one set of plates and utensils for her and her husband, and a second set for her servants.[63] Juana González, daughter of Martín Gutiérrez, insisted on

---

[59] See AHN Inquis. legajo 183, expediente 19, AHN Inquis. legajo 154, expediente 30; Beinart, *Conversos*, 277–278.

[60] Olive oil has long been produced in the Mediterranean, but only in the sixteenth century did olive oil production become affordable enough that it could be a regular part of most people's diets. Clifford A. Wright, *A Mediterranean Feast: The Story of the Birth of the Celebrated Cuisines of the Mediterranean* (New York: Morrow, 1999), 35.

[61] Beinart, *Conversos*.

[62] AHN Inquis. legajo 154, expediente 30; legajo 183, expediente 19, and elsewhere.

[63] Ibid. legajo 183, expediente 19. Since nonkosher foods were prepared in their own pots, such a kitchen might still be considered kosher. There were, however, no refer-

putting one of her pots in the fire to remove any lard after it had been used accidentally. Old Christian defense witnesses claimed that they did the same as a method of cleaning, but this defense was not sufficient to protect her.[64]

Food, then, served as a marker of identity as clear as, and perhaps more emotionally profound than, attendance at weekly mass. The deeply ingrained resonances of food preparation and consumption, linked to memory, ritual, and religious identity, all encouraged Old Christians and conversos observing Jewish law to maintain religious dietary regulations, even (in the case of New Christians) despite major and minor difficulties in doing so. For those New Christians whose conversion was reluctant or forced, observing the complex dietary regulations of Judaism was a means of honoring one's ancestors. Furthermore, as more public observances of Judaism became difficult or even dangerous to continue, *kashrut* provided a consistent link to one's Jewish identity. Keeping kosher not only allowed one to live, to some extent at least, in obedience to Mosaic and Talmudic injunctions; it also provided a constant reminder of the Jewish faith to which one adhered.

Life Rituals: Birth, Marriage, and Death

BIRTH

If Christian and Jewish dietary regulations were central to the consistent maintenance of one's religious identity, then rituals surrounding birth were critical in welcoming one into that community. Christian baptism was long established as one of the earliest rites of the Christian church; even infant baptism had been practiced for centuries. By the end of the fifteenth century, the Jeronymite friars in Guadalupe had begun recording all the local baptisms in large bound volumes. Avoiding this rite was unthinkable. And indeed, the evidence suggests that all Christians in the Virgin's town—both Old and New—participated in the rite of baptism.

New Christians attempting to observe Judaism to some degree might engage in one or two acts: first, they might circumcise a male child; and second, they might symbolically undo the Christian ritual of bap-

---

ences to separate sets of "milk" and "meat" dishes. Gitlitz, *Secrecy and Deceit*, 540, believes that this was extremely rare among New Christian practices.

[64] Ibid. legajo 154, expediente 20. The practice attracted attention because she insisted on cleaning her pot in this fashion even after a visiting pilgrim offered to clean out the pot with a spoon he had. The process described here is *libun*, one method of kashering cookware.

tism by washing off the oil and chrism.[65] Circumcision was a central part of male Jewish identity, and its importance is underlined in its perpetuation among converso families, despite the obvious dangers involved. In later centuries, for the occasional adult converso males who decided to return to Judaism, circumcision formed a key element in their rededication to the faith.[66] And certainly the danger of circumcision, inherent in the ultimate inability of a Judaizer to hide his circumcision, added to its importance as a symbol of devotion to Judaism. At the same time, the importance of circumcision as an irrevocable sign of Jewishness also made it less common and more incriminating than other Jewish rituals that were less obvious and less permanent.

There are only a few references to circumcisions taking place in Guadalupe. Manuel González, owner of the Mesón Blanco, was probably the most prominent example. Manuel stated, both before and after he was tortured, that he imagined he had been born (at about mid-century) without a foreskin; only after the court made the formal accusation of circumcision did he ask his father if he had been circumcised.[67] In a second trial, Juan González (no relation to Manuel) was accused of circumcising his son. Seven or eight years before, several witnesses saw a number of men entering Violante Alonso's home with the infant, who soon began to cry.[68] In both cases, the circumcision was a family event. In Juan González's case, the men who were identified as being with him were all members of one family, and it is implied that González was part of that family.[69] While it is possible that there were other circumcisions that did not come to the attention of the inquisitors, or only appeared in Guadalupense trials lost to us, it seems more probable that circumcision was a relatively uncommon practice in Guadalupe, due to the watchful eyes of the friars and the Virgin.[70] Inquisitors, seeing circumcision as the Jewish equivalent of baptism, certainly would

[65] There is no reference in Guadalupe to "hadas," a ceremony celebrated the night before circumcision. It is mentioned by both Encarnación Marín Padilla, "Relación judeoconversa durante la segunda mitad del s. XV en Aragón: nacimientos, hadas, circuncisiones," *Sefarad* 41 (1981), 273–300; and Beinart, *Conversos*, 279–280.

[66] For example, Yosef Yerushalmi, *From Spanish Court to Italian Ghetto: Isaac Cardoso: A Study in Seventeenth-Century Marranism and Jewish Apologetics* (New York: Columbia University Press, 1971).

[67] AHN Inquis. legajo 154, expediente 24. See the discussion of this event in chapter 6.

[68] Ibid., expediente 14, 5r–6r.

[69] No witness specified whether as many as ten men—a *minyan*, or quorum—were present.

[70] One witness claimed that Juana González circumcised one of her sons, but this claim is uncorroborated, and Juana González never admitted to it, even under torture. See ibid., expediente 20. Four friars were accused of being circumcised, but none had been raised in Guadalupe. Unlike in the secular court, those accused in the ecclesiastical inquisitorial court were examined by a team of friars, including a physician. The ecclesiastic Inquisition, and circumcision within the friary, are discussed in chapter 7.

have made every attempt to seek out circumcisions and circumcised conversos.

More common, apparently, was the folk rite of washing off a child's baptismal oil and chrism—a kind of "unbaptism." To Christian priests—and to Jewish rabbis—such an action had no practical effect; once baptized into the Roman Catholic Church, one could not "unbaptize" oneself and resign from the community of believers. But the spiritual and emotional implications of such an act were obvious, making it one of the more serious acts committed by Judaizing conversos in Guadalupe. Like circumcision, or any of the Judaizing acts described here, it is difficult to ascertain the frequency with which such acts were committed. But the frequency with which they were reported to the Inquisition does provide a comparative scale. Given this circumstantial evidence, washing off a child's oil and chrism was more common than circumcision. Typical is the description provided by Inés González, daughter of Mari Sánchez, the wife of Diego Jiménez the butcher:

> Inés . . . said that at the time that her mother was in bed after the birth of her son [Inés's brother], her mother allowed Elvira González *la francesa* and Isabel López wife of Gonzalo López to enter into her room, and they brought in a small pot of warm water and closed the door, and then this witness heard the child cry; and this was the day that it had been baptized, and she knows that they washed the oil and chrism off of the baby, and she knows this because, as she has said, she heard the cry of the child and because when she saw it later its whole head and face were damp. And this witness also knows it, because she and her mother have discussed it, and her mother has confessed to her that it is true.[71]

Unlike circumcision or baptism, unbaptizing a child was not a community event, or an act with a set series of rituals attached to it. Both circumcisions and baptisms were performed by male religious figures before the community. By contrast, the unbaptisms described were furtive actions performed by women in front of few witnesses. As with the dietary restrictions of *kashrut* and other Jewish ritual practices involving the maintenance of the house, such as cleaning the house on Friday or lighting oil lamps for the Sabbath, women were again portrayed as the primary figures maintaining and perpetuating Jewish traditions. As else-

---

[71] AHN Inquis. legajo 183, expediente 20, 8r. "Inés . . . dixo que al tiempo que su madre dela cama [después del nacimiento de su hijo] e quedaron dentro la dicha su madre e elvira gonsales la françesa e ysabel lopes muger de gonçalo lopes y metieron dentro una calderuela de agua caliente y çerraron la puerta e luego oyó llorar este testigo [este?] niño e hera [este?] día que le avían traydo de bautizar e que sabe que le lauaron la crisma e olio e que esto que lo sabe porque como dicho tiene oyó llorar al niño e porque le vió luego mojada toda la cabeça, e la cara. E asy mismo porque este testigo, e la dicha su madre lo han traydo en habla e ella le ha confesado que es verdad."

where, however, this desire to preserve Jewish ritual and belief was expressed in traditional women's domains. In this case, it is hardly surprising that it was women who washed away the baptismal oil, since they, and not men, were with the infant almost constantly. What is perhaps more interesting is the initiative expressed by these women. Not only did men not participate in these actions, but they also seemed not to instigate or encourage them. In a second case, a girl was accused of washing the oil and chrism off of her infant sibling while returning home from the baptism. In this case, no mention was made as to whether a family member instructed her to perform such an act or she acted independently, and the court did not consider the question.[72] Given such a small number of examples, however, it is impossible to argue that men were unequivocally excluded from removing the baptismal oil from their children.[73] In the case Inés described above, she implied that her father was unaware of his wife's actions; Inés, however, takes pains at all points to describe her father as a devout Christian, despite some contradiction from other witnesses.

MARRIAGE

Unlike the relatively strong evidence available about the various rituals surrounding birth and death, marriages attracted less attention. Certainly this is due in part to the changing place of marriage in the church for Castilians. Christian marriage rites were a more recent innovation, and in Castile earlier practices frequently still obtained. Furthermore, the place of marriage in secular and sacred society was still in flux; definitive practices were unsettled for Christians of all kinds and in many places. Municipal ordinances issued in the fifteenth century recorded the friary's still rather unsuccessful struggle to move marriages into the realm of the church. The friary repeatedly banned unions that had not been blessed by a priest, such as those involving secret vows or lay officiators. Furthermore, the friars mandated that a priest verify that each couple was in accord with the church's regulations, including stipulations on consanguinity, before marrying.[74] Given the transitional nature of Christian marriage rites, therefore, it is not surprising that the inquisitors heard or generated few accusations of "Jewish weddings."

A bigamy trial held in Guadalupe in 1476–77 clearly demonstrated

[72] See ibid. legajo 158, expediente 5. Isabel was fifteen or sixteen in 1485.

[73] Certainly Martín Gutiérrez and Bartolomé Rodríguez Narices, among others, took an interest in the Jewish upbringing of their children.

[74] AMG codex 76 (unfoliated), 1r–2v; codex 77; codex 78, capítulo 2; codex 79, capítulo 2.

the range of marriage practices accepted as valid, if not legitimate, at the end of the fifteenth century. Bartolomé de Fuenteovejuna secretly married Isabel at her home one afternoon. Bartolomé's brother recited the ritual marriage phrases, and, with no witnesses or any further actions by either party, the couple was united. The term for such unions was *desposado*, which signified a type of lay-officiated engagement with all the obligations of marriage.[75] This was reminiscent of medieval practices, which affirmed that parties were wed simply by reciting vows to one another.[76] After their espousal, Bartolomé and Isabel returned to their homes as before, and Bartolomé began the difficult and ultimately unsuccessful process of trying to persuade Isabel's father to approve a formal marriage, *casamiento*. No one outside the immediate family knew of the *desposorio*. Frustrated by his father-in-law's resistance to the union, Bartolomé eventually gave up trying to win Isabel's father over and instead turned his attentions to Catalina, a daughter of the smith to whom he was apprenticed. Catalina's mother liked Bartolomé and encouraged him to marry her daughter since she was not aware of the first *desposorio*. Bartolomé and Catalina were also *desposado* in a lay-officiated, semiclandestine ceremony, this time at night.[77] Only after the ceremony did the couple approach a priest to confirm that there were no impediments to the marriage, and to begin the reading of the marriage banns for a *casamiento*. It was this public announcement of the *desposorio* and impending marriage that alerted Bartolomé's first set of in-laws to his bigamy.[78] The case above was clearly atypical, but the practice of *desposorio* apparently was not. The friary's capitulary records, for example, include numerous references to dowry money given to

[75] The status of being *desposado* was technically not equivalent to that of marriage; couples already *desposado* do at times go on to participate in a ceremony of *casamiento* (marriage). But to be *desposado* was not merely a formal "engagement"; rather, it was a relation as binding as marriage and may even have included all the rights and privileges of a *casamiento*. The formula recited by the lay officiator in both ceremonies, and repeated by the couple, is repeated in the following: "Juan Alfonso de la Morena que les tomó las manos disiendo 'Vos, Catalina, otorgáys vos por esposa & muger de Bartolomé que aquí está presente' & que ella dixo 'Sy, otorgo.' & que preguntó al dicho Bartolomé 'Vos, Bartolomé, otorgáys vos por esposo y marido de Catalina que aquí está presente' & que él dixo 'Sy, otorgo.' Et que asy están desposados." See AMG codex 163, 27r–v.

[76] See, for example, James Brundage, *Law, Sex, and Christian Society in Medieval Europe* (Chicago: University of Chicago Press, 1987).

[77] Catalina's father was not present, but her mother and uncle (Juan Alfonso de la Morena, mentioned in note 75, above) were.

[78] A useful introduction to recent research on bigamy in early modern Spain can be found in Allyson Poska, "When Bigamy Is the Charge: Gallegan Women and the Holy Office," in *Women in the Inquisition: Spain and the New World*, ed. Mary E. Giles (Baltimore: Johns Hopkins University Press, 1999), 189–205.

women already *desposada* who wished to marry, *casarse.*[79] Only after a formal marriage and, apparently, acquisition of sufficient funds did Guadalupenses celebrate their *casamiento* with a large feast.[80]

Given the possibility of such an informal, lay ceremony, it is not surprising that no records of distinctive Judaizing marriage practices exist.[81] It is likely that conversos also had formal *casamientos* and celebratory feasts, with a Jewish ceremony serving as the *desposorio*. Jewish practices that might have continued among conversos, such as writing up marriage contracts, *ketubbot*, would not attract much notice; with relatively little lay attention paid by Old Christians to the stipulations of the church, there would be little external psychological pressure to retain and reinforce Jewish rituals in opposition to Christian ones.[82]

The only reference to marriage by an inquisitorial witness occurred in the trial of Mari Flores, the deceased mother of the sometime *procurador* of Guadalupe, Andrés González de la República. A female fowl-seller from nearby Alía related that around the time of the marriage of Mari Flores's daughter Leonor, Mari Flores removed several small images from a chest and placed them around the home. Upon being questioned by the woman, Mari Flores replied that they were images of saints, an explanation that left the fowl-seller unconvinced. The accusation is confusing. The significance of these images for the marriage, if any, is obscure, and no mention was made of such a practice in other trials. Some of the woman's suspicion seemed to originate with the fact that the images were normally kept in a trunk. It is possible that Mari Flores and her husband kept saints' images in the chest and removed them when Old Christians came to visit. Certainly Mari Flores's explanation of why they were in the chest—"they are there to adore when I go to take something out of the chest"—seems unlikely and even derisive of Christian practice.[83] In short, the townspeople and inquisitors in

---

[79] AMG codex 74, Actas Capitulares 1499–1537, for example 39v. On Friday, March 22, 1504, the monastery gave "limosna a Andrés Gonçales de la República de tres mill mrs. para casamiento a una su hija. El qual es vezino de Cañamero."

[80] Municipal ordinances set limits on the numbers of guests and length of the feasts. AMG codex 78, chap. 3, "de los que han de comer en las bodas."

[81] As indicated above, marriages had very few witnesses. Bartolomé's first marriage had only one witness (his brother, who performed the marriage); his second had fewer than ten witnesses. Encarnación Marín Padilla also made no mention of marriage in her two-part article on fifteenth-century converso practices. Gitlitz, *Secrecy and Deceit*, 243–270, brings together what documentation there is on the topic.

[82] Whom conversos might marry, together with other questions of endogamy and exogamy, are addressed in chapter 3.

[83] AHN Inquis. legajo 148, expediente 9, 9r. The woman stated, "este testigo tiene mala sospecha que cree que heran ydolos." She was there to deliver birds for the wedding. Mari's defense was "que los tenían para adorar enellos quando yua a sacar algo dela dicha arca."

Guadalupe do not seem to have considered marriage to be an important site of Judaizing practices, in part because of its changing status in the Christian church. In other words, marriage seems not to have had the profound religious significance of rituals surrounding birth.

DEATH

Unlike marriage, mourning included well-developed ritual practices among Christians and Jews; unlike circumcision or unbaptisms, mourning was an accepted time for large public gatherings of family and friends, both Old and New Christian. And mourning, particularly when there was a surviving spouse, was often organized by and directed to older generations—that is, those best positioned to remember Jewish traditions and feel most strongly connected to the Jewish customs of their parents and grandparents. In the surviving evidence, one can distinguish between customs relating to death and burial, on the one hand, such as how one spent the last moments of life or prepared the body for burial, and those pertaining to the actions of the survivors, such as mourning, on the other. Not surprisingly, less evidence exists concerning the former than the latter. Only servants and immediate family members would have witnessed any unusual customs surrounding the death itself; the funeral and mourning, however, attracted much more attention and included a much larger circle of people. In the case of funerals that incorporated Jewish elements, mourners might sometimes include devoutly Christian conversos or Old Christians who had married into the family.[84]

In the last days of a New Christian's life, he or she was probably required to make a final confession and receive communion and extreme unction. Last rites were among the most important of Christian rituals; despite the private nature of extreme unction, it is unlikely that it could have been avoided without comment from Old Christians. Anecdotal evidence from the Inquisition held within the friary, although admittedly a different context from the surrounding lay community, provides an insight into the horror that refusing last rites could generate. Prior Gonzalo de Madrid, posthumously accused of favoring conversos and even of Judaizing, created a stir by his actions on his deathbed: "When he was about to die, vicar Diego de París brought prior Gonzalo the unction and the body of Christ. And after prior Gonzalo had received extreme unction vicar Diego wanted to give him the Host, but prior Gonzalo did not want it, saying, 'Don't give it to me, I don't

---

[84] For example, Mari González, an Old Christian who had married into the family, was present at Alonso Fernández Gigante's funeral. Alonso Fernández Gigante was the grandfather of Manuel González of the Mesón Blanco.

have the stomach to take it.”[85] . . . And when they gave him the communion prior Gonzalo feigned that he was vomiting and could not take
the sacrament, which I took to be a very bad example.”[86]

There is little direct evidence of a distinctive New Christian burial. In
one case, a servant told the inquisitors that the body was ritually washed
before interment by a group of family members.[87] This charge was
consonant with other studies that have argued that in late-medieval
Castile washing a corpse was considered a Jewish practice. Others have
suggested that Iberian Jews were unique only in washing the corpse in
warm water, although I have not seen this claim substantiated.[88] Suspicions about Judaizing preparations of the corpse and the burial seemed
limited to washing the corpse, however. Neither Old nor New Christians described other practices, and in Guadalupe at least, in no other
way did Old Christian neighbors view New Christian deaths and burials
as odd.

What seems to have most struck Old Christians in Guadalupe are
more properly considered rituals of mourning, which began after the
interment. These practices were similar to those found in other Inquisition trials from this early phase of the activity of the Holy Office, and
they seem to reflect practices common among Jews throughout the
peninsula, although their origin is not clear, since not all have a specific
Talmudic basis.[89] As always, the practices described below reflect the
totality of Judaizing burial practices available in the second half of the
fifteenth century, rather than a “typical” converso burial. It is difficult to
know how different families chose to incorporate various rites, although
the individual nature of many of these rites suggests that individual
mourners themselves made the choice of how to mourn.

Mourning rituals began as soon as the body was removed from the
house. Immediately after the burial, all the standing water in the house

[85] AMG unnumbered, Internal Inquisition, 188. Testimony of Diego de Burgos el
viejo. “Quando ouo de morir traxóle el vicario fr. Diego de París la unción & el corpus
christi. & des que ouo tomada la unción quería darle el sacramento de la hostia & non
lo quiso deziendo ‘non me lo des, que non siento el estomago para lo tomar.’ ” This is
the same Diego de Burgos who was sentenced to perpetual punishment for Judaizing
activity.

[86] Ibid., 166. Testimony of Pedro de Lequetio. “E como le diesen la comunión en-
fingió que tenía gómitos & començó a dar arcadas & non quiso tomar el sacramento
delo qual yo oue muy mal exemplo.”

[87] AHN Inquis. legajo 148, expediente 9. This was the burial of Diego González de la
República, husband of Mari Flores.

[88] See Beinart, *Conversos*, 280–283; Gitlitz, *Secrecy and Deceit*, 280–282; and Marín
Padilla, “Relación judeoconversa.”

[89] See, for example, Gitlitz, *Secrecy and Deceit*, 277–315; Marín Padilla, “Relación judeoconversa”; Melammed, *Heretics*; and Beinart, *Conversos*.

might be thrown out "to purify the house of the spirit of the deceased," as one woman described it.[90] An immediate family member, often a sibling and his or her spouse, might move into the home of the deceased and live there for nine days, providing food and drink for the deceased, who was believed to stay in and around the home for nine days after death. This was evidenced in Inés González's testimony against Mencía, who observed traditional Jewish burial and mourning practices upon the death of her husband: "When Alonso Montalbán died his wife Mencía threw out all the water in the house, then for nine days put a table in the *bodega* with bread and water and an oil lamp burning; and she said that those nine days her husband went there."[91] For Christian witnesses, the most notable of all mourning rituals was the practice of sitting *shiva*. Family members and probably friends of the deceased would gather in the home of the deceased, often after the funeral, to share a meal. Meat was not eaten, but fruits, vegetables, milk, and fish were.[92] Out of respect for the dead, those present ate on the floor. Other scholars have found references suggesting that this meal was taken not only on the floor, but also in doorways; no witnesses in Guadalupe were so specific, however.[93]

There were also more public expressions of mourning. New and Old Christian women probably followed the body to burial, publicly crying and lamenting. No specific mention is made of such activities in the inquisitorial records, but the silence of the records suggests that New Christian practices were in accord with Old Christian ones in this regard. Old Christians maintained this practice in town until at least 1553, when the town *procurador* petitioned that the practice be prohibited since it led to inappropriate activities.[94] A second, related practice was

[90] AHN Inquis. legajo 183, expediente 19; legajo 155, expediente 8; legajo 148, expediente 9; and elsewhere.

[91] Ibid. legajo 155, expediente 8, 7r. Note that the *bodega* has once again been used as a site in which to carry out Judaizing activities. "yten que al tiempo que fallesçió Alonso Montaluán que su muger mençía vertió toda el agua desu casa, la qual puso nueve días una mesa en una bodega con pan e agua e candil ençendido e desía que aquellos nueve días venía allí su marido."

[92] In other words, the meal did not entirely conform to Christian ideas of ritual dietary restrictions, since at that time avoidance of meat included milk, eggs, and cheese. Of course, Christian practice did not in any case demand that mourners fast. *Shiva* should last seven, not nine, days, though variations were common, even before 1492; see Gitlitz, *Secrecy and Deceit*, 292–303.

[93] Marín Padilla, "Relación judeoconversa durante la segunda mitad del s. XV en Aragón. Segunda Parte: enfermedades y muertes," *Sefarad* 43 (1983), 314.

[94] AMG codex 75, 188r (bis; unnumbered). The *procurador* petitions that the prior "probea y mande que quando alguna persona fallesçiere ninguna muger de las que antel llorar & lloran al defunto al tiempo que le fueren a enterrar no bayan con el cuerpo pues es de tanpoco fruto antes [ere?]. que es en desseruiçio de dios nuestro señor y

the singing of mourning chants, *endechas*, for the deceased. This was
also an activity reserved for women, and women were recorded as having sung for both family members and friends.[95] Witnesses' statements
were not entirely clear but suggested that the lament was sung soon
after the individual's death. The *endecha* seems not to have been related
specifically to the *shiva* or burial, and the witnesses' descriptions did not
indicate whether the singer was alone or with others while singing. In
both trials where the practice was specifically referred to, witnesses
quoted the same song. Indeed, Alonso Rodríguez, the son of Antón
Rodrigo Ballestero, quoted merely the first phrase,[96] suggesting that the
chant was familiar to Old and New Christians in Guadalupe, although
whether all Guadalupe's Christians sang it is unclear: "I collected the
herbs, I collected them; I collected the herbs; / they were not useful to
me and I threw them away."[97] The meaning of the *endecha* is cryptic,
and its origin is equally so. In another trial, cited by Renée Levine
Melammed, a description of mourning included crying and singing "I,
the ill-married woman, went to the field and collected herbs!" But Melammed was also unable to provide any explanation of or context for
the images used, and there was no clear Biblical or Talmudic source for
the words.[98]

All Guadalupenses—both Old and New Christian—marked each new
stage of their lives by ritual acts. The relative importance of these rites
varied, to themselves and to others, but the importance of rite per se
was unquestioned. For each resident of the Virgin's town, those rites
could reaffirm a link to ancestors and to the past, connections particularly dangerous for New Christians. While all conversos celebrated,
with greater or lesser enthusiasm, at least some of the rites of their
Christian faith, others also chose to unite with some family members

---

porque van diziendo tantas cosas que alas vezes se notan y rrien y aconteçe ocupar el
culto divino y suçeden otros ynconbenientes y con probeerse sobre esto ellas quedarán
libres para que no se ve y enpute culpa y adelante en sus casas les queda tiempo para
llorar y sentir sus perdidas y esto se usa en muchas partes." Related practices continued
in Guadalupe until almost the present day. Recently, a woman died in Guadalupe who
had made her living from mourning and praying the Rosary for the deceased.

[95] See AHN Inquis. legajo 184, expediente 1; legajo 154, expediente 30. Modern practice includes repeating a memorial prayer (*El Maleh Rachamim*) and the ninety-first
Psalm.

[96] AHN Inquis. legajo 154, expediente 30, 4v. "cogí las erbas, cogílas; cogí las erbas,
non me aprovecharon y vertílas."

[97] Ibid. legajo 184, expediente 1. Testimony of Mencía Sánchez from Alía.

[98] Renée Levine Melammed, "Some Death and Mourning Customs of Castilian Conversas" in *Exile and Diaspora*, ed. A. Mirsky, A. Grossman, and Y. Kaplan, 157–167
(Jerusalem, 1991). The refrain quoted is cited as AHN Inquis. legajo 158, expediente 9
(1520–1523), "fuy al campo la mal casada e cogí las yeruas!"

and with the family's former faith through unbaptisms, circumcisions, and traditional burials. At the same time, those New Christians affirmed, to some extent, a separate identity from their Old Christian neighbors, a distinct sense of religious community that compelled them to act in ways undeniably dangerous to themselves if discovered.

The Acts of Community Life:
Holidays, Festivals, and Processions

Parallel to the rites that marked individual life-experiences—birth, marriage, and death—were the collective rites that helped forge a common sense of community. These might incorporate the whole town, as in the case of the extensive festivities surrounding the feast day of the Virgin of Guadalupe, or some smaller community, such as the activities of the various confraternities of Guadalupe, or the secretive collective practices of Judaizing conversos. No matter what the specific act, these rites served to unite people with a sense of a common identity, as townspeople, as special devotees of an advocation of the Virgin Mary or the Passion, or as secretly Judaizing New Christians in opposition to their Old Christian neighbors.

Most collective ritual activity involved the large majority of Guadalupe's residents. The quintessential community celebration for Guadalupenses was, of course, the feast of the Virgin of Guadalupe, a religious celebration/market that drew pilgrims, merchants, and buyers from around the Iberian peninsula, especially Castile and Portugal. Local ordinances record that special regulations were in effect for markets in town during the two weeks before and after the birthday of the Virgin, September 8, when the Virgin of Guadalupe's feast was celebrated.[99] As the inns, roads, and market districts swelled with pilgrims and merchants, everyone in town felt the effects of, and almost necessarily participated in, the bustle of activity surrounding the primary celebration for the Virgin of Guadalupe. Extant documents record little of the festivities, other than the brief mentions of economic concerns, but special sermons and processions would be typical elements in any religious holiday of this type.

A better idea of the specifics of processions and celebrations comes from a municipal ordinance, enacted in 1475, describing a new procession for the feast of the Ascension. Since the surrounding towns celebrated the Ascension with a procession, the ordinance declared, the

---

[99] Today, the feast of the Virgin of Guadalupe of Extremadura is celebrated on October 12.

town of Guadalupe would also begin such a practice. The ordinance detailed an extensive and carefully constructed route for processing through all the major streets, both uphill and downhill from the church, and through almost all the town's gates.[100] This new procession united the population both physically and metaphysically, tracing out the town's streets and landscape even as it brought Guadalupenses together to celebrate a common belief in the bodily ascension of Jesus into heaven. Of course, how residents understood the theology that they were ostensibly celebrating is unclear, but even the mere fact of their participation indicates the equation of Christian devotion and community identity. For those participating who might have disagreed with this or other Christian doctrines, by contrast, the sense of alienation from that community would have been even greater. The same would have been true of the smaller, annual pilgrimages to shrines just outside of town, to Mirabel, the chapel of Saint Catherine, and others.[101]

For some Christians in Guadalupe, an equally strong sense of common religious identity came from participation in at least one of the several confraternities that were present in town by the latter part of the fifteenth century. Unlike many other communities in late-medieval and early modern Europe, Guadalupe has preserved little documentation regarding these groups, but the limited information available suggests their extensive role in the religious life of Guadalupenses.[102] The earliest reference to confraternities in Guadalupe dates to 1438, in a Cordoban bequest of wax to the "confraternities of Guadalupe."[103] One small volume at the friary in Guadalupe, in what appears to be a fifteenth-century hand, includes scattered information about confraternities dedicated to Saint John, to Our Lady of the O, and to the Holy Eucharist.[104] By the mid-sixteenth century, and probably before, the town also supported a confraternity devoted to St. Bartholomew.[105]

By the end of the fifteenth century, though, the most active confraternity seems to have been the Confraternity of the Passion. Estab-

---

[100] AMG codex 79, Ordenanzas Municipales, 76r–77r.

[101] The confraternity brethren of Saint John, for example, gained pardon for visiting the chapels of St. Catherine (on her feast day), Mary Magdalene of Mirabel, and St. Cecilia of Valdefuentes. AMG codex 67, 288v–290r.

[102] For a useful comparison from the nearby provincial capital, see Claude-Marie Gerbet, "Les Conféres Religieuses à Cáceres de 1467 à 1523," *Mélanges de la Casa de Velázquez* 7 (1971), 75–113.

[103] AMG legajo 49, loose sheet entitled "Cordoba, visperas 26 agosto 1438."

[104] AMG legajo 49. The confraternity of St. John seems to have incorporated devotions to both St. John the Baptist and St. John the Evangelist. See, for example, AMG codex 67, 290v.

[105] AMG legajo 49, "Carta de troque y cambio de unas casas que este monasterio dio por una viña a los cofrades sant bartolome," 25 febrero 1552.

lished in 1462, the confraternity members—men and their wives—pursued an active agenda in town. The *cofrades* owned vineyards outside of town, maintained a hospital where they cared for those ill with the plague, and, especially at Easter, held a number of processions and ceremonies associated with their primary devotion (fig. 3).[106] During Holy Week, confraternity members dressed in white robes with cowls, with a linen or colored cross stitched to the front and a grass rope belt. They held one procession to adore the cross, another for Good Friday, and a third procession to flagellate themselves (although their ordinances specifically stated that confraternity members were not to flagellate themselves without their habits, or outside of the procession). They also invited thirteen beggars to dinner and on several holidays kissed the feet of five poor people. Like many confraternities across western Europe, they also took care of burials for members and their families, and those found dead within the city limits. Although Villacampo states that several friars were *cofrades*, there is little evidence of this in the fifteenth century. In any event, for Guadalupenses under the authority of the Virgin and her friars in matters both secular and religious, confraternities must have provided a unique outlet for independent religious devotion and organization.

Some New Christians who remained devoted to Judaism developed their own alternate religious communities, organized around secret observance of some of the primary Jewish holidays, including Yom Kippur and Sukkoth. It is important to keep in mind two observations about these Judaizing practices. First, they were particularly oriented toward penitence—understandably, given New Christians' dual status as simultaneous Christians and Jews. As Yirmiyahu Yovel has noted, the duality of New Christians' status as both Christian and Jew created a crisis of identity.[107] It is not surprising that these observances demonstrated, through elements like their emphasis on penitence, a strong influence of Christian theology.[108] Second, these practices should not be considered an organized, reified "crypto-Jewish religion." Rather, they ad hoc practices with common tendencies and sentiments, but not a coherent theology, practice, or even body of members.

The first question, for many conversos, was how precisely to observe Jewish law. This meant not only to what degree was it possible to observe Jewish law without detection by Old Christian neighbors, but also a more fundamental question, namely, what were the requirements

---

[106] AMG legajo 51 "Ordenanzas de la cofradia de la santa Pasion . . ."; P.C.G. Villacampo, OFM, *Grandezas de Guadalupe* (Madrid, 1924).

[107] Yovel, "New Otherness."

[108] For more on the Christianity of New Christians, see chapter 3.

FIGURE 3. The hospital of the Confraternity of the Passion, now a private
residence, on Calle Pasión. Photo by the author.

of observant Judaism, how could one learn and follow them away from
a Jewish community and rabbinic authorities, and what significance
might such observance hold? The dates on which Yom Kippur and
other Jewish festivals are celebrated change annually. A determination
of when to celebrate these holidays requires complex calculations based
on solar and lunar cycles and usually a rabbi or resident elder—in other
words, participation in a Jewish community—to identify the dates.

To resolve this challenge of how to be both a baptized Christian and
an observant Jew, New Christians in Guadalupe resorted to a number of
strategies. Some conversos acquired books or other written materials to
help them calculate festival dates and learn the proper rites. These
books were of great importance to their owners in maintaining a correct practice of Judaism, even though discovery of such books put the
owner in grave danger. When Juana González was threatened with torture, she admitted that "her husband Lope de Herrera had a book of
the law of Moses in which was written all the feasts and holidays and
fasts for the whole year based on the law, and how to do them and in

what manner, and there were prayers in the said law of Moses."[109] With such a text, Lope de Herrera, a cloth merchant himself and son-in-law of another, could observe the cycle of annual feasts, as well as the Sabbath. Juana may not have spoken honestly with the inquisitors: the book may not have existed, or it may have belonged to her and not to her spouse. It seems doubtful that Juana would have invented this book under torture, however, since she might be tortured again if she could not produce it. In fact, several New Christians in Guadalupe apparently owned texts like the one she described. Manuel González (no relation to Juana González) of the Mesón Blanco had collected Jewish or "Jewish-type" prayers in a little book confiscated by the inquisitors, as mentioned above. And enough of these books were confiscated by the inquisitors to be burned in two filled trunks at the last auto de fe in Guadalupe. Such works would have been essential for conversos hoping to observe Judaism without the benefit of resident rabbis, trained in matters of Judaic law, to rule on correct observance.

Others made use of the expert knowledge of visiting Jewish merchants. Martín Gutiérrez, a generation earlier, had questioned Jews who came to Guadalupe on business. Later, Manuel González at the Mesón Blanco had frequent contact with Jewish visitors from other towns; he sat and recited a mealtime blessing, *berahkah*, with them and apparently ran a kosher kitchen.[110] Jewish authorities also apparently worked to advise New Christians living away from Jewish communities. Fray Diego de Marchena, a converso friar, informed his brethren that two rabbis visited the shrine site specifically to counsel conversos attempting to observe Jewish law.[111]

However, relying on Jewish authorities could bring its own anxieties. When Jews were unable to fulfill religious obligations due to outside political pressures, some Jewish authorities made allowances for lack of compliance with Mosaic law. Those in such a position, however, were under a certain obligation to fulfill the law to the greatest extent possible, and, in essence, not to become excessively comfortable living outside the parameters of Jewish law. Under such provisions, conversos like those in Guadalupe did not have a clear status. To what extent were converted Jews—and especially their descendants—being coerced or

[109] AHN Inquis. legajo 154, expediente 20, 11r. "tenía su marido Lope de Herrera un libro dela ley de moysén enel qual estaban escriptas todas las fiestas e pascuas e ayunos de todo el año de la dicha ley e como se avya de fazer e en qué manera e que avya oraçiones enel dela dicha ley de moysén."

[110] Ibid., expediente 24.

[111] AMG, unnumbered, Internal Inquisition, 104. Testimony of fray Alonso de Plasencia against fray Diego de Marchena. This incident is also mentioned in chapter 7.

forced to live as Christians, and to what extent could conversos have acted more forcefully to live fully and openly as Jews? The range of practices and devotion of conversos to Judaism, and the infrequent contact with rabbis, only compounded the moral and theological problems for Judaizing New Christians.[112]

A common response among Judaizers to this moral dilemma emerged in celebrating the annual fast on Yom Kippur. Together with Passover, Yom Kippur is one of the most important holidays in the Jewish ritual year; conversos referred to it in Inquisition documents as the "major fast." For New Christians attempting to observe Judaism, though, Yom Kippur held additional significance. Yom Kippur and Rosh Hashanah celebrate the Jewish new year, and an integral part of that celebration is atonement for actions of the past.[113] For actively Judaizing New Christians, who could not fully participate in Jewish ritual activity, the annual fast of atonement was an important means of reconciling to and maintaining their covenant with God, despite a life lived largely outside of Jewish law. In such a context, it is easy to understand the prominence of Yom Kippur and other penitential fasts in inquisitorial statements.[114]

In considering the role of Yom Kippur for New Christians, it is important not to overlook the place of fasting and atonement in Christian society. Atonement was not only an important element of Jewish theology; it was also highly important to Christians of the time. While conversos in Guadalupe had some connection with Jews and even rabbis, maintaining a distinct theological tradition would have been difficult. New Christians attended mass and participated in other Christian rituals. As a result, it is likely that conversos absorbed Christian preoccupations with sin, atonement, and ultimate salvation to some degree. Even if the content and context of Christian teachings were rejected, conversos born and raised in Christian Guadalupe, far away from practicing Jews, may well have been influenced by exposure to sin and atonement as commonplace concerns. This increased sensitivity to sin and atonement on the part of conversos, combined with their own uncomfortable position with respect to Jewish law, could be resolved in part through the Jewish ceremony of Yom Kippur.

Some New Christians also applied these Christian ideas of sin, fasting, and atonement to their own ambiguous status under Jewish law.

---

[112] This is why Netanyahu argues that they are not Jews. Yovel also explores this moral and theological problem in "The New Otherness" and "Converso Dualities in the First Generation: The Cancioneros," *Jewish Social Studies* vol. 4, no. 3 (1998), 4–28.

[113] Rosh Hashanah, literally "head of the year," is the two-day celebration of the new year. This is followed by seven days of atonement, which proceed Yom Kippur, the final day of fasting, prayer, and atonement.

[114] See, for example, Melammed, *Heretics*, 24, 28.

References abound to additional fasts, adapted from provisions of Jewish law, that seem to have served a similar purpose to the fast of Yom Kippur but appear almost Christian in conception, if Jewish in execution. Conversos claimed in conversation that such fasts were an important means of "saving one's soul"—a decidedly Christian theological concept.[115] Even if the phrase were used to explain these fasts to a Christian audience, which seems unlikely, it is striking that New Christians were sufficiently immersed in Christian doctrine to describe a Jewish fast as allowing one to "save one's soul." Haim Beinart specifically mentions Monday and Thursday fasts, although conversos in Guadalupe were not so specific.[116]

Weekly Sabbath services, Yom Kippur, and Rosh Hashanah were common elements of Jewish practice among conversos, but other Jewish holidays received considerably less attention on the part of both conversos and Inquisition witnesses. Passover was rarely mentioned, and when it was, it was referred to in passing, as when one woman was accused of keeping the Jewish feasts, *pasquas de los judíos*.[117] It is possible that the close coincidence of Passover and Easter may have made it a less noticeable holiday, and thus out of range of detection by the inquisitors. It is certain that the inquisitors were aware of the existence of Passover, one of the best-known of the Jewish holidays. Unleavened bread or matzah, a staple of Passover observance, appeared only in a very few of the witnesses' statements. New Christians during this period almost certainly knew about matzah, as did Christians generally, and references to unleavened bread appeared in other inquisitorial courts.[118] It is possible, though unlikely, that no New Christians in Guadalupe made matzah; more probable is that people simply did not mention it before the court.

Some Guadalupense conversos may also have observed the autumn festival of Sukkoth. Commemorating the wandering of the Jews in the desert, Sukkoth also served as a celebration of the fall harvest. In one trial, two witnesses accused Mari Sánchez, wife of Juan Esteban, of participating in a Sukkoth celebration, mentioning it by the name "feast of the huts," *fiesta de las cabañuelas*. One witness claimed that the event took place two years previously; another witness thought the celebra-

---

[115] For example, Mari Flores, AHN Inquis. legajo 148, expediente 9.

[116] Beinart, *Conversos*, 175, 270.

[117] La Cebriana, AHN Inquis. legajo 154, expediente 30. "Pascua" in Spanish can mean Passover, Easter, or, by extension, any of the major feasts involving Jesus, or any major Jewish feast. The most specific reference I have found is in the reconciliation in ibid., expediente 1.

[118] Matzah, or *pan cenceño*, receives some discussion in Gitlitz and Davidson, *Drizzle of Honey*, 286–296. See also Beinart, *Conversos*, and Andrés Bernáldez, *Memorias*, 97.

tion had occurred four or five years previously.[119] Despite the witnesses' knowledge of a Jewish festival that included building huts, however, it is not clear what the Old Christians witnessed. Both witnesses, peculiarly, placed the time of the event during the late spring or early summer: around the time of Corpus Christi, but before the feast of Saint John the Baptist, June 24. The defense counsel drew attention to this seasonal discrepancy in his questions to the defense witnesses. In addition, a time span of "three or five days" does not fit with proper celebrations of Sukkoth, although the secret practice of Judaism may have forced participants to observe a truncated holiday. Mari Sánchez, through her defense counsel Juan de Texeda, argued that both Old and New Christians, men and women, were present. Although clearly the event aroused the suspicions of some Guadalupenses, without further information it is impossible to determine what took place, why it took place, and even if it was exclusively a New Christian activity.[120]

While there is no evidence to support Baer's contention that Christians in Guadalupe explicitly went to view the converso community there as a kind of "living exhibit" of Jewish practices, it is also inappropriate to dismiss the converso presence in Guadalupe as exaggerated, or as merely an example of the kind of disruptive antisocial elements present at any pilgrimage site.[121] The documentation preserved from the inquisitorial court suggests a wide range of Judaizing practices engaged in by conversos in Guadalupe and overall provides a composite image of the elements of Jewish life most important, and most adaptable, to the hidden practice of Judaism.[122] A hierarchy of Jewish practice developed that emphasized "basic" practices and safer activities over "less important" and riskier Jewish actions. And even in the fifteenth century, corruptions of Judaism apparent in later centuries can be detected in the statements of Guadalupense conversos. Attention to sin, repentance, and ultimate salvation, and a focus on fasting as a means of atoning for one's sins, all suggest the influence of Christian doctrine. Despite these caveats, however, the volume of evidence demonstrates the desire of some Guadalupense conversos to live as Jews. That these New Christians had to struggle with assimilated conversos as well as

---

[119] AHN Inquis. legajo 183, expediente 19. Trial of Mari Sánchez, wife of Juan Esteban de Maestre Pedro, shoemaker.

[120] A second possibility is that the celebration is not of Sukkoth, but of Shavuot, held fifty days after Passover. Building huts by a river, however, is a completely irregular practice for Shavuot.

[121] Baer, *History*, 2:337. García and Trenado, OFM, *Guadalupe*, (Seville, 1978), 95–96.

[122] Renee Levine Melammed. "The Ultimate Challenge: Safeguarding the Crypto-Judaic Heritage," *Proceedings of the American Academy for Jewish Research* 53 (1986), 91–110; and *Heretics*.

Old Christians to maintain Jewish traditions only emphasizes their devotion to Judaism.

Guadalupenses living in the shadow of the Virgin saw themselves as part of numerous religious and secular communities—Old Christian and New Christian, devoutly Christian and lackadaisical in observance, devoutly Christian conversos and New Christians concerned to observe Judaism. Townspeople united as confraternity members, as participants in secret circumcisions, as fellow citizens making their annual procession celebrating the Day of the Ascension. But how they understood their participation in these activities can never be known.

In this chapter, we have closely examined the religious communities present in the Virgin's town. It is evident that these were not monolithic communities: Christians of all types—New and Old Christian—held a wide variety of opinions regarding Christian doctrine and ritual practices. Indeed, it is essential, if we are to understand the religious, cultural, and political ferment in Spain at the dawn of the early modern period, to resist notions of reified, discrete "Old Christian" and "New Christian," or worse yet "Judaizing" communities. Some documentary evidence, particularly from the Inquisition, would tend to reinforce the image of pervasive Judaizing and distinct religious and ethnic communities. And by examining separately the distinct religious practices of Christians (both Old and New) and Judaizers, as we have just done, we run the risk of perpetuating a sense of distinctness between Old and New Christian communities. But in looking at ritual activity in the shadow of the Virgin, we begin to see the variation within as well as between Old and New Christian practices—and we begin to understand the enormous power in the hands of the inquisitors to define ambiguous attitudes and acts in either/or terms. As we turn now to Guadalupe's secular communities, and the place of conversos in them, what may still appear to be boundaries between New and Old Christians will blur even further.

THREE

CONVERSOS IN CHRISTIAN AND
JEWISH SOCIETIES

LIKE ALL Christians in Guadalupe in the second half of the fifteenth century, New Christians belonged to a number of overlapping communities in town—families; fellow shoemakers, hostellers, or pot makers; and, for conversos, a common heritage as descendants of Jews. We have seen the ways in which religious practices emerged in some of these communities and helped to define them. Yet too often New Christians have been defined exclusively as a converso or, worse yet, wholly Judaizing "community"—a reified, unified whole, with *a* religion, *an* ideology, a singular identity. Complicated interactions with Jews are acknowledged, yet many assume that, generally speaking, converso loyalties lay with Jewish "co-religionists." Both the contemporaries of New Christians and later scholars have assumed that resistance to assimilation was natural or inherent, and in many cases more natural than genuine conversion and assimilation. Historians' assumptions of the naturalness of Judaizing are confirmed by the nature of the documentary evidence, in which the only easily identifiable conversos are those tried by the Inquisition, and therefore, by extension, those about whom there is the most evidence of Judaizing practices. Other historians, by contrast, have argued just the reverse—that conversos were exclusively Christian, with absolutely no interest in Judaism whatsoever. But such assumptions, no matter how qualified, deemphasize the fundamental duality of New Christians' lives in the Iberian peninsula. New Christians were *Christian*, most often, by the end of the fifteenth century, baptized at birth. Many New Christians were increasingly isolated from declining Jewish communities. This does not mean that all conversos were devout Christians or that their religious heritage was hidden from view. But it does mean that the lived experience of Iberia's New Christians is not necessarily easily defined or categorized. It means, moreover, that to understand religious, cultural, and political change in Spain at the end of the fifteenth century, we must understand the interactions of conversos with Old Christians as well as with Jews—that New Christians lived *in* a Christian world, rather than merely coexisting with it.

The experiences of conversos living near the Virgin's shrine in Guadalupe reveal the importance of considering to what extent New Christians saw themselves as Christians, rather than exclusively examining connections between conversos and Jews. By contrasting the relationship of conversos to Christians and Jews, we can consider how New Christians redefined themselves and their beliefs in the context of the Christian society in which they lived. In this broader panorama, the story of New Christians in Guadalupe can be understood as part of a larger narrative of converso assimilation into Christian society, a process in which both Jews and Christians played a role.

Converso Connections to Jews

Like several cities with converso populations at the end of the fifteenth century, Guadalupe was an exclusively Christian city; no Jews lived in town.[1] New Christians did not have regular access to kosher meat, to a synagogue, or to any Jewish community that openly maintained Jewish observances. Furthermore, since there had never been a Jewish community in Guadalupe, all the town's conversos had arrived as New Christians. Of these, many had been baptized at birth, rather than being converts from Judaism themselves. In other Iberian cities, conversos might live near friends or extended family in their own separate neighborhood—often at or near the local "Jewish quarter."[2] In Guadalupe, however, New Christians who moved to town during the fifteenth century lived scattered among Old Christians, selecting residences in the rapidly expanding town on the basis of trade rather than ancestry.

It is not clear when conversos first appeared in Guadalupe after the forced conversions of 1391, but New Christians had played a significant role in Guadalupense society for at least forty years before the arrival of the Inquisition. Conversos or recognizable family names of Guadalupense conversos began to appear at midcentury, about forty years before the Inquisition, but those New Christians of midcentury were not necessarily even a generation older than those tried by the Inquisition.[3] Some New Christians mentioned family in Trujillo; it is reasonable to assume that at least some came from there, or from other Jewish or converso communities nearby, where people knew about the oppor-

[1] See Beinart, *Conversos on Trial*.

[2] On relations between New Christians and Jews in late fifteenth-century Castile, see Melammed, *Heretics*, chap. 1.

[3] They are probably contemporaries of the deceased parents of those tried by the Holy Office. Most New Christians had unremarkable last names—Sánchez, González, etc.—though a few families, notably the Gigantes and the Narices, had unique and recognizable family names.

tunities in Guadalupe and were close enough to transplant themselves easily. Most New Christians visible in the Inquisition records made their living feeding, clothing, and housing the thousands of pilgrims who came to town. Presumably, these conversos came to Guadalupe for economic reasons. Certainly, the Jewish merchants who traveled to the shrine site to trade were aware of the economic opportunities available to residents.[4] Whether conversos arrived at the beginning or middle of the fifteenth century, economic information in ecclesiastical and inquisitorial records indicates that New Christians were well established and economically integrated into Guadalupe by the end of the century. Furthermore, in the volume of statements by prosecution witnesses, no one described the New Christians as "newcomers" or "outsiders" in the town—perhaps because so many Old Christian Guadalupenses were newcomers themselves.

Some conversos in Guadalupe maintained links to Jews and Jewish communities, particularly through family relationships. A few New Christians had practicing Jewish family members at some distance, in southern Castile or in Muslim-controlled Málaga where New Christians were free to live as Jews.[5] Guadalupense conversos occasionally traveled south to places like Seville, Alcocer, or Belalcázar to visit with family or share briefly in a Jewish lifestyle. Catalina Rodríguez, the wife of Bartolomé Rodríguez Narices, had traveled to Seville to spend time in the Jewish quarter there before her family fled south permanently.[6] For others, Jewish family members were as close as the nearby community in Trujillo.[7] Beatriz Núñez, for example, moved to Guadalupe from Trujillo when she married.[8] Mari Sánchez, wife of Diego Jiménez the butcher, gave oil to the synagogue in Trujillo and traveled to visit the synagogue and members there.[9] The modern road linking Trujillo and Guadalupe is over eighty kilometers, but these towns, and particularly the Jewish and converso communities, may have been closer than that distance

[4] Jewish traders were not uncommon in Guadalupe. Mari Sánchez, wife of Diego Jiménez the butcher, took in visiting Jewish merchants, and Jews are recorded as staying at the Mesón Blanco for kosher food while visiting Guadalupe.

[5] Connections between Castilian New Christians and Jews in Málaga are discussed in chapter 6.

[6] AHN Inquis. legajo 177, expediente 10.

[7] This Jewish community has been studied in depth by Haim Beinart, who made use of Trujillo's large municipal archive. See Beinart, *Trujillo. A Jewish Community in Extremadura on the Eve of the Expulsion from Spain* (Jerusalem: Magnes Press, 1980).

[8] AHN Inquis. legajo 169, expediente 2.

[9] Ibid. legajo 183, expediente 20. In addition to Beatriz Núñez and the possible family connections of Mari Sánchez, there were also at least three additional families whose surnames indicate family in Trujillo and Talavera.

suggests. Trujillo was not only one of the largest, closest, and most active Jewish communities in the region; it was also Guadalupe's closest point of access to the old Roman road, which had served as a route for reconquering armies, immigrants, merchants, pilgrims, and others. Given the economic importance of Trujillo and its probable role as a waystation for pilgrims traveling to Guadalupe, it is not surprising that there were continuing family connections between Trujillanos and Guadalupenses.

The economic prosperity of Guadalupe and Trujillo, and the mercantile activity present in both towns, provided a second reason for links between conversos in Guadalupe and Jews in Trujillo. Among Guadalupe's numerous merchant visitors were Jews, many of them from Trujillo. Several witnesses for the Inquisition reported that these merchants had frequent contact with several of Guadalupe's New Christians, to the dismay of the friars and the inquisitors.[10] Furthermore, it is possible that these business connections held a personal significance as well. Recent studies provide increasing evidence for the frequency and sophistication of extended-family business ties between Jews and New Christians. In Mark Meyerson's analysis of Jewish and converso communities at the time of the Expulsion, he described the divisions between Jews and conversos and detailed the motivations of those Jews who converted to Christianity rather than face expulsion in 1492. Some young Jewish men who chose to convert were not necessarily cut off from their families; on the contrary, their access to Christian privileges enabled them to aid their families financially.[11] Pilar Huerga Criado, in her study of sixteenth- and seventeenth-century conversos in Ciudad Rodrigo, noted the extended family business networks created by New Christians in the Iberian peninsula. Families moved frequently, not merely for reasons of religious repression, but also to further extended-family business strategies, or to increase profits within one nuclear family.[12] Given these practices elsewhere on the peninsula, it seems likely that Trujillano Jews with converso family members in Guadalupe might have maintained and exploited those connections for economic as well as personal reasons. Those links in turn may have fostered Judaizing activity among New Christians in Guadalupe.[13] Unfortunately, there is insuf-

---

[10] These include the Jewish merchant friends of Mari Sánchez, wife of Diego Jiménez, as well as the merchant whom Martín Gutiérrez calls upon for advice on observance.

[11] Mark Meyerson, "Aragonese and Catalan Jewish Converts," 131–149.

[12] Pilar Huerga Criado, *En la raya de Portugal*, chap. 3. See also Jaime Contreras, "Family and Patronage: The Judeo-Converso Minority in Spain," in *Cultural Encounters: The Impact of the Inquisition in Spain and the New World*, ed. Mary Elizabeth Perry and Anne Cruz (Berkeley: University of California Press, 1991), 127–145.

[13] We know that some New Christians were in at least intermittent contact with

ficient documentary evidence to confirm economic links between Guadalupense conversos and Trujillano Jews, and the Inquisition left no
record of such activity.

For actively Judaizing New Christians, therefore, Jews from Trujillo
provided spiritual and moral support unavailable from residents in Guadalupe. The links between conversos and Jews varied from person to
person: some retained contacts with Jewish family members, while others
met Jews in professional contacts, like Manuel González the innkeeper.
Still others relied on more casual connections, like Martín Gutiérrez,
who questioned Jews he met on the street. Whatever the depth and
consistency of those contacts, however, the cumulative picture they provide is one of Jewish inclusion of at least some New Christians in Jewish
communities, rather than isolation of conversos. Even conversos who
were separated from traditional Jewish communities could, if they wished,
maintain contact with Jews and Jewish ceremonies to some degree.

LINKS BETWEEN NEW AND OLD CHRISTIANS

Some Guadalupense New Christians may have had occasional contact
with Jews, but Old Christians were much more prominent and more
important in the lives of local conversos. In part this was due merely to
the preponderance of Old Christians at the shrine site, and the absence
of any Jews in residence; but the close personal, social, economic, and
political connections between New and Old Christians also reflected the
degree to which conversos had assimilated into Christian society. Contact between New and Old Christians could run the gamut from casual
acquaintance to business relationships, from hostility to friendships and
even to marriage. An examination of professional and personal relationships among these New and Old Christians helps set the stage for an
examination of converso assimilation into Christian society in Guadalupe. Close relationships between New and Old Christians also helped
shape responses to New Christian assimilation by Old Christians and
Jews.

Trades and markets provided the medium for much of the contact
between Old and New Christians in Guadalupe, particularly for men.
Once the first wave of mass conversions to Christianity had begun,
recently converted New Christians throughout Castile and Aragon had
moved quickly into previously unattainable Christian markets. The eco-

---

Jewish visitors to Guadalupe, and while there is no direct evidence, it is certainly plausible that Jews attended, and perhaps acted as consultants for, the circumcisions and
burials described in chapter 2.

nomic benefits of trading as a Christian may have encouraged conversion among some converso tradesmen; however, whatever the motivation, conversion brought New Christian merchants into close contact with their Old Christian co-religionists. Guadalupe, with its steady influx of pilgrims and active regional market, only encouraged that professional contact.[14]

Due to the relatively large numbers of conversos in Guadalupe, Old Christians could not avoid depending on converso merchant families for some goods.[15] Like Old Christians, New Christians tended to marry within their profession, which they then passed on to their children. As a result, converso artisans and merchants clustered around a few trades: shoemaking, tailoring, cloth-selling and trading, and silversmithing.[16] Other families gravitated to more literate labor for the friary. Two families in particular, the Gigantes and the family of Diego González de la República, counted among themselves five scriveners; in addition, Diego González served as mayor, and later his son Andrés served the friary as the town public defender. Old Christians bought bread, wine, cushions, and probably shoes and cloth from conversos. New Christians did not dominate any of these trades, and they worked together and in competition with Old Christians in plying their wares. When bringing civil suits against each other or the friary, Old Christians relied on the converso public defender. Given these numerous links to the broader Old Christian community, it is not surprising that New Christians tried by the Inquisition mentioned their professions and their ties to other locals when defending themselves.

Conversos were also required in all phases of their work to interact with Old Christians. Some tailors may have purchased cloth solely from converso cloth merchants, *traperos*, but most trades demanded working relationships with Old Christians. Some jobs in town were comprised exclusively of Old Christians, it seems, such as the pot makers who hammered out Guadalupe's distinctive copperware. Other professions included some conversos but required collaboration with Old Chris-

[14] For more on economic contacts between Jews and Christians generally, see Nina Melechen, "The Jews of Medieval Toledo: Their Economic and Social Contacts with Christians from 1150 to 1391" doctoral dissertation, Fordham University, 1999.

[15] Between 5 and 10 percent of Guadalupe's total population was New Christian. On the percentage of conversos in Guadalupe at the end of the fifteenth century, see chapter 1.

[16] Of those whose trade is mentioned, some twenty were shoemakers, fifteen were tailors, four were cloth-sellers, two were silversmiths, and one, Manuel González, ran an inn known as the Mesón Blanco. There is no record of coppersmiths or builders—both of relatively common professions among Old Christians in Guadalupe—but it is possible that there were a few. Guadalupe has long been famed for its copper pots and still retains a street for the *caldereros*, "pot makers."

tians. Shoemakers were dependent on others for leather and wood to fashion into shoes and took on Old Christians as apprentices as well as New.[17] These Old Christian apprentices later proved to be key witnesses in either proving or refuting inquisitorial claims against Guadalupense shoemakers.[18]

Not surprisingly, these institutional connections tended to involve men more than women—though women were active in much of the family's business doings.[19] Less expected, perhaps, was the lack of evidence of contact between Old and New Christian men outside of these professional situations. It is possible that Old and New Christian men segregated themselves from their neighbors, but it seems more probable that the distinction may be due to a difference in the kinds of evidence provided about men and women. Witnesses in men's trials tended to be family or male business associates, who provided information about public appearances, such as those at mass, or professional activities. A variety of conversations, both personal and professional, might take place between Old and New Christians walking the vineyards, for example, but those involved an employer and a servant or apprentice. Conversations in the tavern, if there were any, or outside of relationships structured by employment, were not recorded in the Inquisition documents. Male conversos may have hired Old Christians and spoke casually with them, but neither master nor apprentice left evidence that they were friends, as did many women who were tried.[20]

Witnesses in women's trials, by contrast, were usually social companions or female family members and therefore could provide intimate details of families and friendships—perhaps since women's Judaizing behavior took place in the home and involved women's everyday labor

[17] From municipal ordinances setting prices for products sold in Guadalupe, it appears that shoemakers made both cheaper, wooden shoes and higher-quality leather shoes. The wooden shoes may also have been sandals used to protect finer shoes made of cloth. See AMG codex 76.

[18] See chapter 4.

[19] Since the inquisitors had little interest in the details of New Christian economic dealings, there is relatively little evidence provided for women's activity in the family business, other than feeding and caring for the apprentices. Examples from around Europe, however, suggest that women were intrinsically involved in premodern family businesses.

[20] Distinctions of status may have affected these relationships, though other, more socially equivalent relationships also seem to have been uncommon. There is no clear evidence as to whether Old Christians hired conversos. Servants, generally young girls (from age eight, according to the Inquisition material), were from small, poor towns nearby; there were no conversos there to hire out their children. Conversos tried by the Inquisition were largely self-supporting and did not work under anyone, Old or New Christian. Old Christians who could testify to New Christian apprentices or servants were outside the interest of the inquisitors, so the evidence of the Holy Office does not address that question.

(as opposed to men's Judaizing, which tended to occur outside of a work or more "public" context).[21] Whatever the reason, though, witnesses for and against conversos mention in passing, and seem to accept as a given, the intimate daily contact of neighbors and friends. When asked to describe their relationship with the accused, women carefully set out the range of friendships as they saw them.

"We were neighbors, and spoke in the street, but we didn't go in each others' houses."

". . . when I was at her house, kneading with her . . ."

". . . she came to visit, but wouldn't eat the food I made her [because of the lard]"

". . . we were in the street, talking . . ."[22]

These comments described more than casual meetings at the public ovens, or in the street, and attempted to detail the extent of a friendship. There was great variation in these careful accountings of friendships and neighborliness, but it seems clear that Old and New Christian women led lives that were largely integrated. At least some women of all religious beliefs chatted in the street, spoke at mass, and, in some sense, became friends.

Food preparation was one place where these personal connections became evident. A wide-ranging community was forged in the collective preparation of food, a community that included wives, mothers, daughters, and servants. Preparing meals in the premodern period was labor-intensive, difficult work, and women and girls relieved the drudgery by working together—hence the frequent references to kneading bread together. If Old and New Christians had been eating fundamentally different diets, preparing food together would have been potentially dangerous. New Christians might have engendered suspicion among their servants and neighbors. And in some cases, as with the reports of kosher eating habits, that occurred.[23] Yet for the most part there is little evidence of a radically distinct "Jewish" or "New Christian" diet. Differences in diet tended toward distinctions of emphasis—no pork, more meat alternatives like eggplant, more olive oil—rather than clear distinctions of preparation, style, or ingredients.[24] And in these communal preparations of food, Old and New Christian women met frequently to talk. At the family hearth, preparing bread and other foods, or at the public ovens where women had their bread and pies baked, women and

---

[21] My thanks to Mary Elizabeth Perry for her ideas on this point.

[22] AHN Inquis. legajo 181, expediente 16; legajo 148, expediente 9; and others, passim.

[23] See chapter 2.

[24] Gitlitz, *Secrecy and Deceit*, 549–550; and Gitlitz and Davidson, *Drizzle of Honey*.

their servants worked, waited, and chatted together. Indeed, this deep and frequent interaction of Old and New Christian proved to be a challenge for some New Christians trying to avoid Christian observances. One woman sent her servant boy with a pie to the public oven, only to have him chastised by the women there for bringing something that smelled like a meat pie on a fast day.

The most profound and intimate—and rarest—indication of close contact between Old and New Christians was marriage. Actively Judaizing conversos encouraged marriage with other New Christians to avoid marrying Gentiles, and the general practice of endogamy among conversos has been used to help demonstrate the fundamentally Jewish nature of New Christians.[25] Although Old Christians might resist marriage to a potentially heretical Christian, in practice resistance has been understood to originate among converts as much as among Old Christians.[26] Indeed, among Castile's and Aragon's elites, intermarriage between Old and New Christians was not uncommon, particularly in the first half of the fifteenth century, as Old Christian noblemen sought to gain renewed financial resources, and New Christians sought the status of ancient titles. Even King Fernando had Jewish blood.[27] Without marriage records and clearer indications of Old or New Christian identity, evidence for converso exogamy in Guadalupe is slim, but not nonexistent. Converso exogamy existed, for example, among the socially prominent and apparently Judaizing Gigante family. When the patriarch of the family died, all went to mourn in the Jewish manner, even Mari González, an Old Christian who had married into the family. Her discomfort with the rituals she witnessed stayed with her, and years later she testified about them to the Holy Office.[28] In a second case, Inés González testified before the inquisitors that "her father was a good

[25] Haim Beinart has often mentioned endogamy in connection with the converso desire to live as Jews. His most interesting evidence of this comes from the Inquisition trial of the prophetess Inés from Alía, a town located just a few kilometers from Guadalupe. Inés, a New Christian, had visions of devout Jewish men being made available to marry all conversa women. See Haim Beinart, "Inés of Herrera del Duque: The Prophetess of Extremadura," in *Women in the Inquisition*, ed. Giles, 42–52; "The Conversos of Halía and the Movement of the Prophetess Inés," [Hebrew] *Zion*, 53 (1988), 13–52; and "The Prophetess Inés and Her Movement in Puebla de Alcocer and Talarrubias," [Hebrew] *Tarbiz* 51 (1982), 633–658.

[26] See Beinart, *Conversos*; see also Kenneth Moore, *Those of the Street: The Catholic-Jews of Majorca. A Study in Urban Cultural Change* (South Bend: University of Notre Dame Press, 1976).

[27] On King Fernando's Jewish ancestry, see Roth, *Conversos, Inquisition, and the Expulsion* 150–152.

[28] AHN Inquis. legajo 169, expediente 2, 7r.

Christian, but her mother was entirely Jewish."[29] The implications of this statement are not as obvious as they might appear. Perhaps Inés hoped to do her mother great harm before the inquisitors—and, in fact, her mother was executed later that year. Or perhaps Inés wanted rather to protect herself from charges of Judaizing as well. Other witnesses also affirmed the Christian behavior of Mari's husband, Diego Jiménez, though some accused him of Judaizing behavior as well. Yet the inquisitors found him guilty, too, and sentenced him posthumously.[30] Some difference in attitude toward Judaism may well have existed in this household, but it is unclear whether this was a marriage between Old and New Christian.

It is dangerous to characterize from one or two cases, but these relationships suggest a certain confidence that they would not be punished either for their intermarriage or for their relatives' poorly hidden Judaizing. While New Christian–Old Christian mingling could cause tensions, these marriages and other signs of Old and New Christian interactions demonstrate the necessity of interaction among New and Old Christians, as well as, perhaps, a certain level of confidence and comfort among some of those participating. Living in a town run by friars, and without any Jews to rely upon, conversos of necessity associated with Old Christians, despite the risk for some of being discovered to be secret, active Judaizers. This imperative for survival (among active Judaizers) or perhaps confidence (among assimilated New Christians) is apparent throughout the inquisitorial material.

PERCEPTIONS OF ASSIMILATION

Recent studies have attempted to examine more closely who among Jewish converts assimilated into Christian society and who did not. Mark Meyerson's article is one of the best examples of this work.[31] Work like Meyerson's is difficult to accomplish, though, given the available documentation. Guadalupe provides an excellent example of the challenges involved. Of some two hundred–odd trials held in 1485, the records of only thirty-seven are extant today. While these seem to have been randomly preserved, there are insufficient trial records preserved to draw statistical, or even more than general, conclusions. An inven-

[29] Ibid. legajo 183, expediente 20, 6v.

[30] Ibid. For more on this trial, see Gretchen Starr-LeBeau, "Mari Sánchez and Inés González: Conflict and Cooperation among New Christians," in *Women in the Inquisition*, ed. Giles, 19–41.

[31] Meyerson, "Aragonese and Catalan Jewish Converts."

tory of the Guadalupense Inquisition files compiled by the friars in 1513 is of use but provides little information on those who assimilated. At most, it provides a kind of anecdotal evidence, showing that few were deemed innocent Christians beyond doubt, and that a sizable minority were executed for Judaizing.[32]

Despite the lack of hard demographic or numerical evidence, however, some general fissures demarcated those more or less likely to assimilate into the Christian society around them. The most striking distinction was surely that between men and women. The willingness of women to maintain Jewish traditions while men showed less fidelity to Judaism has become almost a topos of recent literature about conversos. Mark Meyerson and Yirmiyahu Yovel have commented on the greater tendency toward Judaizing among women, and Renée Levine Melammed has greatly expanded our picture of female Judaizing activities.[33] Information in Guadalupe presents much the same picture. More women testified, more women were tried, and women were increasingly responsible for the transmission of Judaism as it moved out of the synagogue and into the home. Actively Judaizing women's devotion to maintaining a traditional kitchen, to traditional patterns of living, and even to the books and studies of Judaism all characterized Judaizing practices in Guadalupe. Women, in maintaining the home, raising children, and indeed transmitting Jewish identity to their offspring according to Jewish law, were seen as more traditional than their male counterparts, who left Judaism for assimilation and the Christian world of business and life outside the home. Melammed has also commented on this distinction, noting that men lost much of their ritual activity—and, by extension, their centrality in Jewish life—with the move to clandestine observance, while women's experience of Judaism remained largely unchanged.[34]

The predominant role that women played in Judaizing activities was indicated in an anecdote Andrés González de la República told about his mother, Mari Flores. One evening the family was eating when neighbors informed them that it was a Christian fast day, and that it was time to attend mass. Responsibility for remembering the fast, preparing the meal accordingly, and organizing the family's participation was his mother's, not his father's. In his retelling of the event, his father was put to one side, becoming almost irrelevant in the narrative. Mari Flores was evidently to blame. Even if one could attribute the emphasis on Mari to

---

[32] AHN clero legajo 1423, expediente 93.

[33] See Meyerson, "Aragonese and Catalan Jewish Converts"; Yovel, "The New Otherness," section entitled "Women as 'Semi-Rabbis'"; and Melammed, *Heretics*, 15, 166–167.

[34] Melammed, *Heretics*, 31–32.

the fact that the anecdote comes from her trial, the absence is still striking. Over and over again, in Guadalupe and elsewhere, demands of domestic daily observance—whether Christian or Judaizing—fell to women.[35]

Men were not absent from Judaizing activity, however. Without the synagogue, there was a smaller role for converso men, and while some tired of restricted diets for a faith their parents or grandparents had renounced, others forged a new role for themselves in leading secret services, collecting half-remembered prayers from passers-by, and following the faith of their elders as best they could. Martín Gutiérrez and Bartolomé Rodríguez Narices are only two examples of men devoted to Judaism.[36] Similarly, some women ignored the complexities of Jewish practice, left behind the mikvah bath or the kosher kitchen, and adopted the practices of the Christians around them. Inés González, the embittered daughter of Mari Sánchez, provided one of the most extreme examples of this shift.[37] Juana González, daughter of Martín Gutiérrez and wife of Lope de Herrera, practiced Judaism in her home, but under torture she claimed—how honestly is difficult to know—that her husband was more insistent on following Jewish rites than she was. Once, she told the inquisitors, she complained that there should not be "two laws," Christian and Jewish, in the house, but just one, because her husband followed the law of Moses.[38] Of course, by claiming that she was merely following the lead of her (already executed) husband, Juana not only protected herself but also fulfilled the gender expectations of the inquisitors, who may well have assumed that men, not women, determined a family's religious practices.[39] Some women, married to Old Christians or to devoutly Christian conversos, attempted to link their fortunes to their husband's family and leave behind their Judaizing relatives. Mari Sánchez, wife of Diego Sánchez, tanner, did not leave for Málaga with her sister, son, nieces, and nephews. Instead she stayed with her remaining children and her apparently devoutly Christian husband.[40]

[35] AHN Inquis. legajo 148, expediente 9. Women's trials do include material on the Judaizing activities of their spouses.

[36] Martín Gutiérrez is discussed at length in chapter 2. Bartolomé Rodríguez Narices and his family are discussed in chapter 6.

[37] See Starr-LeBeau, "Mari Sánchez," 19–41.

[38] AHN Inquis. legajo 154, expediente 20.

[39] My thanks to Mary Elizabeth Perry for her thoughts on this issue.

[40] AHN Inquis. legajo 184, expediente 1. Parenthetically, conversa women in Guadalupe who married assimilated New Christians or Old Christians were more likely to share their husbands' name. In this period, there was no standard naming practice for surnames. Husband and wife often held different surnames, and children might carry the surname of one or the other or of neither of them. This suggests that women

Generational differences as well as gender differences were a marked trend in attitudes toward assimilation. Andrés González's testimony against his mother did not necessarily indicate eager assimilation into Christianity. Many children were forced to testify against deceased parents to protect themselves. But for other children of conversos, increasing generational distance from the open practice of Judaism, together with the submersion in a Christian community, weakened already tenuous links to the faith of their ancestors. Not surprisingly, children were more likely to assimilate to Christianity than their parents. Juana González's less consistent attempts at Judaizing do not compare to the effort her father, Martín Gutiérrez, made to learn and practice the rites of Judaism. The family of Mari Sánchez, wife of Diego Sánchez, tanner, again provides an example. Mari's son Martín testified against his family members who fled to Málaga, using largely the same language that his mother did. Unlike Mari, however, Martín seems to have more fully rejected Judaism. When his mother Mari was herself called before the inquisitors, Martín testified at length against her and his sisters, carefully detailing their Jewish practices to the Holy Office. Unlike Andrés González, Martín Sánchez showed no hesitation in condemning his mother.[41] Inés González, daughter of Mari Sánchez and Diego Jiménez the butcher, had moved with her husband to one of the exclusively Old Christian villages nearby, and, like Martín, also testified with apparent eagerness against her mother. Whether religious or personal motivations were at the forefront of their minds when Martín, Inés, and others testified against their families, it is likely that, as families became more removed from lived experience as Jews, it became easier to assimilate to Christianity. The resulting strain on family ties, particularly when inquisitors encouraged family members to testify against each other, only exacerbated the pain and disruption that the Inquisition brought in its wake.

ATTEMPTS TO SLOW ASSIMILATION INTO CHRISTIAN SOCIETY

Perhaps the most significant sign of the lure of assimilation, and the threat that it posed to continued Judaizing, were the attempts of con-

---

assumed the surname of their husband to avoid association with their converso family, but the evidence is too weak to say with certainty. Spanish women currently do not take their husband's name. A woman keeps her maiden surnames (consisting of her father's first surname followed by her mother's), and any children take their first (more important) surname from the father, and the second from the mother. On New Christian men who desired to assimilate, see Melammed, *Heretics*, 25.

[41] AHN Inquis. legajo 184, expediente 1.

versos to keep Jewish practices alive, and the evidence of pressure exerted by active Judaizers on their fellow New Christians not to assimilate. This activity was both organized and unorganized, ranging from traveling rabbis ministering to isolated converso communities, to pressure coming from within a family or within a marriage. In this range of fidelity to Judaism, and particularly in the tensions evident among New Christians themselves, the inherent ambiguity of religious practices among New Christians becomes evident.

One friar's testimony is illuminating in this regard. Fray Pedro de Trujillo, who presented a long, well-organized statement to the inquisitors in 1485,[42] opened his statement with an extended discussion about fray Alonso de Nogales, who was accused, among other things, of being overly sympathetic to conversos.[43] In one instance, fray Pedro was responsible for the baptism and Christian education of a new convert from Judaism named Jerónimo.[44] The conversion was an isolated event, and prior Diego de París and fray Pedro apparently felt that the conversion was genuine. Jerónimo had journeyed to Guadalupe to be baptized, as Abraham Seneor, a crown official, would later do in the company of Fernando and Isabel in 1492. Prior Diego asked fray Pedro to teach Jerónimo the catechism and inform him about Catholicism, but then fray Alonso asked to speak with the convert. Fray Pedro de Trujillo told the inquisitorial court that

> inter alia [fray Alonso] told [the convert Jerónimo] two things which concerned me greatly. I forget the first one. The second one was . . . that Jerónimo should feign with the conversos here who were originally from the place [where he was from] that he was a bad Christian, or that his conversion was fictitious. And thus Jerónimo could take from [the conversos] the most that he could. To which I responded, and with some anger, that Jerónimo should not do any such thing, but that he should

[42] His account ran twelve pages (six folios) and was highly organized, moving from one friar to the next, apparently in order of importance as he perceived it, and discussing all issues pertinent to one friar at the same time. He spoke again for the Jeronymite inquisitorial court in 1488.

[43] He was not accused of Judaizing per se. Some refer to him as a "heretic," but his own tendency to turn to the church fathers to defend his views supports the suspicion that he was not a Judaizer, although he may have been a converso. Only one friar of fifteen testifying against him referred specifically to Jewish practices, saying that Luis de Madrid said that fray Alonso was "bueno rabi, y non consagraua." As discussed in chapter 7, this is a suspicious source. Both the number of testifiers and his own extensive confession, however, indicate that his was not an exemplary record in Guadalupe, even though one could argue that Pedro de Trujillo's testimony was motivated in part by personal dislike.

[44] Jerónimo probably received his Christian name in honor of the founder of the friary where he went to be baptized.

always show himself to be a true and Catholic Christian with all people and in all places, and that [the other advice] was poor counsel . . . that later [Jerónimo] should begin, having just been baptized, to do that which all these evil heretics had had and done, that is, with Jews show themselves to be Jews, and with Christians Christians.[45]

Even in the friary itself, therefore, conversos faced the competing pressures and contradictory advice of the friars. Fray Alonso's eminently pragmatic advice might have made sense from a social or professional point of view, but it was hardly religiously consistent. Elsewhere, fray Alonso suggested that he was suspicious of the beliefs of all converts, although the inquisitors later questioned fray Alonso's own understanding of the Virgin birth. Ultimately, fray Pedro and fray Alonso were united in doubting the sincerity of converso beliefs—whether Jewish or Christian. And while fray Alonso's advice to Jerónimo indicated, on the one hand, the imagined strength of the Judaizing community in Guadalupe, it also suggested that Judaizing practices could be as much the result of community pressure, and perhaps even as feigned, as the Christian activities of active Judaizers. This accusation that all New Christians held beliefs as un-Jewish as they were un-Christian is reminiscent of the polemics of the *Libro del Alboraique*, which described New Christians as being neither Jewish nor Christian, but equally false to all.[46]

This pressure to Judaize could also be found at home. Both Inés González's hostility to all Judaizers, especially her mother, and Martín Sánchez's willingness to testify against family members who fled to Málaga to live as Jews while he stayed in Guadalupe as a Christian may express a resentment of family and friends that stemmed in part from being forced to live a Jewish life instead of a Christian one. Whatever the specific motivations of these two assimilated conversos, family con-

[45] AMG unnumbered, Internal Inquisition, 54. "inter alia le dixo dos cosas de que mucho me pesó. La una [se lo olvidó]. La otra [fue] . . . que se simulase con los conversos de aquí del lugar que era mal cristiano, o que era ficto. & así sacase de los lo más que puediese. A lo qual yo respondí, & aún con algund enojo que no lo fiziese aquello sino que siempre se mostrase con todos & en todo logar por verdadero & cathólico cristiano diziendo que aquél era mal consejo . . . luego començase acabado de baptizar lo que todos estos herejes malvados han tenido & fecho, e.g., con los judíos se mostrar judíos, & con los cristianos cristianos."

[46] The *alboraique*, the beast who carried Muhammad to Heaven, was renowned for including the features of many animals yet truly belonging to no one species. Likewise, the tract argued, conversos voiced the beliefs of many faiths and included many negative traits without adhering to any one religion. See transcriptions and analyses of this work in Isidore Loeb, "Le Livre d'Alboraïque," *Revue des Etudes Juives* 18 (1889), 238–242; Nicolás López Martínez, *Los Judaizantes Castellanos* (Burgos, 1954), 391–404; David Gitlitz, "Hybrid *Conversos* in the 'Libro llamado el Alborayque'," *Hispanic Review* 60 (1992), 1–17; and Benzion Netanyahu, *Origins*, 848–854.

flicts regarding what to practice in the home did find their way into the Inquisition records. Women often explained that men resented being forced to abide by kosher dietary restrictions. Juana González, wife of Lupe de Hemera, grew up thinking Christianity was true, until one Yom Kippur, when she was perhaps around age twelve, she was told of her family's true beliefs. This pattern was repeated throughout the peninsula as a measure of protection for both parents and children, but it may also have created tensions if the child were unwilling to accept the family's faith. In any event, children, like all family members, were expected to hold to a family's beliefs, be they Christian or Jewish, rather than stake out an independent position.

The charge of "imposing Judaism" on family and friends was a commonplace in inquisitorial trials. Mari Flores, mother of Andrés González de la República, was accused of encouraging conversa women to observe the Jewish fasts and to maintain a kosher kitchen.[47] Many women were charged with forcing Judaism on other, less Jewish conversos, leaving the impression that a few vocal and active Judaizers were responsible for encouraging, prodding, and shaming fellow New Christians into following the path that Judaizers believed would (employing a Christian theological concept) lead to "true salvation." Of course, like all accusations asserted by the prosecution, these charges must be carefully evaluated. New Christians hoping to protect themselves might accuse deceased mothers and aunts of the vague charge of "imposing Judaism," thus demonstrating their own willingness to cooperate with the inquisitors. And younger Judaizers caught in the gaze of the inquisitors might accuse others to protect themselves. Even testimony that exaggerates the influence of others suggests the kinds of tensions present within a New Christian home. Alonso the teacher claimed that he had oil lamps lit on Fridays and kept kosher because his mother, with whom he lived, forced him to do so. It is possible that she did maintain that kind of authority in the home—witnesses could identify little in Alonso's behavior that suggested a devotion to Judaism—but the excuse seemed designed largely to turn attention from himself.[48] And yet for those active Judaizers who had been raised in a Jewish environment, or even as Jews, the frustration with declining Jewish observance among New Christian family and friends must have been palpable. Surrounded by

---

[47] AHN Inquis. legajo 148, expediente 9.

[48] Alonso was also shadowed by questions regarding his atypical lifestyle. He was unmarried, despite his age, and lived alone with his mother. He may also have had a married sister. Some accused him of incest, rather than Judaizing, but there seems to be even less evidence for the former than for the latter. The use of the Inquisition as a site to point out all types of unusual and suspicious behavior, whether identifiably Judaizing or no, is discussed in chapters 5 and 7.

Catholic doctrine, and with the children growing up at least nominally
in the Catholic church, actively Judaizing practices were hardly sponta-
neously self-sustaining, even in the fifteenth century, when Jews were
still available to teach doctrine and provide advice. Occasionally, one
senses genuine irritation among active Judaizers. As Mari Sánchez, wife
of Diego Sánchez the tanner, exclaimed in the street one day, "there
aren't ten good conversos left in Guadalupe who haven't confessed to
the Inquisition!"[49]

Community encouragement and support of Judaizing also took more
organized forms, thanks to the support of Jewish communities around
the peninsula. In Guadalupe, this kind of activity was less obvious than
in towns that included both a Jewish and a converso community; at the
shrine site, links to Jews came primarily through visiting Jewish traders
or semiclandestine trips south to Seville and Málaga. Even in Guadalupe, at least intermittent support for conversos from itinerant rabbis
and other travelers existed. Fray Diego de Marchena described one example of this support to his stunned fellow friars. Fray Alonso de Plasencia remembered it thus:

> speaking with Marchena, with the man from Durango, and with fray
> Estevan, the man from Durango said, "Something has happened in this
> town that has not happened in all Castile." And the man from Marchena
> said, "I will tell you what it is. Two rabbis have been walking all through
> Castile visiting [conversos to see] if the Law of Moses was being observed
> properly, and they came to this town and asked if they kept the law of
> Moses. And some said yes and others said that they could not keep it
> well because they were poor. And [the rabbis] granted them a dispensa-
> tion so that they could work on the holidays, and these were the poor
> shoemakers and other poor people."[50]

This testimony of fray Alonso and others about fray Diego's statements
is the only mention I have found of such activity in Castile in the
fifteenth century. Baer and others make no mention of itinerant rabbis
visiting Castilian converso populations.[51] Such an activity, presumably

---

[49] AHN Inquis. legajo 184, expediente 1. See also Baer, *History*, 2:337–338.

[50] AMG unnumbered, Internal Inquisition, 104. Testimony of fray Alonso de Plasencia
against fray Diego de Marchena. "fablando con Marchena, él de Durango, & fr. Esteuan,
dixo él de Durango, 'Una cosa se ha fallado en este pueblo que non se ha fallado en
toda castilla.' & dixo él de Marchena, 'yo vos diré. Que andauan dos rabíes por toda
castilla visitando si se guardaua bien la ley de moysén & vinían aquí a este pueblo &
preguntauan si se guardaua bien la ley de moysén. & algunos dezían que sí & otros que
non podían buenamente porque eran pobres. & ellos dispensauan conellos que traba-
jassen las fiestas & estos era[n] los çapateros pobres & los otros pobres.'"

[51] There is a parallel in the Muslim *al-faqim* who traveled in Christian territories

sponsored in part by a large Jewish synagogue in Castile, Málaga, or North Africa, must also have relied on the hospitality of converso communities through Castile. Assuming that fray Diego did not invent this visit, the incident suggests significant Jewish awareness of and concern for converso communities and their attempts to Judaize. It may also suggest, however, that Guadalupense conversos were not alone in living without access to someone able to rule on Jewish law. The rabbis reportedly traveled through "all of Castile" checking people's ability to keep the law of Moses, perhaps visiting small, isolated Jewish communities as well as converso ones.

Also of note was the rabbis' decision to grant "dispensations" to those who due to circumstance were unable to follow Mosaic law. These included poor shoemakers and "other poor people." The only acceptable excuse for assimilating to Christianity was poverty. We can only guess at how those conversos who did not attempt to observe the law, or who did not feel strongly about Judaism, participated in this visit. Perhaps they did not meet with the rabbis, or perhaps they requested a dispensation from full compliance with Jewish law, willing to see how much could be lawfully avoided while still remaining, in some eyes, a Jew. Whatever the attitude of these more assimilated conversos, it is clear that Jews and active Judaizers could on occasion work together to bolster the observance of Judaism, and to aid as much as possible the Judaizing of those far from strong Jewish institutions.

In a few cases, even some Jeronymites encouraged Judaizing. This was generally the result of the efforts of individual Judaizing friars or friars who sympathized with active Judaizers, who used the institutions of the church to promote their own proconverso, and even pro-Judaizer, attitudes. Only fray Diego de Marchena encouraged conversos to stew rather than roast their chicken on Fridays, to prevent detection by the friars. But more than a few friars chastised their parishioners for speaking poorly of conversos in the confessional, and many were known in and out of the friary for their sympathy to conversos no matter what their religious beliefs.[52] Indeed, the leniency prior Diego de París expressed toward active Judaizers in the 1470s and 1480s not only would heighten local political tensions, but may have affected Judaizing practices within the converso community as well. There was little reason not to believe fray Alonso de Nogales when he suggested that the safest path was to act a Christian with Christians and as a Jew with Jews.

Even the Inquisition, whose purpose was to identify and punish Juda-

---

ruling on Islamic law. See Kathryn A. Miller, *Guardians of Islam: Muslim Communities in Medieval Aragon* (forthcoming), chaps. 3 and 6.

[52] This is discussed in greater detail in chapter 7.

izing behavior among converts, could indirectly encourage the accused to voice support of Judaism. In forcing New Christians to identify solely as devout Christians or heretics, and with the court designed to identify guilt rather than innocence, the inquisitors at times achieved quite the opposite result to what they had intended. Isabel González, who exaggerated her devotion to Judaism to satisfy the inquisitors and returned from exile two years later, provides a particularly potent example of the power of the inquisitors to create a Judaizing heresy where none existed. Ironically, Isabel's case suggests the intense pressure on conversos both to break decisively from Jewish society and simultaneously to confess to alienation from Christian society, even when New Christians considered themselves devoutly Christian. Like the advice fray Alonso had for Jerónimo, Isabel González avoided suspicion by hiding her religious beliefs under the mantle of assumed and expected practices. For Jerónimo this would have meant feigning Judaism with Judaizers; for Isabel it meant a false confession to the inquisitors and a sentence of perpetual exile.

Isabel's return to Guadalupe after a brief exile was destined to be short-lived, for in 1488 she was once again brought before the Holy Office. The charge against her was not violating her sentence of exile. Instead, she was charged with falsifying and later denying her 1485 statement of reconciliation, that she was like a wolf in sheep's clothing—*parecía por que venía debajo de piel de oveja.*[53] This time, there was little hope of absolution, given what the inquisitors perceived as a hardened disdain for Christianity and the sacrament of confession, and an unwillingness to acknowledge her wrongs. Isabel González was permanently exiled from Guadalupe.

There was no mention of children or other family in her file, and without a spouse or family to help protect her, Isabel was particularly vulnerable. In such a climate, Isabel bowed to pressure from all sides to "admit" that her identity as a converso meant she was also a Judaizer, albeit an inconsistent and repentant one. The sparse evidence of Judaizing in Isabel González's file supports her claim that she was a devout Christian. Even so, her postinquisitorial remarks and the evidence of pressure on New Christians to Judaize lead into a "hall of mirrors," where nothing is quite what it seems to be.[54] Evidence that suggested

---

[53] It is possible, but unlikely, that her sentence of exile was commuted. All the Inquisition files were held in Guadalupe until 1513, and they were updated as the cases required. In fact, the record of her second case was put in her file in front of the first. Isabel González's trial is discussed at greater length in chapter 8. See AHN Inquis. legajo 154, expediente 6.

[54] Inga Clendinnen uses this metaphor in *Ambivalent Conquests* to discuss how Mayans and Spaniards understood and misunderstood one another, but it might apply equally to the inquisitorial trials Clendinnen describes.

the existence of several active Judaizers in Guadalupe, such as older women proselytizing among young conversos to observe Jewish rituals, also indicated the difficulties Judaizers had in maintaining those practices. The inquisitorial year of 1485 in Guadalupe was in itself a kind of proof of the presence of Judaizers in the Puebla; yet at least some of those tried lied to the court, falsely claiming to have participated in Judaizing activity to avoid torture and an extended trial. For many of Guadalupe's New Christians, it seems, observance of both Judaism and Christianity was a matter of constant negotiation with family, neighbors, local authorities, and their own consciences. Somewhat fewer New Christians show evidence of being as unwaveringly Jewish as Mari Sánchez, wife of Diego Jiménez the butcher, or as unshakably Christian as her daughter Inés González. Most, like Isabel González, were caught between competing pressures, and with a sense of ever more limited options.

In part, the distinctions between what Old and New Christians saw in Guadalupe—rampant Judaizing as opposed to a scandalous degree of assimilation—can be traced to a difference of perspective. Old Christians lamented any evidence that their New Christian neighbors maintained an affinity for Judaism. For actively Judaizing conversos, too many of their brethren were assimilating into Christianity and Christian society, ignoring the faith and laws of their parents and grandparents. To a degree, both sides unintentionally encouraged the uncommitted to act as "Christians with Christians, and Jews with Jews," though it is only fair to add that the advantage lay with the Christians. Some conversos were clearly assimilating into Christian society before the Expulsion of the Jews in 1492, despite intentional or unintentional resistance caused by both Old Christians and Jews. In Guadalupe, where conversos were already somewhat isolated from contact with Jewish communities, the fifteenth century offered a glimpse of the challenges that all Judaizing conversos would increasingly face after the Expulsion. Without the opportunity to practice Judaism openly, without the possibility of learned elders collecting and transmitting Jewish traditions, and with constant exposure to Christian doctrine, New Christians' Judaizing practices had already begun to erode. In Guadalupe, intraconverso tensions threatened solidarity among Judaizers, a process that might have been somewhat delayed elsewhere until the sixteenth and seventeenth centuries.

But Guadalupense conversos, while prefiguring challenges faced by Spanish converso communities of the sixteenth and seventeenth centuries, were not simply members of an anachronistic converso community lacking the support of Jews. By the end of the fifteenth century, many Jewish communities had been decimated by anti-Jewish riots, increased pressures from the Christian majority, and forced and voluntary conversions. In counterpoint to growing numbers of conversos, people who were generally separated from regular contact with rabbis and synagogue life, were shrinking Jewish communities, with decreasing power over their own affairs and, occasionally, without rabbis and contacts with the wider Iberian Jewish community themselves. These weakened Jewish communities shared some of the challenges of fifteenth-century Judaizing conversos. While not denying the rupture that the Expulsion caused in Christian and Jewish lives in Iberia, Guadalupe provides an example of one kind of continuity for those conversos of all religious beliefs who stayed in Spain after 1492.

The religious practices and sentiments of most New Christians remain unclear, since they depended in part on the opinions of family, friends, and friars, as well as the changing attitudes of the individuals themselves. Yet it is safe to say that some conversos seem to have followed the admonition of fray Alonso to live as Christians with Christians and as Jews with Jews. In contrast to these complex expressions of religious beliefs were the attitudes of inquisitors and to a much lesser extent devout Jews, both of whom by the late fifteenth century had begun to demand more consistency of religious practice among New Christians. The history of the town of Guadalupe revealed the complex negotiations of religious practice that so many New Christians engaged in, negotiations which enabled them to assimilate to some degree into Christian society, but also earned them the suspicions of the devout among both Christians and active Judaizers. As tensions in town escalated, the local political implications of these negotiations became more and more untenable, as we will now see.

FOUR

POLITICAL CONFLICTS, SOCIAL UPHEAVAL, AND RELIGIOUS DIVISIONS: THE ORIGINS OF THE GUADALUPENSE INQUISITION

THE CULTURAL COMPLICATIONS of having a sizable converso minority in town were substantial, but they were only one part of the challenges facing Guadalupe in the second half of the fifteenth century. Rapid population growth in town, financial difficulties for town and friary alike in the wake of the civil war between the future Queen Isabel and her niece Juana la Beltraneja, factionalism among the friars themselves, and frequent social unrest all combined to keep the Virgin's guardians occupied. The specifics of Guadalupe's history were of course unique, but tensions between Old and New Christians, and between townspeople and local authorities, were on the rise throughout Castile. On the surface, Guadalupe's local political conflicts were typical of the upheavals faced by western European towns at the end of the Middle Ages as citizens attempted to wrest authority away from local lords. In that light, the arrival of the royal Inquisition in late 1484 seems at first glance coincidental to these ongoing conflicts, yet events in the two decades preceding the arrival of the inquisitors indicate that the opposite was true. The decision to initiate the Inquisition in Guadalupe did not have its impetus solely in royal policy; while the Catholic Monarchs approved of the Holy Office's activity in Guadalupe, the request for the Inquisition may well have originated with local clerical authorities concerned with local problems.

These local problems stemmed from the evolving relationship among Old Christians, New Christians, and the friary in Guadalupe. Entering the second half of the fifteenth century, ancestry, particularly Jewish ancestry, was only one of many fault lines dividing the population into numerous overlapping, conflicting groups. Resentment toward the friars as both the religious and secular authorities in town was a far greater source of conflict. However, in subsequent decades the prominence of the New Christians within the town and the friary increased. This process was abetted by the Jeronymites' traditional sympathy toward conversos and by the New Christians' financial support of the friary during the political turmoils of the 1460s and 1470s. As a result, the hostilities of Old Christians toward New Christians and toward the friars were increasingly linked, and resentment of New Christians grew stronger. In the wake of the prior's election of 1483, a new way emerged to resolve this increased resentment of conversos and to distance the friars from New Christians—the Holy Office of the Inquisition. Only the presence of the inquisitors could assuage the twin resentments of New Christians and of the friars' lordly authority and restore the status of Old Christians in the town and in the friary.

The seismic tensions that regularly threatened to disrupt community relations in Guadalupe in the second half of the fifteenth century reveal the multiplicity of conflicts that existed in Iberian communities before the arrival of the Inquisition. Indeed, the challenges to local authority— which came primarily from Old Christian artisans in Guadalupe—were not atypical of towns throughout western Europe in this period. In the two decades before the arrival of the inquisitors, we can see the contingent, conditional nature of community identity and individual allegiances. As the century wore on, though, this typical urban unrest was increasingly supplanted by this conjunction of religious and secular grievances. Furthermore, analysis of the friars' attempts to control the townspeople before the arrival of the royal Inquisition suggests a complicated mixture of religious and secular motivations behind their actions as well. The decades that preceded the establishment of the Inquisition in Guadalupe were important in securing the Virgin of Guadalupe's place as the preeminent devotion of fifteenth-century Castile. But even more importantly, those years reveal the religious and secular motivations that would affect the presence and actions of the inquisitors as well as contribute to the creation of Isabel and Fernando's image of Spain as a "sacralized state." Thus, to understand events in Guadalupe in 1484 and beyond, it is important to go back for a moment to the first efforts to establish an inquisitorial court in the Virgin's town.

THE JERONYMITES AND THE ESTABLISHMENT
OF THE SPANISH INQUISITION

While the royal Inquisition established by Isabel and Fernando officially heralded the beginning of the modern Spanish Inquisition, the idea of an ecclesiastical Inquisition had been known to Iberians since bishops and friars had sought out heretics in the thirteenth century.[1] Regionally

---

[1] These courts are best known for their trials of the Cathars of southern France, but ecclesiastical Inquisitions tried a variety of cases throughout the late medieval period. The literature on these medieval inquisitorial courts is immense. Some good starting

organized inquisitions under the authority of the local bishop or the mendicant orders were still familiar in western Europe. The medieval inquisitorial court operating in the Crown of Aragon, for instance, had theoretically remained in existence through the end of the fifteenth century, although it was largely moribund during this period.[2] But even though inquisitorial activity had largely ceased, some Spaniards at court in the middle decades of the fifteenth century saw in the medieval Holy Office of the Inquisition a solution to the social upheaval of their age. In the 1450s and 1460s, the Castilian court became a center of debate about these issues, particularly the nature and place of conversos in Iberia.

A key figure in this debate was the one-time Guadalupense friar Alonso de Oropesa.[3] Fray Alonso de Oropesa rose rapidly to prominence in the order: he was still a young man when he was elected, first, as prior of Santa Catalina in Talavera in 1451 or 1452, and then general of the Order of Saint Jerome in 1457.[4] From his election as general of the order until his death in 1469, fray Alonso unceasingly used his position in the order and at court to support and defend conversos. His opposition to anticonverso sentiment was well known before he took up leadership of the order, and the support of his fellow Jeronymites suggests that he spoke for many of his brethren.[5] Under his leadership, the Order of Saint Jerome supported conversos and their gradual assimilation to Christianity. In addition, the Jeronymites, like other orders in Iberia at this time, counted a number of conversos among its brethren. The order's links to the Trastámara court and Castilian elites further encouraged elite conversos to enter. By the late fifteenth century, the Order of Saint Jerome had gained a reputation as a relatively sympa-

---

points include Giovanni Gonnet, "Bibliographical Appendix: Recent European Historiography on the Medieval Inquisition" in *The Inquisition in Early Modern Europe: Studies on Sources and Methods*, ed. Gustav Hennigsen, John Tedeschi, and Charles Amiel (De Kalb: Northern Illinois University Press, 1986), 199–223; Edward Peters, *Inquisition* (New York: The Free Press, 1988); and Richard Kieckhefer, "The Office of the Inquisition and Medieval Heresy: The Transition from Personal to Institutional Jurisdiction," *Journal of Ecclesiastical History* 46 (1995), 36–61.

[2] Mark Meyerson, *The Muslims of Valencia in the Age of Fernando and Isabel: Between Coexistence and Crusade* (Berkeley: University of California Press, 1991), chaps. 1 and 2, discusses the medieval Inquisition, as does Roth, *Conversos, Inquisition, and the Expulsion* 203–212.

[3] Pedro de la Vega, OSH, *Crónica de los frayles de la orden del bienaventurado nuestro padre sant Hieronymo* (Alcalá de Henares, 1539), 47v.

[4] See Luis Díaz y Díaz, "Introducción general," in Alonso de Oropesa, *Luz*, 7–8, and Luis Díaz y Díaz, "Alonso de Oropesa y su Obra" in *Studia Hieronymiana*, 1:253–313.

[5] See Díaz y Díaz, "Alonso de Oropesa y su Obra," 264–268. Fray Alonso was asked to write his work on conversos by the prior of Guadalupe; see chapter 1.

thetic home to conversos and their Muslim counterparts, *moriscos*. Jeronymites provided both an intellectual defense of the gradual conversion of conversos and the practical benefit of a sympathetic home for would-be converso friars. So entrenched was the belief that the Jeronymites were a refuge for Judaizers that Guadalupense friars were openly questioned on the street about the religious beliefs of their converso brethren.[6]

The primary support for a punitive Inquisition came from the political and religious rivals of the Jeronymites, the Franciscans. Emblematic of the Franciscan argument was the *Fortalitium Fidei*,[7] a tract against religious heresy authored by the Franciscan friar Alonso de Espina in 1459. Fray Alonso concluded his attack on heretical groups, including conversos, by arguing for the reinvigoration of the Inquisition to root out those people "endangering" Iberia. It is probable that Fray Alonso envisioned a revival of the medieval inquisitorial courts with which he was familiar, rather than the development of a new, more powerful, and far-reaching inquisitorial system. Anticonverso sentiments among the Franciscans were widespread, even among New Christians within the order, some of whom were among the most zealous proponents of a new Inquisition.[8]

The Jeronymites refused to support the Franciscans' condemnations of conversos, or their calls for a punitive Inquisition, as is revealed in letters between the two groups. The Franciscans wrote to Alonso de Oropesa, who as General of the Jeronymite Order served as a key adviser and confidant to King Enrique IV (reigned 1454–1474).[9] In these writings, the Franciscans described the many ills of the kingdom and linked the mingling of Christians and non-Christians to contemporary

[6] For one example, see AMG, unnumbered, Internal Inquisition, 79. Testimony of fray Juan de Carranza. While in Guadalajara three *escuderos* stopped him at the duke's gate and asked if he was from Guadalupe. When fray Juan said yes, the *escuderos* asked why the friars allowed fray Diego de Marchena to serve as a confessor.

[7] The *Fortalitium* was a large work divided into four parts, each of which addressed one of the groups "contaminating" Iberia. These fray Alonso defined as witches, Muslims, Jews, and heretics, by which he meant conversos. For a useful summary, see the discussion in Jocelyn Hillgarth, *The Spanish Kingdoms, 1250–1516*, 2 vols. (Oxford: Oxford University Press, 1976, 1978), vol. 2, part 3, chap. 3, "The Crown and Religion." Netanyahu, *Origins*, 814–847, offers a cogent analysis of Alonso de Espina's life and work.

[8] Fray Alonso de Espina himself was reputed to be a New Christian, although Netanyahu argues otherwise; see Netanyahu, *Origins*, 726.

[9] Pedro de la Vega, *Crónica*, 47v. King Enrique was one of the Jeronymites' staunchest supporters, perhaps following the lead of his mother, who like her son was devoted to the Virgin of Guadalupe. Enrique also founded San Jerónimo el Real, a Jeronymite friary whose church still stands on a hill overlooking the Museo del Prado. Enrique's aunt, María Queen of Aragon, also depended heavily upon her Jeronymite confessor and adviser while her husband, Alfonso the Magnanimous, was fighting in Italy.

unrest in Castile. The letter then asked the Jeronymites to join them in two demands: first, that Enrique IV require all Jews and Muslims to live according to Christian dictates and royal statutes; and second, that an Inquisition be established "as is done in France, and in many other Christian kingdoms and provinces."[10] In consultation with his order, fray Alonso responded that the king was already doing much to address this problem, and that it was important that Enrique IV rein in Old Christian persecution of New Christians, as well as the Judaizing of conversos. Fray Alonso de Opoesa's activity in the royal court was informed by the themes of his masterwork, "Light for the Revelation of the Gentiles" (*Lumen ad Revelationem Gentium*), which expanded on his ideas of the proper balance between education in doctrine, reform, and discipline. When the Jeronymites debated the status of conversos with the Franciscans, fray Alonso de Oropesa argued for the importance of tolerance for gradual assimilation, gentle correction of those who erred, and stern punishment for those who wrongly accused New Christians out of ill-will.[11] A wrongful accusation of conversos at Enrique's court served to bolster fray Alonso de Oropesa's argument. On that occasion, a Franciscan at court claimed that he had in his possession a hundred foreskins of circumcised converso boys. Fray Alonso urged the king to demand to see the foreskins as proof of the friar's story. Enrique IV complied. His bluff called, the Franciscan was forced to admit that he had invented the tale. Fray Alonso's suspicion that many accusations of converso wrongdoing were unfounded seemed proven.[12]

When fray Alonso de Oropesa is remembered by scholars today, it is usually for taking up the converso standard against the Franciscans at court. However, Fray Alonso de Oropesa was not averse to the idea of an Inquisition; rather, he argued in his written works and in his statements at the court of Enrique IV for an Inquisition whose purpose would be to reform rather than to punish.[13] Fray Alonso de Oropesa resisted wild and unproven accusations against New Christians, but he did believe that when New Christians did not correctly practice Christianity, they should be encouraged to reform and be disciplined if neces-

---

[10] José de Sigüenza, OSH, *Historia*, 1:363–365.

[11] José de Sigüenza discussed this event at length in his history of the Jeronymite order; see ibid., 361–373. Fray José's ambivalent attitude toward fray Alonso and these events during the reign of Enrique IV is revealing: José de Sigüenza acknowledged the order's and Alonso de Oropesa's importance to events of the time but seems unconvinced of the appropriateness of fray Alonso's actions. See also the more positive, extended discussion of fray Alonso de Oropesa in Pedro de la Vega's *Crónica*, 69v–70r. Netanyahu analyzes fray José's account of fray Alonso in *Origins*, 894–895.

[12] José de Sigüenza, *Historia*, 1:366–367, and William D. Phillips, Jr., *Enrique IV and the Crisis of Fifteenth-Century Castile, 1425–1480* (Cambridge: Harvard University Press, 1978).

[13] See Phillips, *Enrique IV*, and Netanyahu, *Origins*, 855–896.

sary. The proposed second half of *Lumen ad Revelationem Gentium*, which fray Alonso described in passing in the first volume but never wrote, was to discuss the practicalities of discipline and pastoral care, in contrast to the theological thrust of the first volume.[14] When Enrique did attempt to establish a royal Inquisition in the early 1460s, he turned to fray Alonso de Oropesa to organize it. The Jeronymites and the Franciscans debated the degree of sincerity of Jewish converts and how best to address the presence of conversos in the general community, but both sides agreed that those who disobeyed the teaching of the church should be instructed and disciplined. No documents remain concerning fray Alonso's attempts to organize this first Inquisition. It is possible that fray Alonso never began work on structuring his inquisitorial court, with its emphasis on education and reform over harsh discipline. Without a papal concession permitting him to marry a clerical inquisitorial court to the secular Crown, Enrique may have chosen to put plans for his Crown-controlled Inquisition aside, and fray Alonso would have had little time or reason to plan without approval from Rome. In any event, Enrique's moves on this front were poorly timed. Throughout the mid-1460s his attention was increasingly occupied by the civil war brewing over questions of succession. By 1469 fray Alonso, a key motive-force behind Enrique's policy, had died, and Enrique's dreams of an Inquisition, whether reformative or punitive, were set aside.[15]

Meanwhile, unrest surrounding the place of New Christians in Christian society only continued to mount. Increasingly, individual cities and lords sought to quiet tensions involving conversos through existing court structures. Some of Enrique IV's retainers and associates at court may have encouraged local clergy to use their own religious judicial authority to respond to a variety of social, political, and economic issues that involved conversos; on the other hand, local responses to contemporary disturbances may have encouraged Enrique IV to act as well. Little is known of these actions, which involved both civil and eccle-

[14] See, for example, Alonso de Oropesa, *Luz*, 96, in which fray Alonso states that the second half of his work will build on the conclusion of the first that all Christians are equal in the faith by explaining "how to punish any person who errs in any way, and that in this one must observe the same rule for all without any differentiation of ancestry or station" (intentaré exponer cómo ha de ser castigado cada uno que cayese en cualquier error y que en esto hay que observar una misma regla para todos sin ninguna acepción de personas, . . . sin hacer diferencias de raza o persona). Díaz y Díaz, "Alonso de Oropesa y su Obra," 281.

[15] Phillips argues that Enrique IV was effective in the first ten years of his rule, but ineffective in the second ten. On the reign of Enrique IV, his plans for an Inquisition, and the civil war between supporters of Isabel and Juana la Beltraneja, see Phillips, *Enrique IV*, chaps. 4–6.

siastical courts, though the trend can be related to the parallel debate over purity of blood statutes first enacted in Toledo in 1449.[16] Whatever the motivation and status of other courts, however, it is clear that the friars at Guadalupe had initiated at least one short-lived ecclesiastical inquisitorial court by 1462.

The Ecclesiastical Inquisition in Guadalupe in 1462

The timing of Guadalupe's early, limited ecclesiastical Inquisition makes it almost exactly contemporaneous to fray Alonso de Oropesa's period of greatest activity at Enrique's court. Fray Alonso may have encouraged events in Guadalupe, given a confluence of local and royal interest in the practices of New Christians. Indeed, fray José de Sigüenza states in his history that King Enrique IV ordered fray Alonso to establish a general Inquisition in the realm, and that "this was the first general investigation carried out by the bishops in the kingdoms of Castile."[17] Whatever the circumstances surrounding its origins, however, this early inquisitorial court in Guadalupe set the stage for later developments for both the town and the kingdom. The only extant statements about these earlier inquisitorial courts come from comments made by witnesses during the trials of 1485. References by friars and vecinos suggest that the Guadalupense Jeronymites organized an ecclesiastical inquisitorial court in the early 1460s and tried and sentenced a few conversos for Judaizing. The clearest evidence for the activity of this court comes from testimony relating to Fernando González the scrivener, *escrivano*, also known as Fernando González the heretic, *hereje*. His case demonstrates the anxieties caused by the Judaizing practices of New Christians in town.[18]

[16] Ricardo García Cárcel addresses the early history of the Inquisition in Valencia in his *Orígenes de la inquisición española: el tribunal de Valencia, 1478–1530* (Barcelona: Ediciones Península, 1976), but neither he nor any other scholar I have read discusses in detail the civil and ecclesiastical precursors to the modern Inquisition. This is due in part to the paucity of sources for the period (particularly in Castile), and in part to the extensive regional and local archival work such a study would demand. On the purity of blood statutes, see Sicroff, *Controverses*.

[17] "Fue esta la primera inquisicion general que se hizo por los Obispos en los Reynos de Castilla, a lo que yo he podido entender, y no he hallado mas noticia della, desto que consta por los libros de los actos capitulares desta religion." José de Sigüenza, *Historia*, 1:366. Fray José adds that the only record he has found of this first Inquisition is in the Capitular Acts of the Order of Saint Jerome.

[18] Fernando González Gigante, an important Guadalupense converso, was also tried in the 1460s. Fray Juan de Guadalupe sets the date of that earlier Inquisition in 1462.

Fernando González worked as a scrivener for the friary in the 1450s and 1460s, and possibly even as early as the late 1440s. Through his position at the friary, González spoke frequently and informally with the friars; the friars' own testimony during their internal inquest reflects his lack of deference toward them. This collegiality eventually created problems for the scrivener, however, when during the priorate of Gonzalo de Madrid (1447–1450, 1456–1462) Fernando González began to reveal to some friars that he practiced Judaism. In 1485 fray Juan de Segovia—himself punished for Judaizing practices—recounted that Fernando González had spoken disrespectfully of the Virgin during the priorate of Gonzalo de Madrid; moreover, González had told the friar to repeat his heretical words to two other friars in the house.[19] On another occasion González mentioned his practice of Judaism to friar Diego de Marchena. Fray Diego began to spread word around the friary of a Judaizing functionary, although he would not reveal the converso's identity.[20] Prior Gonzalo de Madrid demanded that fray Diego speak:

> one Friday, in the chapter room [at the weekly capitular meeting], fray Gonzalo de Madrid ordered the friar from Marchena to say who were those people who had said those [heretical] things, and fray Diego said

Like Fernando González the scrivener, who was probably a relative, Fernando González Gigante spoke out against fray Diego de Marchena. See AMG unnumbered, Internal Inquisition, 6. Testimony of fray Juan de Guadalupe.

AMG legajo 52 is described in the catalogue as "Santa y General Inquisición, 1455–1726," but I found no materials predating 1485 and none concerning the Guadalupe court of 1485. Rather, the *legajo* includes a few documents concerning Jews in other towns, such as Hervás, and printed leaflets sent out by the Holy Office in the sixteenth and seventeenth centuries.

[19] AMG unnumbered, Internal Inquisition, 82. Testimony of fray Juan de Segovia. Presumably Fernando González believed that those two other friars were also sympathetic to his Jewish loyalties. In 1485 all friars were required to make a statement to the Inquisition detailing any evidence of Judaizing activity they were aware of, and confessing if appropriate. Juan de Segovia's testimony is unusual in that he mentions only lay functionaries of the friary, and no friars.

[20] Fernando González's specific actions were never described, either in the clerical Inquisition records or in the summary of his 1485 trial. Fray Diego de Marchena is consistently described by other friars as inciting controversy, and as delighting in reporting Judaizing activity throughout the friary. In another conversation between the two recorded in González's trial in the 1460s, González reportedly took fray Diego's habit, saying, "One day I'll see you without your habit [that is, defrocked], and then I'll make fun of you." Ibid., 199. Testimony of Juan de Guadalupe the third (not to be confused with the Juan de Guadalupe who served as prior from 1472 to 1475). Juan de Guadalupe read this in González's trial records while looking for other documents in the prior's rooms. The statement actually is in reference to fray Diego's Judaizing activities and apparently implies that fray Diego would be found out and punished as well as (if not before) Fernando González. In fact, both were burned at the stake. Fray Diego de Marchena is discussed at greater length in chapter 7.

that he would not say. Then prior Gonzalo ordered him by the precept of [obedience?] and under penalty of excommunication to say who it was, and how many there were, and fray Diego said that he would not say anything. And some rose to say that [prior Gonzalo] was not obliged to command him, nor was fray Diego obliged to say it.[21]

Fray Diego de Marchena did reveal González's identity, though he later told fray Martín Vizcayno that he had done ten years of self-assigned penance for accusing Fernando González.[22]

Fernando González the heretic became intimately associated with the friary, and a symbol of Old Christian suspicions about conversos in and out of the Jeronymite foundation.[23] González's case not only revealed Judaizing activity in the friary's subject town of Guadalupe, but also highlighted the links between conversos inside the friary and those outside its walls. The erstwhile scrivener's notoriety came from fray Diego de Marchena's resistance to name the guilty party as much as from his original revelations, and it was difficult to avoid drawing awkward conclusions about friars unwilling to discipline heretics. After describing the tense scene in which fray Diego revealed González's name under threat of excommunication, fray Juan de Carranza listed several friars who seemed unhappy disciplining the scrivener, together with those leaders of the order aware of events at Guadalupe and also discomfited by the disciplining of González. Fray Alonso de Oropesa, defender of conversos and general of the order, headed the list.[24]

As a result of these revelations of Jewish practices by their converso scrivener, the friars initiated a local ecclesiastical inquisition in the early years of the 1460s. González and others were tried, probably by prior Gonzalo. The existence of files mentioned by Juan de Guadalupe to-

---

[21] Ibid., 80. Testimony of fray Juan de Carranza. "un viernes mandó fray Gonzalo de Madrid en camara al de Marchena que la dixiese quien eran aquellos que dezian aquellas cosas y el dixo que no las diría. Despues le mandó en precepto de [?], & so pena de excomunion que dixiese quien era, & quantos y dixole que non le diría cosa alguna. & levantaronse algunos a desirle que no era obligado a le poner aquel mandamiento nin el a desirlo."

[22] Ibid., 178. Fray Martín testified that he felt it wrong for fray Diego to do penance for accusing a heretic and revealing the heretic's actions.

[23] See, for example, ibid., 60. Pedro de Trujillo testified that fray Lope de Villareal favored conversos, "especially Fernando González the scrivener."

[24] Ibid., 80. "Los que yo sentí que les pesaua desta emienda son estos: prior Gonzalo de Madrid, Hernando de Ubeda, Luis de Madrid, Rrodrigo de Seuilla, Gonzalo de Laredo, Alonso de Guadalajara. . . . De los de la orden a quien supe que les pesaua son estos: Rvdo. general fray Alonso de Oropesa, Juan de Ortega, Sancho de Cuellar, y Juan de Villaviçiosa." Fray Fernando de Ubeda is discussed at length later in this chapter; fray Alonso de Guadalajara was posthumously accused of Judaizing activity during the internal Inquisition of 1485.

gether with the indication of multiple defendants suggests a formal, operating court. Fernando González and others were assigned penances as punishment, and Judaizing conversos as a whole were sent a message that the days of openly practicing Judaism were over. Twenty years later, the *beata* Mari López, a lay holy woman, cited this earlier period as a time when conversos had been much more open about practicing Judaism.[25] Certainly it seems reasonable that after some active Judaizers were disciplined in public trials, others would be more circumspect. Fernando González, known since the 1460s as "the heretic," disappeared from the records until 1485, when he was burned at the stake for supposedly not having completed his penance from twenty years earlier.[26] His wife, Beatriz Núñez, and her stepson, Manuel González of the Mesón Blanco, were also sentenced to death that year. Two more sons, Gonzalo de Madrid and Martín, were exiled.[27]

This early inquisitorial court apparently fulfilled the relatively limited goals it set for itself, yet even the scant evidence available suggests the multiple fault lines it revealed in the Jeronymite community and the town. Fray Diego de Marchena, a man who by all accounts incited intense frustration and anger among those who crossed him, had uncovered a secretly practicing Jew under the friary's nose yet refused to name the offender. The friars in Guadalupe were faced with an embarrassing resistance within their own house to identifying or disciplining the accused Judaizer. Some felt that the prior himself was hesitant to act too severely, and rumors persisted about his own supposed devotion to Judaism twenty years after his death.[28] Even the general of the order, fray Alonso de Oropesa, was rumored to be uncomfortable with events taking place in Guadalupe.[29] For perhaps the first time, the friars in Guadalupe were forced to witness a division within their ranks over the subject of conversos. Fray Diego de Marchena may have served as the catalyst for this and other disturbances, but he cannot be held solely responsible. The friars at Guadalupe included New Christians with

[25] AHN Inquis. legajo 184, expediente 20.

[26] AHN clero legajo 1423, expediente 89. Fernando Gonzalez's trial records no longer exist, but this summary of sentences states that he was burned at the stake on June 11, 1485.

[27] AHN Inquis. legajo 169, expediente 2. It is probable but not definite that Manuel González was the son of Fernando González. Manuel was innkeeper of the Mesón Blanco and was tried in AHN Inquis. legajo 145, expediente 24. The trials of Beatriz Núñez and Manuel González were published by Fidel Fita in "La inquisición en Guadalupe," 283–343.

[28] AMG unnumbered, Internal Inquisition, passim. Prior Gonzalo may have hesitated to act for fear of civil unrest, but converso scriveners, at least in later years, did not receive the support of the town as a whole.

[29] Ibid., 80. Testimony of Juan de Carranza.

varying levels of devotion to Christianity as well as Old Christians with their own range of beliefs. This volatile combination of attitudes, together with the friary's dependence on lay converso functionaries, meant that suspicion and submerged conflict were a constant concern. In short, this early inquisitorial court unintentionally revealed that, like the town that they governed, the friars were deeply divided among themselves. Those divisions complicated the tensions between friars and townspeople considerably, as evidenced by events in the subsequent two decades.

PRIOR DIEGO DE PARÍS AND CHANGING CONDITIONS IN GUADALUPE

Events in Guadalupe in the early 1460s highlighted the presence of Judaizing conversos in town, particularly conversos with ties to the friars, but converso residents and converso links to the friary seem to have changed relatively little in its immediate aftermath. Judaizers may have attempted to assimilate into Christian society somewhat further, or at least to be less open in their practice of Judaism, as some witnesses in 1485 averred; but New Christians continued to play an important role in the economic life of Guadalupe and retained a significant percentage of lay offices in town. The 1460s and 1470s in Castile witnessed an economic decline, as bad weather and civil unrest combined to affect harvests. In these challenging times, fiscal support for Guadalupe's Jeronymites came from Guadalupe's wealthiest conversos, who apparently lent the friary money during that period. The first round of fighting stopped in 1467, but the unrest had not come to an end. After Enrique IV's death in 1474, civil war resumed as Enrique's daughter, Juana la Beltraneja, and her supporters fought to regain the throne from his half-sister Isabel. The Jeronymites in Guadalupe were careful to remain neutral during the civil war, but times were difficult.

In addition to the external challenges of the 1470s, the Jeronymite friars were facing internal struggles as well. A new prior, elected in 1475, soon divided friars and vecinos with his arbitrary exercise of power. Diego de París (prior 1475–1483) heightened resentment and divisions among Guadalupe's vecinos and fostered the belief that favoritism determined his actions. During the course of prior Diego's tenure, Jeronymite authorities isolated conversos socially by linking them to special favors from the friary, ultimately making their place in Guadalupe untenable. In the widespread unrest that inevitably ensued, resentment of New Christians and of the prior's poor government melded, endangering the friars' control over the Puebla and clearing the way for the arrival of the royal Inquisition in late 1484. What might elsewhere in Europe have been a typical hostility on the part of citizens toward lordly authority at the end of the Middle Ages was complicated here by the increasing association of New Christians and arbitrary secular governance by the friars.

Prior Diego's election in itself signaled the latest swing in attitudes toward conversos and the friars' government generally. In 1447 Juan de Zamora (prior 1444–1447), one of Guadalupe's harshest and least popular friars, was succeeded by fray Gonzalo de Madrid (prior 1447–1450, 1456–1462) of the ecclesiastical Inquisition. Prior Gonzalo exercised a less rigid, more conciliatory authority than prior Juan and was known for his sympathy for New Christians.[30] A similar dynamic occurred in the election of 1475: fray Diego de París's predecessor, fray Juan de Guadalupe (prior 1472–1475), had taken a much harsher stand toward conversos in town; he exiled two New Christians for their financial improprieties and, according to one friar, attempted to initiate a second inquisitorial court.[31] Ten years later, fray Juan's statements before the inquisitors confirmed his deep suspicion of converso devotion to Christianity.[32] Those electing fray Diego de París could hardly have overlooked the differences in philosophy and temperament between the two, and prior Juan's removal from the priorate after a single term suggests a collective desire for a leader less critical of New Christians.

Prior Diego's conciliatory style of government became apparent immediately after the election in early June. Within his first month of holding office, prior Diego had reversed several minor decisions of his

[30] On Prior Gonzalo's method of governing, see AMG legajo 82, leather-bound file with 47 folios (unnumbered) titled "En este cartapacio esta çiertas petiçiones y juramentos de los vezinos desta puebla de guadalupe y çiertas respuestas de los priores fr. Juan de Çamora & fr. Gonçalo de Madrid." On his sympathy for New Christians, see above. On the priorate of Juan de Zamora, see discussions of the 1447 popular uprising in Vizuete Mendoza, Guadalupe, 50–51; and Sebastián García, OFM, and Felipe Trenado, OFM, Guadalupe, (Seville, 1978), 86–88. Evidence for changing practices under different priors is given in the case of Alonso Rodríguez de los Encensos (AMG codex 74 bis, 12v–13v). Alonso Rodríguez de los Encensos, a converso, had been awarded special water rights by prior Gonzalo de Madrid. (The water pipe carrying the water was turned on by means of a key.) Prior Juan de Guadalupe revoked those rights, claiming that the friary should receive payment for the water, and furthermore, that the water was going to Alonso's barnyard, corral, as well as to a building that Alonso Rodríguez had theoretically given to the friars as a donation. On or after Feb. 20, 1478, Rodríguez de los Encensos appealed the decision to prior Diego de París. The prior restored Alonso Rodríguez's rights to the water with the further provision that the friars would pay him eighty maravedís each year for use of the building and barnyard both. The buildings would revert to property of the friars only after the end of his family, an event, as the document notes, perhaps 150 to 200 years in the future.

[31] On the expulsion of conversos Alonso de Córdoba and Juan de Segovia, see AMG codex 74 bis, 1r–v. On the second inquisitorial court, see AMG unnumbered, Internal Inquisition, 220.

[32] See AMG unnumbered, Internal Inquisition, 6–7.

predecessors, especially concerning residents' demands. Particularly significant was his action toward two wealthy converso cloth merchants, *traperos*—Alonso de Córdoba and Juan de Segovia—whom prior Juan had exiled.[33] The first record in prior Diego's journal of capitular acts is June 12, 1475,[34] in which he temporarily lifted Alonso de Córdoba's exile so that he could bring in items he had bought at Medina del Campo for the Mendoza countess of Medellín. He could stay, it was ruled, until she sent for her goods. Four days later, Juan de Segovia was given permission to return to town temporarily; some had begun to protest that he should not be permanently exiled from town. A few days later, on June 25, the friary collected its annual tribute from the townspeople and dealt with local business. That day several people from the Puebla begged the prior to pardon Alonso de Córdoba and Juan de Segovia; merchants, possibly other converso traperos, wrote letters of petition asking prior Diego to end the sentence of exile. Prior Diego and his deputies agreed, and the sentence was lifted.[35]

Even in this relatively routine action the tendencies of fray Diego's priorate were evident. Eventual pardons were not uncommon, but such rapid pardons were unusual, particularly for people as notorious as Alonso de Córdoba, a converso cloth merchant who continually ran afoul of the friary until his death at the first auto de fe in 1485. By contrast, Pedro García, who was exiled in 1476 for challenging the authority of the prior, was not pardoned, although the magnitude of his crime was dwarfed by the pattern of disobedience of Alonso de Córdoba.[36] One difference between these two men was their support in the community: the *Capitular Acts* specifically note that prior Diego received no letters supporting García, as compared to the many merchants who wrote in support of Alonso de Córdoba. In addition, Pedro García had specifically challenged the authority of the current prior, while Alonso de Córdoba's misdeed had occurred during the tenure of prior Juan de Guadalupe. Finally, Alonso de Córdoba's economic role in town made it easier to bend the rules in his favor. Alonso de Córdoba

---

[33] Although both use place names as surnames, I have found no evidence that either was a Jeronymite friar, as Adèle Perrin suggests. See Adèle Perrin, "Moines et villageois en Extrémadure au XVIe siècle." The role of converso cloth merchants in Guadalupe is discussed below.

[34] This is the first extant collection of *Actas Capitulares* for the friary of Guadalupe and covers most of prior Diego de París's tenure, particularly his first years as prior. After his death, no similar records remain until the more formal *Actas Capitulares* began in 1499.

[35] AMG codex 74 bis, 1r–3v.

[36] Ibid., 10r, 6 Oct 1476. This man, identified as Pero García *calderero* in AMG legajo 83, 13v, was a local coppersmith/pot maker. I would speculate that he was an Old Christian, given his history and the lack of evidence that conversos in Guadalupe worked as coppersmiths—a common local profession.

and the other, largely converso cloth merchants were among the wealthiest residents in this artisan community. Not only did they play an important role in maintaining Guadalupe's pilgrim economy, but these were the vecinos who helped support the friars during the civil war (1474–1480), when the number of pilgrims coming into town dropped and the friars' crops suffered.

Prior Diego early established a pattern of departing from established laws and traditions when he wished to exempt those who soon came to seem his favorites. In some cases he might have been rectifying the past severity of the previous prior; economic motivations probably colored his early rulings; and a desire to support conversos in town may also have played a role in his decisions. Whatever the motivations, however, they should not be confused with the theological defense of New Christians voiced by Alonso de Oropesa and others. While prior Diego may have agreed with fray Alonso de Oropesa's attitudes toward integrating New Christians into Christian society generally, those beliefs had little or nothing to do with pardoning people who had disobeyed secular law, a stand fray Alonso opposed.[37] Prior Diego's misuse of power—his willingness to make extra-legal, arbitrary judgments in response to personal pressure—was to become a hallmark of his tenure as prior and earned him the resentment of many outside the friary, as well as the suspicion of one faction within it. This appearance of arbitrariness and favoritism, particularly toward conversos, greatly exacerbated tensions in Guadalupe and created the conditions that made it possible to introduce the inquisitorial court of 1485.

CONVERSO FUNCTIONARIES AND RESISTANCE TO THE FRIARS' OVERLORDSHIP

The preponderance of lay converso functionaries serving the friary further heightened popular impressions of favoritism toward New Christians in the decades before the Inquisition. The mayor, Diego González de la República, and his son Andrés González de la República, a public defender, were only the most prominent examples of official converso intermediaries between friary and town.[38] At least some counselors,

---

[37] By the same token, his decree of exile by itself did not identify fray Juan de Guadalupe as an anticonverso prior, although his actions may have reflected both his desire to see local ordinances followed and his suspicion of conversos as members of Guadalupense society.

[38] It seems likely that the term *república* refers to Guadalupe itself, since vecinos continued to refer to the town as a republic, despite its changed status.

fieles, and probably the bailiff, *alguacil*, were also conversos.[39] Given the prominent status of New Christians in town governance, and the apparently arbitrary justice meted out to protect them, it is not surprising that resentment of Jeronymite authority and suspicion of conversos grew together in Guadalupe. Any support or sympathy for conversos, however justified, might have generated criticism from some Old Christians, but the variety of political, social, religious, and economic resentments of Old Christian vecinos in fifteenth-century Guadalupe became increasingly intermingled in Old Christian rhetoric, at the expense of the converso functionaries and peace in town.

The exercise of Jeronymite authority through converso functionaries, combined with the image of favoritism toward certain wealthy conversos in the community, led to conflict a year after prior Diego took office. In September 1476, during the week leading up to the feast of the Virgin of Guadalupe, three Jews who had come to town made a complaint to the mayor. While on the royal road to Guadalupe, a man had attacked them, killing their father and stealing the goods they were bringing to trade. Now, they said, the murderer was present in Guadalupe. The grieving sons asked the mayor to seize the murderer until they could bring a charge against him. In short order the mayor seized the alleged murderer, who admitted to the charge without torture. He added that after the ambush he and his companion had gone on to Trujillo to sell the victim's possessions, and that they had stayed there until he had come alone to Guadalupe, he said, in penance for his sin.[40] The mayor ordered the bailiff to hold the prisoner, and, as was apparently typical in criminal cases, the bailiff kept him in chains and seated on an ass.[41]

Not all Guadalupenses were pleased with this justice, however, as a contemporary account from the friary indicates.

Some walked about inciting people, asking how they could kill a Christian for [murdering] Jews, and up to 150 or 200 armed men assembled and went to the house of the bailiff and opened by force the doors of his house and prison. And they took the said man from the ass and with his

[39] A *fiel* was another town official, who served as an adviser to the mayor and as a witness to local decisions. All lay local officials were named by the friary and answered to the Jeronymites. This includes the *procurador*, who theoretically acted as a public defender even for vecinos bringing suit against the friary. Identifying conversos in these positions is difficult, since they can only be distinguished through references in passing, or through inquisitorial documents.

[40] AMG legajo 83, document titled "Insultos y movimientos q eneste pueblo fueron fechos en tiempo de Rvdo padre Fr. Diego de París . . . [1476]," 2r. For an abbreviated account, see AMG codex 74 bis, 8v–10r.

[41] The meaning of this passage is a bit unclear.

chain they carried him out of town, where they broke his chain and released the prisoner. And from there all of them together with great boldness and audacity and with great shouts went to the house of the said mayor, saying that he should get out and that they didn't want him as mayor; others said that they should kill him and his wife and children and burn down the house, and that they should go to the plaza and Seville street and kill and rob the converso merchants and officials. And coming to agreement they decided to put the plan into play. Some who knew the evil that [these men] had done, and other good people who found themselves there at that time obstructed the way and refused to let them pass a blockade. And thus they dispersed that assembly and assault.[42]

This incident was notable for joining anticlerical and anticonverso sentiments through actions against converso merchants and the friars' converso functionaries. By 1476, resentment against the friary's tight control of the town and converso favoritism were linked in the minds of many vecinos. As Francisco García Rodríguez has noted, the friary exercised unusual control over the actions of vecinos. This high level of control engendered bitter resentment among Guadalupenses, many of whom were newcomers to Guadalupe.[43] The friary, for its part, was often equally frustrated with the difficulties of relying on lay townspeople to provide food, shelter, and clothing to pilgrims and would have made the town smaller and more manageable, if possible.[44] By targeting converso "merchants and officials," the rebellious townspeople moved the focus of attack away from local officials and clerical government to the converso minority in Guadalupe; but by wanting to do away with the office of mayor, the vecinos also challenged the authority of the friary

---

[42] AMG legajo 83. "[Algunos] andovyeron Inçitando, disiendo que como avia de matar un cristiano por judios e ayuntaronse fasta çiento e çinquenta o dozientos ombres armados e fueron a casa del dicho alguasil e abrieron por fuerça las puertas de su casa e carçel. Et tomaron el dicho ombre de ençima del dicho asno e con su cadena lo levaron fasta fuera del lugar, a donde quebrantaron el candado e soltaron el dicho preso. Et de ally todos juntamente con grand osadía e atrevimiento e con grandes gritas se movieron fasia la casa del dicho alcalde, diziendo que fuese fuera e que non querian que fuese alcalde; otros desian que lo matasen a el e a su muger e fijos e le quemasen la casa, e que fuesen a la plaça e ala calle de sevilla e matasen e rrobasen a los mercadores e ofiçiales conversos. Et viniendo todos a una bos a lo poner en obra, algunos que conosçieron el mal que avian fecho. Et otros buenos que ala sazon ally se fallaron lo estorbaron e los non consintieron pasar do una barrera. Et asy se desbarataron de aquel ayuntamiento e ynsulto."

[43] Francisco García Rodríguez, "Ordenanzas Municipales de la Puebla de Guadalupe," 31–33.

[44] See trial of Pero Gago, AHN Pergaminos, clero 411.2; AMG codex 169; and the discussion in Perrin, "Moines et villageois."

to exercise control over the Puebla. Even their gathering was a threat to the hegemony of the Jeronymites. The term used by vecinos and friars to describe this and other meetings was *ayuntamiento*, which means "assembly, meeting" but in other contexts serves as the term for "city hall." Any public gathering where collective policy decisions were made could be considered an attempt to create an independent governing authority and was therefore forbidden.

It should be stressed that resentment of conversos centered around those who appeared to benefit from a privileged, higher status under Jeronymite rule; religious beliefs per se were not necessarily at issue. Old Christian anger with conversos, in this and other cases, stemmed not only from religious beliefs but also from the apparent political, economic, and social position of conversos in Guadalupense society. Because of ancestry and in some cases religious and social attitudes, conversos were identified as a "community"—a group of people linked by political, social, or religious attitudes and disposed toward mutual support because of those links. Individual converso religious practices, and indeed most individual differences, diminished in importance compared to questions of potential political clout. Once some members of this perceived "converso community" had been identified with political favoritism, other conversos without particular authority in town—and irrespective of their devotion to Christianity—were equally liable to the attack of an angry mob, as the converso shoemakers who lived on Seville Street nearly discovered. Clearly, the ethnic identity of Guadalupe's residents was known to most of those present in town and for some held a potentially dangerous significance.[45]

The prior's response to the crisis shifted rapidly from meting out punishment for wrongdoers to placating angry vecinos. Prior Diego exiled a dozen ringleaders, imprisoned up to thirty more townspeople, and demanded an investigation to identify other wrongdoers. Soon, several of the town's most honorable men came to the prior, acknowledging their errors and pleading for forgiveness.[46] Even the converso mayor, who was ill, sent a petition to the prior advising that "to him it seemed that he should pacify his Puebla [rather than punish it further] because he saw that it was quite necessary"; in his petition the mayor himself pardoned those who had wronged him and asked the prior to do the same.[47] The prior decided on a public ceremony of town pardon and

---

[45] On the importance of violence, and threats of violence, in maintaining social and religious boundaries, see Nirenberg, *Communities of Violence*, especially chap. 7.

[46] This was typically how Guadalupenses initiated the process of pardon for collective town wrongs.

[47] AMG legajo 83, 2v. "le enbió otra su petiçion disiendole su paresçer que deuia paçificar su pueblo porque el veya que era mucho nesçesario."

reconciliation. All the vecinos gathered on their knees in front of the prior and other officials of the friary, with those found guilty singled out by their bare feet. Collectively, the town publicly acknowledged its errors and guilt and begged for mercy. After a long, harsh sermon pointing out that the proper sentence was death, the prior pardoned his townspeople.[48] The vecinos were required to swear, first, not to form any confederation or league against the prior, friary, or its goods; second, not to speak against persons or goods or differentiate on the basis of persons or lineages; third, to take any debates between vecinos to the prior to decide; and fourth, to obey the decrees of the prior, including the above oath.[49] In response, the prior ordered that according to local ordinances, all local lay offices, including the mayor, bailiff, and counselors, would be vacated every January first. In essence, the townspeople were asked not to challenge the friary's authority by meeting independently, or to single out conversos, while the prior promised not to create a local converso elite. Widespread local resistance to lordly control was typical of western European towns at the end of the Middle Ages and the beginning of the early modern era, but in Guadalupe that picture was being altered by the increasing association of a religious minority with political favors.

The ruling acknowledged vecino grievances but did little to resolve underlying concerns about converso favoritism or to provide vecinos with more independence. Both Old and New Christians avoided following local ordinances, and punishments were mitigated by pleas for mercy. The friary made no move to change its restrictive control over the Puebla. Furthermore, conversos continued to control local positions of power, with any changeover in authority not destined to take effect for at least three more months. The presumed, though not necessarily actual, links between wealthy conversos and other New Christians, and between conversos and friars, remained intact, and there can be little doubt that local tensions concerning elite conversos and the friary continued to smolder. Within a few weeks Pedro García, a local pot maker, was exiled for saying in the presence of the prior that he did not acknowledge the prior as lord—quite probably a statement generated by recent events in the town.[50]

Almost exactly one month later, on October 8, 1476, the vecinos staged another uprising. This time, the focus of discontent was the friary, rather than converso links to it. Prior Diego had initiated a new

---

[48] This sermon no longer exists. All that remains is a mention of it in the record of the uprising.

[49] Ibid., 3r.

[50] Ibid., See also above, and AMG codex 74 bis, 10r. He is also known as Pero García.

tax to pay for a legal settlement with the region's archdeacon.[51] The legal record emphasizes the attempts that were made to soften the blow of the new tax, though the friary's efforts were of little effect. "The greater part of the vecinos of the town were scandalized, saying that it was tribute for the archdeacon, and that they neither wanted nor intended to pay. And that if someone began to pay they would knock over their house. And they even said that they wanted rather to pay tribute to the king and not to the friars nor to the archdeacon."[52] The ink had barely dried on their agreement with the prior when a large group of vecinos met and signed a new agreement among themselves, determining not to pay the tribute requested. Some residents went even further. A second, smaller group met to complain about the town's consent to the exile of Pedro García the pot maker. Some said that they should go to the prior with their complaint, since he had previously met with the Puebla in similar situations; others advised bringing people from outside Guadalupe for armed resistance to the prior and his tribute request. Alternately, they suggested, help could be sought in Trujillo.[53] Still others blamed all the evils of the town on the conversos who lived there. Ultimately, the group at this second meeting united behind a radical plan of action: they went to the house of the pot maker and, ignoring the prior's ruling, told his wife to send for García. The majority of townspeople defended the group's rebellious act, which set off another wave of resistance to the friary. Women in particular were cited in the legal documents as playing a large role in criticizing the prior's justice and demanding change. Subsequently, several vecinos again met illegally; this time they denounced the money paid to the mayor, bailiff, public defender, and public doctor.[54] Their salaries were to be paid by the friary, they argued, or the positions should be eliminated

---

[51] The settlement was designed to eliminate intermittent fighting (including robbery and murder) between the friary's vassals and the vassals of the archdeacon. AMG legajo 83, 13r. For evidence of the lawsuits leading up to this crisis between the friary and the archdeacon of Plasencia, see AMG codex 74 bis, 7v–8r.

[52] "la mayor parte delos vezinos del pueblo se escandalizaron diziendo que era pecho para el arçediano Et que non lo querian nin entendian pagar. Et que sy alguno començase a pagar que le echarian la casa ençima. Et aun diziendo que mas querian pechar al rrey que non a los frayles nin al arçediano." AMG codex 74 bis, 13r–v.

[53] Trujillo was very closely linked to Guadalupe in the later Middle Ages. It was an independent town, but all its scriveners were named by Guadalupe, and the two towns were often engaged in legal disputes.

[54] Such a move would certainly affect the converso population in Guadalupe, and the statements above suggest the continued anticonverso strain in resistance to the friary's government. But I would argue that this complaint is primarily, though not exclusively, aimed at the friary and its fiscal demands on vecinos. The public doctor, for example, was apparently not a New Christian.

altogether. For the second time in as many months Guadalupenses challenged the friary's government of the town.

This time, with the unrest centered on financial matters rather than converso functionaries, the friary answered with an iron fist. The ringleaders were imprisoned and placed in the stocks. More than a score of vecinos fled to the fields to avoid imprisonment and to regroup for another attack, though with little success. They soon returned home after sending the prior messages asking for his pardon.[55] They too were imprisoned as the mayor began his investigations. Although prior Diego lightened some punishments, the sentences remained more severe than before; more than 150 vecinos were punished, with either exile, imprisonment, or loss of goods. After several weeks, "good men" of the Puebla again came in the name of the town to ask pardon. Over 60 kept their sentences of exile, but the rest were pardoned after attending another penitential mass. The friary's harsh response, tempered by mercy, had the desired effect: with the exception of a few townspeople, Guadalupe "remained very calm and fearful and obedient and the majority of those in the town came to make an offering and to oblige the lord prior."[56]

At this point the record falls silent. The outbreaks of violence from Guadalupe's townspeople apparently ceased for the next few years, and after numerous records for events in the early years of prior Diego de París's priorate, there is no further mention of widespread popular unrest until a pair of lawsuits brought against the friary in the sixteenth century.[57] This apparent calm may have been due to changes in the friary's actions, but the few extant local documents suggest no such change. Capitular acts include no reference to rotation of local office holders; Andrés González de la República, public defender in 1476, also held that office before his trial in 1485.[58] Documents of further uprisings may have been lost over time, or the friary's harsher response may have had the desired effect of silencing opposition to their government.[59]

---

[55] Prior Diego de París forgave them only their flight, not the crimes of which they were accused.

[56] "quedo muy sosegado & atemorizado e obediente e viniendose todos los que mas era enel pueblo a se ofresçer & obligar al dicho señor prior." AMG legajo 83, 15v.

[57] These are the Pleito de los Bonillas and the Pleito de los Gagos, discussed in detail in chapter 8. Both trials are available at the AHN (pergaminos clero 410.3 and 411.2) and the AMG (codices 167–169).

[58] He is mentioned as *procurador* in a bigamy trial of 1476. See AMG codex 163.

[59] The Guadalupe archive holds a relatively high number of documents for the early years of prior Diego de París's rule; few documents in the later years of his rule and during the rule of his successor, Nuño de Arévalo; and then an increase in documentation at the end of the century. The friary's *Capitular Acts* follow the same pattern: Diego de París's early years are closely documented while entries for later years are thin. No

Then, too, the kingdom was also entering a new period of calm. Isabel and Fernando were well on their way to reestablishing order in Castile, and urban rebellions were in decline across the kingdom.

In the second abortive uprising of 1476, conversos were not the object of hostility that they were in the first uprising, but tensions surrounding the uncomfortable relationship among the friary, converso functionaries, other local conversos, and Old Christians remained below the surface. Some Guadalupenses were ready to blame their troubles with the friary on the conversos in town; of all those accused or punished by the friary for the second revolt, only one, Andrés Alonso Trujillano, can be definitely identified as a New Christian.[60] Like their Jewish ancestors in Iberia, Guadalupense conversos were dependent on local authorities for their safety, their well-being, and even, whether directly or indirectly, their employment. Their grievances with the friary would not likely take the form of protests against its actions. Once again it is clear that, while New and Old Christians had much contact in day-to-day life in town, there were limits to social assimilation of New and Old Christians.

Guadalupenses' resentment of the friars' overlordship, and particularly of the friars' arbitrary, unjust rule, became personified, not only in prior Diego de París, but also in his assistant, the Old Christian vicar fray Fernando de Ubeda. For both the townspeople and fellow friars, fray Fernando represented the misrule of the friars at its worst—the kind of misrule, in fact, that townspeople were attempting to shrug off throughout western Europe. As vicar, fray Fernando held an important administrative and governing position. Second only to the prior, fray Fernando received complaints of misdeeds and acted for the prior within the friary, as well as serving as a means of relaying information between the friary and the Puebla.[61] Fray Fernando's policy of favoring a few wealthy converso vecinos, of using the resources of the friary to support

---

Capitular Acts exist for prior Nuño, but a large volume with consistent entries was begun in 1499. This pattern may reflect record-keeping in the friary, or it may simply be due to the difficulties of preserving documents.

[60] AMG legajo 83, 26r. See also his Inquisition trial, AHN Inquis. legajo 132, expediente 11. Andrés Alonso Trujillano was one of the few conversos in town to be absolved of any Jewish activity. His trial included testimony that he did not speak with New Christians, only Old Christians.

[61] This task of serving as an intermediary is apparent in the story of Juan de Texeda, below. This intermediary status was shared by another friary official, *portero*, whose literal position at the entrance to the friary kept him in frequent contact with the vecinos. Indeed, the *portero* nearly matched the vicar's importance in Jeronymite houses, with the vicar's duties focused primarily on internal issues and the *portero's* on external ones. See the survey in Vizuete Mendoza, *Guadalupe*, 145–156, and Josemaría Revuelta Somalo, *Los Jerónimos*.

his lover and their illegitimate child, and of forging alliances with some well-placed New Christian residents to gain their support for his political ambitions all heightened tensions in town between New and Old Christians, and between friars and vecinos.

It would be too easy, and misleading, to try and fit these tensions into a simple dynamic of Old Christians vs. New Christians, or friars vs. vecinos. Some Old and New Christians worked together, like the Old Christian friars and their converso functionaries, or the women described in the preceding chapter. Similarly, some friars and vecinos made common cause for their mutual benefit, as the Old Christian fray Fernando de Ubeda did with some wealthy conversos in town. Ethnic identity was not the overriding determinant of conflict in Guadalupe. Rather, what these tensions show us is that over time, one marker of difference (religious ancestry) became associated with vecino grievances about their traditional, lordly governance, drawing additional suspicion upon both parties. Even conversos who earned the hostility of the friars could be seen as having special connections with certain factions within the friary, and thus contributing to the friars' arbitrary and restrictive governance.

The resentment of arbitrary rule as expressed by Fernando de Ubeda is apparent in a witness's statement given in the Jeronymite Inquisition of 1488. Juan de Texeda, a lay Old Christian scrivener, had worked for the friary in Guadalupe for over twenty years when he testified before the inquisitorial court. Among his other tasks, Texeda was charged with the collection of house taxes owed to the friars by the vecinos. One day, he testified, prior Diego de París asked him to collect some *reales* owed by Alonso de Paredes, a wealthy converso trapero who was burned at the stake in 1485. In addition, prior Diego warned Texeda to be on the lookout for underweight *reales* that Alonso de Paredes was supposedly circulating in town. But Texeda ran into problems from the moment he entered Paredes's shop in its prime location on the plaza. Alonso de Paredes and his companions, all conversos, began to trade insults with Texeda; Texeda pulled out his knife and, still holding the account book, advanced on the trapero. The cloth merchant, in turn, reached for his scissors but then stooped down and picked up two stones from the ground instead. Before Juan de Texeda could reach Alonso de Paredes, Paredes hit Texeda in the face with one of the stones. With blood streaming down his cheek, he lost his footing, tripped, and fell to the ground. Meanwhile, the trapero and his friends dashed to the nearby Mesón Blanco. Since the inn was also on the plaza, and furthermore was owned by fellow converso Manuel González, it made for a good refuge.[62] When Texeda finally arrived at the prior's audience hall, blood

---

[62] AHN clero legajo 1423, expediente 79, 1v. "[Five or six years ago Juan de Texeda]

still caked on his face, he discovered Alonso de Paredes and Alonso de Córdoba already with the prior and vicar, telling their side of the story. The vicar, fray Fernando de Ubeda, quickly took charge of the situation, giving Texeda no immediate reparation but, ominously, suggesting an investigation.[63]

Quickly, the investigation turned into a series of humiliations for the scrivener. Statements were taken from the conversos and their families, but not from Juan de Texeda, and Texeda was informed of his accuser's claims much later than legal provisions stipulated. Soon Texeda was placed under house arrest. Then, as he later reported, "two honorable men from here [Guadalupe] went to my house and told me in the presence of my wife, 'fray Fernando sent us here to get your dagger'"; all honorable vecinos were permitted to carry daggers during the day, and seizure of his weapon was a grave insult. When Texeda refused,

---

cogía los ençensos delas casas que este monasterio tiene en esta puebla. Los cogí tres años. Un alonso de paredes que este otro dia quemaron por hereje çerçino grand copia de reales. [When de Texeda saw the prior, prior Diego told him] catad que nos guardedes de tomar destos reales de alonso de paredes. Et dixo yo 'señor en quanto yo pudiere sy fare. Mas ya tan poca moneda que avia el honbre de tomar algunos reales aun sean faltos, etc.' Et dende a un dia o dos yo ove de demandar lo que de mi a un confeso que se llamaua garçia gonsales tendero, el qual quemaron este otro dia por hereje y dauame çiertos reales çerçenados. E yo le dixo, 'por dios non me dys estos rreales que non me los quieren en el arca.' Et luego salió un confeso que se llama diego xastre que estaua fablando con alonso de córdoua a su puerta e dixo aunque non querays los tomareys que el prior manda que non se defechen. Que soys un zizañador del pueblo y de la moneda. Y yo dixe le, 'por çierto yo non soy zizañador del pueblo nin de la moneda que yo sé el contrario deso que nos dezis. çierta desta moneda de nuestro padre y callad en ora tal que non teneya nos aquien que fazer y fablays muy mal.' Et dixo él, 'yo fablaré tanbién como vos.' Y yo ove grand enojo de las dichas palabras y fuy me fasía él y él tomó unas tijeras de su ofiçio para me dar. E yo eche mano a un puñal y saqué lo y él fuese me entre unos dos postes y tomó una piedra o dos y tiró la una y dió me en el rostro con ella y non echó toda fuerça del miedo que yo yua en pos del saluo que me desolló un poco de la mexilla e fuese me fuyendo al mesón blanco. Y yo fuy trás él y como lleuaua el libro abierto en la una mano y el puñal en la otra cayóse me la casa [caxa?] y entropeçe dos vezes en ella con la cobdiçia y enojo que lleuaua del por le dar y doy en un foyo o montón de tierra y fuese me fuyendo por las paredes del mesón blanco."

[63] "Et asy ydo yo me fuy a quexar al señor prior con mi sangre en el rostro y quando fuy fallé al señor prior y a fray fernando que era vicario y a alonso de córdoba que ya es quemado qual les estaua f[aci]endo relación del negoçio como el quiere y como le ví ally dixe pese en tal paresçe que nos fisistes este pues tan presto venistes a fazer esta relación que fazeys por aquel confeso [?] que yo. Y paresçe que aparejada teniades la puerta mas que yo. Et dixo non vine a eso que a otras cosas vine. Y dixe otra ves pese a tal con el villano o judio traydor que sy non se me fuera por las paredes del dicho mesón blanco yo le cortara una pierna. Et a esto respondio fray fernando y dixo, 'podrá ser que se fallara que vos ouistes la culpa.' Et dixe yo, 'no la tengo.' Y dixo él, 'pues saber se a la verdad' y a esto nunca el prior fabló palabra. Saluo sy algunas fabló fauoresçiendo al dicho fray fernando. Et asy yo me salí del capitulo."

they added: "Texeda, the honorable thing to do is to give it to us and
not do anything else, because you know that the vicar can do much
more to you." Texeda gave up his weapon, after which fray Fernando
ordered it broken in pieces to demonstrate Texeda's shame. The bailiff,
another converso, exhibited the broken dagger outside the church on
Sunday at high Mass and ushered everyone out together so that they
would see it.[64] Later, fray Fernando, in the name of the prior, ordered
Texeda but not his accuser into prison to await the results of the inquiry.[65] When Texeda and his accuser were ordered before the prior and
vicar to hear the results of the inquiry, fray Fernando took the opportunity to humiliate the scrivener once more. As if Texeda had already
been found guilty, the vicar forced Juan de Texeda to walk from the
prison to the friary without shoes or cape. Various conversos followed
him; then, taking him to the friary, they made him walk on his knees
without his hat to the chapter room. As is apparent throughout his
narrative, the Jewish ancestry of his accusers did not escape Texeda's
notice. "They did to me" said Juan de Texeda, "as the Jews did when
they took Our Lord before Pilate to be judged."[66]

---

[64] "Et enbiaron por el liçençiado de çibdad que era [alled?] a la sazon y por diego
rrodrigues alguasil los quales non me tenia tan buena voluntad como era menester por
algunas cosas que en este pueblo injustamente fazian las quales yo en alguna manera les
dezia que non eran bien fechas. Y mandaron les que fiziesen la pesquisa. La qual ellos
fizieron entre los mismos confesos con quien yo oue la question y con sus parientes y
con un escrivano confeso y lo que dixeron de mi non lo supe fasta muchos dias despues
de pasado el negoçio. Y luego que fecho este yo me fuy a mi casa por que salia el dicho
alcalde y dixo que aquellos señores me mandauan y el con ellos que non saliese de mi
casa fasta que se viese este negoçio. Et estando asy en mi casa fueron alla dos honbres
honrrados deste lugar y dixeron me en presençia de mi muger, 'aca nos enbia fray
fernando que nos deys el puñal.' El qual yo non les queria dar. Y dixeron, 'texeda, lo
que cunple a vuestra honrra es dar le e non fagays otra cosa. Por que ya sabeys que
contra quien toma tenia el dicho vicario echa le a perder y otras muchas cosas.' Et yo
oue les de dar el dicho puñal el qual me mando quebrar en la picota un domingo. Y por
mas vituperio el alguasil fizo de tener toda la gente que salia de misa por que saliesen
junctos por que lo viesen por que fue sacado para un confeso. Esto non mirando a
venyte e tanto años que avia seruido a esta casa de nuestra señora e fasiendo muchos y
buenos y leales seruiçios. Y poniendo me como me he puesto a muchos y grandes
peligros por ella en los tiempos passados e ensalçando mas que otro."

[65] "Item non basto esto que ovieron de tornar luego por rrodrigues fiel que dios aya o
maestre pedro que non se me acuerda viendo todos tras que los dos fueron e dixeron
me que mandaua fray fernando en nombre de nuestro padre que me fuese a la carçel.
Et dixeles yo, '¿mandolo el prior?' E dixeron, 'non, sino el vicario en su nombre.' Y esto
se me fizo tanto enojo que non pudo ser mas. Et yo queria cavalgar en mi cavallo e yr
me. Et estos buenos honbres me dixeron y dieron tantos buenos consejos que me
queria perder e todo lo que avia ganado en grand tiempo que lo perderia en una hora e
otras muchas cosas. Et que ya sabia que segund mis seruiçios que avia fecho que non
estaria sy non una hora en la carçel, etc."

[66] "Et yo ove de forçar mi coraçon e fuy me a la carçel pensando que fazia bien como
me dezian y desque me touvieron en la carçel el dicho fray fernando dio orden como

Once Juan de Texeda and his accuser were alone before the prior and vicar, however, the scrivener described a change in his fortunes. Prior Diego de París asked Alonso de Paredes if he had attacked Texeda with a stone, and the trapero confirmed Texeda's version of events. Fray Fernando de Ubeda also acknowledged Juan de Texeda's version of events, and Texeda was pardoned.[67] But tensions still ran high over the incident. Friends complained to Texeda about converso influence at the friary through the Old Christian fray Fernando. With the weight of the inquiry's decision behind him, Texeda began to complain to prior Diego and other friars of the mistreatment he had received at fray Fernando's hands, and he threatened to attack anyone who treated him poorly again. Presently he spoke again to the prior, who was able, at least temporarily, to silence Texeda's criticisms of fray Fernando and the traperos. As he described it later, "the said lord prior spoke such good words to me that he gave me to understand, clearly, that he could not do any more for me, and he took me into his chamber and gave me a fine sword with silver fittings, and a pair of spurs and some clothes of the best [cambric?] and a cape, saying, 'For God's sake, Texeda, don't be angry any more!'"[68] In Texeda's mind, it seems, various disparate

---

yo fuese desde la carçel fasta el monasterio descalço y syn capa y con mucha [guarda?] que ally yua y todos los mas confesos y leuaron me fasta la puerta asy e desde la puerta fasta el capitulo fizieron me yr de rodillas y sin bonete e çierto e fizieron de mi como los judios fizieron quando leuauan a nuestro señor ante pilato a lo jusgar."

[67] "Et llegando al capitulo falle al señor prior y a fray fernando asentados. Et dixo me fray fernando, 'Pues, texeda, venis mas manso que el otro dia que nos avia descalabrado y ferido diego xastre e non se fallo por la pesquisa asy que nos lo fisestes y nos distes con el puñal quando caystes y por eso y por que dexistes tantas vezes pese a tal se [vos?] da esta pena.' Et dixe yo, 'Gracias a dios, pero lo que yo dixe çerca de diego xastre es verdad y asy se fallara y venga aqui el dicho diego delante mi y el dira la verdad sino yo ge la fare conosçer por tiempo.' Et llamaron le el qual estaua ally con muchos confesos en el dicho capitulo. Et preguntandole el prior, '¿Nos distes a texeda con alguna piedra?' Et dixo el, 'Vuestra merçed: me perdone que yo dire la verdad.' Et dixo el prior, 'Dezid.' Et dixo el, 'Sabed señor: que texeda desechaua aquellos rreales e yo dixe que vuestra reuerençia mandaua que los tomasen todos y el dixo que no lo [mandauades?] e de ally ouimos palabras. Y yo tome dos piedras y arroje le la una e non le di. Y tire ya que yua como fuyendo la otra y di le en el rostro e entonçes el fue tras mi y cayo en un foyo o tierra que estaua amontonada que estaua cabe las casas de alonso de cordoba.' Et entonçes dixo el prior, 'Padre fray fernando, ¿que nos paresçe?' Et entonçes dixo el dicho fray fernando encogiendose como buen religioso, 'Ya lo veo señor.'"

[68] "Et despues desto andando algunos dias algunas personas que bien me querian dixeron me: 'Texeda, guardadnos destos confesos que muy mal [vos?] tractauan delante de aquellos señores que dixeron e juraron que quando caystes que estauades beodo.' Et desto yo me quexe al prior y a otros rreligiosos del dicho fray fernando porque el dio tal horden para me deshonrrar por tantas maneras que bien sabian ellos mi criança, etc. Et aun dixo juro a tal que sy tanto me haze de lo aguardar un dia ençima de mi cavallo e dar le çinquenta lancadas lo qual los dichos religiosos y aun otras personas dixeron que non seria bien fecho. Et el dicho señor prior me dixo tantas buenas palabras a que

groups—converso officials, like the bailiff, who had an official status and the support of all the friars; converso traperos, whose support was limited to a small if influential faction of friars; and the Old Christian prior and vicar—all could be understood as a single, powerful entity that united within itself unjust governance and suspicious ancestry. Not surprisingly, Texeda and Old Christians like him had little sympathy for either.

FRAY FERNANDO DE UBEDA, CONVERSO TRAPEROS, AND THE MISUSE OF POWER

Texeda's story, which he told to the Jeronymite inquisitors in 1488,[69] mentions two of the elements that contributed most to local tensions in the period immediately preceding the Inquisition of 1485: first, the presence of a small group of conversos with apparent undue influence in the friary; and second, fray Fernando de Ubeda's "favoring" of conversos in his administration of the Puebla—apparently with the acceptance and even support of prior Diego de París. It is no coincidence that the conversos who appeared in Juan de Texeda's well-remembered—and, one senses, oft-repeated—tale of humiliations were traperos. Literally, the word means "cloth-seller," or perhaps "draper," but in Guadalupe traperos formed an economic elite.[70] These cloth-sellers attended the major markets in Medina del Campo and sold rich cloths, wine, and other luxury wares in the profitable regional market in Guadalupe.[71] There are some indications that traperos such as Alonso de Córdoba, freed from exile at the beginning of Diego de París's priorate, even lent

---

me dio a entender (3r) por punctos llanos que non podia él mas fazer y metio me en su camara e dio me una espada muy bien guarneçida y plateada y un par de espuelas y una ropa de contray mayor e un sayo diziendome, 'Por dios, texeda, non ayays mas enojo. Que lo que yo vos pudiere aprouechar lo fare.'"

[69] The Jeronymite order initiated an orderwide Inquisition in 1488 to root out Judaizing friars; fray Fernando de Ubeda was one of those accused. Juan de Texeda's narrative was not included in the 1485 testimony against the friars, perhaps because lay testimony against friars was not sought out or consistently recorded.

[70] These merchants certainly had elite professional links that extended beyond the friary's walls: Alonso de Córdoba's work as a buyer for the Mendoza countess of Medellín, mentioned above, is one example.

[71] See, for example, Huerga Criado's analysis of small businesses. Guadalupe was awarded a number of royal concessions granting the Puebla the right to hold frequent markets in town. See Vizuete Mendoza, Guadalupe, 53–83. Lope de Herrera, one local trapero, was described as selling wine and turkeys, among other items. See the trial of his wife, Juana González, AHN Inquis. legajo 154, expediente 20.

money to the friary during the civil war.[72] Whatever their money-lending status, these merchants were among the wealthiest vecinos in Guadalupe. Fray Fernando's support for the traperos held political and economic implications clear to all. With the support of this powerful faction of vecinos, fray Fernando's influence over the town—and indeed over factions within the friary—increased.

The economic and, by extension, political influence of these cloth merchants is evident in legal records dating from around the time of the Juan de Texeda incident. In 1482 Alonso de Córdoba, Alonso de Paredes, Juan de Segovia, and eleven other converso cloth merchants held meetings to organize a local monopoly.[73] They promised to buy cloth only from each other and to permit no one else to come into town to sell cloth, including visiting merchants who came annually from Seville, Toledo, and Córdoba. Apparently, they also excluded at least two Old Christian cloth merchants resident in Guadalupe. Like the Old Christians of 1476, the cloth merchants were accused by the friary of having held an *ayuntamiento* and of challenging the authority of the friars, who mandated the prices of food and clothing sold in the Puebla.[74] The penalty for meeting and writing laws independently of the friary was death and the seizure of all one's goods, but the prior imposed a six thousand *maravedí* fine, which he later reduced to a fine of one thousand *maravedís*, accompanied by a donation of cloth to the friary and a half-year's exile.[75] Once more, vecinos challenged the lordly authority of

[72] Enrique Llopis, a scholar of the economic and social history of Guadalupe during the Ancien Regime, suggests that conversos dominated gold and silver trades as well as money lending. See *Guadalupe: 1752*, 23. The internal Inquisition material includes one friar (Francisco de Belmonte) who questioned who would be left in Guadalupe to trade and sell, *tratará y venderá*, with all the conversos in prison. Yet to support his statement about the economic importance of New Christians in Guadalupe, Llopis cites only the thesis by Perrin, whose archival work is less sure. Vizuete Mendoza makes no mention of converso loans to the friary but asserts that, at least in this early period, the friary lived within its means. See *Guadalupe: 1752*, 293. The later decades of the fifteenth century may have been different, however, given references elsewhere to financial hardship during those years. While the economic strength of the traperos was relatively minor compared to that of the friary, it is possible that the friars went to local converso merchants for short-term cash loans.

[73] Juan de Segovia was the same man who had been exiled with Alonso de Córdoba at the beginning of prior Diego de París's priorate. AMG legajo 83, unfoliated, 7 folios, titled "Aqui estan çiertas sentençias que se dieron siendo prior fray Diego de París el ano Mccclxxxii contra unos traperos desta puebla que hizieron çerca monipodio & leyes para vender sus paños. . . ."

[74] See the extensive price lists included in the *Ordenanças Municipales* in codices 75–79.

[75] AMG legajo 83, 3r–4r. The sentences of exile were terminated slightly in advance of the six-month end date, after the guilty submitted a petition and public declaration of guilt. The fine was reduced again, this time from one thousand *maravedís* to a donation

the friars, though in this case the challenge came from a small group of elite converso *traperos*.

In this incident, converso merchants acted against the interests of the friary, rather than with the support of the friars, to consolidate their own economic position in town. In that, they resembled nothing so much as the Old Christian *vecinos* in Castile and elsewhere who were struggling for increased, independent authority in the late-medieval and early modern period. Yet once again New Christians found themselves associated with local misuse of power. Perhaps because of the *traperos'* importance to the local economy, or because of the support the merchants had from some friars, the severe penalties initially handed down by the prior were greatly reduced; soon, the cloth merchants were able to continue their business in town as before. Despite occasional attempts to wrest more economic power from the friary, the influence of these merchants created a powerful local faction tempting to any friar trying to unite economic support behind himself. It is not surprising that fray Fernando de Ubeda saw an alliance with local cloth merchants as critical for his political designs within the friary.

Converso success, and the special treatment conversos received from the friary, were due not only to their own initiative but also to friars sympathetic to them, such as fray Fernando de Ubeda. Judging from the Inquisition statements made against him, fray Fernando was greatly disliked in and out of the friary. Although no one accused him of Judaizing, or even of being a converso, many vecinos and friars believed he favored conversos, and that conversos were allied—either politically through positions as lay officials or economically as merchants—with fray Fernando's ambitions for power. Friars and Old Christian townspeople criticized Fernando's abuse of his power as vicar, his ambitious maneuvering to become prior, and his arbitrary judgments and vindictiveness. Several friars complained that fray Fernando took advantage of the Jeronymites' holdings to maintain a lover and their daughter.[76] He was first censured by the inquisitorial court in 1485; in 1488, three years after the two most prominent Judaizers in the friary had already been punished, fray Fernando was the prime target of the internal Jeronymite Inquisition.[77]

---

of food for five, or in some cases ten, poor people. Food for each poor person was expected to cost half a *real*.

[76] AMG unnumbered, Internal Inquisition, various pages, but especially testimony of fray Fernando de Moneo, 170, 172–173. See also AHN clero legajo 1423, expediente 79, 3r–v (testimony of fray Juan de Salamanca) and 4r (testimony of Diego Jiménez). Fernando's illegitimate daughter by *la Cambiadora* married a converso. This converso son-in-law received an office as notary from his father-in-law but was later found guilty of heresy.

[77] Fray Diego de Marchena was burned at the stake in August 1485; fray Diego de

Juan de Texeda's narrative indicates how fray Fernando was viewed by some Old Christian vecinos in Guadalupe, but fray Fernando's harshest critics came from within the Jeronymite community. To the friars, fray Fernando's primary motivation was lust for power. The political and economic benefits of the priorship were as clear as fray Fernando's attempts to gain that position. Particularly alarming to those friars not in fray Fernando's camp was the control that he wielded as vicar over prior Diego. Certainly in the case of Juan de Texeda, it was fray Fernando, not prior Diego, who publicly humiliated him and created his difficulties. In the friary's internal investigation, prior Diego's errors were often blamed on fray Fernando. In part this may be an attempt to salvage the prior's reputation at the expense of an unpopular friar, since prior Diego had created a number of local crises from the outset of his rule. But even relatively sympathetic friars' accounts agree on fray Fernando's links to and support of the converso community.[78] And fray Nuño de Arévalo, who succeeded Diego de París as prior, openly admitted his dislike for fray Fernando in the two inquisitorial courts he presided over in 1485 and 1488.

Fray Fernando was, as vicar, second in command behind prior Diego de París, but one friar claimed that fray Fernando controlled the friary even before prior Diego's death. So great a hold did fray Fernando have over prior Diego, said fray Fernando de Moneo, "that he [fray Fernando] made him [prior Diego] err and make a mistake, which he should not have done; for he caused to be carried out here an act of punishment that was never found nor written in law, because of which he became ineligible for the office of prior, and was not prior when he died, because of a very significant thing that they said to one another concerning a [certain] man, which amazed the queen and all the court when they knew about it."[79]

The "mistake" mentioned by Fernando de Moneo was the exile of a wealthy and possibly converso vecino.[80] A wealthy resident of Guadalupe had mentioned to Queen Isabel that the friary could afford to

---

Burgos the Elder was sentenced to perpetual imprisonment at the same time. See chapter 7.

[78] AMG unnumbered, Internal Inquisition, various, and AHN, clero legajo 1423, expediente 79.

[79] AMG unnumbered, Internal Inquisition, 172. "que le fizo caer en un yerro & caso que non deuiera. Ça fizo fazer aqui una justiçia que nunca fue fallada nin escripta en derecho. Por la qual se fizo incapaz del prioradgo. Que non era prior quando murio, por un cosa muy leve que se dixieron de uno de lo qual se espanto la reyna, & toda la corte quando lo supieron." There is no corroborating reference in the *Actas Capitulares*, but (with one exception) the *Actas* include only references from 1475 to November 1478. My thanks to Joe Jones for his help in translating this passage.

[80] Ibid., "un hombre el mas rico deste lugar aunque creo que era mal cristiano."

send two hundred to three hundred mounted fighters for the war in
Granada, something that the friary was reluctant to do.[81] When fray
Fernando learned of this Guadalupense's costly and possibly embarrassing statement to the queen, he forced prior Diego to exile the vecino.
But this punishment proved even more embarrassing to the friary than
the man's original statement to the queen; the court disapproved of
exiling someone who voiced approval of the Crown's actions. Fray Fernando's attitudes and his relationship with prior Diego, though, weath-
ered this and other storms. Fray Fernando continued to deal harshly
with his political opponents and swayed the prior to employ arbitrary
methods of justice when he felt it necessary. Not a few friars felt that
prior Diego was under the influence of fray Fernando de Ubeda to such
an extent that "he was not prior when he died."

Even if the friar's testimony exaggerated the significance of that event,
the image presented of fray Fernando and prior Diego is consistent with
other accounts. As in Juan de Texeda's encounter with fray Fernando,
fray Fernando and prior Diego used personal, arbitrary means of reaching judicial decisions, acts of justice "that [were] never found nor written in law." At a time increasingly concerned with the observance of
written law, the actions of the prior and vicar were a serious infraction.
This arbitrary exercise of authority rankled. Whatever complaints residents had with the friary's tight control, there was at the minimum an
expectation of adherence to codes of justice. It would be a mistake to
think that prior Diego was an innocent in the hands of his vicar, but
neither was fray Fernando merely a scapegoat for his superior's mis-
steps. Prior Diego was willing to treat the law in an arbitrary fashion,
while fray Fernando saw to it that this capriciousness worked to the
benefit of his allies and himself. The suspicions of favoritism toward
conversos, the resulting doubts concerning institutions and legal sys-
tems designed in some measure to support vecinos, and the appearance
of unjust, arbitrary decisions by prior Diego and fray Fernando helped
foment local tensions and anticonverso actions.[82]

These accusations of favoritism fit into the larger pattern of fray Fernando's exercise of power over New and Old Christian alike. Certainly
the wealthy converso exile discussed above was not one of fray Fernando's favorites. But some conversos, especially wealthy cloth merchants like Alonso de Córdoba and Alonso de Paredes, quite likely
played a specific and concrete role in fray Fernando's governance of the

---

[81] Ibid. The war against Granada, which culminated in the conquest of that last Muslim kingdom on the Iberian peninsula, lasted from 1482 to 1492.

[82] There is a parallel here with the argument made by Greg Dening in *Mr. Bligh's Bad
Language: Passion, Power, and Theatre on the Bounty* (Cambridge: Cambridge University
Press, 1992).

friary and town of Guadalupe. The wealth of merchants like Alonso de Córdoba or Alonso de Paredes and the support network they participated in could prove particularly useful to fray Fernando as he governed the Puebla. At the same time, the network of reciprocal ties created between fray Fernando and the traperos aided the merchants. Close, sheltering links to the political, economic, and even spiritual center of Guadalupe could only help business.

The actions of fray Fernando de Ubeda bore little in common with fray Alonso de Oropesa's impassioned defenses of conversos and their place in society from a generation earlier. Despite the number of friars willing to testify against fray Fernando, no one accused him of being a converso, let alone a covert practitioner of Judaism.[83] Simple ethnic considerations cannot explain his actions with Juan de Texeda and others. Nor is there evidence of the theological motivations that directed the activities of fray Alonso and others within the Jeronymite order. Rather, fray Fernando's attitudes suggest the complexity of the place of conversos in fifteenth-century Castile, and more specifically within the Jeronymite order. Theological, personal, and economic motivations coexisted in the Virgin's community of friars and townspeople, and those motivations were directed toward altruistic and selfish ends, both for and against the interests or well-being of conversos, who were themselves divided along economic, professional, and personal lines. Images of monolithic "converso communities" do little justice to the attitudes of New Christians, though the increasing association of various New Christians with ecclesiastical government, particularly ecclesiastical misgovernment, brought a new hue to the image painted of New Christians. Indeed, it was this tension between a narrowing vision of conversos among some people, on the one hand, and the very multiplicity of attitudes, opinions, and options evident in Guadalupe, on the other, that led, through the actions of men like fray Fernando, prior Diego, and Alonso de Córdoba in 1484, to the arrival of the Inquisition.

The Prior's Election of 1483

Vicar Fernando, Alonso de Córdoba, and other traperos had created a powerful, if controversial, network of reciprocal obligations and opportunities. When it was time to elect a new prior, they were ready to act.

[83] Haim Beinart, "The Judaizing Movement in the Order of San Jerónimo in Castile," *Scripta Hiersolymitana* 7 (1961), 183–189, includes an analysis of fray Diego de Zamora, whose trial was apparently trumped up for political reasons. Note, by contrast, that the Guadalupense friars did not choose to generate false accusations of Judaizing per se against fray Fernando.

In 1483 prior Diego de París died after serving almost three triennial terms as prior. The tensions that had swirled in and out of the friary during his tenure—relations between Old and New Christian, factional struggles within the friary, vecino unrest, economic problems—rose up again after his death. An election had to be held within forty days of the death of prior Diego, and any member of the order from any house who had spent at least twenty years in the habit was eligible. Election could be held by open acclamation, secret ballot, or agreement of the capitulars (friary officials); all friars could participate.[84] Fray Fernando de Ubeda quickly emerged as one candidate for the position. His long-term status as vicar bolstered his claim, as did the support of the wealthy conversos in town. Others nominated fray Nuño de Arévalo, a Jeronymite who had professed in Guadalupe and had held various positions of authority there before assuming the priorship of Yuste, a Jeronymite house a few days' ride to the northwest.[85]

Extant documents mention little of the atmosphere of the friary before the election and do not describe the election itself, but later testimony before the inquisitors includes an account of some of the events at this time. Some conversos had publicly offered their loyalty to fray Fernando on bended knee even when prior Diego was alive—an act verging on treason. After prior Diego de París's death, several wealthy conversos promised gifts to the friary in the hopes that Fernando de Ubeda would be elected prior. A silversmith named Diego Núñez even offered to provide the friary with a mule worth ten thousand *maravedís* if the friars would elect fray Fernando.[86] But the favors that had passed between fray Fernando and the wealthy New Christians were not sufficient to keep fray Fernando in office. In July fray Nuño easily won the election and returned from Yuste to serve as Guadalupe's new prior. Fray Fernando and his supporters in and out of the friary lost their control over the friars and the town, and all of Guadalupe's New Christians earned prior Nuño's resentment for the attempt of some to bribe the friary. In September, just two months after the election, King Fernando of Aragon stopped at Guadalupe while traveling from Córdoba

---

[84] Vizuete Mendoza, *Guadalupe*, 145.

[85] See the brief summary of the election in Rubío, *Historia*, 112. Testimony in AHN clero legajo 1423, expediente 79, suggests that fray Fernando de Ubeda was also in contention for the office of prior; see below.

[86] Testimony of fray Juan de Salamanca, AHN clero legajo 1423, expediente 79, 3v. "et aún a la electión deste nuestro padre fray Nuño de Arévalo pensaron de lo aver por señor. Y tenían fechas muchas mandas y cosas para fazer alegrías. Y aún uno dellos el qual era Diego Núñes platero avía mandado una mula que valía dies mill mrs. si el saliese por prior. . . ."

and met for several days with the new prior.[87] Within fifteen months of
that meeting, the inquisitors had arrived in Guadalupe from Ciudad
Real and, with prior Nuño as Chief Inquisitor, had begun the Holy
Office's work.

When was the decision made to bring the inquisitorial court to Guadalupe? The documentary record is unclear. The Inquisition had so far
visited only a few large cities in southern Castile, sites presumably chosen by Fernando and Isabel. No documentation survives that indicates
the process by which Guadalupe was chosen as a site for the Holy
Office, but the impetus for that decision can plausibly be traced to
Fernando's visit of September 1483. Both king and prior would have
seen benefits in bringing the Inquisition to Guadalupe. And as King
Fernando and prior Nuño talked, it seems inevitable that the conversation would have turned to New Christians and the Inquisition. At that
time the attempted bribery of the friars would still have been the focus
of much discussion; the new prior's anger about the position of New
Christians in town, and about events surrounding his election, must
also have been at their height in the months following his election and
arrival in Guadalupe.[88] The early trials, and especially the execution
rather than exile of Guadalupe's most independent and influential conversos, indicate that traperos and other wealthy New Christians were a
particular focus of the inquisitors under the direction of prior Nuño.[89]
Indeed, King Fernando's visit may have initiated the first discussions
about appointing prior Nuño as chief inquisitor. Prior Nuño de Arévalo's eager participation shows him to have been at the least a willing
participant, and it is easy to imagine that prior Nuño requested the
Inquisition himself. Moreover, friars' statements to the inquisitors suggest the depth of hostility on the part of some friars toward excessive
converso influence in town; this hostility could only have encouraged
King Fernando to order the Inquisition to Guadalupe.

Once the Holy Office arrived in Guadalupe, the hostility of some
friars toward the traperos in particular became evident. Despite the fact
that evidence at their trials did not equal that against other supposed
Judaizers in town, and in some cases was almost nonexistent, traperos
were the first New Christians selected by the friars for trial. Traperos
like Alonso de Paredes, who apparently exhibited no Judaizing practice

---

[87] García and Trenado, *Guadalupe*, 95.

[88] Prior Nuño's hostility toward fray Fernando, fray Diego de Marchena, and Guadalupe's converso population is evident in his testimony before the inquisitors in 1485.
See AMG unnumbered, Internal Inquisition, 5.

[89] On uses of the inquisitorial court in local political conflicts, see Jaime Contreras
Contreras's groundbreaking study, *Sotos contra Riquelmes*.

whatsoever, were redefined by the Inquisition as heretics solely on the basis of their ancestry and economic status.[90] The inquisitors had begun the process of demarking clear differences in the complex religious, political, and social climate of the period.

At midcentury Guadalupe faced what appeared to be a typical series of urban uprisings against traditional lordly authority. Like many late-medieval and early modern towns, Guadalupe was rocked by frequent unrest. The combustible mix of a rapidly swelling population and arbitrary governance, combined with civil war and frequent poor harvests, threatened to ignite on several occasions. These were, to a large extent, local problems, and problems familiar to many Iberian towns in the fifteenth century. Yet what began as ordinary local unrest was changed by the presence of New Christians among the artisans, clerical functionaries, and merchant elite of the town. For Old Christian Guadalupenses, the second half of the fifteenth century seemed to demonstrate that arbitrary governance and an influential religious minority worked together against Old Christian interests. Prior Nuño de Arévalo, in consultation with the king, found a way to quell these local political and social conflicts, to settle immediate grievances, and to sever the link between clerical ill-governance and an influential New Christian minority—the Holy Office of the Inquisition. The inquisitors would indeed resolve these local political and social conflicts.[91] In the process, though, the inquisitors would also fundamentally alter the balance of power in town between the friars and vecinos, and between New and Old Christians. Prior Nuño turned away from the arbitrary and divisive policies of his predecessor, prior Diego de París. But in so doing, the prior also reaffirmed the distinct status of New Christians in Old Christian society. The inquisitors, with their unique view of the residents of Guadalupe, would reify that distinction, and in the process set new standards of secular and religious practice that would affect all of Guadalupe's residents.

[90] While some converso traperos, like Lope de Herrera, had numerous specific charges and much evidence brought against them, others, like Alonso de Paredes, were executed on very flimsy evidence. On Lope de Herrera, see appendix and AHN clero, expediente 1423. On Alonso de Paredes, see introduction and AHN clero, expediente 1423.

[91] Netanyahu also argues for the importance of social and economic reasons in the origins and successes of the Inquisition; see *Origins*, 950–974. But it is important to note that his argument is somewhat different and in any case is minimized in his own analysis in comparison to Old Christian racism.

FIVE

THE INQUISITORS' GAZE

ON THE twenty-sixth of December, 1484, little more than a year after prior Nuño met with King Fernando, the friars of Our Lady of Guadalupe welcomed the arrival of Fernando and Isabel's Inquisition.[1] Two days later, as fray Diego de Ecija described it in his history of the friary, the town gathered in the church for the inauguration of inquisitorial activity there. One of the Jeronymites, fray Juan de Trujillo, preached a sermon, and then everyone raised his hand and swore in a loud voice to tell the truth about whatever he or she knew or had heard spoken against the holy Catholic faith.[2] The next week the inquisitors began their work. During the year that followed, at least 226 local conversos were tried before the Holy Office of the Inquisition. In most respects, the inquisitors here operated as they had elsewhere, though the presence of prior Nuño as chief inquisitor meant that Guadalupe's Inquisition would be unlike any other.[3]

In their attempts to identify active Judaizers in Guadalupe, the inquisitors necessarily acted from the standpoint of their own understanding of the nature of New Christian beliefs, attitudes, and practices; but that standpoint influenced more than just themselves. The inquisitors' vision of Old and New Christians redefined and categorized those over whom the inquisitors' glance passed; at the same time this vision transformed how Old and New Christians saw themselves and each other. The actions of friends, neighbors, and rivals were reexamined through the lens of inquisitorial activity. Inquisitors, friars, and townspeople all participated in the event, but the inquisitors' vision of Guadalupe and its Inquisition became the model by which all residents identified and clas-

---

[1] The inquisitors brought with them a newly written set of instructions, composed by a group of inquisitors and canon lawyers, including Francisco Sánchez de la Fuente, one of the inquisitors in Guadalupe. These instructions served as the basis for inquisitorial procedure until the court was closed in the nineteenth century. See, for example, AHN Inquis. libro 1225.

[2] Ecija, OSH, *Libro de la invencion*, 345; German Rubío also discusses this event in his *Historia*, 112–113.

[3] Nuño de Arévalo may not have been selected under papal authority. He was, in addition, the only member of an early inquisitorial court who was not a Dominican friar. See Lea, *Historia de la Inquisición española*, ed. Angel Alcalá (Madrid: Fundación Universitaria Española, 1983), 1:180.

sified the potential political and religious wrongdoing of their neighbors. Like the inquisitors, vecinos might apply these standards to conversos out of religious concern, personal or political grievance, or some combination thereof. The source of this new view of the community was the activity of the inquisitors, who established their authority—and by extension the authority of the Crown—by constructing differences out of ambiguities. As Talal Asad has noted, "[t]o secure its unity—to make its own history—dominant power has worked best through differentiating and classifying practices. . . . Furthermore, its ability to select (or construct) the differences that serve its purposes has depended on its exploiting the dangers and opportunities contained in ambiguous situations."[4] Examining the actions of the inquisitors and the effects of their gaze on Guadalupe and the Guadalupenses reveals not only the perspective of the inquisitors themselves, but also a new view of conversos that was to gain increasing importance among lay Guadalupenses as well.[5] This new view spread across the Iberian peninsula as word spread of the trials and as the smoke from the autos de fe rose over the mountains. As a result of this activity, both friars and townspeople saw their relation with one another and with the Crown with new eyes. On December 26, 1484, life in Guadalupe was about to change.

THE HOLY OFFICE IN GUADALUPE

The Holy Office of the Spanish Inquisition had been operating for a little over a year when the inquisitors arrived in Guadalupe. The Inquisition had been organized under the authority of the Crown and with permission of the pope in 1481, and the first inquisitors set out two

---

[4] Talal Asad, *Genealogies of Religion: Discipline and Reasons of Power in Christianity and Islam* (Baltimore: Johns Hopkins University Press, 1993), 17.

[5] Recent studies of the Inquisition have added a new dimension to interpretations of inquisitors and their role in the communities where they operated. See, for example, Bartolomé Bennassar, *La inquisición española. Poder político y control social* (Barcelona: Editorial Crítica, Grijalbo, 1981); Jaime Contreras, *El Santo Oficio de la Inquisición en Galicia, 1560–1700: poder, sociedad, y cultura* (Madrid: Akal, 1982); Jaime Contreras, *Sotos contra Riquelmes*; Jaime Contreras and Gustav Hennigsen, "44,000 Cases of the Spanish Inquisition (1540–1700): Analysis of a Historical Data Bank" in *The Inquisition in Early Modern Europe*, ed. Henningsen et al.; Ricardo García Carcel, *Orígenes de la Inquisición;* Carlo Ginzburg, *The Cheese and the Worms. The Cosmos of a Sixteenth-Century Miller* (Baltimore: Johns Hopkins University Press, 1980); Carlo Ginzburg, *The Night Battles. Witchcraft and Agrarian Cults in the Sixteenth and Seventeenth Centuries* (Baltimore: Johns Hopkins University Press, 1983); Stephen Haliczer, *Inquisition and Society in the Kingdom of Valencia, 1478–1834* (Berkeley: University of California Press, 1990); Stephen Haliczer, ed., *Inquisition and Society in Early Modern Europe* (London: Croom Helm, 1987); and Peters, *Inquisition.*

years later. The first court operated in Castile, beginning at Seville and Córdoba before moving on to Ciudad Real.[6] In late 1484, as the inquisitors and their assistants arrived in Guadalupe, the Inquisition was undergoing a profound transformation. Up until this time the inquisitors had operated through a series of sequential ambulatory courts, without a permanent base. By late 1484, however, the Holy Office had begun to acquire a more permanent character. A first edition of the inquisitors' manual, a procedural guide used throughout the three-hundred-year history of the court, was completed in November 1484 in Seville. That same year, the Inquisition made its first foray into Aragonese territory with a court at Zaragoza. During 1485 the Holy Office transferred its files and offices from Ciudad Real to Toledo, the first permanent court with a specific, regional jurisdiction. In the following decades, the Inquisition developed a more elaborate system of regional offices responsible for occasional visits, *visitas*, into the region for which each court was responsible. The inquisitorial court in Guadalupe, therefore, came at a time when the Holy Office was becoming a more permanent fixture in Iberian society.[7]

Even in an age of transition for the Inquisition, however, the operation of the Holy Office in Guadalupe was unique. Nowhere else were local secular authorities so involved in the decision to hold a royal inquisitorial court, and nowhere else was local secular and spiritual authority so closely tied to inquisitorial authority. Elsewhere, contemporary local officials tended to see the introduction of Fernando and Isabel's inquisitors as the beginning of increased royal control in their local domains. Members of the town councils, *cabildos*, both Old and New Christian, resisted the introduction of the Holy Office. In Aragon the court was seen as a fundamentally Castilian institution as well, and Aragonese cities like Teruel resisted its introduction strenuously. In other communities, therefore, the arrival of the inquisitors was seen as a diminution of local power in favor of the Crown.[8] By contrast, Gua-

---

[6] Some penitents from Seville and Córdoba made the pilgrimage to Guadalupe as part of their penance. See AMG unnumbered, Internal Inquisition, passim.

[7] Henry Charles Lea remains the basic text on the history of the Inquisition. The Spanish translation, *Historia de la Inquisición Española*, has a new introduction, an updated bibliography, and updated archival references, and is particularly useful and important. Also on early Inquisition history, see Bennassar, *La inquisición española*; Ricardo García Carcel, *Orígenes de la inquisición española*: and Jaime Contreras and Jean-Pierre Dedieu, "Geografía de la inquisición española: La formación de los distritos (1470–1820)," *Hispania* 40 (1980). Because it lacks the methodical records available after the mid-sixteenth century, this earliest period of Inquisition history is still not well studied.

[8] On resistance to the imposition of the Inquisition by local officials, see Lea, *Historia*, and William Monter, *Frontiers of Heresy. The Spanish Inquisition from the Basque Lands to Sicily* (Cambridge: Cambridge University Press, 1990).

dalupe was insulated from fears of royal intercession in local affairs. The Crown could do little to exercise its authority in a town controlled exclusively by the Order of Saint Jerome; the friars were to an extent immune from the jurisdictional worries of independent, secular towns. Furthermore, Guadalupe and the Jeronymites' close links to the Trastámara dynasty meant that the friars actually benefited from the support and continued close relationship between the Crown and the friary. Prior Nuño's role as spiritual and temporal leader of Guadalupe, together with his position as chief inquisitor, was a sign of the friars' strong ties to the Crown, rather than their weakness before the Catholic Monarchs.

The reasons behind the Holy Office's arrival in Guadalupe were unique, as was the embodiment of local secular authority, ecclesiastical authority, and chief inquisitor in one person; but a complex mixture of royal and local concerns was often present in the actions of the Inquisition. From its inception, the Inquisition had alternately taken advantage of local conflicts and been incorporated into them. In Teruel, Aragon, for example, local politics were intimately bound up with the establishment and activity of the inquisitors. City councilors resisted the imposition of the Inquisition for ten months in 1484; the only supporter of the inquisitors was a local *hidalgo* named Juan Garcés de Marcillán. In response to Garcés de Marcillán's support, King Fernando of Aragon named the *hidalgo* captain of Teruel and granted him dictatorial powers. Garcés de Marcillán allowed the establishment of the Holy Office there and became the court's "secular arm." Captain Garcés de Marcillán's power enabled the Inquisition to function in Teruel during 1485 and 1486; in return, the captain used the Inquisition to settle personal and political debts. As William Monter has described it, "the Inquisition became a lethal and ultimately double-edged weapon in settling family quarrels."[9] Garcés de Marcillán soon fell from power, and two years after their establishment the inquisitors left as well, in 1487. Even from afar, however, the Holy Office continued to take advantage of Teruel's political rivalries for much of the sixteenth century.

The role of local political conditions in the establishment of a royal Inquisition was not limited to the Inquisition's earliest years. Jaime Contreras has provided one example of this in his study of the inquisitorial court in Murcia during the sixteenth century. At this time, when the Holy Office was otherwise largely inactive, the Inquisition in Murcia became a battleground on which local political conflicts were fought. Rival Murcian families, one New Christian and one Old Christian, used the Inquisition as a means of gaining the upper hand in their ongoing

---

[9] Monter, *Frontiers of Heresy*, 6–10.

rivalry during the middle decades of the sixteenth century. Only when both families united in using the Inquisition to attack Murcia's converted Muslim, or *morisco*, population did they cease fighting each other through the Holy Office.[10]

Despite the central role of politics in the establishment and activity of inquisitorial courts, religious concerns were not absent from the work of the inquisitors. The political dimension involved in the establishment of new inquisitorial courts was not surprising, given the Inquisition's status as an arm of the royal government, but the influence of political concerns also reflected the religious ambiguity at the heart of the inquisitors' mandate. The inquisitors were expected to identify heretical beliefs and attitudes—that is, intention—among Iberia's New Christians on the basis of their words and actions alone. Asked to deduce intention from action, the inquisitors were forced to rely upon the statements of conversos themselves, as well as Judaizing activities witnessed by others, to prove their case. Acts that the Holy Office interpreted as Judaizing could be used as evidence against New Christians, but in a Christian society political subversion as well as Jewish ritual activity could potentially be defined as heretical. For the inquisitors, a broad range of social, political, and religious practices could identify the practitioner as a Judaizer. Few inquisitors would have identified themselves as pawns in local power struggles; but given the intertwined political and religious conflicts in Guadalupe, as well as the Inquisition's dual role as instrument of royal policy and reformer of religious practices, it is understandable that political as well as religious concerns motivated inquisitors.

At every level of the Inquisition's activity in Guadalupe, local appointees and royal officials worked in tandem, and their individual histories indicate the prestige and breadth of experience of those involved. This was especially true of the inquisitors themselves. Two inquisitors from the Holy Office's temporary base at Ciudad Real served with prior Nuño de Arévalo: Francisco Sánchez de la Fuente, canon lawyer, and Pedro Sánchez de la Calancha, lawyer, *licenciado*. Sánchez de la Fuente served as an inquisitor at Ciudad Real for a year and a half before coming to Guadalupe, but his work as an inquisitor was just a footnote to his illustrious ecclesiastical career. In 1492 the canon lawyer was elected bishop of Avila, and in 1496 he became bishop of Córdoba.[11] By contrast, Sánchez de la Calancha's time in Guadalupe launched a long career as an inquisitor for the Holy Office. Almost immediately after the

[10] Contreras, *Sotos contra Riquelmes*.
[11] Fidel Fita, "La Inquisición en Guadalupe," 283–343.

Inquisition concluded in Guadalupe, he spent a year as an inquisitor with the ad hoc inquisitorial court in Belalcázar and Pueblo del Alcocér, both towns in southern Extremadura.[12] After his year in Belalcázar, Sánchez de la Calancha helped establish inquisitorial courts in Valencia and Murcia.[13]

Francisco Sánchez de la Fuente and Pedro Sánchez de la Calancha brought with them a bare-bones staff to assist in the work of the court. First among these was the prosecution lawyer, *promotor fiscal*, Diego Fernández de Zamora. Fernández prepared the court's accusations and argued for the guilt of the accused. As in Spanish secular law, the prosecutor was of a higher status than the lawyer for the defense, or *letrado*; during trials the prosecutor was seated to the left of the judges, while the *letrado* sat below the judge's dais and in front of him.[14] The prosecutor brought with him an assistant named Tristán de Medina, who probably took care of much of the day-to-day work. Medina argued only part of one of the extant cases; otherwise his participation was not recorded on paper.[15]

In many respects Inquisition courts mirrored the practices of secular courts, and the counsel provided for the defense was no exception. Those accused by the Inquisition were allowed to select a defense counsel. In Guadalupe, this role was inevitably filled by the lawyer, *letrado*, Doctor de Villaescusa.[16] Doctor de Villaescusa was, like the prosecutor and the inquisitors, an official of the Inquisition, and during his tenure assisting the Holy Office he filled multiple roles. After leaving Guadalupe, Doctor de Villaescusa served as a judge for the inquisitorial court in Toledo.[17] As lawyer for the defense, Doctor de Villaescusa had two major roles in the activity of the Inquisition. First, he represented the accused at formal statements before the inquisitors, usually at the beginning and end of the trial. In other words, the defense attorney was

[12] Contreras and Dedieu, "Geografía," 72.

[13] Contreras and Dedieu, "Geografía," 73 and 80. Sánchez de la Calancha moved on to Valencia in February 1487, and finally to Murcia in May 1488.

[14] See Richard Kagan, *Lawsuits and Litigants in Castile, 1500–1700* (Chapel Hill: University of North Carolina Press, 1981). This work should soon be available in its entirety at libro.uca.edu.

[15] AHN Inquis. legajo 132, expediente 18. Trial of Andrés Alonso Trujillano. Tristán de Medina also began several inquisitorial courts. See also Contreras and Dedieu, "Geografía." Medina later reappeared in Guadalupe in 1488 to complete some trials begun in 1485; see chapter 8.

[16] A "lettered person," that is, a lawyer. On *letrados* and their place in Castilian society, see Nader, *The Mendoza Family*, and Kagan, *Lawsuits*.

[17] See, for example, AHN Inquis. legajo 132, expediente 11, 17r (1490), where Doctor de Villaescusa appears as one of the judges deciding the case of Rodrigo Alonso *tundidor* in Toledo.

the formal advocate for the defense in the courtroom. Second, the defense attorney explained the actions of the inquisitors to the accused and elicited his or her responses to each phase of the trial. The accused remained in prison between the first accusation before the Holy Office and the sentencing. During the trial itself the accused learned of the progress of his or her trial through an attorney; the counsel for the defense apprised the accused of his or her rights and solicited appropriate legal responses. The attorney assigned to the defense, therefore, served as a mediator between the Holy Office, of which he was a part, and the defendant, whom he represented.

Another assistant who arrived with the inquisitors was a bailiff, *alguacil*, named Antón de Castilla. For decades, the friars in Guadalupe had appointed a bailiff who served with the Jeronymites' other lay functionaries; he presumably continued in his role during 1485 and after. The inquisitors' bailiff, by contrast, was responsible for the prisoners of the Inquisition. Antón de Castilla appears in the documents when the inquisitors confronted the accused in person. Castilla participated in the initial arrest, chaperoned the prisoners from the prison to the inquisitors' court and back, guarded the prison, and either participated in or witnessed any acts of torture.

The men who arrived from Ciudad Real formed the nucleus of the Holy Office in Guadalupe, but they did not carry out the Inquisition's activity alone. To aid in their work, the inquisitors employed several Guadalupenses. Most important of these was Juan de Texeda, the longtime lay employee of the friary, whom we met in the previous chapter.[18] Five or six years after his humiliation at the hands of fray Fernando de Ubeda and some local conversos, Texeda served as an assistant to the defense attorney. His position was that of solicitor, *procurador*. As such, Texeda was responsible for the daily work of the defense. While Doctor de Villaescusa served as a liaison between the accused and the court, Texeda organized the defense for the accused. He argued the case, found witnesses, and prepared questions for the court to ask of the them.[19]

---

[18] AHN clero legajo 1423, expediente 79, 2v. "veynte e tanto años que avia seruido a esta casa de nuestra señora e fasiendo muchos y buenos y leales seruicios."

[19] The *procurador*, like all of these positions, was also a feature of civil courts of the period. In *Lawsuits*, Kagan states that lawyers for the prosecution and defense in early modern Spain preferred to have assistants perform most of the work; the relationship between Doctor de Villaescusa and Juan de Texeda fulfills that pattern. The amount of work performed by Texeda seems unusual, however. From the extant records, it appears that Texeda not only prepared the arguments for the defense but also presented them before the inquisitors. There is no obvious evidence of negligence in his work, but one wonders how his previous experience might have affected his activities with the defense.

Texeda was only the most prominent of a number of locals employed by the court. A cleric, Juan Blásquez, aided the prosecutor in the preparation of statements. Several local scriveners, both friars and laymen, received and verified statements of reconciliation and performed the court's clerical tasks. In addition, all the Guadalupenses mentioned above, as well as some of the friary's servants, served as official witnesses to the various actions of the court. The salaries for all these people were paid from the goods seized by the court, as was the practice of the Inquisition throughout its existence.[20]

THE TRIALS

The inquisitors arrived in December 1484; by January 1485 the Inquisition had begun its work. The Holy Office inevitably began its ad hoc court visits by announcing a period of grace, *tiempo de gracia*, during which all conversos were invited to confess their sinful practice of Jewish customs and receive forgiveness. Some New Christians dictated their confessions to the friars serving as notaries for the inquisitors; many others submitted a confession in writing. If the notary had not written the confession himself, he questioned the penitent on what he or she had written, occasionally eliciting further information. As was the case in any other confession to a priest, a penance was assessed, and one was—in theory, at least—absolved of all taint of wrongdoing. Approximately 226 people reconciled in the *tiempo de gracia*.[21] Of the 37 extant trials that include a dated reconciliation from the *tiempo de gracia*, these occurred between January 2 and 25, with most occurring on January 13, 14, and 15. At the end of January the period of reconciliation closed. On February 4 a public hearing against heretics occurred at one of

[20] The collection and disbursement of the goods seized by the Inquisition continued in Guadalupe long after the inquisitors had left. This work can be traced in the "Cuenta de todos los bienes de la inquisicion que yo reciby," the accounts ledger kept by the friary on the Inquisition. See AHN clero legajo 1423, expediente 89. There is no record of *familiares* assisting the inquisitors in Guadalupe.

[21] AHN clero legajo 1423 lists all those tried by the Inquisition and their punishments. This material has been tabulated in Isabel Testón Núñez and María Angeles Hernández Bermejo, "La inquisición de Llerena en la centuria del quinientos," *Actas del congreso: Pedro Cieza de León y su época* (Llerena, 1991). Diego de Ecija in his *Invención* claims over 230 reconciled ("230 y tantas"), 344–345. Eugenio Escobar Prieto, in "Los Judíos en Guadalupe y otros pueblos de Extremadura," *El Monasterio de Guadalupe* 1 (1916), 269–272, states that 282 reconciled. Testón Núñez and Hernández Bermejo's numbers include adult men and women, as well as a few adolescents; see, for example, AHN Inquis. legajo 158, expediente 5. These numbers also include those who reconciled and were not tried. It is unclear why a few adolescents were singled out for trial. It appears that most conversos participated in this first phase of the Inquisition.

the friars' hostels, a site known as the House of the Good Christian Woman.[22] A week and a half later, on Sunday, February 13, those who confessed were officially reconciled. Barefoot and carrying a lit candle, they walked in a penitential processional to the church, where they were subjected to an unspecified public punishment.[23] In addition the reconciled were to continue their penance after the official reconciliation, although it is unclear just how many did. Most made no mention of it during the trials.

The statements of reconciliation themselves were formulaic rehearsals of Judaizing activity. Most statements opened with the penitent announcing his or her sorrow for any actions opposed to the Christian faith and church and disavowing any continuing interest in Judaism or Jewish practices. The penitent further requested pardon for any additional heretical acts which he or she had forgotten to mention. This opening statement was followed by a list of acts that merited pardon for their Jewish significance. Statements of reconciliation could run from a half page to two pages, depending on the specificity of the claims, and how willing penitents were to accuse other New Christians. The inquisitors or their assistants must have explained the proper form of reconciliation to Guadalupe's New Christians; none provided a prose accounting of wrongdoing, and all were careful to ask pardon for any act unintentionally left out.

Neither the inquisitors nor the accused expected that the reconciliations would absolve New Christians and free them from going to trial. From the very beginning, all the participants in the inquisitorial trials were calculating potential advantages and liabilities. This is apparent in the reconciliations themselves. The actions of the Holy Office were predicated on an assumption of guilt rather than innocence, and statements of reconciliation reflect that fundamental assumption, as well as a desire to identify all culprits. New Christians revealed all that they felt they could disclose with impunity, averred their unwavering devotion to Christianity, and often attributed any incorrect actions to the evil influence of family and friends, particularly those who were deceased. When conversos did not immediately respond to the pressure to identify those who had led them astray, the inquisitors or their scriveners asked for the information themselves. Usually a marginal note was added at the end of a statement, adding a parent's name and identifying them as the source of the illicit knowledge. Alonso the teacher, who almost cer-

---

[22] "La Buena Cristiana" was a convert from Islam to Christianity, who escaped from North Africa to Guadalupe after seeing a vision of the Virgin of Guadalupe. For more on her and other converts, see Starr-LeBeau, "The Joyous History of Devotion."

[23] Rubío, *Historia*, 115.

tainly prepared his own reconciliation in his neat, formal hand, stated at the outset that he had fasted in a Jewish, rather than Christian, fashion. On the back, a different, scribal hand added (apparently while reviewing the initial statement of reconciliation, and therefore before any trial) that "his mother made him fast, has done it all his life, and he confessed it to his confessor. His mother is Marina Alonso."[24] Similarly, Mari Sánchez wife of Diego Jímenez the butcher, was asked during her reconciliation to specify with whom she had visited the synagogue in Trujillo. Mari was careful to mention the presence of Old Christians, including listing one by name.[25]

Ostensibly the *tiempo de gracia* allowed conversos who considered themselves to be good Christians the opportunity to repent any wrongdoing and to prove their devotion to Christianity. In fact, rather than serving as a sign of genuine faith and remorse, a statement of reconciliation was usually taken as a sign of exactly the opposite—an indication that the penitent was anything but remorseful or devoutly Christian. For the inquisitors, statements of reconciliation were almost expected from local conversos and were seen as a sign of guilt rather than repentance. They served as an introduction to the paradoxical world of the inquisitor, where coercion made possible, then profoundly tainted, all communications between the court and the accused. The Holy Office recognized the instinct for self-preservation, as had inquisitorial and secular courts for centuries; here it became joined to stereotypes of shifty, dishonest New Christians that had their origins in stereotypes of Jews. Coercion and, more commonly, threats of coercion were employed to insure honesty from dishonest and secretive Judaizers. Yet coercion did little to assuage the concerns of inquisitors, who realized that under torture the accused might create whatever image of heresy the inquisitors wished to see.[26] Reconciliations, as the first contact between inquisitor and New Christian, and the first means of defense for conversos, provided inquisitors with their first suspicions of which New Christians might be guilty of Judaizing activity.

For the inquisitors, the statements of reconciliation gained during the *tiempo de gracia* served as a first opportunity to probe potential inaccuracies in the confessions of conversos, and to begin to compile a list of names of potential heretics. The ceremony of reconciliation that closed the *tiempo de gracia* on February 13 had scarcely ended when the inquisitors began the long process of comparing statements of recon-

[24] AHN Inquis. legajo 146, expediente 6.

[25] Ibid. 183, expediente 20, 2r.

[26] This is apparent in the strictures regarding testimony gained under torture, namely, that torture sessions had to be limited and that any information gained under torture had to be confirmed later, in a confession not made under torture.

ciliation and compiling lists of possible false and simulated, *fingida y simulada*, confessions. Using the careful details provided by conversos and scriveners, inquisitors identified individuals and families of New Christians who seemed particularly suspect. Some reconciliations included spontaneous denunciations of fellow conversos, and the names of those denounced were recorded as potential witnesses for the prosecution. Even deceased members of some families were mistakenly called as witnesses, a sign that the inquisitors were working from documents rather than from the personal knowledge of their staff or from the verbal testimony of witnesses.[27] A few of those who confessed were deemed genuine Christians and received no further attention from the inquisitors. For most New Christians in Guadalupe, however, the statement of reconciliation marked only the beginning of their contact with the Holy Office. Indeed, rather than "reconciling" a New Christian to proper observance of Christianity, these statements initiated precisely the opposite process—the nominally voluntary self-denunciations formed the basis of the inquisitors' prosecutions.

Using the statements of reconciliation, the prosecutor prepared an initial list of New Christians to investigate. Alonso de Córdoba, Lope de Herrera, Alonso de Paredes, and the other cloth merchants were singled out for early attention from the prosecution. With an initial list of the accused settled, the prosecutor began to search out and interview witnesses, building a case for the prosecution. From these witnesses the prosecuting attorney drew up his formal accusation, listing all substantiated charges. The charges were listed from most to least important, based on the evaluation of the prosecutor. Typically, the charge began with the general claim of issuing a false and simulated reconciliation, and illegitimately enjoying the privileges of Christianity while following the law of Moses. From there, the prosecutor would list a specific series of charges, beginning with those activities not permitted by the church. This was followed by activities that were not specifically un-Christian but might indicate the active practice of Judaism.[28] Once the accusation

---

[27] This is apparent in the record of AHN Inquis. legajo 132, expediente 11. Trial of Rodrigo Alonso *tundidor*. His file includes the public notice calling him and several others before the Holy Office. Among the other names is the deceased father of Juan de la Barrera.

[28] Melammed and Beinart also have noted this trend; see Melammed, *Heretics*, and Beinart, *Conversos*, 237–238. It is important to note at the outset the distinction between Judaizing avoidance of Christian activities and the active practice of Jewish ones. Both Beinart and Melammed note the paradox of inquisitorial interests in this regard. Although inquisitors were theoretically concerned more with promoting correct Christian practice, Beinart and Melammed note that in the early years of the Holy Office's activity the inquisitors were concerned primarily with manifestations of Jewish practices, rather than with revealing Christian sins. For example, many inquisitors operated on the

was prepared, the formal trial began. The bailiff and a small number of witnesses walked to the home of the accused or, in the case of a posthumous trial, the deceased's next-of-kin and issued the formal accusation. The bailiff took the accused into custody and informed the defendant or his or her relatives that he or she needed to begin to prepare a defense within a certain number of days.

From references in passing in the Inquisition documents, it seems likely that all the inquisitors' prisoners were kept together in one prison, with separate rooms for men and women.[29] The Inquisition documents themselves specify nothing more about the whereabouts of their prisoners, but it is likely that they were kept at the town prison on Bailiff Street, calle del Alguacil, not far from the friary. There was no prison in Guadalupe throughout most of the fifteenth century, and this structure may have been built to meet the needs of the inquisitors. It included an open central space, *corral*, with room for stabling animals; three small rooms in the *corral* totaling 24 square meters served as the men's prison. The *corral* was encompassed by two corridors; one included the kitchen and the women's prison—a room of 64 square meters. Underneath the second corridor was the torture chamber.[30] The difference in the structure of the men's and women's rooms suggests that not only were there perhaps more female than male prisoners, but also there was more concern about controlling male prisoners. The men were separated into smaller rooms whose doors included a heavy lock and key.

Conditions in the cramped inquisitorial prison are not documented, but some general observations can be made. From the extant trials, it appears that witnesses and prisoners were called individually, as each was accused by the Holy Office in turn. Entire families were not accused and arrested collectively. In this way, at least initially, households

---

assumption that not working on Saturday merited greater punishment than working on Sunday, although working on Saturday was in no sense mandated by the church. In other words, inquisitors punished Judaizers more severely for engaging in acts that were not forbidden than they did for avoiding the responsibilities mandated by Rome. In part, this tactic reflected the realities of Christian practice in the pre-Reformation period. Little was specifically demanded of Christians except annual confession and communion, and although typical expectations of Christian practice exceeded those simple guidelines, it was easier to identify New Christians by what they did as Jews rather than what they did not do as Christians.

[29] See, for example, AHN Inquis. legajo 183, expediente 10, in which the accused discussed with her fellow female prisoners how to respond to the accusations of the inquisitors.

[30] Perrin, "Plenitud del Guadalupe en el siglo XVI," *Guadalupe* 715 (1992), 70. Note, however, that the Inquisition documents refer to a "Casa de Tormentos," which was apparently distinct from the prison. See, for example, AHN Inquis. legajo 182, expediente 20.

were able to maintain their professions, and prisons were less crowded. One exception to this policy may have been made in sentencing spouses. Although they were not mentioned often, there is evidence that in some cases wives were sentenced with their husband.[31] Children under suspicion by the Holy Office were not imprisoned but rather housed individually with "good Christian families," who were reimbursed at a set rate.[32] Throughout 1485 the prison population rose and fell with the shifting tides of additional accusations and completed trials. Those sentenced to death were kept in prison until the next auto de fe, the ceremony that concluded the trials.[33] Those sentenced to exile may have been forced to leave town within a few days of their sentencing, although it is possible that they remained until the official decree of exile was issued on December 3. Since trials tended to run weeks or even months, with an additional wait between sentencing and carrying out the sentence, one would assume that the prisons became quite crowded, particularly before the autos de fe.[34]

From the initial accusation and imprisonment to the final sentencing, the inquisitors oversaw the activity of the Holy Office. Collectively, the judges were responsible for listening to the arguments of the prosecution and defense, the witnesses' statements, and the sentencing. In practice, the judges met together during any given trial only for the initial accusation and final sentencing; the management of each trial was delegated to a single judge, who listened to the arguments and witnesses and perhaps played a leading role in deciding the guilt or innocence of the accused. Of the thirty-seven extant trials, none was delegated to prior Nuño; they were roughly evenly divided between Sánchez de la Fuente and Sánchez de la Calancha.[35] The court met in the audience room of the prior, at least for the accusation and sentencing; references in the trials indicate that the judges convoked the court Monday through Saturday for a morning sentence at terce and again for a session "in the afternoon."

With the accused imprisoned and notified to prepare a defense, the trial began. The inquisitors, prosecutor, defense attorney and solicitor,

---

[31] This is discussed in greater detail below.

[32] See, for example, Isabel de Montalbán and Gutiérrez, AHN Inquis. legajo 158, expediente 5. In this case the child testified in her own defense, but the family to which she was assigned did not testify.

[33] A useful analysis of the auto de fe is available in Maureen Flynn, "Mimesis of the Last Judgment: The Spanish *Auto de fe*," *Sixteenth Century Journal* 22, 2 (1991), 281–297.

[34] It seems improbable that these small cells could have held hundreds of prisoners, which also suggests that those exiled left town soon after their sentencing.

[35] There is no specific record of delegating trials, but the practice is apparent in references throughout the trials to one particular judge who listens to witnesses and shepherds the case through court.

and bailiff were all present at the initial hearing. The judges asked the bailiff to bring in the defendant, and the accused for the first time stood before the court and the prosecutor. A scrivener or notary was present to record events, and additional witnesses, usually *clérigos*, or servants of the friary, were also present. The prosecutor read his statement of accusation, prepared using information from the witnesses he had previously questioned. After reading the accusation, the judges asked the defendant to name a defense attorney and solicitor and allowed a set period of time to organize a defense, usually three to nine days. The accusation and statement of defense were added to the file newly created by the scrivener, and the accused returned to jail to talk with his or her attorney. In the time allowed, the defense prepared an opening statement responding to the charges of the prosecutor. From these two statements the judges decided whether or not there was sufficient reason to hold a trial.

Although it cannot be confirmed, it is plausible that the defense also began to identify and prepare witnesses before the trial officially began. Even if the defense did not begin to prepare until the official start of the trial, there was little likelihood that the attorney and his solicitor would have insufficient time to prepare. The court never reconvened after only three days, and rarely after nine. Occasionally, a file records that the defense requested additional time to prepare their case; more frequently, the trial resumes as much as four to six weeks later, but in all other respects without evidence of a break.[36] When the trial did resume, the defense attorney read the defendant's response before the full court, challenging the prosecution's charges point by point, and arguing pro forma that there was no need for a full trial. The prosecutor responded briefly that there was good reason to go to trial, and the judges then invariably approved the trial, allowing it to continue. It was presumably at this time that the judges decided which inquisitor would handle the day-to-day management of the case.

The process did not change substantially if the defendant were deceased or absent. Not all absent Guadalupenses faced active prosecution by the court; certainly the inquisitors made no attempt to track down or compel the appearance of these former residents. This reinforces the sense that the inquisitors were most concerned with eliminating a perceived nexus of Judaizing in Guadalupe itself. This is also consistent with the ad hoc and intensely local nature of these early inquisitorial courts.[37] In cases of absent defendants, then, the defense was charged to

---

[36] It seems likely that the delays were caused by the high volume of cases and small number of staff.

[37] Absent defendants included Rodrigo Alonso *tundidor*, AHN Inquis. legajo 132, expe-

the next of kin, who were responsible for appearing in court for the opening and closing of the trial, and for formally engaging the services of the resident defense attorney and solicitor. The Inquisition was a supremely legalistic organization, and no defendant could be without a defense. Family members were required merely to organize a pro forma case; while some testified for the defense themselves, they were under no obligation to do so. Coordinating at least a nominal defense was mandatory, however. If the family did not fulfill its responsibilities before the Holy Office, each family member could be cited for contempt, *rebeldía*, and imprisoned. The ritual of the inquisitorial trials demanded participation by both prosecution and defense to gain a secure answer and insure that justice was done, even if the defense's participation was obtained under duress. In the midst of the uncertainty involved in determining the validity of charges of Judaizing, the forms of the trial helped to routinize and clarify what was inherently amorphous and obscure. Beyond their historical or juridical importance, the legal procedures helped the inquisitors to organize and reshape Guadalupenses' understanding of one another and their place in society. Notably, a relative who helped to fulfill the Inquisition's formalized roles did not necessarily cast suspicion on himself or herself. Family members might engage the defense attorney and solicitor to defend deceased relatives, for example, and then serve as witnesses for the prosecution.[38]

Witnesses for both the prosecution and the defense were judged in part on the quality of the testimony—whether it was personal knowledge, eyewitness knowledge, belief, or hearsay. However, Henry Charles Lea noted that these distinctions, which had their origins in canon law, and ultimately Roman law, were considered crucial only for the defense. While theoretically the prosecutor had to provide two witnesses for each accusation, and hearsay evidence was insufficient in and of itself to prove a case, the prosecutor was in fact often given more leeway. Still, in Guadalupe the defense made every attempt to use these criteria to discredit testimony for the prosecution. In theory, these classifications were designed to provide an objective standard for evaluating testimony; in practice, the attitudes of the inquisitors could weaken the effect of those strictures.

The process of collecting testimony, particularly for the prosecution, began even before the official start of the trial. Names for prosecution witnesses could be culled from references made in reconciliations during the time of grace, or townspeople could offer to testify against

---

diente 11, and the Narices family, ibid. 177, expediente 10. For more on Rodrigo Alonso, see below in the section on the autos de fe.

[38] See the trial of Mari Flores, ibid. 148, expediente 9.

specific conversos. Conversos already imprisoned could also be asked or ordered to speak at the trials of others. Family members were customarily asked to testify against the accused; since a refusal to do so could indicate one's own guilt, siblings and children often spoke out against their family, if only briefly and in vague terms. Spouses, however, never testified for the prosecution or the defense. Notes posted on the church doors asked these witnesses to appear before the Holy Office by a certain date or risk being accused of contempt. But the prosecution also found voluntary witnesses or encouraged people to speak against a particular person, since testimony also came from individuals who would be difficult to track down any other way—pilgrims, most obviously.[39]

The Inquisition also benefited from the accumulation of witnesses' testimony. A witness who proved helpful in one case might stay on to testify against others. Although people with a direct bearing on any one case might be relatively small, willing participants could recall events or hearsay related to almost any significant case the court tried. Servants, in particular, provided an intimate picture of family life that the Inquisition mined extensively. Not only did they observe converso families at close range, but they seem not to have felt any strong loyalty toward their former masters. In addition, servants frequently compared notes on their common experiences, meaning that they could provide hearsay evidence against the masters of their friends, as well as firsthand testimony against their own masters. For example, Isabel, the daughter of Juan Vaquero and servant of Alonso López trapero, was a key witness in the trial against her former master, Ruy González de la Corte.[40] Once she had testified against her own former masters, however, she went on to testify in other cases as well. Less than two weeks later, Isabel was in front of the court again, testifying against Mari Sánchez, wife of Juan Esteban de Maestre Pedro. She did not work for the accused, but she had heard about their Judaizing practices from one of Mari's servants.[41] In short, the Holy Office utilized temporal and spiritual coercion, together with the active support of some townspeople, to locate prosecution witnesses and persuade them to testify.

Finding witnesses for the defense was more complex. Friends, family members, and servants might be called in to testify, and defendants often suggested possible acquaintances, clients, and others who, it was hoped, would testify favorably. Witnesses requested by the defense may

---

[39] See, for example, ibid. 154, expediente 20.

[40] Ibid. 155, expediente 13.

[41] Ibid. 183, expediente 19. The first testimony was entered into the record on April 20, 1485; the second, May 3. It is true that hearsay evidence was worth less than eyewitness testimony, but a sizable number of people willing to testify to the Judaizing practices of the defendant was always a benefit to the prosecution.

have been impelled to appear, since not all seemed favorably disposed to speak for the accused. Even with that assistance the task of the defense was challenging, since, at Queen Isabel's insistence, defendants could not know the names of their accusers. Isabel's most significant innovation in inquisitorial practices hinted at her belief that prosecution witnesses might hesitate to speak openly.[42] It also meant that, unbeknownst to the defense, witnesses might speak grudgingly for the accused and then testify vigorously for the prosecution.[43] The advantages that this afforded to the prosecution are manifest in extant trials. Prosecution witnesses could speak freely, while witnesses for the defense may have worried that their defense of another might ultimately work against themselves. The organization and coercive force behind the prosecution meant that the prosecutor could produce and interview all his witnesses in one day. The solicitor, however, could only find and bring in a few witnesses at a time over several days, suggesting the relative difficulty of locating people willing or able to testify productively for the defense.

Whether speaking for the prosecution or for the defense, witnesses' testimonies were officially recorded in the presence of the inquisitor presiding over the case, often after the witnesses had already provided the information once before. At that time, those testifying would come before the inquisitor, swear an oath, and, in the presence of a notary and probably the prosecutor or solicitor for the defense, relate their testimony. The testimony of the defense and the prosecution differed markedly, both in content and in form. The role of the solicitor in an inquisitorial trial was to refute, by logical argument, the charges of the prosecution. Defense witnesses, then, were most important in challenging or denying acts of Judaizing charged by the prosecutor. Only secondarily did the defense attempt to prove positively that the accused was a good Christian, and then most frequently in the context of their general reputation within the community as a whole. The solicitor sought refutation of specific accusations, and so defense witnesses were asked to respond to a series of questions that addressed the accusations made by the prosecuting attorney in his opening statement. The solicitor prepared the questions for the witnesses in advance and presented them to the court. The inquisitor or notary administered the oath to the witnesses and officially questioned them.

Defense questions always began with a request that the witness explain how long he or she had known the accused, and in what context

[42] See Peggy Liss, *Isabel the Queen. Her Life and Times* (Oxford: Oxford University Press, 1992), chap. 10.

[43] See Lea, *Historia*; Beinart, *Conversos*; and Yitzhak Baer, *History*.

they knew each other; the solicitor always closed his questioning with a request that the witness comment on the reputation of the accused. Additional questions were formulated as a list of Judaizing acts which the defense witness could refute. For example, a witness might be asked to confirm that the accused did not wear clean clothes on Saturdays. In addition, defense witnesses were asked to confirm the accused's participation in the Christian community. In either case, witnesses might simply agree or disagree, or else provide a more elaborate explanation within the narrow topic provided. The solicitor also frequently asked the witness to specify how he or she had learned this information, to insure that the defense was not relying merely on hearsay. For example, Juana González, daughter of Martín Gutiérrez, had been accused of asking alms, *limosnas*, for conversos in what was described as a "traditional Jewish fashion," that is, solely for the benefit of New Christians. The solicitor, therefore, asked his witness "if he knew, saw, believed, or heard tell that Juana González was a Christian and a person of much kindness and charity, and that she asked *limosnas* like other Christians and gave them to both Old Christians and conversos."[44] The structured nature of defense testimony meant that the solicitor only learned about that which might aid the accused and minimized the possibility that a defense witness might inadvertently introduce additional incriminating evidence.

Prosecution witnesses, on the other hand, were free to speak on whatever topic they wished, once they, like the defense witnesses, had taken an oath in front of the cross and on the gospels. Witnesses for the prosecution apparently spoke without receiving specific guidance, and their statements reflected a broader range of concerns and interests. The more unstructured format afforded these witnesses greater opportunity to discuss their concerns about any unusual or unacceptable behavior, and prosecution witnesses explained at length their opinions on the personality and character of the accused. This relative latitude to discuss what interested them also provided a sharper image of the witnesses themselves. In particular, a witness's willingness to participate was reflected to a certain extent by the length of his or her testimony. Some witnesses, like servants, clearly expressed a certain resentment of the defendant, or a suspicion of the depth of the defendant's Christian beliefs. At the same time, the grudging or compelled participation of family members was indicated by their terse commentary, which served more to exonerate themselves than to condemn their parents or relatives.

The statements of witnesses for the prosecution also differed from

---

[44] AHN Inquis. legajo 154, expediente 20.

the statements of defense witnesses in the more frequent changes and retractions evident in prosecution statements. In some cases, a witness offered a second, supplementary statement. It is probable that the second testimony was offered later, after the publication of the witnesses' testimonies.[45] After a witness heard the testimony offered by other witnesses, or after further consideration of his or her own attitudes toward the accused, he or she might make a second statement for the prosecution. The witness's two statements might overlap in some details, but usually the second statement was much harsher and more damning than the first. Occasionally, but less frequently, a prosecution witness would retract his or her testimony. On a very few occasions, the solicitor proved that the testimony entered described someone other than the defendant. In other cases, the witness apparently decided that he or she preferred not to speak against the defendant. Generally, those who retracted their testimony were family members, and any number of personal reasons might have informed that decision. It is possible that retractions also occurred after the publication of witnesses' testimonies, although the record does not make that clear.

When the inquisitors approved a case and determined that it should go forward, they provided a set date by which all testimony had to be presented. During that time the defendant was also free to confess to any additional heretical acts and ask forgiveness for them. This deadline, like the others, could be changed relatively easily. In some cases a record exists in a defendant's file noting that the defense requested an extension; in other cases, the dates of the witnesses' testimony indicate that this phase of the trial lasted longer than was originally stipulated.[46] Once the prosecution and defense finished identifying and interviewing witnesses, however, the pace of the trial quickened. The inquisitor in charge of the case officially confirmed that the prosecutor and the solicitor were finished presenting witnesses, and he authorized the publication, *publicación*, of the witnesses' testimonies. Inquisition records were kept hidden from the public, but during the *publicación* the prosecutor and solicitor formally presented each other with the testimony they had collected. Both the prosecution and the defense were given three to nine days to present their materials.

With the testimony of the opposition's witnesses in hand, both parties could begin to draw up their responses. At the same time, the publication of the witnesses limited the freedom of the accused to change his or her approach to the case. The court reasoned that a

[45] See Lea, *Historia*, 2:555.
[46] Of course, the defense lawyer or solicitor might have requested the extension in those cases as well, but it is impossible to determine that now.

reconciliation made after the accused had heard the generic charges against him or her might be genuine, and not merely an act of self-interest. But once specific details of Judaizing acts had been mentioned in individual statements, there was little sympathy for a reconciliation that mentioned only and exactly those new acts charged in the witnesses' statements. Such a reconciliation did little or nothing to change one's sentence. The inquisitors held little sympathy for defendants who did not fully and humbly confess their guilt. If the accused had aroused particular suspicion, and there existed significant discrepancies between the defendant's claims and those of the prosecution's witnesses, the accused might be tortured in an attempt to learn the truth about his or her activities.

Of all the stereotypes surrounding the Inquisition in Spain, that of the specter of torture is one of the most ominous and persistent.[47] As in other, secular courts throughout western Europe in the medieval and early modern periods, torture was an accepted part of the judicial procedure of the Inquisition. Yet the inquisitors themselves understood the paradoxical nature of testimony gained by coercion, whether that coercion was threatened or performed. The fear that led the witness to speak the truth could also lead him or her to lie, and much of the inquisitorial procedure surrounding the use of torture was designed to insure that the torture victim spoke the truth, as much as it was designed to protect the accused from abuses on the part of the inquisitors.[48] The inquisitors followed a specific procedure before, during, and after torture, beginning with the decision to subject a defendant to torment. Like inquisitorial procedures generally, elaborate ritual was used to control, structure, and make meaningful both the torture and its results—to convince the inquisitors that they would be gaining a glimpse of a hidden reality. What motivated the court to resort to torture is not always obvious; some serious offenders were not tortured, while others charged with relatively less serious offenses were. Like the ordeal in earlier periods, torture seems to have been used most often in cases where serious, irresolvable discrepancies arose between the charges of the prosecution and the counterclaims of the defense.[49]

The actual torture of a defendant, with its heavy ritualism and delib-

---

[47] The best introduction to the subject is Edward Peters, *Torture*, expanded ed. (Philadelphia: University of Pennsylvania Press, 1996). Also available is Henry Charles Lea, *Torture*, intro. by Edward Peters (Philadelphia: University of Pennsylvania Press, 1973).

[48] See Jean-Pierre Dedieu, "Los cuatro tiempos de la inquisición," in Bennassar, *La inquisición española*, 15–39; and Lea, *Historia*, 1:195. Guadalupe and its sister ad hoc court in Belalcázar are notable for their speed, efficiency, and brutality.

[49] See Robert Bartlett, *Trial by Fire and Water: The Medieval Judicial Ordeal* (Oxford: Clarendon Press and Oxford University Press, 1986).

erateness, was designed to be a psychological as well as a physical torment. The torture session began by removing the prisoner from the
prison. Escorted by the bailiff, the inquisitors, the prosecutor, and the
defense attorney, the accused was led to the door of the torture chamber. There he or she was asked for the first time to confess, although in
no extant trials did the accused do so. Then the prisoner was led to the
escalera, the only torture instrument used in Guadalupe. The prisoner
was stripped and tightly bound to the *escalera* at the arms and legs and
then positioned so that the feet were higher than the head. This in itself
was quite humiliating and painful, with the leather restraints intended
to cut off one's circulation almost completely. At this point, the prisoner
was asked a second time to tell all. A few confessed at this point, but
most often the prisoner continued to refuse to speak, and the torture
began in earnest. A jar of water, measuring slightly more than a liter,
was poured into the mouth of the accused, provoking a sensation of
choking and suffocation. Intermittently, the accused was allowed to
catch his or her breath to enable a confession. The severity of the session was measured in how many jars of water were used. Lea notes
that a typical amount was one to three jars, but when recorded in the
Inquisition files in Guadalupe the amount was generally six to eight
jars.[50] There is no evidence that the court in Guadalupe extended its
torture sessions over more than one date, even when the accused admitted nothing under torture.[51]

After the torture was finished, the accused was led or carried back to
the prison. The ordeal was not complete, however. Because testimony
gained under torture was seen as suspect, one had to ratify one's testimony after the fact for it to be legally binding. In Guadalupe, this
meant that at least one full day after the torture, the accused came
before the court in its audience chamber and confirmed the statements
made under torture. This final act of the torture session demonstrated
the Holy Office's desire for certainty and clarity even while revealing
the inquisitors' suspicion of their own methods. According to the court's
instructions, this second statement had to be made free from any threat
of torture.[52] Because of the physical distance from the torture chamber,
the accused appeared genuinely penitent and willing to cooperate freely,
thus creating the vision of the compliant, willing penitent that the inquisitors wished to see. This willing penitent embodied the resolution

[50] Lea, *Historia*, 2:513–514.
[51] AHN Inquis. legajo 184, expediente 2, is only one example. Theoretically, the Inquisition courts in Spain could only torture an individual once; this provision was skirted,
however, by "interrupting" a so-called single torture session for up to a period of days.
There is no evidence this happened in Guadalupe, however.
[52] Lea, *Historia*, 2:524.

of ambiguity into difference that was a hallmark of the inquisitorial court. In theory, one could retract statements made under torture at this time, although the continued implied threat of coercion probably dissuaded most defendants from recanting. In fact, rather than merely confirm what he or she had said under torture, the accused often volunteered additional names and information.

Torture was at best a difficult method of achieving the court's goals. While brute force might provide missing details about local Judaizing, no one could avoid the problematic question of how the testimony had been gained. This was clear not only in the demand that the accused "ratify" his or her testimony later, but also in the progress of the case after a defendant was tortured. Testimony given under torture was not seen as freely given; this meant that any confession of wrongdoing was not sincere and did not prevent the accused from being found guilty and unrepentant of Judaizing, and thus relaxed, *relajada*, into the hands of the political authorities for execution at an auto de fe.[53]

Torture as it was practiced by the inquisitors represented a compromise between the desire to uncover the extent of heresy and fear of the effect of coercion on the testimony of the accused. The highly formalized actions surrounding the use of torture indicate both its significance and the profound ambivalence with which the inquisitors viewed it. Inquisitors believed that heretics might go to great lengths to hide their heretical actions and beliefs, and that in some cases only torture would convince heretics to reveal their wrongdoing. Officials of the Holy Office also understood, however, that physical force might lead some prisoners to fabricate accounts of heretical activity. In Guadalupe, torture was reserved for those cases in which the inquisitors confronted the greatest differences between the accusations of prosecution witnesses and the protestations of innocence made by the defense. Only then could the seeming, superficial clarity of a confession made in the torture chamber outweigh the inquisitors' lingering suspicions.

RENDERING A VERDICT

After the witnesses' statements were published and any torture carried out, the trial moved into its final stages. In a few cases, usual legal practices were cut short by the decision to render a verdict through compurgation. In traditional Germanic law, compurgation was the process whereby one's innocence was proven through the sworn statements of others. By the end of the Middle Ages compurgation had largely fallen into disuse in Europe, but the practice was retained in

---

[53] Ibid., 2:487.

some situations. In the extant inquisitorial records, compurgation was used only when the accused was strongly suspected to be innocent. The accused would bring five or ten witnesses before the court, all of whom swore on the cross or the gospels that the defendant was innocent. If all the compurgators testified to the innocence of the defendant, the case was closed and the accused released. The force of compurgation came in the value placed on one's oath, particularly when witnessed by God.

The only extant case that includes a compurgation is that of a devoutly Christian conversa. Rather than fasting as Jews did, by not eating until sundown, Mari Gutiérrez avoided meat and ate only bread and water on one day of the week as part of an oath to God to help heal her son. Similarly, witnesses for both the prosecution and the defense noted that they saw her only as a good Christian woman, rather than as a conversa. After the witnesses' statements were read, the court called for a compurgation, nine people testified to her character, and Mari was released shortly thereafter.[54]

In Guadalupe, compurgation seems to have been used only to ratify and publicly establish the inquisitors' conviction of innocence. In no other extant trial was there so little evidence of Jewish activity. In a second trial, where a man named Alonso Andrés Trujillano was found innocent, the trial was completed without compurgation; but in that case there were slightly more significant accusations on the part of the prosecution.[55] It is difficult to draw firm conclusions from only two examples, but the rarity of compurgation suggests that it occurred only when the innocence of the accused was apparent to the inquisitors. The gender of the participants may also have made a difference. The trial that ended in compurgation was of a woman, but the two extant trials where the accused was absolved of all wrongdoing after facing the inquisitors were men. Sadly, Mari's adamant insistence on her innocence— she denied even knowing what "the great fast" of the Jews was—came at a high price; the inquisitors preceded Mari's compurgation with a torture session. It is possible, though, that she was tortured because she had said that the devil had brought the inquisitors to Guadalupe.[56]

Except in the rare instance of compurgation, the trial moved into its

<hr />

[54] Trial of Mari Gutiérrez, wife of Gonzalo Bueno, AHN Inquis. legajo 156, expediente 10.

[55] Trial of Alonso Andrés Trujillano, AHN Inquis. legajo 132, expediente 18.

[56] Trial of Mari Gutiérrez, wife of Gonzalo Bueno, AHN Inquis. legajo 156, expediente 10. For her statement that she "non sabe que cosa es el tal ayuno e niega aver lo ayunado," see 3r. Her torture session follows the pattern evident with others, namely, that torture was employed when there was a significant discrepancy between the statements of the accused and those of the prosecutor. Mari Gutiérrez was so confident of her devotion to Christianity that she did not even file a reconciliation during the *tiempo de gracia*.

final stages with the closing statements of the solicitor and prosecutor. The court reconvened as a whole in the audience chamber, and both the defense and the prosecution spoke. First the solicitor responded to the statements provided by the prosecution's witnesses. If the accused decided to confess all, hoping for leniency, the solicitor indicated this by asking for the inquisitors' mercy; otherwise, the solicitor proceeded witness by witness, responding to and challenging or explaining the charges leveled by each one. To close, he asserted once again that the prosecutor had not proven his charges against the accused, and that the accused should be released. In response, the prosecutor issued a short statement, affirming the strength of his case and refuting the claims of the defense. The court retired once again, usually for three days, to decide upon a verdict and sentence.

At this point in the trial, the documents fall silent. Often all that appears is the final, official statement given at the next auto de fe, summarizing the presentations of the prosecution and defense, and giving the court's conclusions—usually a summary of the misdeeds of the defendant and the court's sentence. This very polished document indicates little about what happened in between and is often dated weeks or months after the trial must have been decided. In only one case were the intermediate scribal notes preserved, and this evidence, while unique and thus perhaps suspect, does provide one example of the functioning of the court in between the closing arguments and the sentencing. Three days after the inquisitors heard the closing arguments, the court reconvened. The accused and her husband were brought before the court, and the judges pronounced the defendant guilty. At the same time the inquisitors ordered that both she and her husband be exiled from the Puebla. It is noteworthy that her spouse was sentenced with her, even though he was being tried separately. After the sentencing, they were returned to prison, where they waited until the next auto de fe. Only then was the full, formal sentence read.[57]

Although the first generation of inquisitorial courts were generally harsher than those of later years, the verdicts rendered by the inquisitorial court at Guadalupe are notable in the history of the Inquisition for their relative severity.[58] Only a lucky few were totally absolved of Judaizing by the court. The absolved were permitted to continue their lives as before, the records of their cases were sealed, and all involved were forbidden to speak of the trial. In Andrés Alonso Trujillano's case, for example, his innocence was so clear that the prosecution and the defense agreed to dispense with the traditional closing arguments, the

[57] AHN Inquis.
[58] See, for example, Dedieu, "Los Cuatro Tiempos," 16–21.

court found him innocent, and he was simply enjoined to obey the church.[59]

But the vast majority of those tried by the court were not found innocent. Seventy-one people were found guilty, "relaxed" to local officials, and executed in one of the autos de fe held in 1485. Another forty-five were found guilty either posthumously or in absentia and were burned in effigy at the autos. Only seventeen were found guilty of relatively serious offences and were given a perpetual jail sentence. Some thirty-eight persons were found "partially guilty" and exiled from the town and its surroundings for a distance of ten leagues. Finally, twenty-five were reconciled, absolved, or given only a minor penance.[60]

The distinctions between the acts or perceived intentions of those exiled, imprisoned, or killed were nebulous. Since the goal of the court was to seek out and eliminate wrong intentions as well as wrong acts, the court's findings were particularly dependent on the inquisitors' perception of the attitude of the defendant toward living a proper Christian life. Throughout the Holy Office's tenure in Guadalupe, the court showed a strong suspicion of the intentions of those tried and was unwilling to concede the innocence of the accused. Distrust of conversos, though, was balanced with an eagerness to see contrition. While not without its dangers, apparently sincere contrition and cooperation with the inquisitors was generally rewarded. The sentences given by the Inquisition, therefore, were the product of a complicated, sometimes contradictory mental calculus, where perceptions of intention, behavior, and sincerity all played a role. The difference among execution, imprisonment, and exile depended on the inquisitors' vision of the accused as capable of redemption, or as an obstructionist to the goals of the Holy Office; as an honest, contrite Christian or as a dangerous heretic.

One sentence that was unusually frequent in Guadalupe, though atypical of the Holy Office in general, was that of perpetual exile, which was usually paired with a penalty of twenty to one hundred lashes. This sentence accompanied a verdict that can only be described as "partially guilty." The inquisitors declared that the prosecutor had not fully proved

---

[59] AHN Inquis. legajo 132, expediente 18.

[60] These are the numbers provided by Testón Núñez and Hernández Bermejo in "La Inquisición." Thirty sentences of the 226 New Christians tried were left unrecorded. Other historians, including Diego de Ecija, *Libro*, and Fidel Fita, "La Inquisición," have arrived at other numbers; Diego de Ecija, for example, stated that the vast majority of those tried by the court were exiled. Testón Núñez and Hernández Bermejo were the first to use records available at the Archivo Histórico Nacional, however. An execution rate of 30 percent, while grave, does not quite match the myth of the Inquisition, and of course the instances of torture were much lower.

his case, and that the accused was absolved. However, due to suspicions raised during the trial, the accused could not be permitted to go free. Instead, the court seized all the goods of the accused and exiled him or her to a distance of ten leagues.[61] The ambivalence of this verdict is striking. If the accused were innocent, then there should have been no punishment. If, on the other hand, there were suspicions about the devotion of the accused to Christianity, merely exiling him or her seems to have accomplished little, except to disperse any supposed "converso community" that might exist, and possibly to encourage active Judaizers to form new "heretical communities" throughout Castile. The verdict may have indicated a belief that the accused could live a Christian life and was not truly a heretic, but that his or her past had indelibly affected the ability to function within the community. Lea also discussed the sentence of exile, calling it less severe than a sentence of perpetual imprisonment, although its relative severity is difficult to determine. In secular Iberian courts, a sentence of exile was not usually permanent; this suggests that exile may have been used as a form of punishment, equivalent to a whipping, rather than as a means of reform.[62] Separation from extended family, community, and by extension economic and social support—in addition to the loss of all property faced by all those found guilty—was a grave punishment by any account. Indeed, this may have been the intended effect of exile—an economic and political punishment for what prior Nuño and his Jeronymites may have seen as a political and economic problem.

Like perpetual imprisonment, exile also had its equivalents in the secular courts. The municipal ordinances, *Ordenanzas Municipales*, compiled for the Puebla in the fifteenth century, make occasional reference to exile as a punishment, particularly in later recensions. There is no reference in the *Ordenanzas* to perpetual exile as a punishment, although occasionally the period of exile is left unspecified.[63] Lea stated that a typical inquisitorial sentence of exile was not indefinite but was for a specific period, usually two years. What happened to those exiled? For many, surprisingly little. Unlike most inquisitorial courts, the inquisitors at Guadalupe did not include specific instructions in their sentences as to the ritual of exile or who would be responsible for carrying out the

---

[61] The distance of one league could vary but was approximately equivalent to three miles. According to the twenty-first edition of the *Dictionary of the Real Academia*, one league equals a little over 5.57 km.

[62] Lea, *Historia*, 2:639. The term for this was switch or branch, *cepo*.

[63] Most importantly, in AMG codex 78. The earliest collection of *Ordenanzas*, from approximately the mid-fifteenth century—AMG codex 76—made no reference to exile as a punishment.

sentence. The documents themselves are largely silent in this regard, although in at least one trial the inquisitors announced that the guilty party must leave Guadalupe and its surroundings within nine days of the sentence.[64] In this case, however, there was also no record that the defendant was sentenced to any whippings; the public lashings that usually accompanied a sentence of exile would have been carried out either at the time of exile or on December 3, when the sentences of exile were read.[65] Apparently, it was left to the friary to insure that the exiled had actually left; the only public act involving those exiled was the publication of a decree of exile, which was read the day the inquisitors and their entourage returned to Toledo.[66]

Equally ambiguous was a sentence of perpetual imprisonment, the rarest sentence of the court. All conversos sentenced to perpetual imprisonment had been found guilty and might have been burned at the stake. In these instances, however, the inquisitors decided not to execute the guilty party because of extenuating circumstances. Sentences of imprisonment were given out only at the first and last autos, and this clustering also suggests the unusual role of imprisonment. After three women were imprisoned at the first auto de fe on June 11, the next sentence of imprisonment was delayed until November 20, when sixteen men and women were incarcerated.[67] That is, after an initial flurry of last-minute semipardons, the court became less inclined to a median position or held those more difficult cases until the end.[68]

Mencía Alfonso, wife of Diego González the shoemaker, provides one example of how the court might award the sentence of perpetual imprisonment.[69] Mencía was accused not only of observing the Jewish Sabbath and the major Jewish festivals, but of scoffing at Christianity, saying that "everything the Christians observe is a mockery except to keep the law of Moses until the Savior comes." She denied making the

---

[64] Trial of Juana González, AHN Inquis. legajo 154, expediente 20. Her husband's role as a trapero and associate of Alonso de Córdoba may have affected the inquisitors' decision. It is unclear whether sentences of exile were executed quickly—as is implied here—or whether the exiled had until the auto de fe to leave Guadalupe.

[65] Ibid.

[66] Rubío, *Historia*, 116. Rubío's information came from Ecija, *Libro*.

[67] These figures are from Diego de Ecija, *Libro*, and were repeated by both Fidel Fita, "La Inquisición," and Germán Rubío, *Historia*. The records of files sent to the inquisitorial court in 1513 do not allow us to check these figures, since the scrivener included neither the date of sentencing nor, in some cases, the outcome of the trial. AHN clero legajo 1423, expediente 93.

[68] The rhythm of the autos de fe during 1485 will be discussed in greater detail below.

[69] AHN Inquis. legajo 165, expediente 9. Diego González was the son of Juan Esteban de la Barrera.

statement, but under torture she admitted to saying it, claiming that she had forgotten it before.[70] In their findings, the inquisitors found her a heretic and apostate. She was excommunicated, all her goods were seized, and she was condemned to burn at an auto de fe. At her initial sentencing, however, Mencía shed so many tears and demonstrated such penitence and desire for reform that the court absolved her rather than execute her. Instead, the inquisitors sentenced her to a perpetual jail sentence and ordered her to complete her penance there.[71]

In many ways these "intermediate" sentences were not wholly consistent with the early activity of the court. One cannot deny the severity of the Holy Office in Guadalupe—condemning 71 persons to death—but a comparison with the court in nearby Belalcázar indicates the relative frequency of semipardons in Guadalupe. Of the 226 people sentenced by the court in Guadalupe, 80 were reconciled, exiled, imprisoned, given penance, or absolved; 71 were executed; and 45 were either burned in effigy or exhumed and their bones burned.[72] In Belalcázar, on the other hand, 107 of the 110 persons tried were executed, burned in effigy, or posthumously burned. There are no extant examples of any reconciliation, penance, exile, or imprisonment in the latter court, which included some of the same personnel and operated immediately following the court in Guadalupe.[73]

It would be a mistake, however, to assume that a sentence of perpetual imprisonment meant that the guilty party ended his or her life in jail. As with many of the "perpetual" punishments meted out in fifteenth-century Guadalupe, leniency was often extended to the guilty. In Mencía's case, her file states that on January 21, 1488, she was released—less than three years after she was imprisoned. Other extant cases with a sentence of perpetual imprisonment indicate the same clemency.[74] This parallels secular sentences meted out by the friary, where perpetual imprisonment or exile was commuted to a much shorter period, based on the petitions of those involved or of their families.[75]

---

[70] By claiming she had forgotten the statement, she attempted to explain why she had not confessed the remark during the *tiempo de gracia*. During the trial she also admitted doubts that the Eucharist contained the Body of Christ.

[71] Ibid.

[72] Testón Núñez and Hernández Bermejo, "La Inquisición," 107. The fate of the missing 30 tried by the court is unknown.

[73] The sentences of the remaining 3 people tried in Belalcázar remain unknown. Of the 107 conversos executed in Belalcázar, 60 were exhumed and their bones burned, 16 burned in effigy, and 31 burned to death at the auto de fe. Ibid., 106–108.

[74] AHN Inquis. legajo 181, expediente 16. Mari Ruiz, widow of Francisco Arróquez, was released two days earlier, on January 19.

[75] The *Ordenanzas Municipales* demanded perpetual imprisonment in some cases.

Not everyone escaped with their lives. Nearly a third of those tried were found guilty and executed at an auto de fe. Although almost all had submitted reconciliations at the "time of grace," most had demonstrated little remorse during the trial. These defendants had denied any additional charges of Judaizing suggested by the prosecutor and claimed to be innocent of all charges. The infamous Manuel González of the Mesón Blanco, for example, refused to admit any wrong until compelled by mounting evidence. He attempted to excuse his practice of keeping the Jewish Sabbath and of maintaining a kosher kitchen by saying that he had not realized that it was wrong; he added that the number of Jews who stayed in his home were there because he ran an inn, rather than because of any affinity with his practices. His circumcision was the decision of his father or grandfather, he argued. Manuel even attempted to explain the "Jewish" prayer book found in his possession as belonging to his wife from her first marriage.[76] Only when he was tortured did he admit to willing participation in secret Sabbath services and other acts of Judaizing. In their sentence, the inquisitors noted Manuel González's obvious reluctance to participate or admit to any wrongdoing. The Holy Office ruled that González followed the law of Moses and was a *judío entero*, and it ordered him executed at the auto de fe on July 31.[77]

The sentences of execution meted out to Manuel González and others were an innovation, present for the first time in the Inquisition established by Fernando and Isabel. Medieval, ecclesiastical Inquisitions were not authorized to carry out sentences of execution. Clerics who served as inquisitors for the Spanish Crown were, like their predecessors, not permitted to shed blood. Unlike its medieval antecedents, however, the modern Spanish Inquisition was a royal institution, under the authority of the Crown rather than the pope. Through this secularized inquisitorial hierarchy, inquisitors were empowered to coordinate their sentences with local secular officials, who then executed the condemned. For this reason conversos who were found guilty were literally identified as having been relaxed, *relajado*, or remanded to the secular authorities. From the moment of its arrival to the last auto de fe, the Inquisition bound together religious and political authority, jurisdiction, and interests, both in Guadalupe and elsewhere.

However, the *Actas Capitulares* provide examples of clemency. One was the pardon of the sentence of perpetual exile for Juan de Segovia (AMG codex 74 bis, 1v) and Alonso de Córdoba (ibid., 3v), mentioned in the last chapter.

[76] AHN Inquis. legajo 154, expediente 20, 2r. This prayer book, a collection of prayers using Hebrew Bible images and the word "Adonay" for God, is discussed in chapter 2.

[77] Ibid.

The Autos de Fe

Guadalupe was witness to no less than seven acts of faith, autos de fe, between June 11 and November 22. These highly ritualized events presented the actions of the court to the public and made clear to everyone the inquisitors' vision of Guadalupe and its residents. In the auto de fe the inquisitors' gaze became the audience's as well, reflecting to them a new view of their town as primarily and permanently divided between devout Old Christians and dangerous, heretical New Christians. At the same time, the auto de fe served as the public face for the Inquisition— the moment in which it drew together and presented the temporal powers who carried out the sentence and the condemned, now firmly under the guidance of the ecclesiastical power of the inquisitor (fig. 4). These symbols were particularly vividly wrought in Guadalupe, where one man—prior Nuño de Arévalo—was invested with inquisitorial, spiritual, and temporal power. Prior Nuño's multiple functions as inquisitor, prior of the friary, temporal lord of Guadalupe, and spiritual authority for the town were a unique combination in the history of the Inquisition.

During the autos de fe, a platform was constructed for the officials of the Inquisition and the condemned. Some of the autos were held in front of the church doors, at the literal and spiritual center of town; others, presumably for reasons of space, took place outside the city walls, on the meadows just beyond the Eras Gate (fig. 5). Prior-inquisitor Nuño de Arévalo presided over the ceremonies; next to him were his fellow inquisitors, Doctor Sánchez de la Fuente and *licenciado* Pedro Sánchez de la Calancha, looking down on the condemned and on the crowds of pilgrims and Guadalupenses packed around the platform. Nearby on the platform were the prosecutor, Diego Fernández de Zamora, and several notaries and clerics. Also present was the scrivener of record, who read the sentences of the court. When the autos were held at the entrance to the friary, the scrivener climbed just uphill of the church doors to the cemetery, a position that would have placed him at the highest point in the plaza. One by one the scrivener read out the summary and sentence of each case "in a loud and intelligible voice"; these generally ran one to two folios. Finally, the condemned were led together to the catafalque, and burned to death.

The evocative presence of the autos de fe was not limited to those standing in the plaza; the smoke from the effigies, books, and burning bodies rose from the plaza and was visible for miles around, an impressive feat in this hilly country. The rising smoke carried the presence of the Inquisition far beyond Guadalupe itself, bringing the vision of heretical activity to Iberians far beyond the Marian shrine. One man, Rod-

FIGURE 4. *Auto de fé Presided over by St. Dominic de Guzmán* (1485) by Pedro Berruguete. Museo del Prado, Madrid (photo by Erich Lessing/ Art Resource, NY).

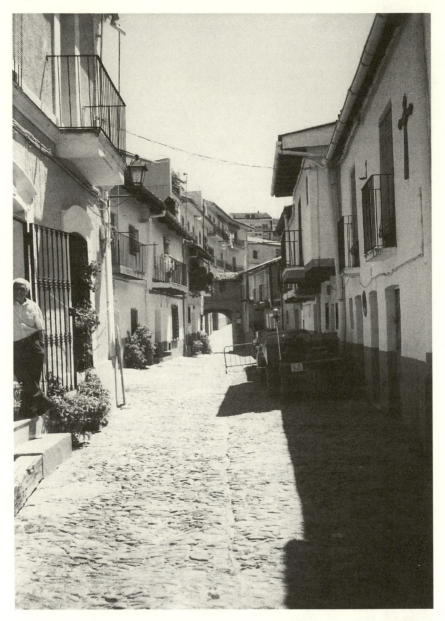

FIGURE 5. Eras Gate. The street, calle Eras, led pilgrims to the church;
beyond the gate were the meadows that held some of Guadalupe's
autos de fe. Photo by the author.

rigo Alonso, saw the smoke as he stopped over in Herrera del Duque. Alonso, a native of Guadalupe, was traveling to the shrine from his current home in Chillón in response to the inquisitors' summons. As one witness described it almost three years later: "He [the witness] saw [Rodrigo Alonso] in this town . . . the day that they burned those from Guadalupe and he saw him stand watching . . . when the smoke rose; and this witness says that they told him that his brother Diego had been burned at the stake and he left in fear."[78] The account, confirmed by four separate witnesses as well as by Rodrigo Alonso himself, suggests that the smoke was visible some 50 to 60 km away.[79]

The pattern of activity of the inquisitors is revealed to a degree in the timing of the autos de fe during the year. The initial auto on June 11 included New Christians who were subjected to a variety of punishments. Nine conversos—many of them the wealthy traperos who had caused prior Nuño such difficulty—were burned to death, three women were sentenced to perpetual punishment, and one innkeeper named Orejuela was burned in effigy.[80] Not until the last pair of autos were such a variety of punishments meted out again, and it seems that after this initial flurry of severe and varied activity the inquisitors planned the remaining autos more systematically. After the first auto de fe, the remaining six came in two groups: the first at the end of July and the beginning of August, and the second at the end of November. The first cluster of autos de fe only included conversos who were condemned to death, either in person or in absentia. It may be that these New Christians appeared more evidently guilty of heresy than those whose trials continued into the fall. This cluster of autos began on Monday, July 31, 1485, two weeks before the Feast of the Assumption of the Virgin, when twenty-five men and women were executed just outside of town

---

[78] See the file of Rodrigo Alonso *tundidor*, AHN Inquis. legajo 132, expediente 11, 15r. "[He saw him] en esta villa . . . el dia que quemaron a los de guadalupe e que lo vido estar mirando . . . quando salió el humo e que [the witness] dise que le dixeron que avía quemado a su hermano diego [gonçales tundidor] e que se fue de miedo." His brother's trial is not extant, although a record of it exists in the catalogue drawn up in 1513. See AHN clero legajo 1423, expediente 93. Diego González's file, from his trial in 1488, contained eighteen folios—a relatively large file—and he was executed.

[79] There was apparently no attempt to track down Rodrigo Alonso or force him to appear before the court, although the Holy Office had requested his presence more than once by means of announcements on the church doors.

[80] These numbers all come from Ecija's *Libro*. Since he was present as a notary and had access to the Inquisition files at Guadalupe until they were moved to Toledo in 1513 (he claims to have been editing his work by 1514), we can assume his numbers are relatively trustworthy. Since so many of the trials are now lost, there is no way to confirm his accounting, although circumstantial evidence tends to support his work. All later accounts (Rubio, Fita, and those who have followed them) derive from this one.

on Eras Street.[81] The next day, an auto was held for the Narices family. Much of their family and some friends had fled to Muslim-controlled Málaga several years before to live openly as Jews.[82] Sixteen people were burned in effigy that day. On Wednesday, August 2, the last of this group of autos de fe was held in the Plaza Mayor for fray Diego de Marchena. His was, not surprisingly, the most elaborate of the autos held in Guadalupe, as the inquisitors' glance turned upon the friars themselves. The long list of his heretical acts was read, and all the Jeronymites of the friary assisted in publicly denigrating and defrocking him before he was finally killed.[83]

After this dramatic event, the inquisitors did not hold another auto de fe until the end of their stay in Guadalupe. At that time, they held three, on November 20, 21, and 30. The first, on Monday, November 20, 1485, was reserved for those still living, that is, those sentenced to perpetual imprisonment or to be burned at the stake. In addition, the remains of a woman who had committed suicide in prison the day before were burned.[84] The next day the inquisitors held an auto de fe for those who were no longer living or present in Guadalupe. The effigies of twenty-five people who were absent from the town and the remains of forty-six people who had been posthumously tried were burned. With them were burned two crates of books confiscated by the Inquisition. Finally, and apparently at something like the last minute, a seventh auto de fe was held for a woman who had claimed, falsely, to be an Old Christian. At the end of the week, on Sunday, December 3, the Inquisition published a decree officially expelling those conversos sentenced to perpetual exile.[85] With that act, the inquisitors and their staff left Guadalupe and returned to Toledo.

The officials of the Holy Office in Guadalupe viewed local conversos through a lens of preconceived expectations. During their year in residence at the shrine, the inquisitors, the prosecution, and the attorney for the defense shared the assumption that Guadalupe's New Christians

[81] That is, twelve men and thirteen women.

[82] AHN Inquis. legajo 177, expediente 10.

[83] Fray Diego de Marchena's trial is not among those kept in the AHN, but there is record of him in the Jeronymite records there, and in the unnumbered manuscript in AMG. Fray Diego's case is discussed at length in chapter 7.

[84] Ecija, *Libro*, cites two men and eleven women who were burned at the stake, and sixteen men and women incarcerated. Unfortunately, he says nothing more about this incident of suicide.

[85] The trials of those sentenced to exile show no fixed date for their final sentencing, unlike those who were burned at an auto de fe. They do, however, cluster before the auto dates, indicating that the court may have organized their standing files before each set of autos.

were, in fact, active Judaizers. The gaze of the Inquisitor, as it passed over New and Old Christians in the town, made sense of Guadalupenses' acts by contextualizing them in a matrix of assumed heretical intentions. The initial confessions during the *tiempo de gracia* only confirmed those assumptions. As the trials progressed, out of the inherently ambiguous language of defendant and witness, speakers for the prosecution and defense were left to construct a reality that fit inquisitorial expectations as well as demonstrated their interpretation of past events. The complexities of this task were not lost on the inquisitors, who struggled to make every aspect of the trial a medium through which the intentions of New Christians could be discerned. Legal strictures and even torture were ritualized and structured and helped the inquisitors to reassure themselves that what they saw had some validity.

At the end of the trials, the autos de fe transmitted this view of Guadalupenses to the residents and pilgrims in town, thus encouraging everyone to reorient their view of the community. The autos de fe also served as a warning of the paramount importance of proper Christian intentions and practices, as well as of the power of the friars to enforce their authority with the help of the Crown. This inquisitorial vision was transmitted throughout the realm, not only by the many pilgrims who visited the Marian shrine, but also by the smoke of the autos de fe that rose over the town. All who attempted to cast their purported acts in a different light, to defend themselves before the inquisitors, would face a difficult task indeed.

SIX

STRATEGIES OF THE ACCUSED

THE COERCIVE POWER of the inquisitors was apparent to all of Guadalupe's residents during the trials of 1485. Defendants were not without recourse, however, despite the legal and psychological pressures placed upon them by the inquisitors. Guadalupe's conversos had been redefined by the inquisitors' gaze as a collective, unified, subversive minority and treated accordingly. As a result, imprisoned conversos were able to use that common experience of trial and imprisonment against their prosecutors. Making use of the organization of the inquisitorial courts and independent, extra-legal initiatives, those accused by the inquisitors employed a variety of strategies in their own defense. Under the rules of canon law, counsel for the defense and standards of witnesses' testimony could work in the defendant's favor. To these few institutional protections, New Christians added their own efforts to secure the minimum punishment possible. During the year, converso defendants acted individually and collectively to challenge and on occasion subvert the goals of the inquisitors for their own benefit. The methods and aims of the Holy Office implicitly sought to weaken the solidarity of those accused and thus more effectively fulfill its goals; tensions among New Christians are as evident in their attempts at defense as in the actions of the prosecutors. In the end, the vision of unanimity seen by the inquisitors was still a fiction, as the range of attitudes, practices, and beliefs of conversos indicated. Survival, as well as concern for family and friends, motivated those New Christians brought before the Holy Office. Patterns of defense among New Christians, however, suggest widespread solidarity among the accused, a common understanding of how best to thwart the inquisitors, and some collective strategies developed over the course of the "inquisitorial year."

THE TRAJECTORY OF RESISTANCE

For most conversos, one's defense began even before one was tried, with a statement of penance and request for reconciliation. Through this statement, which was presented on paper and notarized during the period of grace the truly repentant could confess freely before the official beginning of the inquisitorial investigations. For the inquisitors these confessions served as an initial database of potential heretics; conversos presenting them might have feigned repentance and thus be worthy of further investigation.[1] New Christians, for their part, were equally aware of the potentially dangerous nature of a written confession of spiritual wrongdoing. To refuse to confess might indicate obduracy and disrespect for one's putative faith. To begin the process of reconciliation before the inquisitors, however, was an admission of wrongdoing and entailed the risk of attracting attention to oneself.

For potential defendants, a category that included almost all New Christians, the statement of confession and request for reconciliation demanded that one weigh the relative benefits of appearing contrite in guilt or of maintaining innocence. This concern with appearances was matched by a concern for expectations. Any attempt to maintain complete innocence had to be balanced against a common assumption of guilt and the consequences of conviction. That is, a denial of wrongdoing could only be accepted in a community that had not already decided the accused's guilt. This was particularly true since New Christians were required to defend themselves initially through the act of confession and reconciliation, an act that assumed the guilt of the author. Ironically, this meant that most conversos affirmed their innocence in statements of confession and requests for reconciliation by admitting some degree of guilt. Such an admission fulfilled the inquisitors' expectations of wrongdoing, expressed in the concept of reconciliation itself, while deflecting suspicion of greater heresy.

Extant statements of confession reflect these conflicting motivations. Almost all of those conversos tried by the Inquisition submitted confessions during the *tiempo de gracia*. Generally, these statements reflect a few common patterns of construction. The confessions open with a formulaic statement of repentance, then proceed to a list of specific misdeeds, sometimes organized in a chronological, or biographical format. In closing, the penitent asks forgiveness for any sin he or she may have forgotten to include. Some statements were apparently prepared in consultation with the scrivener who recorded the statement; others were written independently or largely composed before speaking to the Holy Office's scriveners. During the three weeks of the *tiempo de gracia*, Guadalupe's New Christians clearly conferred on how best to respond and confess. A small minority later regretted any penitent statement at all, lamenting that "there did not remain ten good Jews who have not confessed to the Inquisition," but most conversos encouraged vague

---

[1] These issues were discussed in greater detail in chapter 5.

and generic participation.[2] Some faults or minor acts of Judaizing were admitted, with the blame placed on others if possible.

Autobiographical confessions, tracing one's heretical practice of Judaism throughout one's life, tended to fix blame on deceased parents or other relatives who demanded that their children participate in Jewish ritual. For most conversos, implicating the deceased was understandably preferable to endangering the living. Juana González blamed her parents for any Jewish practices in which she may have engaged. She did not know her ancestry until one Yom Kippur, she said, when her father blessed her in a Jewish fashion.[3] New Christians who remained in Guadalupe also placed blame for their heretical acts on absent family members and friends. Like the suspicious percentage of the deceased who encouraged Judaizing, these accusations sometimes ring a bit hollow. Many one-time associates of Martín Bachiller Narices did not hesitate to blame him for their Judaizing activities. Martín had left Guadalupe several years earlier and was presumed dead by remaining family and friends in the town. Prosecution witnesses at his trial frequently cited him as the instigator of wrongdoing, beginning their statements, "As I described in my [request for] reconciliation. . . ."[4] Family and friends who were beyond the reach of the inquisitors, either through decease or absence, provided a convenient excuse for conversos, since they could neither contradict the statement of the defendant nor suffer the wrath of the inquisitors.

The dead or absent received much blame for the Judaizing practices of Guadalupe's conversos, but New Christians strongly resisted naming the living as bad influences. From the first actions of the inquisitors, conversos followed a practice of revealing as little as possible to the Holy Office and of protecting, as much as possible, one's fellow New Christians. Both inquisitors and penitents recognized the importance of naming those guilty of apostasy, and those who heard confessions during the *tiempo de gracia* sometimes encouraged penitents to be more

[2] AHN Inquis. legajo 184, expediente 1. See also Baer, *History*, 2:337–338. Baer also mentions this incident in *Die Juden im christlichen Spanien* (Berlin: Akademie-Verlag, 1929–1936), 2, no. 393. More common were the people who collaborated on creating acceptable and nonincriminating statements. See, for example, the trial of Alonso Fernández the teacher, AHN Inquis. legajo 146, expediente 6, and the trial of Catalina (Mari) Sánchez, AHN Inquis. legajo 183, expediente 10.

[3] AHN Inquis. legajo 154, expediente 20, 11r. This trial, and the complexity of autobiographical confessions generally, are examined in Gretchen Starr-LeBeau "Writing (for) Her Life: Judeo-Conversas in Early Modern Spain," in *Women, Texts, and Authority in Early Modern Spain*, ed. Marta Vicente and Luis Cortegnera (Aldershot: Ashgate, 2002).

[4] His trial began by stating that he was being tried in absentia, but by the sentencing the court had concluded that in fact Martín had died and was being posthumously tried. Ibid. 164, expediente 18.

specific. Alonso the teacher provides one example. Alonso stated at the outset that he had fasted in a Jewish rather than Christian fashion, but he never specified when or where he learned to do these things. On the back, a different, scribal hand added that "his mother made him fast, has done it all his life, and he confessed it to his confessor. His mother is Marina Alonso."[5] When another conversa, Mari Ruiz, was preparing her statement for the inquisitors, she asked her friends what to include. They encouraged her to remove the names of family members identified as engaging in Judaizing practices, and thus spare her family the attention of the inquisitors. Her concern for her family was to no effect; this conversation and her omissions were revealed in the course of her trial, and ultimately she was exiled.[6]

Any omission later discovered by the inquisitors, whether of names of fellow Judaizers or of practices engaged in by the penitent, cast suspicion on the seriousness of one's repentance; but most New Christians also recognized the danger of admitting responsibility for too many heretical acts. When the inquisitors confronted Mari Sánchez, wife of Diego Jiménez the butcher, with evidence of heretical acts for which she had not confessed, Mari acknowledged purposefully omitting them. She admitted that she had chosen not to include these actions—which included desecration of an image of the crucifix—because they were too blasphemous.[7] Most New Christians were not as forthright as Mari Sánchez, but their trials also indicated an unwillingness to reveal too much too early. Local residents happily identified Judaizing activities that the participants themselves neglected to mention.

For most conversos, therefore, the confession helped to define the parameters of the defense of their Christianity. Both inquisitors and potential defendants recognized the importance of a written confession of wrongdoing at the outset of the Holy Office's labor, and both sought to manipulate the confession for their own ends. The inquisitors worked to clarify a specific genealogy of heresy and history of incorrect acts; conversos, fearful of accusation by the Holy Office, established an initial framework of guilt and innocence. In that framework penitents admitted some guilt, assigned blame whenever possible to the absent and deceased, and maintained their current unstained devotion to Christianity. New Christians asserted that any past wrongdoing committed while under the influence of other, less devout Christians, such as parents, spouses, or other family and friends, had been both committed and then set aside in the past. In contrast to any past heretical actions,

[5] Ibid. 146, expediente 6.
[6] Ibid. 181, expediente 16, 2r.
[7] Ibid. 183, expediente 20. See also Baer, *History*, 337–338.

conversos maintained, their present behavior denoted a fidelity to Christianity that required no further examination from the inquisitors. In short, a confession became a carefully worded retelling of one's history that obscured incorrect or heretical actions while fulfilling inquisitorial expectations of some guilt. The careful language required to obscure and reveal only specific elements of one's life suggests once again that at least some New Christians did participate in some Judaizing rituals.

The carefully constructed version of one's spiritual and moral past and present that emerged in these statements underwent a final transformation as the narratives were repeated scores of times for the inquisitorial scriveners. By the final retelling of these confessions to the inquisitors, individual histories were flattened into relatively unrelieved stock narratives of a misguided past subsumed in a repentant present. Through the process of explaining his or her story to a scrivener who was listening for the familiar structure of a confession, the penitent transformed his or her account into a stark portrayal of past wrongs now atoned for and righted. Given the hundreds of statements that were recorded and accepted, and the widespread familiarity New and Old Christians had with the form of the confession, it is not surprising that inquisitorial confessions and requests for reconciliation took on a stark, formulaic cast in the dialogue between the penitent relating his or her confession and the scrivener or notary assigned to record it.

Despite the difficulty and potential danger of confessing, it appears that almost all conversos submitted written confessions and then reconciled during the *tiempo de gracia*. Some New Christians were clearly troubled by the process, but few escaped it. In the trial against Mari Sánchez, wife of Diego Sánchez, tanner, one witness noted that when the accused heard a group of women discussing the Inquisition in the street, she rushed out complaining that not ten conversos remained in town who had not reconciled and given up their beliefs.[8] In fact, Mari Sánchez had reconciled as well. Indeed, there was little reason not to reconcile, and there were a great many reasons to participate. If nothing else, a confession and subsequent reconciliation indicated a certain remorse, or at least recognition of participation in acts prohibited by the church, and even this modicum of penitence could serve one well.

Those who confessed gained only a temporary reprieve from the attention of the inquisitors; most were accused of further heresies in the months following the conclusion of the *tiempo de gracia*.[9] Once Guadalupe's New Christians realized that their confessions had not guaranteed immunity from the Holy Office, strategies of self-protection changed.

[8] AHN Inquis. legajo 184, expediente 1.
[9] The *tiempo de gracia* was discussed in detail in chapter 5.

During the time of grace, New Christians had admitted guilt and contrition. Now, conversos insisted on the veracity of their initial confessions and denied any further wrongdoing. Whatever their religious practices, and whatever other divisions among them, New Christians in Guadalupe were united in their refusal to admit further guilt.

Paired with this vehement claim of innocence was an equally tenacious legal defense. Those accused of wrongdoing by the Inquisition used what resources the Holy Office provided to restate their innocence in the strongest possible terms. In civil courts of the period, stalling tactics and repeated appeals provided an effective means of protection from an early and unfavorable decision by the judge.[10] The Inquisition, with its limited time frame and single-minded focus on one community, brooked no such defensive maneuvers. The Holy Office did provide a legal means of defense, however, based on canon law. A defense lawyer, Doctor de Villaescusa, and a solicitor, usually the lay functionary Juan de Texeda, acted as intermediaries between the court and the defendant; these men also prepared the defense of the accused by writing and delivering statements to the court, interviewing witnesses, and so forth.

The work performed by Juan de Texeda and Doctor de Villaescusa was not considered merely a pro forma or irrelevant part of the inquisitorial process. The Holy Office was a profoundly legal body, and it operated within the rules of canon law. As such, the prosecutor was required to prove his case against the defendant, adhering to legal requirements concerning the minimum number of witnesses needed to verify an event and other elements of the trial. Juan de Texeda, who was most involved in providing assistance to the defense, seems to have worked to fulfill this duty. Given Texeda's hostility to Fray Fernando de Ubeda and the New Christian merchants associated with the friar, one might assume that Texeda had little interest or motivation to defend Guadalupe's New Christians. In fact, the extant trials indicate that, on paper at least, Texeda and de Villaescusa often provided their charges with a strong defense. The two men presented detailed defense statements and questioned numerous character witnesses who might support the claims of New Christians to be genuine participants in their Christian faith. Guilt was determined primarily by whether the prosecution had proved the case through argument. The role of the defense, therefore, was to weaken the arguments of the prosecution by provid-

---

[10] On means of extending a trial in an attempt to turn the issue to one's favor, see, for example, Kagan, *Lawsuits and Litigants*. This technique is also quite evident in the many trials extant at the archive in Guadalupe. See, for example, AMG codex 163 and the *Pleito de las Bonilla*, discussed in chapter 8.

ing alternate explanations of the character and behavior of the defendant. The many conversos who received reduced sentences or were pardoned owed that success in some measure to these two men.

Mari Sánchez, wife of Juan Esteban de Maestre Pedro, provides one example of how this process worked in practice.[11] In his opening statement, the prosecutor made a series of accusations against Mari Sánchez. He claimed that her confession was false and simulated; that Mari had participated in Jewish rites, both in secret and in the open; that she cut the throat of her own meat (a distinctly Jewish method of slaughtering animals); that she attempted to make her children Jews by washing the chrism off after their baptism; and that she observed Jewish feasts. The most serious of the charges against her were the claim that Mari had tried to nullify her children's baptisms and that she had participated in Jewish feasts, particularly Sukkoth, a harvest feast. The prosecutor alleged that Mari, her husband, and several others had observed Sukkoth, known in Spanish as the feast of the tabernacles, *fiesta de las cabañuelas*, by building some huts and eating outside at the Guadalupe River around the Christian feast of Corpus Christi.[12] The prosecutor, Diego Fernández de Zamora, brought forward a number of witnesses to support these claims, the most damning of whom was María, the daughter of Pedro Martín, a maid who had lived with the family for the three years before the inquisitors imprisoned them. María had also spoken to many of her friends about events in Juan Esteban's and Mari Sánchez's home, and they testified to what María had told them.[13]

Juan de Texeda defended Mari Sánchez in two ways: first, by presenting numerous character witnesses who could attest to Mari's Christian character, and second, by challenging the accusation of observing Sukkoth in particular. Texeda's questions for his many defense witnesses demonstrated this. After an initial question to determine how the witness knew the defendant, and for how long, the witnesses detailed whether Mari Sánchez did Christian acts, including attending mass, observing the sacraments, confessing during Lent, and receiving the Eucharist. Witnesses were also asked to confirm that Mari gave much in alms to the poor, to hermits, and to hospitals, churches, and other

---

[11] Her trial is preserved as AHN Inquis. legajo 183, expediente 19.

[12] It is not quite clear what these New Christians were attempting to do. Eating outside in huts certainly sounds like Sukkoth, but that festival is celebrated in the autumn, after Rosh Hashanah, the Jewish New Year. Corpus Christi is celebrated in early summer. It is possible that the witnesses are misremembering or lying. See chapter 2.

[13] See, for example, Isabel, the maid of Catalina García; Inés, the maid (daughter of Alonso de Paredes); Isabel, the maid of Alonso López trapero; and Mari Sánchez, wife of Juan Fernández the tailor. Ibid.

institutions. The questionnaire for defense witnesses closed with a request that the witness affirm that Mari Sánchez did the acts of a Christian, that she was like a Christian, and that she was Christian. Texeda also asked witnesses to confirm that Mari spoke more frequently to Christians than to Jews, and that she honored Christians more than Jews. Subsequent questions refuted specific elements of the claims of the *promotor fiscal*. Witnesses were asked whether Mari Sánchez or her husband killed animals like Christians or like Jews. Texeda also asked witnesses if they knew that Mari and her husband went with a dozen other Old and New Christians to the Guadalupe River bank in the early summer. Witnesses were to confirm that while there they ate lard, and other foods that Jews did not eat, and that the huts were built for fun, not as a Jewish ceremony or to fulfill the law of Moses. The next question asked witnesses whether they knew that Sukkoth was celebrated in September, not in May or June, and that it was celebrated at home rather than in the country. This question was almost certainly aimed at the judges and the prosecution, since it seems unlikely that witnesses would have such a sophisticated knowledge of Jewish law.[14] Finally, as was customary, witnesses were asked to comment on the reputation of the accused.

Texeda's attempts seem to have met with success. Defense witnesses testified to Mari's Christian acts, and many specifically commented on her good reputation in town. Furthermore, while many knew of the cabins at the river, few believed the event was associated with a Jewish feast. When the inquisitors rendered their verdict in the case, they determined that the prosecutor had not proven the worst of the charges, namely, that Mari Sánchez had washed the chrism off her children's heads and that she had celebrated Sukkoth. Mari was absolved of all charges save keeping the Jewish Sabbath, and she had already been pardoned for that offense in her reconciliation. However, the Holy Office decided that Mari had not reconciled out of piety or spiritual rigor— that her confession was to an extent "false and simulated"—and so she was exiled. The reasoning behind the inquisitors' relatively mild sentence is unclear, but Texeda's seven witnesses and clear evidence that Mari had not celebrated Sukkoth must have played some part.

CONFRONTING FAMILY AND FRIENDS

Mari's case is a reminder that no converso could rely on the legal structure of the Inquisition to protect him or her from a guilty verdict, and

---

[14] Indeed, no witnesses responded to that question.

most New Christians labored in whatever way possible to subvert the court's assumption of guilt. In 1485 the Holy Office had only recently begun functioning on a large scale in Castile and Aragon; the means and methods of the inquisitors were still in development. As a result, common strategies of the accused that developed later in the history of the Inquisition were at this time largely absent. Popular knowledge of the Inquisition and how it would come to operate was not yet available, and inquisitors and New Christians alike struggled to routinize the court's activity in the context of life in the late fifteenth century. In the few courts that had already begun to operate, most conversos were found guilty and executed at one of the many autos de fe. The fate of New Christians in Seville, Córdoba, and Ciudad Real provided cold comfort to Guadalupe's conversos.[15]

One technique commonly used during the sixteenth century, but only once in Guadalupe, was the practice of challenging the validity of particular witnesses. When the Inquisition was founded, Isabel insisted that the identity of prosecution witnesses be hidden from defendants. The queen of Castile seems to have believed that only in this way could prosecution witnesses avoid intimidation by the defendant.[16] This change from both medieval inquisitorial practice and the practice of civil law had broad implications for the working of the court, with grave consequences for those accused. Isabel recognized, however, that some might use the court to seek revenge against a defendant, a process made infinitely easier by the rule of anonymity. To provide some mitigating protection to the defendant, the person accused was permitted to challenge the testimony of "known enemies." The defendant listed all those in town who might speak against him or her out of spite rather than to promote honestly the work of the court, lists known as *tachas*. In each case, the accused explained the source of the enmity between them and why this person might testify falsely. If the person listed had indeed testified, their statements were stricken from the record. This practice was in frequent use in civil trials of the period,[17] and Melammed describes its use in sixteenth-century Castile.[18] In later years, this became a staple strategy for the defense, who created endless lists of enemies in an attempt to avoid punishment by the Inquisition. Ulti-

---

[15] Some penitents from Seville made the pilgrimage to Guadalupe as part of their penance. It is possible that these conversos communicated with New Christians in Guadalupe, although there is no evidence of that.

[16] See Peggy Liss's interesting discussion of this decision in chapter 10 of *Isabel the Queen*.

[17] See, for example, AMG codex 163, in which a man accused of bigamy attempts to defend himself by challenging the validity of witnesses called by his first wife.

[18] Melammed, *Heretics*, 113–139.

mately, this protection for the defense was converted into an agonizing
and largely unproductive exercise, as one attempted to guess who might
have presented which piece of testimony to the inquisitors. Whatever
the benefits or difficulties of challenging witnesses, those accused of
Judaizing in Guadalupe appear largely not to have attempted the tactic.
The widespread disinterest in challenging witnesses might have been
due to the practices of the counsel for the defense, or it might simply
corroborate what seems to have been true elsewhere, that this defense
became more common in later trials.

In the single extant trial in which a defendant attempted to guess and
discredit his accusers, it proved to be of little success. Ruy González de
la Corte, one of the first men tried by the Holy Office, clearly took a
strong interest in the progress of his case, and he stamped his personality on his defense more than any other defendant was able to do.[19]
When the prosecutor alleged that Ruy wore special clothes on the Jewish Sabbath, the defendant, through his solicitor, demanded that the
prosecutor specify which Saturday, and say what he wore the rest of the
week, and even "of what color were the clothes that he wore on that
Saturday, because I [wish?] to prove [the case], being necessary for justice."[20] Later, in a moment unique in the extant Inquisition documents
for Guadalupe, Ruy González questioned the quality of the prosecution
witnesses. He asked to be informed "of what reputation and in what
manner and in what form they state and depose [and if they were]
vacillating or changing expression or the color of the face; or if they
come or came with hatred and enmity to state their testimony against
me, the aforementioned. . . ."[21]

Ruy González challenged the prosecutor and the prosecution witnesses to prove the case against him. When the prosecutor's witnesses
alleged that he observed the Jewish Sabbath, he made what might be
considered a formal challenge of the witnesses. He charged that they
were criminals, and he listed a number of family and friends who might
have testified against him out of spite, including one former maid who
was among the prosecution witnesses.[22] Yet González also averred that

[19] It may be that no other extant trial records used this type of defense because of
Ruy González's ultimate failure to defend himself. That is, his early failure discouraged
both the defense lawyers and the accused from attempting this defense strategy.

[20] AHN Inquis. legajo 155, expediente 13, 5v. "& de que color eran las que traya el
sabado porque yo me afresco de prouar seyendo neçesario ala iustiçia."

[21] Ibid., 15r. "de que fama e en que manera & de que forma dizen & deponen sus
dichos vaçilando o mudando el gesto & color dela cara o sy viene o vinieron con odio
& enemistad a dezir sus dichos contra el dicho mi parte . . ."

[22] Ibid., 16r. "y como quiera que para desarraygar este viçio & morbo tan contagioso
dela heretica prauedat rregularmente se admiten & resçiben todos los testigos aun que

it was not believable that he observed the Jewish Sabbath since the defense witnesses had already proved his innocence. He asked that the witnesses for the prosecution be questioned themselves on how they kept the Sabbath. Had none of them ever stopped working for an hour or two on a Saturday, he wondered. Ruy González's combative defense suggests that he was accustomed to wielding influence in town, and the long list of enemies also indicates his political and economic importance in Guadalupe. Given his apparent stature, it is not surprising that he was among the first to be tried by the prior and his fellow inquisitors. That his defense strategy was unsuccessful might also have been expected. Ruy González de la Corte was able to eliminate the testimony of his former servant from the record, but he could not avoid a guilty sentence. In May he was found guilty of heresy and executed.

More common than Ruy's combative hostility toward the Holy Office was the practice of noncompliance with the court, particularly when the trial concerned a friend or family member rather than oneself. Through minimal compliance or noncompliance, Guadalupense New Christians could reduce the efficiency of the court and decrease their complicity in the actions of the inquisitors without putting themselves specifically at risk. For the accused, taken and imprisoned by the court, there was often little choice but to participate.[23] The family and friends of the accused, however, had slightly greater opportunities to avoid the direct pressure to participate, even if they were all in prison together. First, the family members of a deceased relative often shirked the responsibility of organizing the defense of their parent or spouse. The accused was required to defend himself or herself, and the trial could not commence until the accused or the next of kin had named defense counsel (invariably Doctor de Villaescusa and Juan de Texeda). The inquisitors cited those who persisted in refusing the court's summons as being in contempt, *rebeldía*, and if they persisted in their intransigence the court would either take them prisoner or grant the prosecutor license to begin without the defendants.

For most people, though, prison was a difficult launching point for resistance to the Inquisition. The emotional climate within the prison must have been unnerving, to say the least. Prisoners were frequently asked to testify for the prosecution, and the constant traffic between the

---

sean criminosos saluo en çiertos casos pero sy son criminosos & puestos en viçios a los tales non se deue de adibir & dar tanta fe como aquellos que son mayores de toda exçepçion para este efecto & para aquellos que el derecho admite digo. . . ." This comment is followed by a long list of names and the nature of their dispute with the accused.

[23] The sole exception was a prisoner who committed suicide. See Diego de Ecija, *Libro*, 339–341, 345–346.

court and the prison meant that those confined remained relatively well-informed about the day-to-day activity of the court. Almost daily, new prisoners arrived, old ones were sentenced, and statements taken. Prisoners stayed at the prison except during the accusation and sentencing; otherwise they were informed of the progress of their trial by the lawyer in charge of their defense. Conversations between the defense lawyer Doctor de Villaescusa and the defendants occurred outside of the holding chamber per se but were clearly audible to at least the women prisoners inside.[24] And the sounds from the torture chamber would also have been easily heard by all.

Because so many family members were gathered there, the prison itself was an important source of information about family histories and Judaizing practices for both prosecution and defense. The ability to confer among themselves at its best provided families with a chance to consult and create a coordinated defense; at its worst, it allowed those who cooperated with the Inquisition to elicit even more damning statements from the accused, or at the least meant that the temptation to sacrifice a relative's defense to improve one's own was greatly increased. In one case, Manuel González, the innkeeper of the Mesón Blanco, was accused of being circumcised (fig. 6). He denied it, but when he returned to prison he and his father—who was also in prison and accused of Judaizing—discussed the issue. He asked his father, Fernando González, if he had been circumcised; as he later reluctantly described the ensuing conversation for the inquisitors, "His father told him that it was true that he was circumcised, and that he told him [Manuel] that his grandfather Alonso Fernández Gigante was to blame; and that this witness [Manuel] responded, how was this possible since his grandfather had been dead forty years and he [Manuel] was only thirty-five, and that then his father said to him, 'Go on, don't be such a fool.'"[25] Here, Manuel and his father used their time together in prison to discuss the charges against the son, and the relevant family chronology. It is likely that neither imagined the conversation would reach the ears of the court. Manuel González divulged the conversation only under torture, after having admitted first his own Judaizing activities, and then the actions of other conversos he knew. Once Manuel had been forced to implicate his own father by repeating this conversation, together with his conclusion—after prompting—that he believed his father must have

---

[24] The conversations between Villaescusa and the defendants may have been held in one of the rooms next to the women's prison and across from the kitchen, or (less probably) in the *corral*, or garden, behind the prison. See AHN Inquis. legajo 183, expediente 10, discussed in more detail below.

[25] AHN Inquis. legajo 154, expediente 24, 19r–v.

FIGURE 6. View of the plaza from the friary. Seville Street is at the center of the picture, and the modern road to the left marks where Manuel González's Mesón Blanco once stood. Photo by the author.

circumcised him, he begged to be released, which he was.[26] This conversation and its grave effects clearly indicate the perils a common jail could have for inmates of the Inquisition. Not only was Manuel González unable to discover a satisfactory explanation for the alleged circumcision, but instead he heard more damning evidence. Rather than the conversation securing Manuel González's exoneration, the common prison ultimately left him in the agonizing position of confirming his family's guilt.

For others, though, the close quarters and ability to talk freely with family and friends provided benefits. Of course, the progress of one's trial was a frequent topic of conversation among inmates, as scattered references in the inquisitorial files indicate. These discussions, and the accumulated wisdom they disseminated, altered the defense of those

---

[26] "This witness said to him [the torturer] that he [the father] would have done it, and that given how he knew his father he felt that he did it" (segund conosçio de su padre que syntio que el lo avia fecho). Ibid., 19v.

who were accused later, as conversos themselves admitted during their trials. In this way the prison became a key site for gaining information about inquisitorial practices and strategies for resistance.[27] During the trial against Catalina Sánchez, for example, the defense lawyer came to her at the prison and read her the statements of the prosecution witnesses. As the bailiff later testified, she laughed when she heard them and denied them all. But soon after returning to prison, he notes, she called the bailiff over and asked to speak to the judge in charge of her case, and when he and the defense attorney appeared she confessed all and asked for mercy.

The reason for this notable change in attitude became clearer when the next witness, Mari Sánchez, wife of the butcher (no relation to Catalina Sánchez), was called to testify. She stated that when Catalina Sánchez returned to the prison, she told Mari Sánchez that she was worried, because the Holy Office had discovered an incriminating family story—when her youngest son was a child, they had occasionally called him "little Jacob," Jacobito. Part of Catalina's concern must have come from attempting to imagine who the source of this information was—almost certainly a family member or servant.[28] Parenthetically, it is interesting to note that like many of the prison conversations reported to the inquisitors, this one mitigates the guilt of the participants. Catalina explains to Mari Sánchez that Jacobito was not her son's "real," Jewish name, but rather a joke, what they called him when they dressed him up in big clothing and laughed at him.[29] Upon hearing her story, Mari Sánchez urged Catalina to call for the defense lawyer and confess all. Her confidante spoke from experience. Mari had failed to confess to three acts that she felt were too incriminating to mention, assuming that there was no way that the court could learn of them. Mari's own

---

[27] Inga Clendinnen, in her work on the 1570 Inquisition against Yucatecan Mayans (who were charged with reverting to paganism), provides an interesting model for tracing collective responses to Inquisitions through individual trials. See *Ambivalent Conquests.*

[28] In fact, both family and servants testified about this practice. See AHN Inquis. legajo 183, expediente 10.

[29] The humor behind calling a child dressed up in too-big clothing "little Jacob" is obscure. It is possible that Catalina (and/or Mari) is lying, and that this was merely the child's Jewish name. If it was part of a larger joke, it might be related to the Biblical story of Jacob and Esau. To steal Esau's inheritance, Jacob disguised himself in Esau's clothing and wore fur on his arms to simulate Esau's bigger, hairier appearance. Isaac, being nearly blind, was thus deceived into giving Jacob, rather than Esau, his blessing (see Genesis 27). Jewish boys were often referred to by family and friends in the Inquisition documents as Jacob. The tribulations of Jacob (later named Israel) held particular resonance for New Christians; his name also appears in Manuel González's confiscated prayer book.

daughter testified against her, however, and less than two weeks before this conversation with Catalina, Mari had been tortured until she had admitted the truth of her daughter's testimony. Mari was profoundly aware that details of family life, whether real or imagined, could be used to condemn the accused if they came from a witness close to the accused. In this case, her advice was only partially helpful: because Catalina admitted her guilt she was not tortured, but her evident lack of repentance—as indicated by the conversation above, which was added at the last minute by the prosecution—brought Catalina a death sentence.[30]

Catalina Sánchez was not alone in her struggle with servants and family members who testified against her. Many children testified against their parents, both to hide their own guilt and to identify the guilt of their family. Since New Christians were both so heterogeneous in questions of religious practice and under such pressure to testify, it is not surprising that many conversos testified against one another. Both Catalina Sánchez and Mari Sánchez, wife of the butcher, were sentenced to death as a result of the hostility of daughters who willingly detailed their mothers' improprieties. Mari's daughter, Inés González, testified against many of the women in town, listing kosher cooking practices and other Jewish ritual actions that she witnessed among her neighbors; however, her most venomous testimony was saved for her mother. Inés accused her mother of desecrating a drawing of a cross, keeping kosher, and other heretical Jewish activities. As she casually informed the inquisitors and her friends and neighbors in town, "My father is a good Christian, but my mother is wholly Jewish."[31] Others testified against their family, not out of hostility, but less willingly, largely to protect themselves. Andrés González de la República, for example, reluctantly and vaguely testified against his deceased mother to divert attention from his own inherently suspicious status as a New Christian. Often the testimony of Andrés González and people like him was unusually brief and noncommunicative. Not only were these New Christians at risk of losing their own lives to the Inquisition; in addition, they were forced to condemn their parents to improve their own image before the Holy Office. Andrés and others may have participated, but they attempted to say as little as possible. Conversos like Andrés González struggled to strike a balance between the threatening demands of the court and the more personal demands of family loyalty.

---

[30] AHN Inquis. legajo 183, expediente 10.

[31] "Mi padre es un buen cristiano pero mi madre es una judía entera." See ibid., expediente 20. For more on Inés and her mother, see Starr-LeBeau, "Mari Sánchez and Inés González," 19–41.

The inquisitors understood that not all New Christians were necessarily devoted to Judaism. The Holy Office showed some sympathy for those willing to divide their own families and condemn their parents and grandparents; in at least one case, the inquisitors themselves drew a distinction between the practices and beliefs of the parents and the practices and beliefs of their children. In this one instance, a sixteen-year-old named Isabel was tried by the Inquisition for Judaizing.[32] In her confession she admitted to washing the chrism off her newborn sister after bringing her home from church, but the prosecutor claimed that in addition she kept kosher and observed the Sabbath. In this case the inquisitors decided that Isabel could not be held liable for her actions, since she had been wrongly educated in the home and had not had an opportunity to learn to live a proper Christian life. The court sent Isabel to live with "a good Christian family," assigning her no punishment. Rather, the Inquisition laid blame on Isabel's mother and aunt, Inés and Aldonza Gutiérrez. Although they were not specifically tried in the case, they were sentenced as the guilty parties to life imprisonment. Here the motivation for imprisonment rather than execution was their role in teaching another to act wrongly, rather than any wrong actions of their own.[33]

TACTICS OF DESPERATION

As the trial drew to a close, and the defendant learned of the many detailed charges made against them, desperation entered into the acts of many conversos, and the trajectory of resistance changed. The stage in the trial known as the publication of the witnesses served as a significant turning point in this regard. For the first time, the prosecution and defense received a copy of the statements made by witnesses for the opposing side. Legally, this stage also signaled a new limitation on the defendant. The court reasoned that a confession after the accused had heard the generic charges might be genuine, and not merely an act of self-interest. But once specific details of Judaizing had been mentioned in individual testimony, the inquisitors felt no sympathy for an additional confession that mentioned only and exactly those new acts charged in the witnesses' statements; such a confession did little or nothing to change one's sentence. The Holy Office had little patience for defendants who seemed to resist inch by inch, rather than those who fully

---

[32] Trial of Isabel, daughter of Inés Gutiérrez and Juan Alonso de Montalbán, AHN Inquis. legajo 158, expediente 5.
[33] Ibid., 5v.

and humbly confessed their guilt and expressed apparently genuine repentance.

It was the publication of the statements of one's accusers that had the most impact on the accused and seems to have broken the resistance of more than one converso. At the very least, it encouraged some conversos to "cut their losses," as it were, and to admit to all, hoping for leniency. Diego Fernández de Zamora, the prosecutor, was quick to point out when a full statement of contrition followed the publication of witnesses, and to deride its importance.

Even at the end of the long trials endured by conversos in Guadalupe, one could hope to save oneself by begging for the mercy of the court. Few availed themselves of that mercy, however. For those New Christians sentenced to "partial guilt" and exile, there was little chance for final recourse to the Holy Office. Most chose to accept the sentence for the moment, hoping—as other New Christians sentenced for heresy had done in the 1460s—to return in later years. Those found guilty and sentenced to death had even less chance of winning a last-minute appeal. Most did not escape the flames of the auto de fe, but a few survived through an eleventh-hour plea to the inquisitors. Defendants threw themselves on the mercy of the court once the witnesses had been published, admitting all and begging forgiveness. This tactic increased in popularity during the course of the year, as word-of-mouth reports of its efficacy spread. Catalina Sánchez, mentioned earlier, provides one particularly emotional example.

Catalina Sánchez, the woman who had mocked her lawyer and refused to admit wrongdoing until persuaded to do so by her friend, had been sentenced to death for her misdeeds and lack of true repentance. Admitting that she referred to her son as Jacobito had only saved her from being tortured, but that moment of honesty may ultimately have spared her life as well. Generally, sentences were first read before the accused in the audience chamber where the inquisitors met; only some months later was the sentence publicly announced at the auto de fe. At the first reading of her sentence, Catalina burst into tears, sobbing and begging for the mercy of the court. Her lamentations and repentance were so moving that the inquisitors relented and sentenced her to perpetual imprisonment instead. The stay of execution was more generous than it appears at first sight. Those sentenced to perpetual imprisonment were all released within three years of their sentencing, to return to their homes and families in the town. For women—and to a lesser degree men—who demonstrated abject humility and repentance, the inquisitors might acknowledge a change of heart and reward it by sparing their lives.

A final option for the truly desperate was flight. In fact, there is little evidence of people fleeing the Inquisition in 1485; once a New Christian was accused and taken prisoner, there was little opportunity to flee. And given the tight network of interrelationships in Guadalupe, and the obvious difficulty and pain in leaving one's home, there must have been a great deal of pressure to remain in town despite the risk of being taken by the Inquisition oneself. Indeed, there is even evidence that family members living outside of Guadalupe returned to town to reconcile during the time of grace. At least one of these was held in prison during 1485, but there is no evidence that any of them were sentenced.[34] There is one extant example of an accused converso who fled the court: Rodrigo Alonso *tundidor*, who turned back halfway into his trip after seeing the smoke from the auto de fe rising in the sky ahead of him.[35] Intriguingly, Rodrigo Alonso later regretted his decision to flee. He had made the decision in a moment of fear; he changed his mind three years later and returned to Guadalupe to face the Inquisition, in part at the urging of his family in Chillón. After an initial phase in Guadalupe, his case was transferred to Toledo, where his case lingered until he was pronounced guilty and executed in 1491.

Those who chose to flee had made their decision earlier, before the coming of the Inquisition, and had joined the many Jewish families heading south to return to Judaism in the Muslim kingdom of Granada.[36] The best known example to contemporaries in Guadalupe was that of the Narices family. Some years before the Inquisition came to Guadalupe, Bartolomé Rodríguez Narices, his wife Catalina Rodríguez, five of their children, and other family members and friends (totaling a dozen people) moved to Málaga to practice Judaism. This move was the culmination of a series of trips to Seville and other points south to participate in Jewish ceremonies, as witnesses explained to the inquisitors. The story of the Narices also indicates the emotional complexity of such a transfer. The move allowed the family to reunite with other family members who had moved at different times and to different places; the move south also created new ruptures in family life, with

---

[34] AHN clero legajo 1423, expediente 93. There are several such examples in the index of confessions and reconciliations transferred to Toledo in 1513. Anecdotal evidence of the participation of out-of-towners with family, usually parents, in Guadalupe also exists: Inés, daughter of Mari Sánchez and Diego Jiménez the butcher, describes a conversation she had with her mother in prison; though a resident of Valdecaballeros, she describes the situation as though she were being held with her mother. There is no evidence that she was sentenced, or even tried, for that matter; indeed, given her voluminous and apparently voluntary testimony against her mother and other residents, it seems likely that she was not convicted of Judaizing.

[35] AHN Inquis. legajo 132, expediente 11.

[36] The practice is commonly referred to in Spanish as *tornar judío en Málaga*, to revert to Judaism in Málaga. See below and chapter 3 for more on flight to Málaga.

some family members choosing to remain behind as devoutly Christian conversos in Guadalupe.[37]

The decision to flee was also not without its dangers. Once one had been baptized, one was not permitted the option of changing one's mind; a Christian could not revoke his decision to join the community of believers. Those caught making the trip to Málaga to return to Judaism were therefore liable to be held prisoner for their actions. Fray Diego de Marchena, one of the friary's boldest Judaizers, had witnessed the dangers of flight in his own family. In the 1470s fray Diego's family was seized by Juan de Guzmán, lord of Teba, while fleeing to Málaga.[38] One friar later described fray Diego's family as traveling behind Muslims, *detrás de moros*, by which the friar may have meant with or behind a caravan of Muslims. It is plausible that conversos journeying to the Muslim kingdom of Granada might travel with Muslims who could not only act as guides but also help obscure the Christian status of conversos.[39] Fray Diego de Marchena received permission from the prior to make at least two trips south to ransom "a sister and other family members," as fray Diego de Ecija recalled.

Despite his trips to Andalucía, fray Diego de Marchena was unable to rescue his family; at least some of his family members who had fled to Málaga were transported instead to Córdoba to be tried by the Inquisition. Fray Diego de Marchena corresponded with the court on behalf of his family, perhaps hoping that his status as a friar at the prestigious friary in Guadalupe would aid his family's case. As one friar grumbled to the Inquisition in Guadalupe, "he wrote to the Inquisition in Córdoba without our father [prior] knowing anything or seeing the letters." It is unclear if any of the family escaped to Málaga, or if all were tried by the Inquisition. Rumors circulating in the friary suggested that some

[37] AHN Inquis. legajo 177, expediente 10. All those who fled together were tried together in a single trial, including those who were rumored to be deceased. One son, the lawyer Martín, was tried separately, since he left Guadalupe at a different time to *tornar judío*. First he was tried in absentia, but later the accusation changed to a posthumous one when the inquisitors discovered that Martín had died; see ibid. 164, expediente 18. Another daughter, Mari Sánchez, chose to remain in Guadalupe, where she was tried and convicted. See ibid. 184, expediente 1. One of her five children, Bartolomé, went to Málaga with his grandparents; another, Martín Sánchez shoemaker, proved a key witness against both the Narices family in general and his mother in particular.

[38] AMG unnumbered, Internal Inquisition, 8. Testimony of fray Diego de Ecija. Fray Diego de Ecija specifies that fray Diego de Marchena traveled south while fray Juan de Ortega served as general of the Order of Saint Jerome. According to fray Pedro de la Vega, fray Juan de Ortega served two terms as general, from 1472 to 1478. See fray Pedro de la Vega, *Crónica de los frayles*, 47v–48r.

[39] AMG unnumbered, Internal Inquisition, 8. Testimony of fray Diego de Ecija.

family members safely returned to Judaism in Andalucía while others were tried by the Holy Office.[40] Certainly not all of fray Diego's family were untouched by the Inquisition; a close relative, perhaps his brother-in-law, was condemned to death by the inquisitors in Córdoba. Fray Diego brought his relative food as the man awaited execution, to the deep disapproval of fray Diego's brethren in Guadalupe.[41] For every family like the Narices, who had the wherewithal and luck to leave Christian Iberia, another family was unsuccessful in its attempt to avoid the Inquisition and openly practice Judaism in Granada.

Whether in response to the challenges of the inquisitorial trials or in the dangerous trek south, New Christians found that their best hope of success lay in collaboration. Through delaying tactics, the simple accumulation of experience over the course of the year, or even through silence, conversos caught in the gaze of the inquisitors tended to rely upon others in building their own defense. In some small measure these strategies can be considered successful, though of course there were limits to the legal and extra-legal means of defense available to New Christians. Furthermore, not all of Guadalupe's New Christians contributed to this collective enterprise. There had never been a unitary "New Christian community," and many individual New Christians testified against others, either to identify what they saw as wrongdoing or as retribution for personal grievances. Others were forced to testify against family and friends out of self-preservation. Responses to the inquisitors varied; but the anxiety generated by the actions of the Holy Office spread throughout the town, enveloping everyone involved. Even friars who had initially requested the presence of the inquisitors had reason to regret the decision, when the Holy Office turned its attention upon them.

[40] Ibid., 33. "segund dizen de sus hermanos o hermanas y parientes se han ydo a tornar judíos y a otros han quemado."
[41] Ibid. For other accounts of fray Diego de Marchena's family, see ibid., 76, 92, etc.

SEVEN

INVESTIGATING THE FRIARS

TENSIONS in the Royal Friary of Our Lady of Guadalupe were already running high over the ongoing inquisitorial investigation in town when fray Luis de Madrid went mad and died early in 1485. The Jeronymite friars were not immune to the presence of the inquisitors or to their own continuing conflicts with the townspeople; the disruptive nature of the Holy Office had inevitably penetrated the friary. Fray Luis's illness reflected and exacerbated those anxieties. As his mental condition deteriorated, fray Luis began to speak wildly about his brethren in the friary:[1] "'Be quiet, be quiet, be quiet, do not make me speak! If not, I will say things that some will regret.' And some said to him—I do not remember who they are—that they knew that he would say it. And he responded, 'I know that there are two friars here who do not consecrate the Host'"[2] Word of fray Luis's delirious accusations spread quickly through the friary; no fewer than twenty-one friars repeated the claim to the inquisitors later that year.[3] Fray Luis was himself of converso origin, though considered by all a devout Christian. His closest companions in the friary, his cousin fray Pedro de Madrid and former prior Gonzalo de Madrid, were fellow *madrileños* of converso origin, and both were accused of some Judaizing.[4]

---

[1] Fray Luis is referred to by other friars as deceased, although a Luis de Madrid does testify briefly. See AMG unnumbered, Internal Inquisition, 80, 85, 87, 138, etc. It is possible that this is another Luis from Madrid, although usually if there were two Luises from Madrid one would be referred to as "Luis de Madrid mozo" (the younger). Since there is no evidence of a second fray Luis in the friary, I presume that the fray Luis who testified was the same fray Luis who died soon after.

[2] "¡callen, callen, callen, non me fagan fablar! Si non yo diré cosas que a algunos pesara[n]." & que algunos le dixeron (non se me acuerda quien[es] son) que sabían que lo dixiesse. & que respondiera el "yo sé que estan aquí dos frayles que non consagran." Ibid., 24. Testimony of fray Francisco de Ubeda.

[3] Ibid., 24, 80, 85, 87, etc.

[4] On connections between fray Luis, fray Pedro, and prior Gonzalo and their potential Judaizing, see ibid., 7, 19, 30, 78, 148, 220. On the relationship between fray Pedro de Madrid (who died before 1484) and fray Luis de Madrid, see ibid., 85, and Albert Sicroff, "Clandestine Judaism in the Hieronymite Monastery of Nuestra Señora de Guadalupe," in *Studies in Honor of M. J. Bernardete. (Essays in Hispanic and Sephardic Culture)*, ed. Izaak A. Langnas and Barton Sholod (New York: Las Americas Publishing Company, 1965), 102n. 67. Fray Gonzalo de Madrid, former prior of the friary, faced considerably

Fray Luis's insanity came at a particularly troubled moment in the history of the friary. The arrival of the Inquisition had thrown the local conflicts between conversos and Old Christians, between townspeople and friars, and within the religious community itself, into sharp relief. Worse yet were the Inquisition's findings: by March, Doctor Francisco Sánchez de la Fuente, inquisitor in Guadalupe, wrote his fellow inquisitor prior Nuño de Arévalo asking permission to investigate Judaizing inside the friary itself. In the midst of the turmoil caused by the presence of the inquisitors and the introspection forced on the community, fray Luis's devastating claim must have seemed disturbing indeed. In those months when the friars reexamined their brethren for evidence of Jewish sympathies, fray Luis's words were assumed to apply to whomever was considered most suspect. No one remembered to whom fray Luis was referring in his delirium; many said simply that he had cited "two [unnamed] friars." As a result, his words were used to indict all friars of converso ancestry. In their sworn statements to the inquisitorial notaries, the friars included their suspicions of who might not have consecrated the Host during mass. Most assumed that fray Luis meant the two friars who were ultimately those most severely punished by the Inquisition—fray Diego de Marchena and fray Diego de Burgos the Elder—but others offered fray Pedro de Madrid's name, or cast suspicion on the converso community as a whole.

Fray Luis de Madrid's claim and the events surrounding it highlight the numerous divisions among friars at the Jeronymite house in Guadalupe, particularly the increasing suspicion of New Christians within the order. Indeed, we cannot make sense of the fate of New Christians among the townspeople of Guadalupe without considering the friars who collectively controlled the Puebla. The assimilation or continuing separateness of the friars' own converso population had a significant effect upon both the town they ruled and upon the changing way in which they ruled it. These troubled events also provide further evidence of the divisions within the Jeronymite house that encompassed and superseded questions of Jewish ancestry. Fray Luis's accusation highlighted the spiritual power and responsibility inherent in the friars' maintenance of the central rite of Christianity; but it also indicated the vulnerability of both the rite and the friars to those acting with wrong intentions. Indeed, anxiety about Judaizers "infiltrating" Christian offices and functions was rooted in fears like those expressed by fray Luis, that the cen-

---

fewer accusations of Jewish practices than fray Pedro, although whether because untrue, because few remembered him, or out of respect for his position as prior is impossible to say. See chapter 4 for a discussion of prior Gonzalo's policies as prior; see chapter 2 for a discussion of some accusations made against prior Gonzalo.

ter of Christian practice, and the primary, miraculous function of the priesthood, could be endangered by the unbelief or hostility of Jewish converts.

In short, comments like those of fray Luis and others help reveal the internal climate of the friary in Guadalupe. By exploring traditional Jeronymite expectations of community life and how Guadalupe did and did not meet those expectations, it is possible to examine how the organization of Jeronymite community life provided space for converso brethren. Studying the process and impact of the internal inquisitorial trials on the friary sheds light on New Christians and the Inquisition both in the friary and in the town of Guadalupe.

Jeronymite Spirituality in Guadalupe

To understand events in the friary in 1485, it is important to review briefly the foundations of Jeronymite spirituality. The Order of Saint Jerome traced its origins to late-medieval hermits following the example of Saint Jerome in the desert and to the "modern" devotion of the later Middle Ages.[5] By the time the pope approved the order in 1373, the Jeronymites had evolved into a contemplative order, distanced from the poverty of the Franciscans, the preaching mission of the Dominicans, or the occasionally more extreme asceticism of their early roots.[6] Away from population centers and seats of power, Jeronymite friars dedicated themselves to singing the Divine Office, a solemn event that could occupy between eight and fourteen hours a day.[7] In Guadalupe, in addition to the liturgy sung daily in the parish church, masses were held in chapels scattered throughout the cloister. Intellectual pursuits were not encouraged, but readings at meals from the Bible, the church

[5] See my fuller discussion of the origins of the Jeronymites in chapter 1. Links between the Order of Saint Jerome and the *devotio moderna* of northern Europe are intriguing but still unclear and largely unresearched. See Charles Fraker, "Gonçalo Martínez de Medina, the *Jerónimos*, and the *devotio moderna*," 197–217; Castro, *Spaniards*; Nader, *The Mendoza Family*; and Marcel Bataillon, *Erasmo y España*, 2d ed., tr. Antonio Alatorre (Mexico City: fondo de Cultura Económica, 1966, reprinted 1995).

[6] See José de Sigüenza, OSH, *Historia*; Vizuete Mendoza, *Guadalupe*; and Revuelta Somalo, *Los Jerónimos*. On the Jeronymites' separation from more ascetic elements in the order, see chapter 1.

[7] On the role of music in the Order of Saint Jerome, see José López-Calo, SJ, "La música y el rito en la Orden Jeronimiana," in *Studia Hieronymiana* (Madrid, 1973), 1:125–138. Also of interest is Michael Noone, *Music and Musicians in the Escorial Liturgy Under the Habsburgs, 1563–1700*. Since a majority of the friars who established the Jeronymite community at the Escorial were from Guadalupe, Noone's work pays particular attention to practices there.

fathers, and medieval writers provided spiritual nourishment. A well-stocked library was also available.[8]

In the devotions of the Jeronymites, in their focus on humility, and in their resistance to highly intellectualized pursuits, the friars in Guadalupe differed little from their brethren throughout the order. But the Virgin that brought the Order of Saint Jerome to Guadalupe also made this house unique among Jeronymite foundations. The cult of the Virgin of Guadalupe and her large number of pilgrims made Guadalupe much wealthier than other Jeronymite houses, and at the same time demanded much more attention and administrative concern than smaller, less-visited houses. The friars complained bitterly about the demands of serving as lord over the Puebla, and those complaints seem more understandable when the responsibilities of friars in Guadalupe are compared to those of other foundations in the order, which tended to sit in small, out-of-the-way villages. Guadalupe also overshadowed the mother house of the order at court. The friary of San Bartolomé of Lupiana near the Mendoza stronghold of Guadalajara housed the general of the order and might provide advisers to the king, but this first Jeronymite house did not receive the same attention from Iberian royalty as Guadalupe. Lured in part by the area's reputation for hunting and by the shrine of the Virgin, generations of Castilian and Portuguese nobles had spent time in the friary. The royal hospice built after 1485 provided the Catholic Monarchs with a home during their frequent visits to the shrine and prepared the way both for Charles V's retirement to the nearby Jeronymite foundation at Yuste and Philip II's construction of El Escorial.[9]

Conversos in Guadalupe and the Order of Saint Jerome

Guadalupe resembled its brother houses in another way: the significant presence of conversos among the friars. It is difficult to specify the exact

[8] On sources of Jeronymite spirituality, see Ignacio de Madrid, OSH, "Teoría y práctica de la lectura espiritual en la Orden de San Jerónimo," in *Studia Hieronymiana*, 1:139–161; Vizuete Mendoza, J. Carlos, "La Biblioteca de Guadalupe: un reflejo de la espiritualidad jerónima," *En la España Medieval* 5 (1986), 1135–1146; B. Jiménez Duque, "Fuentes de la espiritualidad jerónima" in *Studia Hieronymiana*, 1:107–121. See also José de Sigüenza, *Historia*, and the summaries in Germán Rubío, OFM, *Historia*, and Vizuete Mendoza.

[9] The Royal Hospice, Real Hospedería, was built by the prior in gratitude to Isabel for donating Inquisition revenue to the shrine. The hospice is discussed at greater length in chapter 8. Holy Roman Emperor Charles V (Carlos I of Spain) retired to Yuste in northern Extremadura in 1556. Philip II, his heir, began construction of El Escorial palace and friary, a Jeronymite foundation, a decade later.

number of converso friars in Guadalupe, since in the fourteenth and fifteenth centuries few if any records were kept distinguishing New from Old Christians, in or out of the orders. New Christians were not yet subject to purity of blood laws, *estatutos de limpieza de sangre*, which in the early modern period stipulated that applicants to many civil and religious positions produce a genealogy proving Christian ancestry for four generations. When a popular uprising in Toledo in 1449 did attempt to ban conversos from public life, the Crown and the pope issued stern denunciations.[10] Evidence is if anything harder to come by in the Order of Saint Jerome. As a sign of humility, friars renounced their surnames, identifying themselves only with their place of origin—for example, Diego from Marchena or Nuño from Arévalo. This practice allows us to trace the geographic origins of Jeronymite friars but leaves little evidence of the family connections that might help us identify converso families.[11]

What is clear is that the Jeronymites were an order relatively more sympathetic to conversos, which made the order in general both more likely to include New Christian brothers and less likely to distinguish New from Old Christians. Alonso de Oropesa's strong defense of the Christianity of conversos in *Lumen ad Revelationem Gentium* and his resistance to anticonverso attitudes in the court of Enrique IV are perhaps the clearest indication of the mood of the order he led.[12] Not all Jeronymites supported conversos equally, but most if not all entered with the knowledge that the Order of Saint Jerome was seen as a refuge for conversos. Indeed, some saw the Jeronymites as sympathetic not only to conversos, but also to active Judaizers. This reputation may have been fostered largely by fears and suspicions about New Christians, but the actions of some conversos encouraged it. The bishop of Coria, a Jeronymite with converso sympathies if not a converso himself, was reported to have frequently lavished alms on local New Christians as part of his office's charitable works.[13] The Inquisition was tailor-made to reveal and promote these suspicions.

The reputation that the Jeronymites gained for harboring Judaizers as well as devoutly Christian New Christians may have owed much to the foundation at Guadalupe. Even when the Jeronymites launched their own investigation of Judaizing in the order, no other house contained

[10] Albert Sicroff, *Controverses*. The complicated history of purity of blood laws in the Order of Saint Jerome is discussed in chapter 8.

[11] Of course, surnames by themselves would not identify conversos, since conversos take on Christian names. They would, however, permit further genealogical research.

[12] Alonso de Oropesa and Jeronymite and Guadalupense attitudes toward New Christians were discussed in chapters 1 and 4.

[13] AMG unnumbered, Internal Inquisition, 89, 131, 165, 174, 183, 207.

the same number of friars accused of Judaizing or the extensive contact with lay New Christians that Guadalupe did.[14] Guadalupense Jeronymites who traveled to other cities frequently complained of being questioned about Judaizers in Guadalupe in particular. "I have heard said that in Guadalupe there is a friar who follows the law of Moses and encourages others to do the same," offered one man, after ascertaining the friars' Guadalupense origins.[15] In 1485 the presence of the Inquisition before so many pilgrims helped disseminate vivid images of the Holy Office throughout the peninsula; it is hardly surprising that the pilgrimage site in earlier years would have spread rumors of friars' improper activity.

One might ask why a Judaizing New Christian would enter a friary at all. No motivations are mentioned in the testimonies or confessions, and any latter-day hypothesis is mere speculation. Some possibilities do suggest themselves, however. One answer, of course, is that there were no Judaizing friars. Benzion Netanyahu has forcefully argued for the innocence of New Christians tried by the Inquisition, and even as noted a defender of the Judaism of New Christians as Haim Beinart has acknowledged that some accusations made against Jeronymite friars were false.[16] If we do accept the existence of a small number of Judaizers, it is conceivable that some may have sought out the Jeronymites as a refuge from the suspicions, outright hostility, and even persecution of one's home town. In Guadalupe, those accused of Judaizing tended to come from a very few towns some distance from the Marian shrine, suggesting the importance of "feeder communities" to the house in Guadalupe and the utility of distance from one's family and friends. At least three

[14] There have been a few studies on Judaizing in the Order of Saint Jerome. Haim Beinart, "The Judaizing Movement in the Order of San Jerónimo in Castile," *Studies in History, Scripta Hiersolymitana* 7 (1961), 167–192, uses trial records from the Toledan Inquisition (not the internal Jeronymite Inquisition) to trace the trials of Jeronymites generally. It remains a basic overview of the subject. The study also includes an important discussion of false accusations. Albert Sicroff, "The Jeronymite Friary of Guadalupe in 14th and 15th Century Spain," in *Collected Studies in Honour of Américo Castro's Eightieth Year*, ed. Marcel Hornik (Oxford: Lincombe Lodge Research Library, 1965), examines Guadalupe specifically. He makes use of the book of friars' testimonies from the friary in Guadalupe (AMG unnumbered, Internal Inquisition) to discuss Judaizing practices and responses. Julie A. Evans, "Heresy as an Agent of Change: Inquisition in the Monastery of Guadalupe" (doctoral dissertation, Stanford University, 1998), explores the hermeneutical questions surrounding the investigation of the friars. Diego de Ecija, *Libro*; Gabriel de Talavera, OSH, *Historia*; and José de Sigüenza, *Historia*, should also be consulted for their discussions of Judaizing and the Inquisitorial courts. The 1488 Inquisition is discussed in chapter 8.

[15] AMG unnumbered, Internal Inquisition, 79.

[16] See Beinart, "The Judaizing Movement," and Netanyahu, *Origins*. Less directly relevant but still useful for understanding his argument is Netanyahu, *The Marranos of Spain*.

friars might have entered the friary to try to hide evidence of their circumcision from any potential spouse. Others may have been drawn by the relatively easy and quiet lifestyle of the friary, particularly the comparative luxury of life in Guadalupe. Religious life also afforded the opportunity to read and write, and in some cases to perform other specialized trades, such as illuminating manuscripts or embroidery. Whatever their reasons, it does appear from the evidence that a few Judaizing friars were drawn to Jeronymite foundations throughout Castile, and particularly to Guadalupe.

AN INTERNAL INQUISITION

When prior Nuño arranged for the Holy Office to come to Guadalupe, he had no intention of initiating an investigation of the friars themselves.[17] But as vecinos testified against their fellow Guadalupenses, they did not hesitate to accuse local friars who were rumored to observe some elements of Judaism. Some friars in their role as confessors had urged greater sympathy by penitents for conversos, or even encouraged Judaizing behavior itself. The most experienced inquisitor present, Dr. Francisco Sánchez de la Fuente, wrote the prior on March 3, announcing officially the mass of evidence collected against his friars and requesting permission to investigate actions inside the friary. After negotiating with Sánchez de la Fuente, prior Nuño agreed to permit the Inquisition inside the friary, with some important provisos. The investigation of any friars would be distinct from the lay Inquisition proceeding outside the cloister walls. Proceedings would be kept secret, and separate from the lay Inquisition. Such actions were a further innovation in what was already something of a novelty. The inquisitors sent from Ciudad Real were still in the process of creating inquisitorial conventions, but the establishment of a separate court with distinct files, meetings, etc., made the internal investigation of the friars doubly ad hoc.[18]

Very little documentation remains of the "internal" Inquisition in Guadalupe in 1485, but near-contemporary accounts and the few documents that do remain suggest that prior Nuño succeeded in creating a

---

[17] Benzion Netanyahu has a very different understanding of the investigation of Jeronymite friars in Guadalupe and its aftermath. He believes that prior Nuño was part of a Jeronymite "racist" faction, bent on mercilessly eliminating all conversos from the order in the most efficient way possible. See his *Origins*, 1055–1063.

[18] AMG unnumbered, Internal Inquisition, 1–3; see also Fidel Fita, "La inquisición en Guadalupe," 283–343. Haim Beinart, "The Judaizing Movement," includes some discussion of events at Guadalupe.

parallel investigative structure that kept its activities separate even from the formal "lay" Inquisition with jurisdiction outside the cloister. After the Inquisition had completed its work in Guadalupe, all documents— for both "lay" and "clerical" inquisitions—were left in the keeping of the friary. In 1508 the Office of the Inquisition in Toledo sent a letter requesting that the 1485 trial records be sent to Toledo to become part of the permanent file there. Two additional requests and five years later, the Guadalupense friars responded; they returned all records of lay trials with an index compiled at that time listing all the vecinos who confessed and all who were tried, with a summary of their sentences.[19] Notably, the index does not include mention of those friars tried, nor are any trials of Guadalupense friars extant among the Toledan Inquisition trials. The prior apparently felt that the internal, "clerical" Inquisition did not fall under the jurisdiction of the Holy Office in Toledo, despite the participation of the inquisitors. The only record of the clerical Inquisition that survives is a Jeronymite collection of all the friars' statements to the Holy Office, recopied with an index at the front listing all those sentenced and indexing all references to those friars in the text.[20]

Once the arrangements for this internal Inquisition had been agreed upon, work began. Prior Nuño appointed two friars, Diego de Ecija and Diego de Guadalupe, to serve as scriveners for the internal Inquisition and then ordered all the friars to testify about any Jewish activities they had witnessed by friars living or deceased.[21] On June 30 friars related

---

[19] AHN clero legajo 1423, expediente 80. The records sent include trials conducted by prior Nuño in 1488.

[20] This is the unnumbered codex at AMG. I wish to express my sincere gratitude to the archivist at the friary in Guadalupe, Father Sebastián García, OFM, for allowing me to read this codex. The front cover prescribes excommunication for all who open it or read its contents. At the back is an explanation of how the testimony was to be guarded. There were two copies—one at Guadalupe and one in Lupiana—and each was locked in a box. AMG unnumbered is a clean copy bringing together all the friars' initial testimony before the inquisitors; one page uses the back of a page used to record the torture session of one of the friars—an apparent first draft and the only evidence for torture being used inside the friary.

The codex has a troubled history. At some point, most likely after the *desamortización* of the nineteenth century, the document disappeared from both friaries; one copy eventually came into the hands of the monastery of Nuestra Señora del Perpetuo Socorro in Madrid. Monks at the monastery in Madrid told me that the original was lost during the civil war, but others claimed that fray Arturo Alvarez, former archivist at Guadalupe, photographed an original copy of the document in the 1960s. The photocopy unfortunately was imperfectly done and lacks a few folios; as it now exists, the codex numbers over 250 pages. I use the modern foliation in my notes.

[21] This is the same fray Diego de Ecija who in approximately 1510 composed the *Libro*. Fray Diego de Ecija went on to serve the orderwide Jeronymite Inquisition in the same capacity.

their testimony to the two inquisitorial scriveners. According to Diego de Ecija, all the friars lined up to present their testimony on the same day. Their testimony was sorted by the name of the friar being accused, and trials against those most frequently accused began. Thereafter, trials presumably progressed much as they did in the lay Inquisition, with imprisoned defendants arguing their innocence before an inquisitor with the help of a solicitor. From one fragment of a trial record unintentionally preserved in the book of testimonies, it is clear that defendants and witnesses were directly questioned and that torture was used on some friars who would not confess wrongdoing.[22]

In a tight-knit community like the Jeronymite house at Guadalupe, rumor and gossip were the order of the day. Earlier accusations of Jewish practices spread quickly through the friary and could be used to contribute to ongoing divisions and disputes among the brethren. On the surface, the Jeronymites at Guadalupe might have seemed to be part of a very private group, isolated for the most part from the town that surrounded them and even from the pilgrims who came to visit their shrine. But in another sense the friars existed in a hothouse environment, on display to the town and the world. Their behavior in front of the town was scrutinized, and their every communication with the townspeople closely examined. Given such close attention from outside the friary walls and such close quarters inside them, it is not surprising that the inquisitors quickly elicited a variety of complaints against fellow brethren.

Leading a contemplative life away from family and town, the Judaizing practices of friars would necessarily differ from those of their lay coreligionists. Life rituals, such as circumcision, marriage practices, or mourning, held little relevance for monastic life. Jewish practices linked to the calendar year were also difficult to engage in, since the structured nature of Jeronymite life left little free time in which to celebrate private feasts, fasts, or other celebrations. On the other hand, some practices were facilitated by the quiet life of the cloister where the anonymity of leaving behind one's home provided freedom from suspicion. In short, Jeronymite Judaizing was limited to those practices that were compatible with their chosen life as a Christian friar.

Converso friars created informal networks within the Jeronymite community at Guadalupe. While friars generally came from around Extremadura, Andalucía, and to a lesser extent the peninsula as a whole, those accused of Judaizing tended to come from a few particular towns—most notably Burgos, Madrid, and Segovia.[23] In contrast, none

---

[22] On imprisonment, see AMG unnumbered, Internal Inquisition, 42.
[23] Madrid and Segovia were each the site of Jeronymite houses.

of the six friars born and raised in Guadalupe was accused of any wrongdoing. In some cases the number of friars hailing from one city had to do with family connection—Juan and Diego de Segovia were brothers, for example—but none of the five Burgalense friars was related, and three of the four converso friars from Burgos were accused of observing Jewish practices. The combination of similar family histories, cities of origin, and perhaps religious beliefs encouraged the formation of these smaller groups within the Guadalupense Jeronymite community as a whole. Throughout the friars' testimony, conversos from one city are described talking and spending time together. Unlike among the townspeople of Guadalupe, there is no evidence of groups of friars engaging in collective Jewish activities, but the companionship of brethren from home must have comforted New and perhaps Old Christian friars.

Accusations of Judaizing against converso friars were generally not as elaborate as accusations against their lay counterparts. Most common were accusations of private devotions easy to practice in one's cell. A few friars, like Pedro de Madrid, for example, were said to light oil lamps on Friday evenings.[24] Others feigned a physical inability to eat lard or other pork products, or simply left any pork uneaten.[25] Celebrating the Divine Office and singing in the choir were the primary occupations of friars in Guadalupe, and so it is hardly surprising that converso lack of interest in devotional activities would be most apparent in church. Fray Gonzalo de Alcalá spoke for many when he complained that "converso friars do not sing unless they individually read the lesson or something else."[26] Fray Diego de Burgos the Elder, *el viejo*, earned the resentment of his fellow friars for missing Saturday choir an unseemly number of times. Many accused him of attempting in this way to observe the Jewish Sabbath.[27] Fray Velasco de Villatoro complained that fray Diego de Marchena and Diego de Burgos were "always straying and searching for infinite ways and incredible illnesses so that they could be exempt from the Divine Office. And if they do come there it seems that they come more because they are constrained to do so than with devotion and love for Our Lord."[28] Few friars were as apparently explicit in their

---

[24] Ibid., 9, 87, 107, 127, 131, etc.

[25] Ibid., 42, for example.

[26] Ibid., 48. "[Los frailes confessos] que son desta naçion non cantan salvo si singularmente dizen lection o otra cosa alguna." Other complaints about singing occur on 68, 221.

[27] Ibid., 146.

[28] Ibid., 221. "siempre deviando & buscando maneras infinitas, & enfermedades incredibiles por ser exentos del ofiçio divino. & si ay bienen paresçe que vienen mas [construidos] que con devoçion & amor de nuestro señor." Fray Velasco saw one's

practices as fray Diego de Burgos the Elder. One friar commented that fray Diego did not make the sign of the cross over his meals "until the Inquisition came here." Furthermore, fray Diego occasionally prayed with his head covered with a white cloth as if following "the old law of the Jews."[29]

What life in the house at Guadalupe did offer for Judaizing friars was the opportunity to read and think, and there is evidence that some conversos' most suspicious activities—at least in the minds of their fellow friars—revolved around these more intellectual pursuits. Fray Diego de Burgos the Younger, *el mozo*, provides one example. Fray Diego de Logrosán said he heard fray Diego the Younger use the word *adonay*, a Hebrew term for God, in his prayers, although fray Diego defended himself by saying he was merely praying the verses of Saint Bernard.[30] The Talmud or other explicitly Jewish literature was of course unavailable, but the Hebrew Bible or Old Testament provided a model of Jewish concerns and practices—a reminder of Jewish ancestry and ritual activity if not a description of it. Fray Diego de Burgos the Younger roused the suspicions of fray Lorenzo de San Esteban for owning a copy of the Pentateuch—the first five books of the Hebrew Bible—in Spanish. The vernacular edition of the Pentateuch included lies, thought fray Lorenzo, and his opinion influenced the testimony of several friars who confirmed that fray Diego owned the Spanish book, encouraged others to read it, and spoke highly of Jews. Some said that fray Diego even claimed to read Hebrew, although there was no clear evidence to support that charge.[31]

Not surprisingly, conversos inside the Jeronymite house were accused of making heretical theological arguments more often than were those living outside the friary. Heretical theological arguments also found their way into the Inquisition records, although in a limited fashion. The only specific theological arguments propounded by converso friars concerned the Virgin Mary and the Incarnation of Jesus. Fray Alonso de Nogales believed that the Virgin had conceived her child as did other women. "I heard tell that fray Alonso de Nogales said that Our Lady

---

degree of participation in choir as a key indicator of attitudes toward Judaism. Summing up a short, vague statement about fray Alonso de Nogales, fray Velasco commented, "I do not know if he sings," 221.

[29] Ibid., 68. Testimony of fray Juan de San Sebastián.

[30] Ibid., 99.

[31] Ibid., 44, 67, 69, 99, 103, 155, 191, 200 include testimony about fray Diego de Burgos the Younger in regard to reading and owning books in Spanish. Pages 67, 155, 191 specifically report accusations that fray Diego knew Hebrew. These anxieties about religious literature in the vernacular foreshadow Reform interest in vernacular religious writings a generation later.

Mary had given birth by the same path by which she had conceived or similar words." When he heard this comment, the general of the order wrote fray Alonso's confessor urging him to separate fray Alonso from these errors.[32] Fray Alonso also questioned the doctrine of the Annunciation and the Incarnation; he referred to Joseph as the "father" of Jesus and avowed that Mary gave birth to other children after Jesus. Fray Diego de Marchena frequently affirmed that Jesus had brothers and sisters by Mary and Joseph since the New Testament called Christ the first-born, *primogénito*, of Mary.[33]

Fray Augustín announced his theological conclusions more publicly. In a sermon before the town he proclaimed that Mary did not know she bore the Son of God until she gave birth, thereby denying the Annunciation. Fray Augustín apparently was attempting to draw a moral lesson for the vecinos. According to one friar present, he argued that

> if [the Virgin Mary] had conceived as a virgin that [therefore] other women had conceived as virgins, comparing the Mother of God, who conceived by the Holy Ghost, to the other women, who conceived by the dirty semen of man in prurience and filth. And [Augustín] said thus without other distinction and if she conceived as a virgin others conceived as virgins. . . . [Fray Augustín added that] moral virtues or the moral [?] were better preached in the synagogue of the Jews or in the mosque of the Muslims than in the Church of God.[34]

Whatever his intent, fray Augustín's message was lost on the scandalized townspeople and friars who complained about his sermon. Fray Augustín requested the chance to explain himself in a second sermon, but after horrifying his brethren with the explanation that "men are born from men as horses are from horses," his public explanations of the Virgin Birth ceased.[35]

[32] Ibid., 127. Testimony of fray Pedro de Guadalupe. "[oí dezir] avia dicho el dicho fray Alonso que Nuestra Señora avia parido por donde conçibio, o semejantes palabras." This account is confirmed by fray Pedro de Trujillo, 49, fray Juan de Siruela the Second, 135, and fray Fernando de Osuna, 158.

[33] Ibid., 6, etc.

[34] Ibid., 56. Testimony of fray Pedro de Trujillo. "ça si ella avia conçebido virgen que otras mugeres avian conçebido virgenes comparando a la madre de dios que conçebiera de Spiritu Sancto a las otras mugeres que conçiben de simiente suzia de varon con pruritu y suziedad. diziendo asi sin otra distinçion y si ella conçibio virgen otras conçiberon virgenes. . . . [Dijo que] mejor se predicauan las virtudes morales, o la [phian?] moral en la sinagoga de los judios, o en la mezquita de los moros que en la yglesia de dios."

[35] Ibid., 57. Testimony of fray Pedro de Trujillo. Several other friars testified against fray Augustín for his statements about the Virgin; see 40, 100, 139, 180, 183, 186, 215,

Other friars took advantage of their time outside the cloister and town of Guadalupe to Judaize more openly, although distance from the friary did not prevent rumors from following them on their return. Fray Diego de Marchena was rumored to have entered a synagogue in Seville while Jews were inside praying. Fray Diego explained that he had been asked by an imprisoned Jew in that city to carry a letter to the rabbi explaining how he kept the Sabbath in prison. In the opinion of at least one friar, however, this explanation did little to absolve him. Even if fray Diego had not entered a synagogue to worship, he was still enabling a Jew to observe the law of Moses.[36]

More threatening even than heretical doctrine, perhaps, was the more intimate heresy of circumcision. Usually, circumcision indicated devotion to Judaism on the part of one's parents, since most circumcisions occurred in infancy; therefore, it was at one level irrelevant to an individual's fidelity to Christianity or Judaism. Indeed, circumcision was no barrier to conversion. Yet most inquisitors seem to have considered it analogous to Christian baptism, which fundamentally and irrevocably changed one's nature, and thus aroused suspicions of Judaizing. In the same way that New Christians were responsible for adhering to their Christian status gained at baptism, so too inquisitors might think that conversos were responsible for the covenant signified by circumcision. For the inquisitors, circumcision revealed that the body and soul of the circumcised man were subject to a covenant made according to the law of Moses. Only close questioning could reveal whether a circumcised man's baptism had truly washed away the earlier covenant he had made at birth. Few Guadalupense vecinos seem to have engaged in the practice, but among the Jeronymites, inquisitors found three circumcised friars. In the lay Inquisition court, those few accused of being circumcised argued for the presence or absence of circumcision without, apparently, submitting to a physical exam. In contrast, all brethren in the friary suspected of being circumcised were brought together toward the end of the clerical inquisition, on July 18, 1485, and were examined by a team of four friars, including one doctor. Upon inspection, three friars were found to be circumcised, and one was declared uncircumcised.[37]

---

229. AHN clero legajo 1423 includes a lengthy inquest into fray Augustín's actions. Albert Sicroff mentions fray Augustín in his article "The Jeronymite Friary."

[36] AMG unnumbered, Internal Inquisition, 65. Testimony of fray Pedro de Ribadeo. The letter presumably asked for rulings on what practices were demanded of him while imprisoned by Christians. No one suggests why fray Diego was carrying the letter; perhaps he had easier access to the prison than did the rabbi.

[37] Those found circumcised were fray Diego de Marchena, fray Diego de Burgos the Elder, and fray Diego de Segovia. The brother of the latter, fray Juan de Segovia,

Fray Juan and fray Diego de Segovia provide one example of the anxiety that circumcision or even the suspicion of it could bring. When he was first accused of being circumcised, fray Juan argued that he and his sibling fray Diego had been born after their father's conversion to Christianity and that none of the brothers had been circumcised. Five days later, but five days before the inspection, fray Juan changed his story. He still maintained that he had always been Christian, but he now added that his brother Diego had been "taken out of his company" when he was only eight years old; he did not know whether his brother Diego was circumcised or not. Fray Diego had long expressed his concern about his own circumcision to some friars. He once asked another if it were possible to be born circumcised and later affirmed that to be the case.[38] Nor was fray Juan viewed as completely innocent; several friars considered him to be circumcised, he worked long hours with a lay converso assistant, and he engaged in other suspicious behavior.[39]

Equally serious were suspicions surrounding some converso friars who officiated at mass without showing proper reverence for the Host. Fray Alonso de Nogales was accused of demonstrating little reverence or devotion during mass; one friar claimed that he had watched fray Alonso put his hands on his head and in other ways show little reverence for the Host.[40] Fray Diego de Burgos the Younger and fray Diego de Marchena were also accused of acting improperly during mass.[41] Aided in part by fray Luis de Madrid's vivid deathbed account, friars repeatedly stated that fray Diego de Marchena raced through celebration of the mass, hurrying the formulae so much that many speculated that there was not sufficient time to say the rites necessary to consecrate the Host. Even without fray Luis's suggestions, friars lamented how fray Diego did not lift the chalice or paten fully above his head and

---

silversmith, was determined to be uncircumcised. Ibid., 15–16. For more on circumcision, see the relevant discussion in chapter 2.

[38] Ibid., 85. Testimony of fray Luis de Madrid. Ibid., 126. Testimony of fray Martín de Trujillo.

[39] His brother fray Diego was responsible for some of the rumors about fray Juan's circumcision. Fray Juan ate eggs (i.e., meat) on Friday and spoke poorly of the Inquisition's mission. Despite the common belief among the friars that fray Juan was circumcised, he was found to be uncircumcised by the inquisitors. His sometime assistant in silversmithing, Diego Nuñez *platero*, was tried and exiled by the Inquisition. See AHN Inquisition legajo 169, expediente 3. One impressive example of fray Juan de Segovia's work remains at the friary today. It is a trunk elaborately decorated with silver bas-relief panels. The trunk has been restored recently and is on display at the friary in Guadalupe.

[40] AMG unnumbered, Internal Inquisition, 135. Testimony of fray Juan de Siruela.

[41] Ibid., 230. Testimony of fray Pedro de Vidania.

treated the ceremony perfunctorily when it was performed by others.[42] Fray Juan de Durango testified that "[fray Diego de Marchena] is not devoted to the Sacrament . . . when it is raised he is always squatting. And before the priest officiating lowers the Host or the chalice he sits down."[43] Fray Juan added darkly that during one mass celebrated before the town, fray Diego was responsible for several Eucharistic wafers falling to the ground.

Clearly many converso friars were not ideal Jeronymites, and a few maintained Jewish traditions inside the friary's walls. Only two friars— Diego de Marchena and Diego de Burgos the Elder—appear in the documents as consistently maintaining their devotion to Jewish practices and attitudes, and it is not surprising that they alone were publicly sentenced by the inquisitors. Unlike in the Puebla of Guadalupe, there were few New Christians in the friary who evidenced a desire to live a fully Jewish life. The nineteen friars who were ultimately censured for their whispered criticisms of the Inquisition and its practices, their aversion to pork, and their suspicious prayers and attitudes toward the Virgin Mary and the Mass were clearly not models of Jeronymite devotion or Christian spirituality. Professing Christianity while secretly attempting to live as a Jew was a difficult and dangerous proposition no matter what the circumstances; it was especially challenging in a friary, and it should come as no surprise that despite the high number of conversos in the house in Guadalupe, most did not openly and consistently attempt to live as Jews.

Only one friar in Guadalupe, fray Diego de Marchena, was executed for his Judaizing, and it is worth considering his case in greater detail.[44] Fray Diego was unique in Guadalupe, in the Order of Saint Jerome, and in Castile. His history as a friar at one of Castile's most prestigious monasteries, who was circumcised but never baptized, and who died for his lack of devotion to Christian rites, has been mentioned by many scholars, who use his case as an example of the most radical action taken by conversos who never wished to convert.[45] It is important, however, to consider fray Diego in relation to events in Guadalupe. Diego de Marchena was paradigmatic of the challenges facing Guadalupe in

[42] Ibid., 108, 161.

[43] Ibid., 108. Testimony of fray Juan de Durango. "muy indevoto al sacramento . . . quando alça siempre esta de nalgas. & antes que el sacerdote abaxe la hostia o el calix se mete en la silla."

[44] Netanyahu is inaccurate when he says that "a number of friars were publicly burned" in Guadalupe. See *Origins*, 1311n. 25.

[45] The best summary of fray Diego's career can be found in Albert Sicroff, "El Caso del Judaizante Jerónimo fray Diego de Marchena," in *Homenaje a Rodríguez-Moñino* (Madrid: Editorial Castalia, 1966), 2:227–233.

the fifteenth century, yet he was also a striking exception to practices and attitudes of New Christian friars in Guadalupe and elsewhere.

Fray Diego de Marchena had been a friar in Guadalupe for well over twenty years by the time he was burned at the stake in 1485. That he had been able to stay as long as he did was in itself striking; it suggests both the patience of the friars with disruptive brethren and the friary's unwillingness to punish its own. Indeed, fray Diego may at one time have had powerful patrons within the friary walls: he served in the prestigious positions of cantor and confessor during his time as a friar there. Fray Diego may have had his supporters during the course of his twenty-odd years at Guadalupe, but he was not universally loved: many more friars testified against fray Diego than against fray Diego de Burgos the Elder, the only other friar to be punished publicly. Indeed, criticisms of fray Diego de Marchena's actions extended even to the early 1460s and the first, locally organized inquisitorial court in Guadalupe. At that time fray Diego had supported the scrivener, Fernando González, against charges of heresy; he had taunted his brothers by announcing that he knew of the existence of a Judaizing vecino, but he had refused to divulge his identity. Eventually fray Diego had relented and revealed González's name, although he confided to fray Martín Vizcayno later that he still prayed for forgiveness for this act.[46]

Fray Diego de Marchena seemed to delight in shocking his fellow friars. As previously mentioned, he frequently argued that the Virgin Mary had borne other children, since Jesus was referred to as *primogénito*, first born.[47] The advice he dispensed in the confessional horrified the friars when they learned of it. As one friar ruefully explained to the inquisitors, "Seville already doesn't allow conversos to be confessors."[48] One day, when a friar asked his brethren if they knew of anything new happening in town, fray Diego quickly replied that he knew what was new: two rabbis had come to town to check on the devotional practices of the local converso community, and to console and advise them.[49] Fray Diego made little attempt to conceal his opinions; indeed, he seemed to enjoy flaunting them. Hot-tempered, fray Diego and fray Juan de Andújar kept up a long argument through a series of written messages left on each other's chairs in choir.[50] Until he was investigated by the inquisitors, fray Diego left little doubt as to his opinions of Christianity, Judaism, and his fellow friars. He confidently asserted that Jews and Muslims could be saved in their religion as easily as could

[46] AMG unnumbered, Internal Inquisition, 178. Testimony of Martín Vizcayno.
[47] Ibid., 6 and passim.
[48] Ibid., 29–30.
[49] Ibid., 104. Testimony of fray Alonso de Plasencia against fray Diego de Marchena.
[50] Ibid., 27–34. Testimony of fray Juan de Andújar.

Christians in theirs.[51] His attitudes were apparent not only to the friars in Guadalupe, but also to vecinos and pilgrims, and his notoriety extended throughout the peninsula.

Indeed, it was fray Diego de Marchena's attitudes, as much as his actions, that crystallized others' dislike of him. Fray Diego was never accused of participating in Jewish ritual activity. Other than one friar's testimony that fray Diego avoided a blood sausage, *morcilla*, when he first arrived in Guadalupe, no one suggested that fray Diego lit candles, prayed Hebrew prayers, or engaged in any other "Jewish" practice. Rather, fray Diego infuriated his Old Christian brethren with his mocking of Christian ritual and his use of his clerical authority to support Judaizers in town. Fray Diego appeared uninterested and disrespectful during mass, even as he was theoretically consecrating the Host. He scoffed at Christian and Jeronymite tradition, mocked the practices of the confessional, and cynically took advantage of traditional means of monastic discipline. Further, the friar openly supported Jews and Judaizers and aided them when possible. On numerous trips to Seville he interacted with the Jewish community there, such as when he brought a letter from an imprisoned Jew to his rabbi. When his sister and other family members were taken prisoner while attempting to flee to Granada to practice Judaism openly, fray Diego asked for an extended leave of absence to gain their release. Loyalty to one's family was an admirable characteristic, but aiding family members who avoided their Christian responsibilities was decidedly less admirable, particularly when the friary's funds were used to do it.

Unlike fray Fernando de Ubeda, fray Diego de Marchena did not involve himself in town politics, or aim for the highest offices in the friary. The prestigious position of confessor had been sufficient for him. Like fray Fernando, however, the enmity focused on fray Diego was rooted in fray Diego's easy dismissal of monastic norms of behavior. Fray Fernando challenged traditional means of getting and keeping political power in the friary; fray Diego overturned patterns of behavior in the confessional and among other friars. Both were aggressive men who infuriated their fellow friars. As disliked as both men were, however, only fray Diego de Marchena was sentenced to death by the Inquisition. The emotional upheaval surrounding the arrival and activity of the inquisitorial court brought to the surface ill-will against both men, but the Inquisition was directed against the more explicitly anti-Christian, and ancestrally Jewish, fray Diego.

It was fray Diego de Marchena's opinions, as much as his actions, that eventually caused his downfall. No one but fray Diego ventured to state such controversial claims, and his independence (and occasional

[51] Ibid., 6.

disagreeableness) led to his death for heretical acts. Fray Diego may have spoken to some degree for his fellow *converso* friars, but that assumption is impossible to prove. In fact, his singular fate serves as a reminder that only the rarest converso friars spoke so bluntly. Most assimilated, or attempted to assimilate, and few New Christians attempted to unite life as a Jeronymite with a dismissal of Christianity, or with continued devotion to Judaism.

Fray Diego de Marchena's trial, like all the trials held within the walls of the friary, operated with much greater speed than those for the lay Inquisition. While lay trials usually ran for several months between March and November, verdicts against the friars were reached and sentences read by the end of July, only one month after testimony had been collected. In all, 21 of the 130 friars in Guadalupe were censured for their purported Jewish activities. Nineteen of the 21 were never publicly revealed; their punishment was decided by the prior and in keeping with the internal nature of this Inquisition, revealed only within the friary rather than to the town or kingdom as a whole. The sentences of these friars were relatively light; like their lay counterparts who received relatively mild sentences, their heretical activity had not been fully proven. For fray Diego de Marchena and fray Diego de Burgos the Elder, however, the fates were not so kind. Both men were handed over to the official inquisitorial court for sentencing. Diego de Burgos was sentenced to perpetual imprisonment on July 31, 1485. The next day, August 1, fray Diego de Marchena was sentenced at his own auto de fe on the steps of the church (fig. 7). Under torture, fray Diego de Marchena claimed that he had been circumcised, but never baptized, and that he kept kosher by not eating pork. Like the lay people sentenced in earlier autos de fe, his sentence was read out from a catafalque raised in the cemetery, at the highest point in the plaza, with hundreds of pilgrims and townspeople crowded into the plaza to hear. Fray Diego was then publicly stripped of his status in the order, humiliated by each of the friars in turn, and burned at the stake.[52]

---

[52] A summary of fray Diego de Marchena's confession is available in AHN clero 2160. His lengthy testimony appears in AMG unnumbered, Internal Inquisition, 231–245. Fray Diego de Burgos's testimony before the Inquisition is in ibid., 184–185. Testón Núñez and Domínguez Ortiz both mention documents relative to Diego de Marchena; see Testón Núñez and Hernández Bermejo, "La inquisición de Llerena en la centuria del quinientos," and Antonio Domínguez Ortiz, *La clase social de los conversos en Castilla en la edad moderna* (Madrid: Consejo Superior de Investigaciones Científicas, 1955). Diego de Ecija provides an account of these two trials in his *Libro*. Accounts are also available in José de Sigüenza, *Historia*, and Germán Rubio, *Historia*; a less accurate summary appears in García, Sebastián, OFM and Felipe Trenado, OFM, *Guadalupe*: 95–96 (they claim that Diego de Marchena was not tortured, for example).

FIGURE 7. View of the church porch, steps, and plaza, where fray Diego de Marchena and others were sentenced. In the foreground is the site of the old cemetery, where the inquisitors' platform was raised. Photo by the author.

NEW AND OLD CHRISTIAN PROCONVERSO FRIARS

The Jeronymite house in Guadalupe generally lacked converso friars who attempted to use the cloister as a shield for active Judaizing; what it did not lack were Old and New Christian friars who supported *conversos* and their place in society, even when those New Christians did not practice the faith they officially espoused. These proconverso advocates, intellectual descendants of the tolerant policies of fray Alonso de Oropesa, were more numerous than Judaizers and, as attitudes toward New Christians hardened over the fifteenth century, more and more divisive. Their outspoken sympathies, at times colored by financial, political, or personal self-interest, helped radicalize debate in Guadalupe and the order as a whole between those who favored gradual integration and reform of New Christian populations and those who emphasized punishment for wrongdoing and isolation of converso friars. Proconverso attitudes, expressed in the practices of the friars in and out of the friary, were the most public expression of the friary's converso sympathies and had the potential to damage the reputation of Guadalupe and the Jeronymite Order.

Within the walls of the shrine, friars often urged tolerance for New Christians. Beyond the theological arguments of fray Alonso de Oropesa, however, some friars expressed a support of conversos and concomitant suspicion of Old Christians that almost veered into heresy itself. Fray Diego de Segovia, himself a New Christian, strongly resisted the Inquisition and spoke out against it, an opinion that seemed to some to share little with fray Alonso's concern for correct doctrine among conversos.[53] Fray Diego de Burgos the Elder supported conversos but was said to hate Old Christians, an attitude hardly in line with those who encouraged converso assimilation into Christian society.[54] Other friars complained when they heard their brethren speak poorly of conversos. Such an assertion in itself raised little suspicion, but fray Alonso de Nogales's criticism of fray Lorenzo in the confessional "because [he] spoke poorly of heretics" went beyond defending converts to defending those who resisted Christianity.[55] Twenty years earlier fray Alonso de Oropesa's support for assimilating conversos raised fewer questions; his devotion to Christianity was as clear as his desire to assimilate New Christians gently into their faith. In the increasingly divisive climate in Castile and in the friary in Guadalupe, however, there was less tolerance and support for the moderate opinions of the previous generation.

Perhaps more damaging to the friary than proconverso sentiment expressed inside the friary were converso sympathies stated to the pilgrims and vecinos outside of the walls. One example was the proconverso policies of vicar Fernando de Ubeda. No one accused fray Fernando of participating in Jewish ceremonies or maintaining Jewish practices; but many pointed to fray Fernando as "favoring" conversos over Old Christians. Fray Fernando's close political and personal links to wealthy New Christian merchants, as well as his apparent legal protection of them, earned him the resentment of many of his brethren. Political favoritism for personal gain were hallmarks of his tenure as vicar, and some friars complained to the inquisitors of gifts he made to his mistress and child.[56] While his behavior seemed suspicious and certainly unbecoming of a friar, no one thought to name fray Fernando a converso per se. Still, whatever fray Fernando's personal beliefs, his policies

[53] AMG unnumbered, Internal Inquisition, 79. Testimony of Fray Juan de Carranza.

[54] Ibid., 111.

[55] Ibid., 44. Testimony of fray Lorenzo de San Estevan. "Quando era confessor me reprehendia muchas vezes porque dezia mal delos herege. . . ."

[56] Ibid., 170. Testimony of Fray Fernando de Moneo.

supporting converso merchants brought further lay suspicion upon the house and the order.[57]

Not surprisingly, the confessional was a convenient place for proconverso friars to share their opinions with the townspeople of Guadalupe. Repeatedly, vecinos complained that their confessor exhorted them to treat conversos better and not to criticize or in any way denigrate their New Christian brethren. Some converso penitents claimed that while in the confessional they were encouraged to keep kosher.[58] Wealthy conversos had financially supported the friary during the economically disastrous civil war, and to many vecinos these merchants appeared to benefit from privileged treatment. Confessional urgings to speak well of conversos and treat them fairly held political and social as well as religious significance. But despite the disturbing implications of such confessional advice, the confessional was still primarily a religious site, and support for conversos by friars in the confessional raised profound spiritual concerns. Contact with the spiritual attitudes of the friars was limited primarily to homilies and to the act of confession, and lay suspicion of the friars' beliefs must have come largely from these two kinds of encounters. Fray Diego de Marchena's role as a confessor to pilgrim and vecino certainly did not do him or his house any good; many friars lamented fray Diego's habit of encouraging penitents to boil rather than roast chicken on Fridays. "The smell of cooking chicken is in this way hidden, and you could eat chicken in the plaza itself on Good Friday and no one would know!"[59] Even more upsetting was the cruel "anticatechism" fray Lope de Villareal supposedly practiced in the confessional.

> Mari González widow of Diego González *cardador* said . . . that one day confessing herself with fray Lope de Villareal he asked her some things concerning confession. And as the good woman did not know how to respond to what he asked, fray Lope the confessor said, "Although he is considered a heretic, Fernan González the scrivener knows how to answer better than you. Well, then, what is raised at the altar?" The old woman replied, "What is raised at the altar is the true body and blood of Our Lord Jesus Christ," to which he responded, "It is nothing but bread and wine." And when she heard this and many other things she did not agree with she began to cry out strongly that he would not make her

[57] Fray Fernando de Ubeda and his attempt to control of the town of Guadalupe was discussed at greater length in chapter 4.

[58] See, for example, complaints made against fray Diego de Marchena, AMG unnumbered, Internal Inquisition, 55. Testimony of fray Pedro de Trujillo.

[59] Ibid., 29, 156, 157, etc.

become Jewish. And so having heard this she never confessed with him again.[60]

It is hard to imagine why fray Lope might have forced such a confrontation. Perhaps he mistook her for a conversa or felt that she had been needlessly cruel to a local New Christian. Perhaps Mari González was lying. Whatever their motivations, rumors of such an encounter could hardly have improved the plight of New Christians wrongly suspected of Jewish practices; nor could the alleged incident have improved the reputation of the Guadalupe friary as being a haven for conversos.

Just as proconverso sentiments were unwelcome from New or Old Christians, so too were unconventional understandings of Christian doctrine, even if voiced by Old Christians. Unusual intellectual or spiritual practices, even if not heretical, increasingly came under suspicion by friars worried about moral decay in the friary. Fray Diego de Ecija, one of the two friars named as inquisitorial scriveners, mentioned several conversos in his deposition before the Inquisition. But he also complained that fray Pedro Alemán, Peter the German, incorrectly cited Aristotle. The charge is hardly equivalent to avoiding pork or lighting candles on Friday; indeed, one could question the possibility that a German was a converted Jew at all, since no one else testified against the deceased friar, and no charges were brought against him. However, fray Diego de Ecija's concern does indicate the depth of suspicion of some friars, and the increased suspicion surrounding potentially dangerous intellectual pursuits. Political motivations also played a role in accusations, as fray Fernando de Ubeda and others learned. Old Christian fray Augustín's irregular moralizing on the Virgin Birth, discussed previously, aroused the anxiety of the friars. But once fray Augustín publicly spoke against the traperos, Alonso de Córdoba launched a personal attack, implausibly challenging fray Augustín's devotion to Christianity. Under many circumstances New Christian Alonso de Córdoba would not have been considered a plausible witness, but the friar who heard his remarks faithfully repeated them to the inquisitors without

---

[60] Ibid., 90. Testimony of fray Alonso de Trujillo. "Mari González viuda de Diego González cardador le dixo [a fray Alonso de Trujillo] que un día confesandose con fray Lope de Villareal preguntandole algunas cosas çerca de la confesion. & como la buena muger no le supiese responder a lo que le preguntaua dixole el dicho fray Lope confesor 'digos que aunque tienen por ereje a Ferran González escrivano que sabe mejor responder que vos. Pues veamos que es lo que alçan en el altar.' Dixo la vieja, 'lo que alçan en el altar es cuerpo verdadero & sangre de Nuestro Señor Jesu Christi.' A la qual respondio él, 'aquello non es sinon pan & vino.' & quando ello oyo esto & otras muchas muchas cosas que a ella non se le acuerdan començó a llorar tan fuertemente que [ayna?] la tornara judia. & como ella oyó esto nunca más se confesó con él."

comment.[61] Any accusation might be read through the lens of anxiety
over un-Christian attitudes in the friary and held suspect. Fray Diego de
Burgos the Younger has already been mentioned for reading the Bible
in Spanish.[62] A generation before Luther's Ninety-Five Theses, reading
religious literature in the vernacular was a sign of dangerous religious
tendencies. Among the occasionally anti-intellectual Jeronymites, and in
the context of Judaizing activity in the friary, any reading might be a
cause for concern. Fray Alonso de Béjar reported that he saw fray Juan
de Segovia reading a Bible, "which seems wrong to me."[63]

Under the pressures of a strong converso minority and a small population inside the friary of brethren sympathetic to Judaizers and hostile
to some Christian doctrine, Jeronymite spirituality was changing. Their
focus on humility remained unchanged, but other qualities of the early
Jeronymite movement were challenged by contact with the court and
the world. It would be an oversimplification to argue for a radical,
complete shift in attitude among Jeronymite friars; it is possible, however, to speak of heightened polarization among two increasingly distinct factions in the Order of Saint Jerome. The vision of conversion by
persuasion championed by fray Alonso de Oropesa continued to have
force in the order: fray Hernando de Talavera, first bishop of postcon-
quest Granada, was one of its best-known proponents. Increasingly,
however, his outlook was contrasted with the harsher attitudes toward
New Christians espoused by fray Gonzalo de Toro and others after
1485.[64] An older attitude forgoing excessive intellectualism was now
challenged by a more radical anti-intellectualism, eschewing academic
pursuits entirely for more strictly liturgical ones. During the period of
Catholic Reform and afterward, the Jeronymites were noted for their
lack of scholars, despite the impressive library assembled by Philip II at
the Jeronymite palace-monastery of the Escorial. Fray José de Sigüenza,
historian of the order and librarian at the Escorial, was the exception
rather than the rule.

The internal Inquisition in Guadalupe did not independently engender
these shifts, but the Inquisition's investigations, together with changing
attitudes in Iberia and in the order, helped further these changes. By
focusing attention on the friars who were most controversial or in any

---

[61] Ibid., 148.

[62] Ibid., 103.

[63] Ibid., 76. Testimony of fray Alonso de Béjar. "Lee en la brivia que me paresçe mal."

[64] Fray Gonzalo de Toro was head of the order during the Jeronymite Inquisition; he
was also a strong proponent of *limpieza de sangre* statutes in the order. The imposition
of the statutes is described in chapter 8. Benzion Netanyahu also sees two factions
developing in the Order of Saint Jerome; he calls the faction of Gonzalo de Toro the
"racist" faction. See Netanyahu, *Origins*, 1058ff.

respect unconventional, the inquisitors implicitly encouraged the order to reevaluate how it wished to define itself. For those friars who had long been suspicious of the Jeronymites' more atypical brethren, the Inquisition provided the opportunity for them to confront friars who challenged the order spiritually or socially. In the process, the Guadalupe Inquisition of 1485 provided a new framework through which new labels of correct and incorrect behavior could be applied and enforced.

The year 1485 was a difficult one for the Jeronymite foundation in Guadalupe. The alarming death of fray Luis de Madrid, the presence of external inquisitors, the embarrassment of six autos de fe sentencing over two hundred vecinos for secret devotion to Judaism, and the humiliation of an inquisitorial investigation into the friary itself profoundly shook the order and its friars in Guadalupe. Factions in the friary were challenged and practices altered in subsequent years. Most significantly, conversos became less welcome in an order that had once been their defender. In the aftermath of Guadalupe's inquisitions, the friars, like the vecinos, would move quickly to reestablish a more normal existence. But long after the execution of fray Diego de Marchena, anxiety about the presence of conversos in the Order of Saint Jerome continued. As the fifteenth century drew to a close, however, a developing consensus among the friars at Guadalupe made one thing clear: conflict in the friary would be resolved at the price of acknowledging the difficulty of assimilating New Christians into their midst. Exclusion and punishment would win out over fray Alonso de Oropesa's vision of gentle assimilation. It is to this process, the establishment of a new status quo in the years after 1485 and the broader implications of that new status quo, that we now turn.

EIGHT

GUADALUPE AFTER THE INQUISITION:
ENVISIONING THE EARLY MODERN STATE
IN GUADALUPE

On December 6, 1485, the inquisitors packed their belongings, though not their files, and left Guadalupe. When they had arrived just one year earlier, the Holy Office had been based in Ciudad Real, a Castilian city with a sizeable converso population. From Ciudad Real, Fernando and Isabel's Inquisition still operated primarily as an ad hoc affair, moving from city to city. By the time of the inquisitors' departure, however, the Holy Office had established a more permanent identity for itself. The caravan of lawyers, bailiffs, and doctors of canon law set out from Guadalupe to Toledo, Castile's new, permanent base of inquisitorial activity. From there, the officials were quickly assigned to new duties. Pedro Sánchez de la Calancha returned to Extremadura the following year to serve as chief inquisitor for the ad hoc court in Belalcázar. Sánchez de la Calancha would ultimately organize permanent inquisitorial offices across the peninsula. Doctor Francisco Sánchez de la Fuente, head of the Guadalupe delegation, was appointed bishop of Avila in 1492. Doctor de Villaescusa, chief attorney for the defense, continued with the court in Toledo. Their histories are well documented in Henry Charles Lea's work and elsewhere.[1]

Guadalupe had changed during the "inquisitorial year" of 1485 as well. The court's activity had widened the fissures that divided New Christians and Old Christians in Guadalupe. With the title of chief inquisitor and the concomitant increase in his authority, prior Nuño de Arévalo imprisoned, condemned, and exiled hundreds of residents. The daily rhythm of life in the town must have been severely disrupted in the wake of such an upheaval. Yet in many respects life in Guadalupe changed slowly, if at all. Countering the dislocation of families and the damning testimony of servants and neighbors were the social and eco-

---

[1] On Sánchez de la Calancha, see Jaime Contreras and Jean-Pierre Dedieu, "Geografía de la inquisición española: La formación de los distritos (1470–1820)," *Hispania* 40 (1980), and Henry Charles Lea, *A History of the Spanish Inquisition*. On Sánchez de la Fuente, see Lea and Fidel Fita, "La Inquisición en Guadalupe." See chapter 5 for further discussion of the inquisitors and their careers.

nomic motivations that encouraged coexistence among Old and New Christians. The political, economic, and social transformations that occurred in Guadalupe after 1485 ultimately changed the role of friars, Old Christians, and conversos in town; but those transformations were not immediate. By the middle of the sixteenth century, the friars exercised the kind of authority over the Puebla that they had always hoped to have.

As Guadalupe was beginning to adapt to new social and political conditions, the kingdom was undergoing its own transformation. The coincident presence of royal inquisitors, local religious authorities, Marian devotion, and the interest of the Catholic Monarchs in the town was not accidental. Guadalupe's experiences with these multifarious influences highlighted changes in how Fernando and Isabel's newly united kingdom was imagined. Local officials had taken advantage of the royal Holy Office of the Inquisition to tamp down threats to their authority, and they would continue to employ the authority gained from the Inquisition to consolidate their power. At the same time, the king and queen would make use of Spanish religious personnel and religious devotions—like the cult of the Virgin of Guadalupe and the spiritual power she was believed to convey—to strengthen their own position as leaders of a kingdom that they understood to have a uniquely sacred purpose in the world.

GUADALUPE AFTER THE INQUISITION

Nuño de Arévalo continued as prior for thirteen years after the trials in Guadalupe, until his death in 1498, but little in these years created as much of a stir in Guadalupe as the presence of the Holy Office. The records of transactions of the Capitular Acts for his priorate, if they ever existed, have been lost. Nor do any large trials or court cases remain, as they do for his predecessor, prior Diego de París. Guadalupe was favored with a long series of visits from the Catholic Monarchs, including one in 1492 to celebrate the conversion and baptism of one of their chief advisers, Abraham Seneor; Christopher Columbus traveled to Guadalupe a few years later in fulfillment of a vow to the Virgin of Guadalupe for his successful journey across the Atlantic and to baptize two Americans brought back with him from the Caribbean.[2] Aside from these distinguished pilgrims and the initiation of a new phase of ecclesiastical construction, the last years of the century seem to have been relatively quiet ones in Guadalupe.

[2] My thanks to Jodi Bilinkoff for informing me about the vow that precipitated Columbus's visit.

In the Christian practices of residents, too, little seems to have changed. Sunday mass, seasonal pilgrimages, confraternity activity, celebrations in honor of Jesus, the Virgin Mary, and the saints—all continued as they had before. Pilgrims continued to stream into town, staying in the local inns, buying food, shoes, and clothes. The number of pilgrims may have declined somewhat after 1485 as the activities of pilgrims changed across Europe, but the Virgin of Guadalupe remained a popular cult well into the seventeenth century.[3] The rites that marked out community identity continued to do so, without the conspicuous presence of New Christians.

Not surprisingly, the position of New Christians in town had changed markedly. The first conversos tried and condemned were the traperos who had challenged the authority of the friars. By the end of the inquisitorial year, those New Christians most commonly suspected of Judaizing—people like Mari Sánchez, whose daughter testified against her— had been relaxed to the secular authorities and condemned to death. Even the New Christians who had served as lay functionaries for the friars apparently lost their positions in the aftermath of the trials. With the priorship of Nuño de Arévalo and the dispersion of New Christians, the link between local conversos and ecclesiastical governance, particularly arbitrary governance, had been eliminated. A local power base to rival the friars had gone. Apparently only a few New Christians had evaded sentencing and legally remained in town.

Yet that does not mean that all conversos were gone. Within a very short span of time, no more than three years, many New Christians had returned to Guadalupe. In 1500, the Inquisitor General Diego de Deza lamented that many New Christians had returned, if they had ever left at all. The history of Isabel González, which will be discussed in more detail below, demonstrates how easily some New Christians were able to reestablish themselves in Guadalupe. In that sense, life in the Virgin's town appeared to have returned to the status quo ante; but there were some critical differences. Some conversos—the ones most threatening to Old Christians, both politically and religiously—would never return. Furthermore, those who returned or remained were in a precarious political and social position, forever living under the implicit threat of being exiled once again. This certainly had an impact on the Judaizing practices of Guadalupe's New Christian population after 1485. Mari López, the *beata*, told the inquisitors that before the 1462 heresy trials Judaizers were more open and active in town.[4] In the same way, it

---

[3] Crémoux, "Pélerinages et Miracles à Guadalupe (Extrémadure) au XVIe siècle," chap. 3.

[4] AHN Inquis. legajo 184, expediente 20. See also chapter 4.

seems likely that New Christians who remained in Guadalupe after 1485 were less willing to endanger themselves with Jewish observances. Furthermore, the active Judaizers who encouraged fidelity to Judaism among less interested conversos were gone to the stake, further encouraging New Christian assimilation and more mainstream Christian observance.

The Inquisition was not forgotten; reminders and memories of the trials and autos de fe continued long after the ceremonies of sentencing themselves. The economic transformations caused by the sentencing of some of the town's most prominent merchants, the absence of townspeople imprisoned or exiled, the imprisonment of one friar and condemnation and execution of another—all these changes served to impress the memory of the Inquisition on those townspeople who remained. Reminders of the inquisitorial year also took form in a new royal palace, built as an addition to the Jeronymite friary. When the trials first began, Queen Isabel had magnanimously donated all proceeds from the Guadalupense court to the friary. The gift was as generous as it was unusual. The Holy Office received no financial support from the Crown; inquisitors were expected to survive by the goods taken from the accused. In no other case did inquisitorial revenue return to the site of the trials, one reason for local resistance to the activity of the Holy Office.[5] Isabel's gift suggests her devotion to the prior and friary, and the clerics responded in kind. The friars volunteered to use the funds to construct a palace, or Royal Hospice, Hospedería Real, for the Catholic Monarchs as part of the friary's buildings. The Hospedería Real became an indication of the mutual respect and support between the Crown and the Jeronymite friars as demonstrated by the activity of the Inquisition in Guadalupe.[6]

This striking physical reminder of the Inquisition and of the Catholic Monarchs' link to the friars and friary quickly took form. The friars received one million *maravedís* in income from the Holy Office. Once Isabel and Fernando learned of the friars' plans for the inquisitorial income, the Catholic Monarchs contributed an additional million *maravedís* for the construction of the Hospedería. In short order, the friars

---

[5] See Kamen, *The Spanish Inquisition*, and Lea, *History*. In his study of the Inquisition of Valencia, Stephen Haliczer discusses the frequent financial woes of the Holy Office. See *Inquisition and Society*.

[6] See AHN clero legajo 1423, expediente 89, "Cuenta de todos los bienes de la inquisición que yo reciby." The Hospedería Real is no longer standing. After the exclaustration of the friars in 1835, local residents tore down the building as a hated sign of ecclesiastical power in the town. It is possible that pedestals and other architectural fragments evident in buildings around town are originally from the Hospedería; two examples exist in the Plaza de los Tres Chorros and on Eras Street. María Pescador del Hoyo has researched the probable location and history of the Hospedería in "La hospedería real de Guadalupe," *Revista de estudios extremeños* 21 (1965), 327–343, 493–528.

had not only eliminated the presence of the economically powerful group of traperos, but also employed their confiscated wealth to strengthen the friary's ties with the Crown. The friars set to work collecting funds from the sentenced converso families and the monarchs even as building commenced, and in just six years the hospice was complete (fig. 8). By 1492 Guadalupe had become one of the first clerical houses in Iberia to build quarters specifically for the royal family and the court. In the next half-century this process was repeated at some of the most important shrines in Spain, including Santiago de Compostela, until it culminated at the Escorial, a Jeronymite foundation specifically built as a "monastic palace" for King Philip II.[7] In Guadalupe, meanwhile, the Hospedería Real became a site of ecclesiastical, as well as royal, justice: in the sixteenth century audience rooms in the Hospedería were used to hold monthly meetings where vecinos could bring their grievances before the prior.[8] Once again, the link between ecclesiastical and royal authority was reaffirmed.

Prior Nuño may not have been closely involved in the day-to-day work of the 1485 Inquisition, but he took his role as a member of the court with the utmost seriousness. In part, this may have been due to the similarity between his training and outlook and the outlook of those who had helped initiate the Inquisition. As Helen Nader has demonstrated in her work *The Mendoza Family in the Spanish Renaissance, 1350–1550*, the establishment of the Inquisition coincided with the rise in power of the *letrados*, men trained in civil or canon law.[9] With their growing importance in the second half of the fifteenth century, the *letrados* propounded their belief that Spanish history was a manifestation of divine will. For them, political successes could be attributed to the aegis of divine power and the intervention of religious intermediaries like the Virgin of Guadalupe; political setbacks could be linked to sin or heresy—like the heresies practiced by Judaizing conversos. At the same time, as a result of the influence of the *letrados*, a more professionalized legalism came to characterize activity of the royal court. As Nader notes, "It is no coincidence that this judicial solution [the Inquisition] to a religious problem [conversos] occurred just when the *letrados*, with their views of an all-powerful state, their legal training, and their concern for correct religious beliefs and practices replaced the aristocracy

[7] Of course, since El Escorial was not built by the Jeronymites themselves, this is a somewhat different case.

[8] See AMG codex 75.

[9] *Letrado* meant generically "lawyer," as in the defense lawyer acting for the accused in inquisitorial trials. Here, I wish to indicate specifically the unique training these men received, as discussed by Nader and others, which could lead to careers other than in law.

as principal advisers of the crown."[10] Secular, royal justice had received a religious impulse, even as religious orders became more involved in royal government.

Guadalupe typified the understanding of divine will operating in a political sphere that the *letrados* championed. The town already brought together secular and religious authority in the person of the prior. Furthermore, the miraculous acts of the Virgin of Guadalupe—particularly redeeming Muslim captives and rescuing sailors at sea—emphasized the spiritual import of Spain's political power in the Mediterranean.[11] In both his own authority and the cult that he maintained, therefore, prior Nuño could understand and support the divinely guided state envisioned by the *letrados* who helped construct the Inquisition. Given the complementary political positions of the Virgin of Guadalupe, the friars who maintained her shrine, and the *letrados* who helped create the Inquisition, therefore, it is not surprising that prior Nuño and many of his friars wholeheartedly supported the Holy Office and their role in it.

In fact, the prior and friars understood their continued royal favor to include permanent inquisitorial authority in addition to their many other privileges. In 1488 prior Nuño initiated a pair of inquisitorial investigations in Guadalupe. To assist him, the Holy Office in Toledo sent Tristán de Medina, a minor official present at the first trials who, like Sánchez de la Calancha, helped establish inquisitorial courts throughout the peninsula. No records of official authorization exist, although Medina's presence suggests approval from Toledo. In effect, the trials were primarily information-gathering sessions. Two officials were not sufficient to hold a trial and did not have authority to act on their own. Still, prior Nuño assigned the task of defense to the friary's notaries, while Tristán de Medina acted as prosecutor and prior Nuño sat by himself as judge. Before 1485 and the institution of the modern Spanish Inquisition, prior Nuño would have had the right to authorize a small inquisitorial court under unusual circumstances, much as his predecessor had done a generation before.[12] Prior Nuño, however, clearly saw his 1488 court as a continuation of the Inquisition trials of 1485. He reopened records of the Holy Office (which were still stored in Guadalupe), duplicated the roles and function of the earlier court with friars at hand to fulfill those roles, and ultimately sent one trial to Toledo for adjudication. Apparently, prior Nuño saw himself as a permanent, if largely inactive, official of the Holy Office.[13]

---

[10] Nader, *The Mendoza Family*, 135.
[11] See Starr-LeBeau, "The Joyous History of Devotion."
[12] See chapter 4.
[13] At this early stage of the modern Inquisition, such misunderstandings were possi-

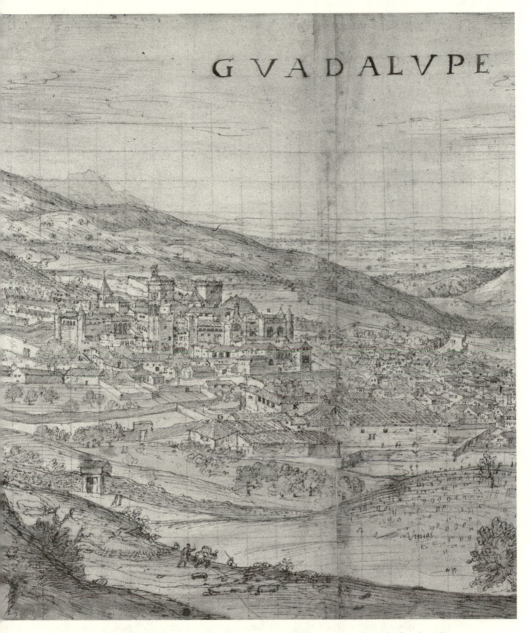

FIGURE 8. The Hospedería Real (above, center), constructed with funds taken from those tried by the Inquisition. The drawing is from 1567. Anton van den Wyngaerde, cod. 41, fol. 24, Bildarchiv der ÖNB, Vienna.

The first of these two trials provides a potential explanation for why prior Nuño chose to reopen the Guadalupe Inquisition when he did. Rodrigo Alonso *tundidor*, cloth cutter, had reconciled before the Inquisition on January 13, 1485, but had then left town. The inquisitors formally called Rodrigo back to Guadalupe, and he began the journey, but halfway home he turned back in fear when he saw the smoke of the auto de fe. Three years after the death of his brother at the hands of the inquisitors, though, Rodrigo began to regret his flight from the Holy Office. With the encouragement of his wife, Rodrigo voluntarily made the trip back to Guadalupe to present himself before the Inquisition and throw himself on the mercy of the court. In response, prior Nuño reopened the Office of the Inquisition in Guadalupe, assigned a scrivener as lawyer for the defense, and collected statements from the prosecution and defense before sending the case on to Toledo for a final verdict.[14] It is unclear from the extant documents why prior Nuño appears to have begun the trial under his own authority, when he lacked trained officers and judges to assist him. It is also unclear why, having begun the trial, he was not permitted to finish it. Perhaps the inquisitors preferred to delegate evidence-gathering to prior Nuño, while leaving adjudication to themselves. Employing prior Nuño and the minor official Medina, the inquisitors were able to question Guadalupenses about the accused without going to the expense of returning to Guadalupe for just one trial. If this was the case, then the inquisitors never intended to permit prior Nuño to decide the case by himself. The trial record itself does not comment on the change of venue (which included a lapse of two years), merely recording that the early actions of the trial occurred in Guadalupe. In 1490, when the trial resumed, Rodrigo Alonso was found guilty of apostasy and condemned.

A second trial in 1488 focused on Isabel González, a conversa who had been found "suspicious" and exiled in 1485, and whose trial seems to have been an opportunistic response by the prior to the combination

---

ble, if uncommon. The inquisitors were based in only a few cities and had visited only a few other sites to establish ad hoc courts. The careful documentation that has recently earned the attention of historians was a product of the mid-sixteenth century, when the inquisitors had gained fifty years of experience and had become a fixture on the Iberian landscape. On the files of the Inquisition, see Contreras and Hennigsen, "44,000 Cases of the Spanish Inquisition (1540–1700)." The Holy Office was apparently unimpressed with prior Nuño's interpretation of his role: after they took control of one of the 1488 trials, the inquisitors never again permitted the prior to exercise inquisitorial authority.

[14] Luis Alonso, the scrivener who defended Rodrigo Alonso, complained that he needed more time to prepare since he was not a lawyer. AHN Inquis. legajo 132, expediente 11. Rodrigo Alonso *tundidor's* trial is discussed in greater length in chapters 5 and 6.

of a sitting inquisitorial court and an unruly penitent.[15] Her trial is interesting, not only for what it reveals about the friars' perceptions of authority in the wake of the 1485 Inquisition, but also for the insights it provides into lay reactions to the Inquisition three years later. In Isabel's trial, begun two days after Rodrigo Alonso's, an Old Christian complained that Isabel had abjured her statement of contrition. At her stall in Guadalupe plaza, Isabel complained to passersby that she had had to invent Jewish activities to confess so that the inquisitors would leave her alone. The prosecutor charged Isabel with feigning contrition for misdeeds; in other words, Isabel was in trouble, not for making up false activities to the inquisitors, but rather for trying to deny her guilt, as the inquisitors understood it. Interestingly, Isabel had been sentenced to exile in 1485 for her relatively minor misdeeds; no one, however, charged her with returning illegally to the town. A quick trial, held entirely in Guadalupe, resulted in confirmation of Isabel's statements in the plaza, and she was again exiled from Guadalupe.[16] Her file records in detail the manner in which she was exiled, which suggests that the sentence was carried out. Prior Nuño and Tristán de Medina ordered "that she be given twenty lashes in the prison where she is being kept, and that she be publicly exiled seated on an ass, and that she not enter this Puebla nor go within fifteen leagues of it for perpetuity on pain of [condemnation as] relapsed."[17]

Throughout Isabel's trial, one aspect of her life was taken for granted: her presence as a businesswoman in the plaza just over two years after her "perpetual exile" from Guadalupe. No one asked how long she had been there, or how she was able to return. And the one complaint received about her did not address her presence, but rather was in reference to comments she made freely about the Inquisition. Had she been pardoned after her exile and officially permitted to return, that information should have been listed in her file.[18] Isabel's presence, and

[15] AHN Inquis. legajo 154, expediente 6. It is possible that someone coincidentally complained about Isabel's behavior in the same week that Rodrigo Alonso returned, but it seems more likely that the friary had not acted on the complaint about Isabel until Rodrigo provided an opportunity to begin the trials again. Isabel González's trial is also discussed in chapter 3.

[16] Isabel was benefited in her trial by the defense of Juan de Texeda. Juan de Texeda had done much of the defense work during the 1485 trials under the authority of Doctor de Villaescusa. Rodrigo, on the other hand, had to make do with the services of Luis Alonso, an admitted novice. This more minor case was not sent to Toledo for judgment because, I believe, Isabel was not the prime focus of the inquisitors.

[17] Ibid., 5v. "le sea dados en la carçel donde era presa veynte açotes e que sea desterrada publicamente cauallera en un asno por esta puebla e que non entre enella non quinze leguas en derrador por perpetuamente so pena de relapsa."

[18] Other pardons were listed, as will be discussed below.

the nonchalance with which the friars and townspeople of Guadalupe accepted it, suggest a sharply different community attitude toward New Christians from what one might expect so soon after the conclusion of the trials. Isabel's heretical activity was minor, even if we accept her original confession (which she herself later disavowed) as true; furthermore, as a poor widow, she was not an economic threat to Old Christians in the way that the wealthy traperos might have been. In short, Isabel's presence was less likely to arouse concerns among Guadalupenses. But her presence raises the question: if Isabel was able to set up shop so quickly after her expulsion, how many others had returned as well? Had Old Christians and the friary turned a blind eye to the return of exiled conversos?

Isabel's comfortable residence in Guadalupe two years after her sentence suggests that with the most egregious offenders burned at the stake or imprisoned, leniency to less economically or religiously dangerous offenders might be tolerated. Defense witnesses in 1485 as well as 1488 included Old Christians as well as New Christians, and friendships among these different groups of Christians were not uncommon before the Holy Office began its work. Guadalupe was not a society rigidly segregated between Old and New Christians, and whether for professional or social reasons, Old and New Christians did intermingle. It seems possible, therefore, that some connections linking Old and New Christians endured after the departure of the Inquisition. Indeed, while some hostility toward New Christians clearly existed (particularly on the part of Old Christian servants of New Christian families) and was growing in Castile generally in the second half of the fifteenth century, and while there had been occasional anticonverso riots in the years before the Inquisition, these riots often expressed hostility toward the friars and especially powerful conversos as much as toward all New Christians per se.[19]

An outbreak of the plague following the trials in 1488 further encouraged reconciliation in Guadalupe. The town cemetery, located at the town's founding just outside the church doors, had to be relocated to accommodate the victims, which fray Diego de Ecija estimated at over one thousand. The economic basis of the pilgrimage site was certainly affected.[20] In the epidemic's wake, prior Nuño pardoned the half-dozen conversos kept in perpetual imprisonment in Guadalupe.[21] Given the

---

[19] The anticonverso violence discussed in chapter 1 is a good example of this.

[20] See Germán Rubío, OFM, *Historia*; Diego de Ecija, *Libro*, 341; García and Trenado, *Guadalupe*. The cemetery remained in its new position uphill from the friary's school until the 1980s. Some of the 1488 cemetery's brickwork can still be seen at the end of the parking lot for the local Parador de Turismo.

[21] This was noted on the covers of the records of those sentenced to perpetual pun-

town's fortunes, it is reasonable to assume that any exiled residents willing to return to Guadalupe and take up their former tasks would have been welcomed. Isabel González was not the first to break her exile and return; other conversos had never obeyed the sentence of exile in the first place, at least not for any significant period of time. And additional New Christians continued to move back to Guadalupe over the years.[22] Both the friars and remaining Old and New Christian townspeople suffered the presence of these returning exiles quietly. In some cases their return may have meant the reunion of families, and in many cases it meant the resumption of jobs particularly suited to Guadalupe's economy, such as shoemaking.

Inside the friary, and throughout the order, the upheaval caused by the Inquisition continued long after the inquisitors had left Guadalupe. In the aftermath of the score of trials at the house in Guadalupe, the Jeronymites confronted their reputation as an order sympathetic to Judaizers.[23] In 1486, one year after the inquisitorial trials in Guadalupe, the triennial chapter meeting of the order was held in Lupiana near Guadalajara. At that meeting, the priors and other leaders of the Order of Saint Jerome passed a statute designed to prevent New Christians from joining the order; they demanded proof of purity of blood, *limpieza de sangre*, from all new members. For the first time, purity of blood laws had been instituted for membership in a religious order.[24] Furthermore, fray Gonzalo de Toro, prior of Montamarta, suggested (unsuccessfully) that any converso friar currently in the order be forbidden to hold the offices of prior, vicar, or confessor. The 1486 ruling by the Jeronymites indicated a radical shift in policy for the friars. Not all Jeronymites were in agreement with the new standards; the General of the Order of Saint Jerome, fray Rodrigo de Orense, also opposed the purity of blood statutes, and even engaged some converso *letrados* to determine the legality of such statutes. Fray Rodrigo personally appeared before the Catholic Monarchs, Fernando and Isabel, to urge them to declare these statutes illegal, and the monarchs voiced their clear disapproval of the ruling. In

---

ishment. See, for example, the trial of Mari Sánchez, wife of Juan de Moya, AHN Inquis. legajo 183, expediente 22; or the trial of Mari Ruiz, ibid. 181, expediente 16.

[22] This is discussed in AHN sello 47/51, the 1500 decree of expulsion for all conversos from Guadalupe.

[23] On Judaizing in the Order of Saint Jerome, see Beinart, "The Judaizing Movement," 167–192. Benzion Netanyahu offers a different interpretation of these events in *Origins*, 1055–1063, and Roth tackles the issue in *Conversos, Inquisition, and the Expulsion*, 229–236. The most recent work on this topic is Sophie Coussemacker, "Convertis et judaïsants dans l'ordre de Saint-Jérôme. Un état de la question," *Mélanges de la Casa de Velázquez* 27:2 (1991), 5–27.

[24] On this issue the classic study remains Sicroff, *Controverses*.

the end, this pressure halted implementation of the statute, although it remained a contentious issue within the order.

While enforcement of *limpieza de sangre* statutes was put on hold, other initiatives of the chapter meeting of 1486 went forward. Most notable among these was the establishment of an internal investigation into the extent of Judaizing in the Order of Saint Jerome as a whole.[25] Selected as inquisitors were fray Hernando de Córdoba, prior of San Jerónimo in Seville, and fray Gonzalo de Toro, who had encouraged the most extreme exclusion of conversos already in the order. Serving as their chief assistant and scribe was fray Diego de Ecija, who had served as one of the scriveners for the Inquisition in Guadalupe the previous year. For over two years, from 1486 to 1488, these men traveled from friary to friary, investigating, taking testimony from other friars, and censuring friars who were determined to have engaged in suspicious behavior. In most cases the grievances identified by the friars were insufficient to warrant investigation by the Holy Office of the Inquisition, although occasionally a friar was remanded to the royal Inquisition for an official trial.[26]

By 1487 the Jeronymite investigators had returned to Guadalupe and the supposedly Judaizing friars there. The inquisitors took testimony from vecinos as well as friars about incorrect practices at the house dedicated to Our Lady of Guadalupe. Diego de Marchena and Diego de Burgos had already been sentenced, and the inquisitors could find no one else to remand to the Holy Office in Toledo. But in reviewing old testimony and taking new statements, the inquisitors underscored the suspicions of Old Christians in the friary at Guadalupe. Fray Fernando de Ubeda and his faction of Jeronymites sympathetic to Guadalupe's conversos were the primary target of the inquisitors. Many of Ubeda's associates were censured by the Jeronymite inquisitors in 1487–88. Combined with the loss of their financial supporters—wealthy converso traperos—in the Inquisition of 1485, the proconverso friars had little hope of returning to their former positions of power in the friary. Both in the friary and elsewhere in Spain, New Christians were facing increasing challenges. Given this context, it is perhaps less surprising that Isabel González and Rodrigo Alonso *tundidor* were investigated in 1488 than that so few other conversos met the same fate.

However, for a brief period after the plague of 1488, there was room

[25] Contreras and Dedieu mention this series of trials in passing in their article, "Geografía."

[26] See Sicroff, *Controverses*, 103–105. These trials are also discussed in José de Sigüenza, OSH, *Historia*, 2:32–33. Those friars who were given over to the Holy Office appear in the records of the Inquisition based in Toledo and are the subject of Beinart's article. Not surprisingly, those trials date to the later 1480s.

amid renewed prosperity in Guadalupe for New Christians quietly plying their trade. The continued presence and attentions of the Catholic
Monarchs brought additional prestige to the shrine. Throughout the
fifteenth century Guadalupe had been a destination for Jews wanting to
convert and for New Christians repentant for lapses into Jewish practices. Conversos journeyed from Seville at the request of confessors or
the demand of inquisitors, and this practice presumably continued during the many baptisms of 1492, when Jews had to choose between
conversion and exile from Spain.[27] Despite the relatively peaceful respite
in relations between New and Old Christians, the broader trend was
toward decreased acceptance and increased suspicion. The new set of
circumstances that obtained in Guadalupe after the 1485 Inquisition—
the friary's increased power, prestige, and increased resistance to New
Christian minorities; the smaller population in town; and the decreased
influence of New Christians in Guadalupense life—all made the position of New Christians in town that much more precarious.

EXPULSION FROM GUADALUPE

It was not long before Guadalupe addressed the issue of its New Christian population for the last time. At the end of the fifteenth century,
Guadalupe was again brought to the eyes of the inquisitors in Toledo.
No records are left as to the motivation for the demand, but on July 13,
1500, the inquisitor general himself, Diego de Deza, issued this order to
the town of Guadalupe: "since many have returned, and some [of those
sentenced to exile] have never left, I demand and order that all conversos from the town of Guadalupe be exiled forever."[28] Officials of the
Holy Office had chosen to act in response to the presence of exiled
New Christians in the town, a fact that would have been difficult for
the pilgrimage site to conceal even if it had attempted to do so. Apparently, either the friars felt unconcerned about most of the exiled New
Christians in town, although they had not been formally pardoned, or
else the Jeronymites found themselves economically bound to accept
the presence of exiled conversos in Guadalupe as the price of serving
the thousands of pilgrims in town. Isabel González may have been exiled anew for complaining about her treatment by the inquisitors, but
apparently other, more circumspect New Christians had been allowed
to stay.

A blanket order of exile to all New Christians, such as the one or-

[27] AMG unnumbered, Internal Inquisition, passim.
[28] AHN sello 47/51.

dered by Diego de Deza, was as difficult to understand as it was unique. Certainly many conversos were expelled by the 1485 inquisitorial court, but no one argued that the entire New Christian population was secretly living as Jews. From the time of the Guadalupense trials some conversos had been permitted to stay by right of their acquittal. Furthermore, at no other time or place did the Inquisition demand the expulsion of all converted Jews, regardless of their guilt or innocence. In fact, the expulsion of an entire community of converts was not repeated until the series of expulsions of converted Muslims, *moriscos*, from all Iberia from 1609 to 1612. It is unclear what precipitated the inquisitor general's decision. Perhaps Guadalupe's unique status as a pilgrimage site as well as its importance as a locus of spiritual power might have motivated Diego de Deza to act on his own initiative. Word of the inquisitorial trials there must have spread quickly. Both for the sake of the Virgin of Guadalupe and for the reputation of the Holy Office, the inquisitors may not have wanted to permit large numbers of exiled New Christians to return to the town and scandalize its pilgrims. Or perhaps the apparent disinterest among the friars sparked concern on the part of the inquisitors. On the other hand, it is possible that the friars requested this edict from the Holy Office. The friars, too, may have grown increasingly intolerant of the continued presence of New Christians in town. Isabel González's trial suggests that this was a long-standing problem, long predating the 1500 decree. The decree from the Holy Office, with its references to the many who have returned and to some who never left, confirms the suspicion that large numbers of exiled conversos were resident in Guadalupe. But it is unclear why the friars would have felt the need to rely on the Holy Office to issue this order, and no evidence remains of any correspondence between the prior and the inquisitor general that might have sparked this move— although of course such correspondence might exist. Furthermore, by 1500 the additional trials in Guadalupe and throughout the Jeronymite Order were long completed, and so it seems unlikely that local events provided the impetus for a final exile for all conversos in town. With so little documentation extant from the 1490s in Guadalupe, we will never know for sure what triggered this highly unusual decree. Isabel González's fate, it seems, came to prefigure that of the converso community in Guadalupe as a whole.

Whatever the reasons, sincere Christians were exiled solely on account of their ancestry. Unlike the earlier popular uprisings or anticonverso riots in Guadalupe, or even the abortive attempts at purity of blood restrictions in Toledo and elsewhere, this was the measured decision of an arm of the Crown, and it signaled more difficult times to come. Never again would outright expulsion be ordered for conversos, who themselves had just been "saved" from the influence of Jews by the Expulsion in 1492; but the growing popularity of the new purity of blood statutes was a sign of the increasingly acceptable and widespread prejudice against New Christians. Within fifty years, most religious orders had excluded descendants of Jews and Muslims. Many secular positions were also denied to conversos and *moriscos*, although false genealogies sometimes overcame these restrictions.[29] The Expulsion, together with the spreading Inquisition, worsened, rather than improved, the status of conversos in Spain. In Spain as a whole, this became evident over time, as the cumulative effect of inquisitorial trials, new legislation, and a changing climate of opinion took hold. For Guadalupenses, this process was truncated by the relatively quick double-blow of inquisitorial trials and mass expulsion.

Unlike the expulsions ordered in 1485, the edict of expulsion of 1500 was almost certainly enforced by the friars in Guadalupe. It is possible that improved economic conditions by century's end made the expulsion conceivable. Fewer conversos lived in Guadalupe after 1485, and they no longer wielded as much economic power. Now, in the face of permanent expulsion, conversos moved their families to nearby villages or more distant cities like Seville and Córdoba. Evidence suggests that even the friary's former *converso* favorites permanently relocated after 1500. In 1504 the friary's book of capitular acts records that a three thousand *maravedí* dowry was given to Andrés González de la República for the marriage of his daughter.[30] The former public defender, *procurador*, for the town was recorded as living in Cañamero, a nearby village. The generous dowry suggests continuing ties between Andrés González and his former employers, twenty years after he had lost his job and was tried by the Inquisition. No other non-Guadalupense was awarded a cash donation by the friars. The gift is a sad reminder of earlier positive interaction between some friars and conversos, and between New and Old Christians, long after the delicate balance of social relations in Guadalupe had been upset.

Still, the immediate overall impact of the 1500 expulsion on Gua-

[29] The relationship between Jews and conversos in the context of the Expulsion remains a contentious issue. Three articles that form a useful starting point are Stephen Haliczer, "The Castilian Urban Patriciate and the Jewish Expulsion of 1480–1492," *American Historical Review* 78 (1973), 35–58; Maurice Kriegel, "La prise d'une decision: l'expulsion des juifs d'Espagne en 1492," *Revue Historique* 260 (1978); and Henry Kamen, "The Mediterranean and the Expulsion of Spanish Jews in 1492." On religious orders and secular offices adopting purity of blood laws, see Sicroff, *Controverses*, 92–122.

[30] AMG codex 74, Libro de las Actas Capitulares, 39v, Friday, March 22, 1504, "En este día hizo el Rreverendo nuestro padre con el convento limosna a Andrés González de la Rrepública de tres mill mrs. para casamiento a una su hija. El qual es vezino de Cañamero."

dalupe does not seem to have been profound. Documents from the period make no mention of the expulsion; indeed, the capitular acts—which are extant for the year 1500—are silent on the question of New Christians in town. After the Inquisition trials of 1485, it seems, conflict over New Christians had greatly diminished. Those conversos most disruptive in local politics, and most financially linked to the friary, had been executed by the Holy Office; men like the traperos Alonso de Córdoba and Rodrigo de los Encensos were no longer a spur to anti-converso activity. Similarly, those conversos most associated with clandestine Judaizing activity—such as the Narices family or Mari Sánchez, wife of Diego Jiménez the butcher—were also gone, either by flight or execution. Diego de Deza's order of expulsion was observed quietly, it seems, because the prominent role New Christians had once played in Guadalupe had largely ceased after 1485.

The decree of expulsion did not extend into the friary itself, but the power of conversos inside the Jeronymite house was also on the wane. Friars who had most noticeably favored New Christians or supported Judaizers before the trials of 1485 and 1487–1488 had already been punished and by 1500 were less prominent in Guadalupense affairs. Furthermore, some Jeronymite Old Christians had continued to move the Order of Saint Jerome toward implementation of purity of blood laws. At a 1504 general chapter meeting of the order attended by Old Christians exclusively, the priors and vicars decided to forbid conversos to enter the order, and then to keep that decision secret from New Christian attendees of the general chapter meeting. As Old Christians gained control of houses previously controlled by conversos, they would be expected to begin enforcing the secret statute.[31] That ruling may not have been public knowledge in the Order of Saint Jerome, but in Guadalupe and throughout their order, converso friars must have known that their days of influence were gone, never to return.

THE HEGEMONY OF THE FRIARS

By the end of 1500 Guadalupe's conversos were gone, but conflicts with the vecinos continued to plague the Jeronymite friars. In the fourteenth and early fifteenth centuries, townspeople had protested their loss of independent decision making. Vecinos responded quickly, and sometimes violently, to attempts by the friars to tighten their control over the town and its residents. Guadalupenses were unsuccessful in their demands for increased autonomy and the right to name their own local officials, but the friars in turn were unable to consolidate their hold

---

[31] Ibid. 107, 4r–v.

over the town. Indeed, the friars were known to lament the necessity for having to maintain a town at all. Without the pilgrims, they noted, they could be surrounded by only a handful of homes. In the second half of the fifteenth century, the growing population, combined with the increasing number of New Christians in positions of secular authority, changed the nature of Old Christian complaints. Critiques of the friars' authority now combined with criticisms of the prominent role of conversos in local government. Popular uprisings explicitly linked and challenged New Christian functionaries and Jeronymite officials. Now, after the expulsion of conversos from local politics, Old Christian townspeople returned to their earlier challenge of the friars' authority.

By the sixteenth century, however, the balance of power between friars and vecinos had fundamentally shifted in favor of the friars. In the wake of the inquisitorial activity in Guadalupe, the friars faced widespread humiliation after the public exposure of Judaizing activity in and out of the friary. Inside the friary, factions realigned themselves in light of inquisitorial revelations and new figures in power. This retrenchment was quickly followed by a new, fundamentally more stable, expression of authority. The prior had stood publicly as spiritual leader, secular authority, and chief inquisitor before townspeople and pilgrims; his power had never been more clearly expressed or more forcefully used. Out of that multiple role, relations between the friary and the Crown were solidified. Each had benefited the other, each had strengthened the other by conjoining the symbols and sources of their power, and the resulting strength of their alliance was evident in the newly constructed Royal Hospice used by friars and royalty alike. Fernando and Isabel had supported the new prior and his decisions, while prior Nuño de Arévalo had promulgated the Crown's new Holy Office of the Inquisition by linking it to the ever-popular Marian shrine in Guadalupe.

The Jeronymites' renewed strength in Guadalupe was matched by a new era of financial independence. During the first two centuries of Guadalupe's existence, the friars—both the secular friars who managed the shrine from 1340 to 1389 and the Jeronymites thereafter—had depended on rents from their many properties and gifts from wealthy patrons for their income. Gifts of land and precious items to the friary, together with purchases made by friars in the fourteenth and fifteenth centuries, helped the Guadalupense friars extend and consolidate their holdings in land, livestock, and precious metals. During the hard economic times of the mid-to-late fifteenth century, the Jeronymites had supplemented these sources of income by loans from the wealthiest conversos in town: the small group of traperos who controlled most of the luxury trades in Guadalupe.[32] After 1500, however, the economic

---

[32] Vizuete Mendoza, *Guadalupe*, 283–304.

base of the friary shifted. Wholesale seizure of converso goods during the Inquisition brought the friars 1,450,233 *maravedís*, as well as effectively canceling any outstanding debt to the traperos and eliminating the possibility of future indebtedness.[33] Records from the friars' book of donations and gifts show the careful management of Jeronymite lands stretching throughout Extremadura at this time, particularly the consolidation of numerous small parcels of land into large, more productive estates with livestock and crops.[34] The years from 1479 to 1520 were the period of greatest growth for the friary, as the friary used income and donations to buy fields, cows, and sheep.[35] Gifts to the friary decreased during the sixteenth century, as did acquisitions by purchase or exchange, but the land the friary already possessed produced an income that only continued to increase. As a result, total income for the Jeronymites increased dramatically during the sixteenth century.[36] Never again would the friary depend on outside income. In effect, the friars were less dependent financially on the vecinos than they had ever been before, an important factor in relations between the shrine and town.

Guadalupe's vecinos, on the other hand, faced a powerful friary that continued to exert what townspeople saw as undue control over life in the town. In the short term, the friars' division of the town into Old and New Christian factions helped the friars to maintain their hold over all the town's residents; but the increasing cooperation of the Crown and friary, the elimination of conversos as a political threat, and the spectacle of the Inquisition may well have served to unite remaining residents more strongly. Whatever their joy, regrets, or exhaustion after the Holy Office left Guadalupe, after 1485 vecinos clearly saw the center of local power in the friars rather than in a suspicious converso minority. When the friars recovered from the chaotic years after 1485—

[33] Diego de Ecija complained in his history of Guadalupe that debts rose precipitously under prior Diego de París. See Diego de Ecija, *Libro*. One friar, in his statement to the inquisitors, said that if the conversos were expelled, "who will sell or lend" in town. AMG unnumbered, Internal Inquisition, 242. His statement may say as much about popular images of conversos as it does of the economic role of conversos in Guadalupe, however. On the amount confiscated by the Inquisition and awarded by Fernando and Isabel to the friars, see García and Trenado, *Guadalupe*, 97.

[34] AMG codex 72, *Libro de Donaciones, Testamentos, etc.* The collection, from c. 1676, includes seventeenth-century notarized copies of land transactions from the fifteenth to the seventeenth centuries. From the fifteenth century well into the sixteenth, the friars engaged in an extended series of land deals designed to create larger, more productive, and more efficient estates.

[35] J. Carlos Vizuete Mendoza, "El Patrimonio del Monasterio de Santa María de Guadalupe (1340–1785)," 598–602. It is important to note that Vizuete is most interested in total revenue, rather than the relative importance of gifts as opposed to income.

[36] Ibid., 603–606.

with their internal struggles, continuing inquisitorial investigations into the friary, and plague—their authority was more apparent and unchecked. Less than a generation after the inquisitors left Guadalupe, Guadalupenses once again began agitating for increased control over their own affairs. Now the battle lines were clearly drawn between townspeople and friars, with both seeking finally to claim the right to exert local authority for themselves.

Almost since the expulsion of the conversos, vecinos had begun agitating for increased power in Guadalupe. A new cast of characters, Old Christians whose names were not mentioned in the revolts against the friars a generation before, took center stage in these new demonstrations. Soon, townspeople started to gather at public spaces in the shadow of the friary to complain about the Jeronymites' policies. As in past years, vecinos held *ayuntamientos*, public meetings with the intent of deciding on a course of action for the town. This time, though, lay functionaries of the Jeronymites were Old Christians, and natural allies of the agitators. With their assistance, the vecinos chose not simply to assault the friary or start a riot. Certainly the participation of local scriveners helped make their ultimate form of battle—a court case— possible. Under the guidance of the scrivener Alonso Fernández de Bonilla, the townspeople wrote and signed a petition asking the friars to cease their harassment of Guadalupe's residents and to allow the townspeople more latitude in local rights and governance. The friars responded quickly, and with force. The Jeronymites ordered that all vecinos who had signed the petition be imprisoned. Some residents were seized and held by the friars, while others hurriedly fled Guadalupe. In response, the townspeople, led by Bonilla, took the friary to court in 1507 and demanded that all prisoners be released. In addition, Bonilla encouraged over a hundred vecinos to sign their names to a nineteen-point petition issued to the friary.[37]

The struggle between friars and townspeople entered a new stage in 1508, when the vecinos of Guadalupe, led by Alonso Fernández de Bonilla, a scrivener for the friary, took their complaints to the royal court of appeals, the Chancillería in Granada. As reorganized and expanded by Fernando and Isabel, the Chancillería was a royal law court created to adjudicate cases appealed from local jurisdictions. Since 1505, judges in Granada had heard cases from throughout southern Castile. Spanish townspeople, like colonists and indigenous people in Spain's American colonies, were aware of and made use of their rights under the law, and were renowned for their litigious nature.[38] Peasants and

---

[37] AHN clero pergaminos, carpeta 409, item 24, 2v.

[38] On law and the uses of the courts in early modern Spain, see Richard Kagan,

artisans like the vecinos of Guadalupe won in court only rarely; but the possibility of success was sufficient to encourage Spaniards to bring an ever-increasing number of cases before the court. The vecinos' court case—known in local histories as the *pleito de los Bonilla*, lawsuit of the Bonillas—involved years of struggle, and represented the last major attempt by Guadalupe's residents to gain independent authority in their town.[39]

In many ways, the grievances listed in the vecinos' petition echoed earlier popular resistance from before 1485. Townspeople gathered against the friary's wishes and against municipal ordinances to organize resistance to ecclesiastical authority and to compose a list of demands.[40] Tensions escalated as both sides marked out their positions more firmly. Townspeople employed both some measure of physical violence as well as formal written complaints in their challenge to the friars' authority. But in other respects the *pleito de los Bonilla* marked a new era in relations between the town and friary. Unlike the uprisings of the 1460s, for example, there were no conversos in positions of authority to attract the suspicion of vecinos. Concern and hostility were aimed squarely at the friars. The Bonillas had worked for the friars as scriveners, a position that had usually been filled by New Christians a generation earlier. Now, Old Christian townspeople may have believed—in this case apparently correctly—that lay officials were more sympathetic to their con-

---

Lawsuits and Litigants. The first Chancillería was in Valladolid; a second court, designed to serve Spain south of the Tagus River, was founded in Ciudad Real in 1494. It was this second court that moved to Granada in 1505. See John Elliott, *Imperial Spain, 1469–1716* (London: Penguin, 1963), 97–98. William Taylor, *Drinking, Homicide, and Rebellion in Colonial Mexican Towns* (Stanford: Stanford University Press, 1979), provides one example of the use of law in colonial Latin America and what court cases reveal about colonial society.

[39] Copies of the *pleito de los Bonilla* are available in Madrid and Guadalupe. In Guadalupe the documents are listed as AMG codex 167; in Madrid, the *pleito* is available in AHN clero pergaminos, carpeta 409, item 24, and carpeta 410, item 2. On pre-Jeronymite government in Guadalupe and earlier demands for vecino self-government, see chapters 1 and 3. Guadalupe historian Germán Rubío, OFM, was the first to refer to the *pleito de los Bonilla* in his 1926 history of the friary. The court case is also discussed in García and Trenado, *Guadalupe*; Sebastián García, *Guadalupe*; and Enrique Llopis, ed., *Guadalupe, 1752*. The court case is also discussed at length in Perrin, "Moines et villageois en Extrémadure au XVIe siècle." A summary of the dissertation, including a discussion of the *pleito*, can be found in "Plenitud de Guadalupe en el siglo XVI," *Guadalupe* 715 (1992), 53–70.

[40] See chapter 1 and especially chapter 3 for a more detailed explanation of these earlier riots. As explained in chapter 3, the term *ayuntamiento* literally means "gathering," but then and now it also signifies "local government" or "city hall." Any large, unsanctioned public gathering could be construed as revolt against ecclesiastical authorities when local government was discussed.

cerns, prompting increased demands of the officials and the friars. In addition, the newly reorganized Chancillería was available to hear legal complaints, to the extent that townspeople could pay the fees.

The lengthy petition composed by the aggrieved vecinos in itself represented a change from earlier demands brought before the friary. More than ever before, the document went to great lengths to explain the wide range of disagreements with the friars over the methods of government of the town. It includes nearly all the complaints registered in earlier petitions, as well as expanding the list in several ways. Those complaints ranged from the details of town management to the most profound questions of ultimate authority. Some requests reflected demands for resources that residents had wanted for decades. Townspeople legally demanded a clarification and extension of fishing rights in the Guadalupejo River, the right to collect firewood in various fields owned by the friary, and certain checks on the rights to pasturage in private fields.[41] Other requests, however, struck at the heart of Jeronymite government of the town. Guadalupenses used the agreement reached between the friary and the townspeople in 1409 to bolster their demands a century later.[42] The vecinos complained about gifts that the townspeople had become obliged to give to the friary as a form of taxation. Not only were vecinos impelled to pay, but the amount had not decreased substantially, despite the recent loss of population due to plague (and, presumably, though the vecinos do not mention it, the loss of conversos in town).[43] Guadalupenses also demanded that the friary pay some share of the salary for the mayor, bailiff, and prison, since these two officers, together with the prison, notoriously acted for the benefit of the friary rather than for the benefit of the townspeople.[44] Most importantly—it was their first demand—the townspeople demanded the right to their own city council, elected by the vecinos themselves.[45] These claims, the most radical that the townspeople would ever put forward, were no less than a call for a return to the rights of the República which had been awarded to the friary in 1340.

The breadth of these demands is striking, but not out of keeping with the attitudes of the times. Increasingly, early modern townspeople across western Europe began to take advantage of growing central authorities to curb the power of local lords. As Helen Nader has made clear in her work on the sale of towns in Hapsburg Spain, town rights

---

[41] See demands 2–7 and 17–19, AHN clero pergaminos, carpeta 409, item 24, 4v–5v.

[42] Ibid., 19v. The uprising, petition, and agreement of 1404–1408 are discussed at greater length in chapter 1.

[43] Ibid., 5r, demand 8.

[44] Ibid., demand 10.

[45] Ibid., 4v, demand 1.

were often sold to municipal councils during the sixteenth century. Charles V (reigned 1516–1555) established the practice first begun by his grandparents, Fernando and Isabel. Despite the loss of direct control over these towns, the Hapsburg emperor gained the towns' steadfast loyalty and a political counterweight to noble possessions elsewhere in the peninsula. Given this political climate and their old history of independence, it is not surprising that Guadalupenses could imagine the possibility of success at court.[46] And while this negotiation most often took place regarding relations among the Crown, the populace, and the nobility, the church was not separate from these discussions. Indeed, events at Guadalupe suggest the complexity of the church's relation to these political and social developments. Unfortunately for the vecinos, their strategy of a lawsuit worked best when the Catholic Monarchs benefited from the sale, gaining an ally against a strong nobleman. The Inquisition had demonstrated that the Jeronymite friars in Guadalupe, at least, were not enemies of the monarchs. On the contrary, prior Nuño and his brethren had bound themselves more tightly to the Crown by accepting and participating in the royal inquisitorial trials of more than twenty years before. Furthermore, Isabel had died in 1504, and Fernando spent his time after the summer of 1507, when he was named guardian of his daughter Juana the Mad, trying to maintain his hold on the united kingdoms of Castile and Aragon. For Fernando, the friars in Guadalupe were guardians of a powerful shrine, useful allies in both the political and the spiritual realms; they were not enemies to be divested of their holdings.

For four years the vecinos and friars battled in the Chancillería. Finally, in 1511, the court ruled against the townspeople. Given the political clout of their adversaries and their weak legal position, it is not surprising that the vecinos' actions at court had little effect. In no way did the final ruling of the Chancillería in 1511 challenge the friary's complete control as it had been awarded in 1389. From the most minor requests to the townspeople's most radical claims, the court sided with the friary and affirmed its rights as collective lord of the Puebla. The Jeronymites were sovereign lords of Guadalupe, under the political authority of no one but the Crown. The friars were not required to respond to the townspeople's complaints about the accessibility of firewood, let alone permit townspeople to determine their own officials or meet independently of the friary. The friars were vindicated almost completely.[47] As soon as the case was won, the friars took steps to re-

---

[46] Helen Nader, *Liberty in Absolutist Spain: The Hapsburg Sale of Towns, 1516–1700* (Baltimore: Johns Hopkins University Press, 1990).

[47] AHN clero pergaminos, carpeta 409, item 24, 22v–31r, ruling of the Chancillería.

cord for themselves the specifics of the legal victory by ordering a copy of the trial documents for their records in Guadalupe.[48] If there were ever another *ayuntamiento*, the Jeronymites would be ready to defend themselves.

Only one part of the ruling of the court came close to acknowledging vecino demands, but even here the court reaffirmed the friars' authority over the town. The judges of the Chancillería acknowledged that Guadalupenses had few opportunities to express their concerns to the friars, or to petition them for changes. The friary had no need to allow an independent city council to rule on local issues, the court affirmed, but as collective lord they did need to listen to town complaints and requests. Therefore, the judges ruled that the friary was required to hold a monthly audience for vecinos. At that time townspeople would be permitted to present petitions, demands, or requests to the prior.[49] Political interaction between friars and townspeople was in effect shifted from the confessional to these new monthly audiences. The friary now expressed its temporal authority in a way that demonstrated the friars' political as well as spiritual jurisdiction. The audiences, held in the Hospedería Real, were dramatic moments heavy with symbols of spiritual as well as political power. The building, with its associations with the Inquisition and the Crown; the position of the prior (or his assistant) in the seat used by the king and queen when they were present in their audience hall; and even the brown-and-white habits of the friars all emphasized that the friars' authority derived from both God and king. The audience codified the political nature of the friars' power over the town and rationalized somewhat their modes of governance.

Yet this new monthly session was not a simple case of "modernized" or "secularized" government. On the contrary, at a time when many villages and towns in western Europe were becoming more independent, and when emancipation of serfs in the West was the rule, the prior's audience seems like an anachronism. As collective lord, the friary was exerting more direct authority over the town of Guadalupe, when one might expect local authorities to wield less and less power. Like the Guadalupe inquisition before it, the Bonilla case reveals that aiding local authorities in consolidating their hold on power might redound to the benefit of the Crown, and that spiritual authority was important in both

[48] This is AMG codex 167.
[49] AHN clero pergaminos, carpeta 409, item 24, 22r–35r. See also AMG codex 75, "Libro de los actos de las audiencias que nro Rvdo padre el prior y sus offiçiales en su lugar y el alcalde han hecho a los del pueblo en prinçipio de cada mes. segund fue mandado por la sentençia dada en granada contra ellos: y en favor desta casa. Desde primero de enero: Año del . . . [1512]."

local and royal settings. As the friars tightened their once-tenuous grip on the townspeople, they were more able to support the Crown in its endeavors and put their collective wealth and spiritual authority behind Fernando and his descendants. The Chancillería, a new royal institution, aided the friars in their political struggles, and the friars were predisposed then to return the favor. In turn, the vecinos gained a clear means of expressing political concerns and discontent directly to the prior, giving townspeople—through their subordinated status—a greater voice in Guadalupense life than at any time since the establishment of the friars in town. Of course, the costs of that voice were great. The ruling reaffirmed the friar's right to rule the town as they saw fit and solidified the Jeronymites' control over the vecinos. The Chancillería introduced a court ruling into the centuries-long debate between friars and townspeople over the proper extent of ecclesiastical control, a definitive ruling that forever changed the nature of Guadalupense political life. From this point forward, all debate began from the point of fundamental control on the part of the friars.

Guadalupe's townspeople had suffered a profound setback in their struggle with the friary, but the vecinos were not cowed. The monthly audience with the prior was quickly taken up by townspeople as a new means of presenting demands to the friary. Residents abandoned their most ambitious demands and turned rather to smaller issues about the quality of Jeronymite governance and life in town. The pattern of these meetings is recorded in a book detailing complaints raised at the meeting. A representative of the prior listened to vecino concerns and issued a response, either immediately or within a week. In the years immediately following the *pleito de los Bonilla*, townspeople used the audience to petition the friary to hire an apothecary, *boticario*, for the town; to demand that the friars provide an independent public defender; and to resolve other, smaller disputes among townspeople. By the late 1510s and early 1520s tensions in the town had clearly quieted, and meetings became less frequent. While the friars granted few of the townspeople's larger requests, the ability to petition in an audience—much like the Crown's Chancillería—seemed to placate the vecinos. The records of the prior's audience suggest that in the aftermath of the *pleito*, Guadalupe's townspeople reconciled themselves to the new balance of power in Guadalupe in which the friary held more clearly defined and more absolute control. The prior's audience, though less than an independent town council, provided sufficient opportunity to voice concerns so that vecino frustrations did not boil over.

This new balance of power is evident in the last legal battle between friars and townspeople in Guadalupe—the *pleito de los Gago*, as Germán Rubío identified it in his 1926 history of Guadalupe. In the 1520s the friary was continuing the expansion begun with construction of the Hospedería Real and the new "Gothic Cloister." As part of the construction of new outbuildings, the friary seized several buildings and a street near the friary to provide more room. Most townspeople rented their homes from the Jeronymites, rather than owning the buildings outright; this fact, combined with the friary's status as sovereign lord, made such a move unremarkable. For those people unceremoniously evicted, however, the seizure seemed much more drastic. The neighborhood claimed by the friars was one of the most attractive and comfortable in Guadalupe; the streets were open and sunny, and the homes well constructed. Repeated complaints by the townspeople at the suddenly revived monthly audience had no effect on the friars, who continued with their plans. Once again, Guadalupe's vecinos decided to take their complaints to court. A participant in the Bonilla case, Pero Gago, together with his family, took the lead for the townspeople before the Chancillería.

The vecinos struggled to make their case and were willing to make sacrifices to do so, but the lawsuit was doomed from the start. As in the Bonilla case, it is likely that Pero Gago was relatively well educated, although the record does not confirm that. Certainly one of the leaders of the townspeople was alert to developments across the peninsula. As a sign of their independence and their desire to be "liberated" as an independent community by Charles V, the vecinos of Guadalupe began paying tribute to the emperor. Guadalupe's residents expressed their willingness to buy their independence, as so many noble towns were doing. In fact, it was only in the 1540s, long after conflict with the friary had ceased, that Guadalupenses began paying tribute to the friars once again.[50] But despite this dramatic gesture, the Gago suit had little legal standing, and less hope of success. The earlier *pleito* had confirmed the Jeronymites' right to rule the town as they saw fit, and little in the vecinos' sad testimony of displacement during the Gago lawsuit challenged that right. More importantly, the friary was better prepared to respond to popular unrest. More than a generation had passed since internal factions and inquisitorial investigations had divided the friars, and even the purity of blood debate had receded. In 1515 the Order of Saint Jerome had finally instituted purity of blood restrictions for new converts, and by 1525 the friars in Guadalupe had begun recording the proofs of purity of blood for their new brethren. The friars in Gua-

---

[50] Rubío, *Historia*, 338. The vecinos continued to pay tribute to the emperor until the priorate of fray Hernando de Sevilla (1544–1547), who successfully petitioned the emperor to award the tribute to the friary once again. It is important to remember that during this period the townspeople still owed the friary tithes, rent, and other fees.

dalupe had entered a new phase of social and spiritual agreement; as a result, the Jeronymites were poised to act quickly. Previous court experience and broad authority sanctioned by the Chancillería also strengthened the friary's hand. When discontent in town rose and vecinos began to pursue their court case, prior Luis de Toledo acted swiftly. Prior Luis called a public meeting in the audience room to discuss the vecinos' complaints. Once there, he demanded that all those in favor of action against the friary sign a piece of paper. All understood that the eye of the friary was upon them. With the swift threat of force, vecino unrest soon dissipated, the court found in favor of the friary, and the record of monthly audiences indicates an almost immediate return to infrequent meetings and political somnolence on the part of the townspeople.[51]

Prior Luis de Toledo's swift response contrasts markedly with his predecessors' methods of confronting vecino unrest. In the last third of the fifteenth century, prior Diego de París exercised little control over the townspeople, his indecisiveness and arbitrary rule exacerbating conflict. His reliance on a proconverso vicar, fray Fernando de Ubeda, further weakened prior Diego's ability to act. Prior Nuño de Arévalo suffered none of prior Diego's indecisiveness; however, his decision to petition that the Inquisition come to Guadalupe suggests the depth of division both within and without the friary. But by 1526 both Guadalupe and Spain had changed significantly. The friars in Guadalupe were Old Christians, not riven by conflict, and firmly in control of their wayward charges in town.

The outcome of the *pleito de los Gago* demonstrates how significantly attitudes in Guadalupe had changed after 1485. No one in this second *pleito* thought to demand any larger rights to self-government through the old rule of the *República*. Even the Gagos's more limited goals of restraining the friary's physical expansion into the town were frustrated. The friary's firm control of the town was assured, and neither vecinos nor friars were willing or able to consider alternate political and social alliances. In the fifty short years since fray Nuño de Arévalo's election as prior, relations between friars and townspeople had changed dramatically. Prior Nuño would hardly have recognized the efficient friars and quiet populace of mid-sixteenth-century Guadalupe. Occasional food shortages and financial crises, as well as the ultimate decline in importance of the town as a pilgrimage site in the modern era, still lay ahead; but the roles established in the 1520s for the friary and townspeople would continue until the nineteenth century. The contentious relationship between Guadalupe's lay residents and clergy, and divisions within

---

[51] AMG codex 75, 60r–64r. 1 Dec. 1525–July 1526.

each of those groups, were replaced in the decades after the Inquisition by a new status quo that placed local authority firmly in the hands of the friary.

GUADALUPE AND THE SACRALITY OF THE
EARLY MODERN SPANISH STATE

The Inquisition fundamentally altered the friars' authority in Guadalupe, but its effects were not confined to any one town. Changes in the production, consolidation, and protection of local and royal authority, apparent in events in Guadalupe in the fifteenth and sixteenth centuries, reflected broader changes throughout Europe. Across the continent, rulers were attempting to consolidate authority around themselves at the expense of rebellious nobles and independent-minded towns—or, as they sometimes saw it, reclaiming royal roles usurped by the nobility.[52] For Fernando and Isabel, as well as their successors Charles V and Philip II (reigned 1555–1598), one means of gaining this authority was by allying with the church, or, more specifically, by sacralizing the kingdom itself. By the term "sacralize," I mean imbuing Castile (and to a much lesser extent the Spanish kingdoms as a whole) with an inherent religious significance and spiritual power that guided the destiny of the kingdom in foreign and domestic policy. For Fernando and Isabel this was particularly important in the wake of the Castilian civil war after the death of Isabel's half-brother Enrique IV. In their concerted effort to tarnish the reputation of their predecessor and simultaneously legitimate Isabel's rule in Castile, they needed to restore the status of the monarchy and justify her position as queen, as opposed to her rival Juana la Beltraneja.[53] In bolstering the image of the monarchy and especially Isabel's position in it, they changed the image of the kingdom as well.

[52] Nicholas Henshall, *The Myth of Absolutism. Change and Continuity in Early Modern European Monarchy* (London: Longman, 1992), 143.

[53] Much work has been done recently on Isabel's propaganda efforts after the civil war in Castile that won her the crown. See Barbara Weissberger, "'Me atrevo a escribir así': Confessional Politics in the Letters of Isabel I and Hernando de Talavera," in *Women at Work in Spain: From the Middle Ages to Early Modern Times,* ed. Marilyn Stone and Carmen Benito-Vessels (New York: Peter Lang, 1998), 147–69; and "'A tierra, puto!': Alfonso de Palencia's Discourse of Effeminacy," in *Queer Iberia: Sexualities, Cultures, and Crossings from the Middle Ages to the Renaissance,* ed. Josiah Blackmore and Gregory S. Hutcheson (Durham: Duke University Press, 1999), 291–324; Elizabeth A. Lehfeldt, "Ruling Sexuality: The Political Legitimacy of Isabel of Castile," *Renaissance Quarterly* 53 (2000), 31–56; and Liss, *Isabel the Queen,* 52–64. Helen Nader also discusses this in *The Mendoza Family,* 34. See also José Manuel Nieto Soria, *Ceremonias de la realeza: Propaganda y legitimación en la Castilla Trastámara* (Madrid: Nerea, 1993).

The sacralized kingdom that Isabel and Fernando helped to create was distinct from medieval precedents of sacred kingship, or from the sacred aspects of monarchy visible in other early modern kingdoms. Scholars have long noted the sacred markers associated with some medieval kings—anointment with holy oil at the coronation, authority to confront heresy, and "the royal touch" of healing, for example.[54] Marc Bloch carefully has traced the evolution of the idea of a sacred, healing touch of kings, who in France were reputed to heal scrofula, and who in England supposedly healed epileptics as well. As Bloch notes, Robert of Blois described Henry II as "the Anointed of the Lord."[55] This clearly was a prerogative of kings as sacred beings, not of the kingdom as a whole. Ernst Kantorowicz's treatment of the political concept of the "king's two bodies" also addresses the intersection of religious and secular authority, although even here the end result is a "quasi-religious glorification" rather than an imbued sacred nature per se. The medieval *corpus reipublicae mysticum* is a borrowing from theologians. It attributed the idea of a transcendental, corporate character to the state as an entity that has a legal status as a kind of "fictive" person. The state's "mystical nature" has to do with its legal status, not with any unique, divine favor.[56] Yet, as Teófilo Ruiz has demonstrated, this image of a "sacred king" was not an active element of royal rituals of power in Castile in the Middle Ages, and the sacralized kingdom envisioned by Isabel and Fernando had little in common with it. Kingship in Castile was not limited to a single family "blessed with thaumaturgical and sacred aspects," but rather was defined by military prowess and celebrated with predominantly secular rites, some borrowing from Muslim practices.[57] The way was clear, in effect, for Isabel to use religion to

---

[54] The classic analysis of sacred kingship and its implications remains Ernst Kantorowicz's *The King's Two Bodies: A Study in Medieval Political Theology* (Princeton: Princeton University Press, 1957). Important for its analysis of the sacred power of kingship is Marc Bloch, *The Royal Touch: Sacred Monarchy and Scrofula in England and France*, tr. by J. E. Anderson from *Les Rois Thaumaturges* (Paris: A. Colin, 1961). A brief overview of these attitudes and their decline in the High Middle Ages is found in R. W. Southern, *The Making of the Middle Ages* (New Haven: Yale University Press, 1953), 92–96. For the early modern period, see Paul Kléber Monod, *The Power of Kings: Monarchy and Religion in Europe, 1589–1715* (New Haven: Yale University Press, 1999).

[55] Bloch, *Royal Touch*, 22.

[56] Kantorowicz, *Two Bodies*, chap. 5, particularly 207–208.

[57] Teófilo F. Ruiz, "Unsacred Monarchy: The Kings of Castile in the Late Middle Ages," in *Rites of Power: Symbolism, Ritual, and Politics Since the Middle Ages*, ed. Sean Wilentz (Philadelphia: University of Pennsylvania Press, 1985), 121, 129. This is reprinted in the Variorum reprints edition, *The City and the Realm: Burgos and Castile in the Late Middle Ages* (Aldershot, England, and Brookfield, VT: Variorum, 1992). A version of this article also appeared in French as "Une royauté sans sacre: La Monarchie castillane du Bas Moyen Age," *Annales E.S.C.* 3 (1984), 429–453.

legitimate her rule, unfettered by conventions of England, France, or even Aragon.

Under Isabel, royal legitimacy and spiritual authority were linked in new ways. First, the Crown, under the impetus of Fernando and Isabel, began systematically to incorporate religious offices, functions, and personnel into the bureaucracy of the kingdom at an impressive rate. As Helen Nader has observed in her work on the Mendoza, *letrados* began to replace the military nobility that had previously filled out the royal bureaucracy. These scholastically minded bureaucrats melded their view of a divinely impelled history with the idea that the kingdom itself exhibited a spiritually significant quality—that it was not merely the recipient of divine good will, but that it was *itself* a locus of spiritual power, a divine agent rather than merely a beneficiary of divine favor. Humanistically trained *caballeros* like the Mendoza did not accept this idea of a divinely ordained plan for Spain and increasingly found themselves pushed to the side.[58] While this change in attitude was not created by the Catholic Monarchs ex nihilo—indeed, Nader indicates that many of the individual actions of the Catholic Monarchs were presaged by earlier reigns—it is in the reign of the Catholic Monarchs, and in their actions in Guadalupe and elsewhere, that the creation of this new, powerful image of Spain takes clear form.

This interpenetration of secular and sacred attitudes, and particularly of hierarchies, is not surprising given the importance that the *letrados* ascribed to a divinely ordained, well-defined hierarchy both in government and in the church. It seems comparable to similar notions of God and of the state in the Holy Roman Empire, as described by David Sabean.[59] In Spain as in the Holy Roman Empire, people understood sacred and secular authority in ways that facilitated "the use of religious institutions for buttressing the lines of political authority."[60] The fabric underlying the sacralized quality of the Spanish state was, in essence, a seamless garment of authority, joining sacred and secular hierarchies in the design of God, as proponents of this vision saw it.

The institution of the modern Spanish Inquisition as an arm of the state further underscores the extension of *letrado* ideas into Spanish political culture, where religious concerns were resolved through political action, and vice versa. Until the ascension of the Valencian Alexander VI as pope, the papacy had been reluctant to grant the episcopal power of investigation to a secular authority. Early in the papacy of Alexander

---

[58] Nader, *The Mendoza Family*, 130–132, and all of chap. 6 generally.

[59] David Sabean, *Power in the Blood: Popular Culture and Village Discourse in Early Modern Germany* (Cambridge: Cambridge University Press, 1984), especially chap. 1.

[60] Ibid., 58.

VI, however, Isabel and Fernando were granted the right to institute the Holy Office of the Inquisition as an office of the secular state. Now the task of regulating, punishing, and altering the behavior of New Christians was part of the role of the Crown. With the support of the *letrados*, the Crown began to exercise this religious role as an intrinsic part of its royal authority. Peggy Liss has demonstrated in her biography *Isabel the Queen* that Isabel saw herself as living at a particularly significant time in the history of the world—and the eagle of John's gospel and apocalypse served as the emblem of her and her husband's reign at this millenarian period.[61] In that sense, Spain and its policies such as that of the Inquisition were the tools of divine prophecy coming to bear in the last days, converting all the world's peoples to Christianity and ushering in the Apocalypse. They and their kingdom held a unique position in the history of the world, foretold by prophecy, and critical to ushering in the millennium.

Further evidence for the sacralization of the kingdom of Spain comes from the Virgin herself, and Isabel's association with her. As Elizabeth Lehfeldt makes clear, the Virgin Mary became a model for Isabel as ruling queen, particularly in the doctrine of the Immaculate Conception—the doctrine that the Virgin Mary was born without sin. Like the Virgin Mary, who redeemed the sins of Eve, Isabel's bearing of an heir to the throne helped redeem Spain from its chaotic recent history. The doctrine of the Immaculate Conception emphasized this redemptive role of Mary and also linked the Virgin Mary to the Woman of the Apocalypse. Similarly, Isabel was associated with the redemptive power of the Immaculate Conception and the Woman of the Apocalypse, who bears a son. Isabel's identification with the Immaculate Conception also helped lessen anxieties surrounding her dual political and distinctly sexual roles, as secular leader and mother of her children. Her impure, sexual role could itself be redeemed, to some extent, by the redemptive power it carried with it. It is hardly surprising, then, that Isabel granted a large sum to the friars in Guadalupe to celebrate the feast of the Immaculate Conception each year on December 8.[62]

Thus, Isabel associated herself in general with the cult of the Virgin Mary, the doctrine of the Immaculate Conception, and by extension particular advocations of the Virgin like the Virgin of Guadalupe, who provided a sacred impulse to Spain's foreign actions as she rescued prisoners, defeated Muslims, and saved ships at sea. For centuries advocations of the Virgin Mary had favored men in battle, but the Virgin of

---

[61] Liss, *Isabel the Queen*, 123–126, 136–137, and 286–287. Lehfeldt has a particularly useful analysis of the symbolism of the eagle in "Ruling Sexuality," 38–39.

[62] Lehfeldt, "Ruling Sexuality," 50–53. The doctrine of the Immaculate Conception was a popular, if controversial, doctrine in early modern Spain. It did not receive official papal approval until the nineteenth century.

Guadalupe, by the very nature of her history, the kinds of miracles she was purported to carry out, and even the national and international nature of her cult, seemed to show more than generic assistance to people in need.[63] Rather, the combination of actions implied a more universal favoritism—namely, of Spain collectively as a recipient of divine power. The elements that comprised her history and her miracles—association with Spain's preconquest Christian past, flight before the Muslims, and miracles that especially benefited those participating in the reconquest or battles with the Turks—all made the Virgin of Guadalupe a means by which Spaniards could understand the relationship between their past, present, and future in a context of divinely mandated conquest. The Virgin and her shrine became a "memory place," or *lieu de mémoire*, in which the remembered past helped explain for Iberians their present and future. In Extremadura, one of the last battlegrounds of the Christian reconquest of Iberia from the Muslims, the Virgin of Guadalupe stood as a vital symbol of the continuity of Christian settlement of the whole peninsula. After 1492 and the final defeat of the Muslims in Granada, the Virgin of Guadalupe and her miracles demonstrated the divine necessity of Spain's Christian mission in the world. As late as the battle of Lepanto in 1571, the Virgin of Guadalupe was invoked to provide aid in battle against Muslim enemies. In short, Spaniards understood her cult as demonstrating the religious significance and power of Spain in the Mediterranean.[64]

In the suppression of religious minorities and the consolidation of spiritual functions under secular authority, the Crown made use of religious institutions and devotions like that of the Virgin of Guadalupe to strengthen itself, both in traditional political alliances and in claiming some of the spiritual strength of the church. This brings us back to Guadalupe and coordination of local and royal, and sacred and secular, to the benefit of both. The implication of this analysis is that both the Crown and, to a lesser extent, local officials in Guadalupe used each other in the process of self-fashioning—in the process of creating an imagined community.[65] The friars who controlled Guadalupe, like many Spaniards to a greater or lesser degree, attempted to use the Inquisition

---

[63] Amy G. Remensnyder is investigating martial aspects of the Virgin Mary. See, for example, "The Colonization of Sacred Architecture: The Virgin Mary, Mosques, and Temples in Medieval Spain and Early Sixteenth-Century Mexico," in *Monks and Nuns, Saints and Outcasts: Religion in Medieval Society. Essays in Honor of Lester K. Little*, ed. Sharon Farmer and Barbara H. Rosenwein (Ithaca: Cornell University Press, 2000), 189–219.

[64] Starr-LeBeau, "Joyous History."

[65] Benedict Anderson, *Imagined Communities: Reflections on the Origin and Spread of Nationalism*, rev. ed. (London and New York: Verso Press, 1991). This community is necessarily somewhat different from the modern nation-state Anderson describes.

for their own ends, in this case the consolidation of their authority over the town. But there was more to the effects of the Inquisition than that. For by challenging and eliminating conversos from Guadalupense society, the friars created a newly imagined community of Guadalupe—one that adhered to an emergent sense of Roman Catholic "orthodoxy" but simultaneously held political implications for all townspeople. At the same time, the Crown was also re-creating an imagined Christian community, legitimated by the Virgin of Guadalupe and other religious devotions that emphasized the unique, sacralized role of the state. In an eminently practical way, Guadalupe was the kind of pilgrimage site that Anderson, drawing from Victor Turner's work, describes, one that created a sense of common identity for townspeople, pilgrims, and in a larger sense Castilians as a whole.[66]

Indeed, not only did the shared experience of the pilgrims help to create a common bond, but the spiritual message of the shrine, which was consciously disseminated by the devotees of the Virgin of Guadalupe, also helped create a community unified in belief and action. Pilgrims traveling to Guadalupe in the wake of the inquisitorial trials were witnesses to the power of the monarchy in the actions and after-effects of the Holy Office, in the Catholic Monarchs' residence at the sacred shrine, and in the supernatural support of the Virgin for Isabel and Fernando's political agenda. What a contrast to Isabel's predecessor! Unlike her half-brother, Isabel reflected the redemptive purity of the Virgin Mary, patronizing the Virgin's shrines at Guadalupe and elsewhere, and identifying and punishing apostate New Christians. At the same time, Isabel basked in the support of the Virgin as evidenced through the assistance that the Virgin of Guadalupe provided in defeating the enemies of Christendom and of Spain. The popularity of the Virgin of Guadalupe may not compare to the print revolution that Anderson describes, but the large numbers of pilgrims who visited the shrine seem to have had a similar effect, spreading the intertwined messages of Isabel and Fernando's spiritual authority and secular power throughout the peninsula, just as they had at one time spread stories about Judaizing friars at the friary.

Sabean's work suggests that this process of "sacralization" was not limited to Spain alone. As secular and sacred authority and religious self-identification changed in the fifteenth and sixteenth centuries, early modern realms could increasingly take advantage of a wellspring of localized religious practices to consolidate their own authority. Whether it was use of the Eucharist as a defining element of community, employ-

---

[66] Ibid., 53–54. See also Victor Turner, *Dramas, Fields, and Metaphors. Symbolic Action in Human Society* (Ithaca: Cornell University Press, 1974).

ment of local religious officials to help implement royal policies, or the role of Marian devotions in fashioning the state, early modern kingdoms acquired a sacralized quality with their new attempts at cohesiveness.

Like the kingdom of which it was a part, Guadalupe changed greatly in the years after 1485. The friars successfully used their connections with the Crown to increase their own authority over the local population. That Old Christians could be quieted through the indirect force of an institution like the Inquisition, which was not specifically directed against them, suggests the growing power and importance of royal authority in Spain at the end of the fifteenth century. Of course, the conjoined interests of royal and local authority benefited the Crown, too. The power inherent in the popular cult of the Virgin of Guadalupe, and the power perceived to inhere in the image of the Virgin herself, strengthened the monarchy by association. In supporting the friars and promoting the Virgin, the Catholic Monarchs imbued their kingdom with a sacralized quality that legitimized themselves as it simultaneously helped define Castile, and to a lesser extent Spain. Ultimately, it was all of Spain—this new, somewhat precariously united state—that lived "in the shadow of the Virgin"; that is, whose existence was supported both politically and spiritually by the religious devotions so important to contemporaries.

CONCLUSION

Wʜᴏ New Christians were—that is, how they understood their religiosity and ethnicity—is a question that engendered strong opinions five centuries ago and continues to attract attention today. The experiences of conversos in Guadalupe at the end of the Middle Ages and the beginning of the early modern era suggest why this is so. It is due in part to the complexity of their attitudes and practices, their distinctness from the general population, and the political repercussions of their presence at the shrine site and elsewhere. From the recorded experiences of New Christians in Guadalupe in the fifteenth and early sixteenth centuries, it appears that conversos were neither entirely alienated from Jews and Judaism nor thoroughly allied with them. These New Christians made their way in the world at the Marian shrine, living among Old Christians, sharing friendships with them, and selling goods to the Christian pilgrims who came to town in such numbers. Some, it appears, had assimilated thoroughly into Christian society, reminded of their Jewish ancestry by the Inquisition and purity of blood statutes, or by Judaizing family and friends. Others made their fortune with the support of the friars and were necessary to the administrative activities of the Virgin's guardians. These, not surprisingly, engendered the hostility of some of the Old Christians in town, who resented the control that the friars attempted to wield over them. Still others apparently felt a strong kinship to Judaism, seeking out knowledge of Jewish practices from visiting Jewish merchants, visiting the synagogue in Trujillo, and maintaining to some extent a Jewish household.

These New Christians, with their divergent practices, beliefs, employment, and economic status, did not apparently see themselves as a singular, coherent community within the larger community of Guadalupenses. Most strikingly, converso officials of the friary worked in the interests of the friars and their governance, while the wealthy New Christian cloth merchants in town challenged the authority of the Jeronymites when it suited their financial interests. Conversa women, in particular, socialized with Old Christians with at least superficially little distinction. Of the multiple ways in which Guadalupenses identified themselves—by occupation, confraternity membership, location of residence, place of origin, ethnicity—Jewish descent did not automatically supersede all others.

Yet neither were the Jewish practices of New Christians mere cultural artifacts. Martín Gutiérrez, who wore a prayer shawl to pray in his home and invited Jewish merchants into his home to explain Jewish observance; Manuel González of the Mesón Blanco, who kept a secret prayer book and invited the Jews who stayed in his hostel to add Jewish prayers; and Mari Sánchez, wife of Diego Jiménez, whose reputation in town for Judaizing behavior was widespread and well-founded—each of these and other conversos seem indeed to have had a deep and abiding personal attachment to the law of Moses. At this most controversial period in the history of New Christians, between the establishment of the Holy Office of the Inquisition and the expulsion of the Jews, connections between Jews and New Christians were neither so distant nor so close as might initially appear. The history of Guadalupense conversos suggests that simple generalizations of any kind fail in the face of such complicated and intractable ambiguities.

It was this very ambiguity that made possible a shift in the understanding of the role of New Christians in town. As Guadalupe grew, so did tensions between the townspeople and the friars who governed the town. Accusations of abuse of power and poor government dogged the friars, and increasingly Old Christians saw a link between the power of the friars and the power of a few particularly wealthy and powerful converso merchants who helped underwrite the Jeronymites during the middle of the fifteenth century. Many townspeople also apparently saw a distinct but related connection between the friars and their well-educated converso functionaries. By the second half of the fifteenth century, a renewed hostility toward New Christians began to emerge. Of course, the friars themselves were deeply divided, but this factionalism, too, began to turn on the issue of New Christians. The political import of conversos—from the shoemakers critical to the continued success of the shrine, to the functionaries carrying out ecclesiastical governance, to the wealthy merchants providing financial support to the friars during the fifteenth century—was not lost on the Jeronymites. Converso merchants in particular became a useful and willing tool for friars looking to increase their influence inside the friary and out. New Christians could not be easily categorized on religious questions, but their political role in town was becoming increasingly clear and increasingly precarious.

The malleable and ambiguous nature of New Christian religious identity also gave the Inquisition its power. The inquisitors' power was fundamentally definitional: it emerged from the ability of the inquisitors to define heresy and orthodoxy, to distinguish faithful from apostate Christians, and then to punish (with the aid of secular authorities) on the basis of those distinctions. For Guadalupenses, this meant that simmering resentments against New Christians could be reimagined as parts of a larger whole of heretical acts. Juan de Texeda's humiliations at the hands of Alonso de Paredes were now not merely a political act, but also part of Paredes's heretical nature as a converso. This makes clear a further implication about inquisitorial activity; namely, that this activity was predicated on the widespread consent and participation of Old Christians in town. Everyone in Guadalupe—Old Christians and New Christians, friars and townspeople—could attempt to take advantage of that definitional power for his or her own ends. Obviously, though, the Holy Office of the Inquisition benefited the political aspirations of some more than others, and benefited prior Nuño de Arévalo most of all.

The actions of Guadalupe's "inquisitorial year" clarified and strengthened some boundaries in town, though other ambiguities remained. Factions among the friars were profoundly reshaped, as those supporting fray Fernando de Ubeda lost their relative position within the friary and their financial support from outside of it. In 1488 a second set of inquisitorial trials in the Jeronymite order, including Guadalupe, further weakened the proconverso faction in the friary, as well as strengthening the position of prior Nuño and those supporting purity of blood laws for the order. The town, too, saw profound if gradual realignment. With Guadalupe's wealthy converso cloth merchants executed, and the friars' New Christian lay functionaries punished and—perhaps temporarily at first—exiled, the hostility of the town's residents turned increasingly toward the friars themselves. Yet with power now consolidated in the hands of one faction of the friars, Guadalupenses had little ability to challenge effectively Jeronymite authority in town. By the middle of the sixteenth century, local uprisings against the friars had ceased; and the friars, with greater economic self-sufficiency and unanimity of purpose, had finally achieved the control over the town for which they had long struggled.

The implications of this narrative are more than simply local. Because of its supreme religious and political importance in late-medieval and early modern Iberia, events at the site of the cult of the Virgin of Guadalupe held significance throughout the Spanish kingdoms. Spaniards understood the Virgin of Guadalupe to offer special protection to those involved in the reconquest of the peninsula from Islam, as well as offering her benediction of the political and religious agenda of the Trastámara dynasty. The Virgin's shrine, and her protectors the Jeronymites, were a critical element of Isabelline propaganda of the late fifteenth century. The friars demonstrated the potential utility for local authorities of royal intervention in local affairs, but the presence of the Holy Office of the Inquisition in Guadalupe also benefited the Crown. Fernando and Isabel not only disseminated news of the Inquisition through the thousands of pilgrims who witnessed Guadalupe's autos de fe; they also reemphasized the link between the Virgin of Guadalupe and themselves—the sacred underpinnings of what they presented as the reestablishment of order and good government to Castile and the peninsula.

Furthermore, the example of Guadalupe sheds light on the complicated political and religious transformations of this period. The town of Guadalupe was undeniably unique; yet the political and social conflicts in evidence there reflected, in microcosm, the upheaval convulsing all of Spain at this time. Was the reign of Isabel and Fernando a time when, as some have described it, the desire for uniformity and orthodoxy annihilated the last vestiges of a multiethnic, pluralist society? Certainly the religious practices of Old and New Christians were a concern to monarchs who saw their lives and their time in a millenarian light. And those who allied themselves with Isabel in the civil war and after hoped for enough uniformity and orthodoxy to help ensure stability. But to see their goal as absolute, identical orthodoxy or broad uniformity does something of a disservice to the Catholic Monarchs. As Guadalupe demonstrates, the programs of Fernando and Isabel, particularly the Inquisition, did not create an external oppressive office, a program of purification with a vengeance, but rather a construction of political and religious identity—and political authority—through definition and distinction. This was, of course, not a benign process; but neither was it an alien imposition upon a wholly unwilling populace. Indeed, this picture of the intentions of Isabel and Fernando does not negate the fact that, even in their lifetimes, these somewhat more moderate goals came under increasing challenge from those interested in a thorough marginalization or even elimination of the descendants of Jewish converts in Iberia.

The Virgin of Guadalupe had a painful history; after centuries of hiding from Muslim invaders, she reemerged in triumph to protect Christians fighting against Muslims. The town founded to serve her interests had a difficult history, too, as rapid growth, thousands of pilgrims, factionalism among the friars, and a sizable population of New Christians made a quiet existence there impossible. But that tumultuous history serves to make clear the fundamental interrelation of the reworking of religious identity and the restructuring of political authority in Castile and Spain at the beginning of the early modern era.

APPENDIX

(1r) TRIAL AGAINST JUANA GONZÁLEZ, WIFE OF LOPE DE HERRERA

reconciled 17 January of 1485
and afterward given penance on 19 November 1485
seen on 9 November being put to torture for what she says of the alms
and the pots and the spoon

Seen on 16 November 1485. That she was asked [illegible] about that which she had said when under the will of the Lords. To the prisoner, exile.

She was exiled and her [husband?] on 19 November. Witnesses the *licenciado* Cristobal de Loaysa and the *licenciado* Juste de Loaysa and the *bachiller* Gonzalo Muñoz his brother.

(1v) [sign of the cross] Very Reverend and Lord Fathers:

¶ I, Juana González, wife of Lope de Herrera, appear before Your Reverences with great pain in my soul and penitence in my heart and greatly shame-faced to say and bear witness to my sins that I have committed in offense of Our Lord Jesus Christ, whom I embrace, and against his Holy Catholic faith, repenting myself of them and I ask pardon of your Holy Piety and ask of Your Reverences penitence.

¶ I say, Lords, my guilt that before I was married, in the house of my father I saw my mother order that the oil lamps be cleaned and order them to be lit Friday evenings, and that they not spin on Saturdays either and thus I saw it in their house, and even after I married. Sometimes and even at times those similar nights they did not do anything and also at times my husband. I beg penitence; and I consented to it in my home. I ask penitence.

¶ I say, Lords, my guilt. Also my mother fasted some days and did not begin to eat until night, and also fasted the Great Fast [Yom Kippur] and one day would stew for eating in [illegible] and that they would eat. I beg pardon for the ones and the others, and I also did it in their house and sometimes even after being married and I consented to it, and I saw my husband do it for reasons of ceremony. I ask penitence.

¶ I say, Lords, that when my period came I left my husband's bed and [illegible] that I don't know as custom [illegible] . . . one bathed me and cleaned my body with ceremony. I ask penitence.

¶ I say, Lords, that sometimes I did not observe some feasts and Sundays of those that the Holy Mother Church orders us to observe, [sifting?] for another day and making other things by hand and I helped to make them. I ask penitence. And I saw my husband make them. I ask pardon.

¶ I say, Lords, that sometimes when I kneaded bread I tossed a little dough in the fire, and I saw my mother do it for reasons of ceremony. I ask pardon.

¶ I say, Lords, that sometimes I heard read in my father's house in a Bible and I read in it and also my husband and also in another book that they had in which it said "Creator" and "Adonay." I saw him read. I ask pardon.

¶ I say, Lords, that sometimes I ate meat and eggs and cheese and milk during Lent and other things on prohibited days with necessity and without, and I consented to do it and [encouraged?] my husband. I ask penitence.

¶ I say, Lords, that sometimes I dressed in new clothes and shirts and shoes, and I dressed my children thus, and I saw my husband dress thus for reasons of ceremony. I ask pardon.

¶ I say, Lords, when my son had been sick for four or five months, having tried all the hardships of the physicians I looked for women who might cure him for money and I did what I could with drops [?] and similar things that look like heresy or witchcraft. I did it for his health. I beg penitence.

¶ I say, Lords, that when some relative or [illegible] died, in that day I did not eat meat and sometimes for longer, for more days. In sorrow if the person was needy I would send him fish and eggs and similar things and also my husband. I ask pardon.

(2v) ¶ I say, Lords, that when my father (may he rest in heaven) [was discredited?] we ate on the floor behind [illegible] and we came with a silver cup in heaviness of desire. I ask penitence.

¶ I say, Lords, when some [illegible] came I kissed his hand putting it on my head, and I saw my husband do it. I ask penitence.

¶ I say, Lords, that at times I stewed in my house on Fridays for the Saturday for reasons of ceremony. I ask penitence.

¶ I say, Lords, my guilt that I stopped eating lard and hare and rabbit and fish without scales and I choked on them and also my husband. I ask penitence.

¶ Of all these sins that I have done I beg pardon and my Lord Jesus Christ and of your Reverend Lords penitence with mercy and justice for all my errors.

¶ In these sins and errors, if in asking I [illegible] that I feel for my sins to our Lord Jesus Christ, to whom I pray and ask for mercy. That thus with Him in the holy [illegible] of the holy [illegible] that is the open arms for receiving meritorious sinners. And pardon me all my sins that I did and consented to against Our Lord Jesus Christ and against His Holy Catholic faith and also I say, Lords, for as much as the ceremony weakens especially for the length of time that I have been in this error, Your Reverences order me to give an end to say what most [illegible] or of [illegible] and I promise by my Lord Jesus Christ to live and die in the Holy Catholic faith and to you other Lords I beg penitence, the which I am bound to comply with as Your Reverences would give and put upon me, to the heart of the Holy Mother Church and with [illegible] below and if some people declare more against me [illegible].

¶ On 17 January 1485, before the Lord Doctor inquisitor [Francisco Sánchez de la Fuente], he said that hearing read in a Bible in her father's house, took something, and also of her mother that she saw her do some things she learned from her and that until she was a girl of twenty years in her father's house she did it and after she married until now. If [illegible] did the said ceremonies and that [illegible] confessed it, which she swore to be the truth. [illegible]

(3r) On the 17 September
Very Reverend and Virtuous Lords:
I, the *bachiller* Diego Fernández de Zamora, prosecuting attorney [*promotor fiscal*] of this Holy Inquisition, accuse Juana González wife of Lope de Herrera, who is herself present, citizen of this town of Guadalupe, who lived in possession and in the name of a Christian, and thus she called herself and enjoyed the privileges and immunities conceded to all those of the Christian religion, is a Judaizing heretic and apostate following the law of Moses in offense and injury of God and of our Holy Catholic faith, furthered when she said in her fictitious and not truthful confession but simulated reconciliation in the following things and cases: asking for alms for the conversos saying çedaca [tzedakah; Hebrew: mercy, alms] like the Jews say; and not praying the *Pater Noster* or *Ave Maria* when she is in church, but says "give me, Lord, what you promised me," as the Jews say; and circumcising and consenting and permitting her son to be circumcised and after this to have reconciled. She burned her pots in the fire because lard had been cooked in them, the which she did last July 4 to observe the ceremony of the said law of Moses and in this law it is prohibited and especially condemned to eat such meat for any person who observes and holds to the said law where clearly it seems and [illegible] to have been and are [illegible]. Item: Judaizing heresy and apostasy and other things and cases that further were said by her in her so-called confession that I will protest and allege in the progress of this trial. For which I ask you and require, Reverend Lords, that for such heresy and false penitence and [illegible] you pronounce and declare her to have incurred a sentence of excommunication and confiscation and loss of all her goods and in all the other penalties and censures for the said offenses both canonical and civil imposed against such persons, relaxing her and ordering her relaxed to the secular arm and justice. I propose that the said accusation and the best form that I can [be accepted] and in all things necessary and complete. I implore your noble and Reverend office and the costs. I ask and protest and overall be made completely for justice.

(3v) ¶ And the accusation thus presented, read by me the scrivener, the said Juana González said that she did not want a defense lawyer [*letrado*] or solicitor [*procurador*] but that she wanted to respond "by word."

¶ And after this on this said day the Reverend Lord inquisitors ordered me, the said notary, go to the prison where the said Juana González was held. And there I read her the said accusation so that she could respond to each item specifically. And the said accusation being read to her by me, the said notary, the said Juana González responded to each item in the following way: that she says that she asked alms saying çedaca: she acknowledged that she never knew that was anything, except that she asked alms for the poor Christians and for the conversos without Judaizing intention, nor saying çedaca. And to the accusation that she did not say in church the *Pater Noster* or *Ave Maria* but "Lord, give me what you promised me," [she says] that she prayed the *Pater Noster* and the *Ave Maria* and other Christian devotions. And that the truth is that being in church and having a son ill at around six months that she said among other prayers, "Lord, give me what you promised me and give health to this son." And that she did have said for him masses for his health. Because she never said with Judaizing intention "Lord, give me what you promised me," except as a Christian. And to the accusation that she agreed to circumcise her son, she denies it, and that never, God, did she want her son to be circumcised nor did she circumcise any son of hers. And to the accusation that she burned the pots in which she had cooked lard after she reconciled, that the truth is that she burned a pair of pots that were oily and dirty with other fats for cooking; and that she always ate lard and eats it now, and that she never [illegible] God that with Judaizing intention; she would do it except to clean her pots like Christians do. And that she reconciled.

¶ And then later the said prosecutor said before the said Lord *licenciado* judge inquisitor [Pedro Sánchez de la Calancha] that, affirming his accusation and denying it prejudices he concluded and asked that it be received to trial. And the said Lord inquisitor said that he concluded with both said parties, and pronounced sentence in which he said, "We find that we will give receipt and receive both parties to the trial after announcements except [illegible] and not admit it, for the which will we proceed after a period of nine days."

(4r) First of October
Very Reverend and Virtuous Lords: I, Juan de Texeda, in the name of and as solicitor that I am of the said Juana González wife of the said Lope de Herrera, ask and supplicate of your Reverences that the witnesses for my party be presented in the cause that the said prosecutor of this Holy Inquisition is conducting against the said my party, order done and do the following questions:
1 ¶ First, if they know the said Juana González and for how long a time up to now.
2 ¶ Item, if they know, saw, believed, or heard tell that the said Juana González, as a Christian and person of much charity, asked alms like other Christians who demand and ask and divide them and give them to Old Christians and conversos.
3 ¶ Item, if they know, etc., that the aforementioned my party said and prayed in church the *Pater Noster* and *Ave Maria* and Creed and *Salve Regina* and other devotions like a good Christian, and that she used to do and did have said masses so that Our Lord would give health to her son who was ill.
4 ¶ Item, if they know, etc., that all the sons of the aforementioned my party from birth are healthy in their members and with whole foreskins and not circumcised, and I ask Your Graces that the aforementioned sons of the aforementioned my party be ordered to show the said witnesses so as to depose how they are entirely healthy and without any fault in their members.
5 ¶ Item, if they know, etc., that the aforementioned my party ate and eats lard like any other Christian.
6 ¶ Item, if they know, etc., that [illegible] Christians [illegible] have some pots of oil or other grease that they put over the fire and burn to clean them.

[7] ¶ Item, if they know, etc., that all of the abovementioned be publicly known in this town of Guadalupe or in the greater part of it.

¶ Furthermore, I ask and supplicate to Your Graces that they be ordered to answer and provide answers for all the other questions pertinent to the case, for which, out of necessity, I implore the Reverend and noble office of Your Grace.

(5r) Witnesses presented on behalf of Juana González wife of Lope de Herrera
On the fifth day of October

¶ Francisco son of Juan Alonso *escudero*, citizen of Navalvillar, witness sworn in, and asked about the first question said that he has known the said Juana González perhaps two years because he lived with her one year and one month. And that he was with them from the age of thirteen years more or less.

¶ To the second question he says that he does not know that.

¶ To the third question he said that he used to see her go to church but that he does not know what she prayed.

¶ To the fourth question he said that he knew the three sons of the said Juana González, and that one called Rodrigo and Gabriel, and this witness said about them that he saw their members but that they were not circumcised.

¶ To the fifth question he said that in that time that he was with them this [witness] did not see them eat lard, the said Juana González and her husband and children.

¶ To the sixth question he said that certain times he saw in Juana González's house that when they had some pot dirty with oil or other grease she used to burn it in the fire to clean it.

¶ To the seventh question he said that he heard tell from many people what [the question] said.

¶ Catalina Alonso wife of Antón Martín of Malagarida, deceased, citizen of this town. The witness being sworn in said that she knew the said Juana González for twenty years more or less but that she had not had other dealings with her except that they sat together in church and talked together.

¶ To the second question she said that she does not know.

¶ To the third question she said that she heard her pray many times and that she prayed loudly. And sometimes she understood her to say the *Pater Noster* and *Ave Maria* and other times she did not understand what she prayed. But to the question she does not know.

¶ To the fourth question she does not know.

¶ To the fifth question she does not know.

¶ To the sixth question she said that she never saw her do it.

¶ To the seventh question she said that it seemed to her that she was a good Christian. And that was what she had heard from other people.

(5v) ¶ Juana Martín wife of Juan Gil Crespo, citizen of this town, witness presented, said that she knew the said Juana González seventeen or eighteen years because she raised one of her sons, giving him milk for twenty days, more or less, and that she had had dealings with her because she was in Juana's house sometimes, and the said Juana González in the house of this witness and slept in her house sometimes.

¶ To the second question she said that she does not know.

¶ To the third question she said that she heard her pray and [illegible] Jesus and "the shame" but to the content of it she has not heard or knows.

¶ To the fourth question she said that she does not know but that the eldest son, to whom this witness gave milk, did not seem to be circumcised.

¶ To the fifth question she said that she never saw them eat lard.

¶ To the sixth question she said that she knows how it [the pots] contained it, and that she has done it [herself].

¶ To the seventh question she said that she knows that she is in possession of a good Christian [reputation], and that to this witness and to other Old Christians she has given alms.

¶ Ínes González wife of Juan de Herrera, citizen of this town, witness presented and sworn in said that she knew the said Juana González about ten years because sometimes she went to buy bread at her house.

¶ To the second question she said that she had seen her give alms to a poor Old Christian woman when she married. Of the rest she does not know.

¶ To the third question she said that she did not see her pray, but that sometimes she said to this witness that she would have [illegible] to her [husband?] when she had gone out.

¶ To the fourth question she said that she saw their [illegible], saw their [illegible] members but that they were like the other sons of Christians and were not trimmed back and that the one of them died and this witness [enshrouded] him and that he looked like the said [illegible].

¶ To the fifth question she said that she does not know.

¶ To the sixth question she said that she knows it and this witness has done it.

¶ To the seventh question she said that she knows it.

¶ Mari Sánchez wife of Miguel Sánchez *tejero*, citizen of this town, witness presented and sworn in, said that she has known the said Juana González about twenty years by sight and conversation and because they sat together in church.

(6r) ¶ To the second question she said that she does not know but that she saw her give alms to a poor Old Christian woman who married.

¶ To the third question she said that she saw her pray the *Pater Noster* in church and that she said to this witness that she came to do two masses for one of her sons that was sick.

¶ To the fourth question she said that she had seen two or three of her sons and that they are healthy in their members.

¶ To the fifth question she said that she does not know.

¶ To the sixth question she said that she knows it, and that this witness has done it.

¶ To the seventh question she said that she knows it, and that this witness held her in possession of good Christian [character].

¶ Juan Alonso [illegible] witness sworn in, and asked about the first question said that he has known her since childhood because the father of the said Juana González lived most all of the time one and a half walls from the father of this witness, and the said Juana González also lives one and a half walls from the mother of this witness.

¶ To the second question he said that he does not know it.

¶ To the third question he says that the said Juana González arrived to fray Pedro de Palencia about a year ago [who] at that season served at the main altar, and she gave him three masses but I do not know if it was before the death of the child. And that she begged this witness saying to him that if she would have [trusted] in her sacrifices for her son and Our Lady would heal him, but that of the prayers that she prayed, he knows it, except that he used to see her in church many times, especially since that Inquisition [arrived] there is more devotion.

¶ To the fourth question he said that he does not know it.

¶ To the fifth question he said that he does not know it.

¶ To the sixth question he said that he does not know it.

¶ To the seventh question he said that from what he has said, he believes that she is of little voice and notoriety.

¶ The Gaga, wife of Pedro Fernández Gago, citizen of this town, sworn in and asked said that she has known the said Juana González about seven or eight years, more or less, because this witness was a midwife and [Juana] bore two sons and a daughter with her.

¶ To the second question she said that she does not know it.

¶ To the third question she said that many times she saw her pray in church and that she understood that she was praying the *Pater Noster* and *Ave Maria*, and this witness heard it. And that when this witness went to her house she pleaded that in her prayers she would plead for her children, that God would minister to them of His holy service.

¶ To the fourth question she said that she saw those two sons that were born with this witness and that they were born healthy in their members.

(6v) ¶ To the fifth question she said that she saw her stew lard in her house but that she did not see her eat it.

¶ To the sixth question she said that she does not know it.

¶ To the seventh question she said that she believes [her] of little voice and notoriety for what is said, and that this witness took her for a good Christian.

¶ María García wife of Rodrigo Martín *albañil* a witness presented and sworn in said that she has known the said Juana González since childhood because they saw her sometimes in church and in this place but by other dealings or conversation. .

¶ To the second question she said that she does not know it except that she heard tell many times how the said Juana González gave alms to the Sevillana, mother of this witness.

¶ To the third question she says that she does not know it.

¶ To the fourth question she says that she does not know it.

¶ To the fifth question she says that she does not know it.

¶ To the sixth question she says that she does know it.

¶ To the seventh question she says that of what is said she believes her to have little notoriety.

(7r) Witnesses presented for the prosecutor

¶ Juan Pérez Vizcayno pilgrim, having been sworn in and being questioned said that this witness and Juan de Astorga, citizen of Salamanca, entered to stew something to eat at the house of Lope de Herrera, who sold wine. And standing stewing the pot he saw that there was a pot put mouth down on the fire to burn. He did not know why and that it seemed to him that it was dirty from others and had been used for stewing.

¶ Juan de Astorga, citizen of Salamanca at the Val de Escuderos, having been sworn in, said that today, Monday 4 July, this witness and another, his companion, went to stew for eating at the house of Lope de Herrera because they sell wine, and saw that two pots that others had been stewing in, that they were recently dirtied, the wife of the said Lope de Herrera put them to burn over the fire, putting them mouth down and they were there until they reburned, to which this witness asked why she burned them, to which she said to get the grease out, because the boys did not wash them well. And because this witness took an iron spoon to skim his pot and she grabbed and took it and threw it on the ground, and ordered a boy to bring a stone [illegible] and clean the spoon.

¶ Antona Fernández, daughter-in-law of Rodrigo Martín, having been sworn in, said that she heard tell that the wife of Lope de Herrera, having recently given birth, one night she circumcised a son of the said Lope de Herrera, that she does not know which but that she heard tell from some peasants [*peones*], namely Alonso de Quantos, citizen of Las Juntas.

¶ Catalina Alonso, wife of Antón Tostado, citizen of this town, was sworn in and said that she saw the said Juana González, that one day she arrived at the home of Diego Sánchez Çerero and filled one cup and she went and Leonor daughter of Andrés Alonso and they said *çedaca* [tzedakah] and showed the cup and said *zanquzda*. And that the said Gonzalo Sánchez and his wife took out four [paths?] and [text ends here]

¶ Ínes González wife of Juan Esteban de la Barrera says in the response to her accusation, she responded to that of which she was accused (that she made fun of those who blessed their children) and how this witness had believed that Juana González was a Jew and not a Christian and that she [Juana] did not have it in her heart to bless her said children, that in seeing them blessed like that she laughed.

(7v) ¶ Leonor Martín wife of the bailiff Maestre Rodrigo said, being sworn in, that being in the church many times she has heard it said by the said Juana González standing praying, "Give me, Lord, what you promised me," and that she said it so loudly that this witness could hear it well and those who were around her and that it has not been two months since she heard it said. And that this past Friday, that was 14 January, she heard it said in church, making prayer for her husband who was not here, "deliver me and free me, Lord, from this strong force," and that she has not seen her pray *Pater Noster* or *Ave Maria* but rather those other words.

(8r) And on 21 October of the said year the said Juan de Texeda appeared before the Lords inquisitors and presented this following response:
(8v) Very Reverend and Virtuous Lords:
I, the said Juan de Texeda, in the name of and as solicitor that I am of Juana González wife of the said Lope de Herrera. I say that by Your Reverences seen and with diligence examined the said depositions of the witnesses presented by the said prosecutor. Your Reverences will find that the said prosecutor has not proven nor proved his said accusation according to the form that he put it. It contains in itself four things of which he accused her: the first saying that she asked alms for the conversos and saying *çedaca* like the Jews say. About this he deposes the fourth witness presented for the said prosecutor whose speech and deposition, I say, does not make a pronouncement against the said my party. The one does not because she is alone and singular; the other because she does not say that the said alms were collected for the conversos as is contained in his said accusation. The other does not [illegible] this to the said my party because the said my party reconciled to many other greater and graver things and thus in consequence this was seen to have been reconciled if it would have been done; but the said my party says that she never said *çedaca* nor *zanquzda* nor did she know it or hear it until this accusation. So that this first case was not proven.

The second of which she was accused (it was saying that she did not pray the *Pater Noster* nor the *Ave Maria* when she was in church but that she used to say, "Lord, give me what you promised me, etc."), about this he deposes the fifth witness presented for the said prosecutor, and there is no other that says such, and so her speech is denied *cur dictum uniq.*, etc. [because it is unique, etc.]. And the said my party said that it is true that she had said it by the means and form that she said and alleged in her exemptions and defense, because Our Lord has promised sinners that in that very hour in which they converted to Him and they asked mercy He would hear them. And so the said my party, because one son had died and another had been killed, and she had another ill to the death [illegible] her sins and repenting herself of them asked God mercy, that He would give to her son, saying "Lord, You promised well to give this to me and heal this son of mine." And so understood the said witness and the deposition of the said witness. It does not [pertain?] to the said my party.

The third item which was accused was saying that she had circumcised, and permitted to be circumcised, her son. About this he deposes the third witness presented by the said prosecutor and there is no other that says such. And so for being alone and singular the said [prosecutor] has not proven anything and because he deposes by hearsay and not by sight, nor by certain knowledge, so he did not prove this third case.

The fourth of these he accused her saying that after the reconciliation she had burned the pots in the fire because he says that lard had been cooked in them. About this the prosecutor deposes the second witness whose sayings and depositions, I say, did not [pertain?] to my party because it is not (9r) proven that she would have done it like a Jew nor for any observance or ceremony of the law of Moses, and I have it proven by the said my party that many of the Old Christians, to clean their pots of grease, burn them and put them on the fire and thus did the said my party, for cleaning. So that this fourth case of which he accused her is not proven. Furthermore, the said my party has proven her exemptions and defenses for where just so it elides and excludes the said accusation.

To conclude, I ask and implore Your Reverences that, pronouncing the intention of the said prosecutor as not proven and that intention of the said my party as well proven, order her absolved and give her as free and wish and do in all according to the said my party and by me in the name of her who is asking. For which, and in necessity, I implore the reverend and noble office of your mercy and ignoring the prejudicial. [illegible] I conclude.

Very Reverend Lords:
I the said prosecution attorney Diego [Fernández] that presented the said [witnesses] and depositions of the witnesses, seen and examined with diligence by Your Graces and I will be found to have well and completely proven my intention for that [which is] contained in my said accusation and the witnesses presented by me well deposed and as they should be in law. And not be alone nor singular as, to the contrary, it says above, conforming and answering the ones to the others, still less to depose by hearsay as, to the contrary, is said, except for certain science and wisdom, and I say they conform and answer, since that they are deposing of all that is heresy and the witnesses presented for the other side are friends and servants and relatives [*familiares*] and contain other *tachas* and [objections?] for which by law they should not be admitted. For which I ask you, according to the aforementioned, I hold to that despite the contrary [argument] alleged, you come to agree that the witness that deposes that the said Juana González asked alms saying *çedaca*, that it does not say that she asked for it for conversos even though it does not say it, it can be inferred from the speech because not only does the witness believe the said alms would not be given to Old Christians given the enmity that they have with them (they would even kill them and rob them if they could, as they do). And given the case that this should stop that, it does not stop, then the petition is proven saying *çedaca* enough for her condemnation. And to prove that as a Jew she asked [alms], how much more then if this witness that says such would be re-questioned she would say the aforementioned, no less persist in saying that she reconciled more grave things and cases of heresy (9v) and that beneath all those are included what is accused by me. Because it does not happen like that in truth. And given and not confessed, I say in kind that so she should be obligated to confess the aforementioned things because it is not enough that they be included among the others, nor is there law that says such, nor less to say that these words, "give me what you promised me," that she said toward the end that she says, nor as she says it, except like a Jew, and received the confession in which she says by me thus in this case, as in all the others by her, confessed. And in the other she used to be eating, I say, nor less say that if she burned the said pots, that it was for cleaning. And to the end

that other Old Christians do it because it is not worth the argument and there is great dissimilarity because these said Old Christian women are not qualified in witnessing to the sin of heresy to which they confessed to be heretics like the said opposing party. For which I ask you according to the above, negating prejudicial intention, ceasing, I conclude.

¶ On 26 October came the said. The said Lords inquisitors, *oidores*, [illegible] of the said parties said that they concluded with the parties; they followed to [illegible] to give sentence on the third day and from there until when they had free.

(10r) On 10 November 1485, seen by the Reverend Lords inquisitors together with the other *letrados* to see the trials of the heretics they alleged, among which they saw that of Juana González, wife of Lope de Herrera, and how the said Juana González was testified and the infamy of the sin for which she confessed and that even that, having been required to say the truth by Your Reverences many times, that she had not wished to say [anything] except quali-fiedly and excusing herself in a manner that was more seen to deny than confess. And for other indications and causes that moved them to order her put to the question of torture. And to the bailiff Antón de Castilla to [bring] her then to the house where they were accustomed to give the said tortures and putting the said Juana González at the door of the said house she was required to say the truth, and if not they would give her the said torture. And never did she wish to say anything until they began to tie her arms, and then she said that her husband Lope de Herrera had a book of the law of Moses in which was written all the feasts and holidays and fasts for the whole year based on the law, and how to do them and in what manner, and there were prayers in the said law of Moses and that this witness said this following prayer: "He that lives hidden in the height in the shadow of the strong I will sleep and I will say 'Adonay, I live; you are my shelter from punishment and aid'; I trust in Him and in His great mercies [rest of prayer is illegible]." And she told [Juana] that if she stopped saying this prayer that she would be deserted. She was called Aldonza Rodríguez, first wife of Alvar López of Alía. And that when she could she used to say sometimes *"en vuas cucuos cados cados adonay sabaoth"*[1] because whoever says it will be saved. And that she gained many days that would be lost. And that this was shown to her and said by Juana Ruiz wife of Rodrigo Alonso of the beehives. And also she said that this witness showed Ínes Sánchez the *bachillera* this aforementioned prayer she came to know, "He that lives in the covering of the High, etc." And her hands being tied she said about the pots that she had burned, that it was true what the witness had said, that it was because of the lard that had fallen in them. And also the spoon. And also the alms she had asked were according to this accusation and deposi-tion of the witnesses saying *çedaca*, and that she had asked it for three old women, two Old Christians and one conversa. Also she said that Lope de

---

[1] [uncertain] qadosh qadosh Adonay Tsevaot; "[uncertain] holy, holy is the Lord of Hosts." This appears to be from the Kedushah (sanctus) doxology from the Amidah prayer. My thanks to Elka Klein for her thoughts on this passage.

Herrera her husband is a great Jew because many times she had words with him saying to him that she did not want two laws in her house and this because he kept the law of Moses, her aforementioned husband. And that how much her said husband knew and did of the law of Moses, which he would show but he is dead. (10v) And being put on the *escalera* before giving her any water she said that she held the law of Moses before she reconciled, not believing the Messiah promised in the law to have come, nor less that the crucified Christ was in the consecrated Host that is raised on the altar, nor less that [illegible] the Virgin Mary was a virgin before or during the birth, nor after the birth. Nor less did she believe that Christ had been received as the Son of God [illegible] the Passion for us other sinners to save, that He is God and also that when she held this bad law and sentence she did not [missing] that the baptism, taking advantage of the children and people that they be baptized [missing]. Also she said that she kept all the Sabbaths until two or three years ago and that she reconciled after this. [Then] she asked that they untie her and let her go. And that she had told the whole truth of what she knew and had done. And then she was untied and released from the *escalera* with protestation that if what she said proved true, and also if she confessed, where they would not continue the torture, and that it [the torture] was considered not given.

¶ On 16 November Juana González wife of Lope de Herrera was brought by the bailiff Antón de Castilla before the Lord Doctor inquisitor at which [time] was read to her the confession that she had given and said at the time that she had been put to torture (which is above). And being asked if that was the truth and if she would ratify it, she said that in regards to the prayer about "being covered," that it is true that she knew it, and that she thought that she had reconciled it and asked penitence for it. And that in regard to what she said that her sister had shown it to her, that this is not true, but that Beatriz González, the first wife of Ruy González, brother of this witness, had shown it to her. And [illegible] that she knew it but that she did not say it and that it is true that she showed this prayer to her sister Ínes Sánchez, wife of the *bachiller*. And that in regard to the said pots: in arriving at the fire, that she snatched it from his hand and gave him another pot since he had the spoon with which she skimmed her pot. And that in that which she said of Pedro González scrivener, deceased, that he had shown her husband, was that he had [illegible] her husband a book of Hebrew prayers. And he told him that the Messiah had not come, that he said it under torture. And that of the sacrament of the altar and of the virginity of Our Lady: that she held it and that she had no doubt about it. And that in regard to the baptism of her children, that she always held it and believed it. And about Saturdays, that she never observed them completely, that if she left off spinning, because it was too much work to do, (11r) still that she did other work. And I swear to say the truth about this as about other people that I remember. And that she [Juana González] always held that the Holy Catholic faith was true and that one day of the Great Fast [Yom Kippur] that she saw her father and mother, that they fasted, not finishing until night, and that this witness kissed his hand and he put it on her head to bless her that day. That for all this I ask penitence.

On 19 November 1485, the Reverend Lords inquisitors being together in the hall where they are accustomed to hold their audience, at the hour of the afternoon, they ordered their bailiff Antón de Castilla to bring from prison, where she was being held, Juana González, wife of Lope de Herrera, before them, who then by the said bailiff was brought. And being present before the said Lords inquisitors and the *bachiller* Diego Fernández her prosecutor, they said and pronounced this sentence that follows (witnesses the *licenciado* Cristobal de Loaysa and the *licenciado* Juste de Loaysa): Having seen a case before us without Nuño de Arévalo prior of this friary of Santa María de Guadalupe, that was handled and pending between our prosecutor and Juana González wife of Lope de Herrera, citizen of this town of Guadalupe, regarding an accusation attempted against her, in which it said that in addition to the cases of heresy that she falsely confessed when she reconciled, that she had done and committed the following: that she had asked alms for conversos saying *çedaca* as the Jews say. And that she did not pray the *Pater Noster* or *Ave Maria* when she was in church, but that she said "give me, Lord, that which you promised me," and that she consented to circumcise her son; and that after she reconciled she put her pots in the fire (because in them lard had been cooked) to observe the law of Moses that prohibits eating the said lard. For which things [illegible] in offense of our Christian law, she was asked to be declared a heretic and relaxed to the secular arm and to be done above all in accord with justice. And having seen how the said Juana González, responding to the accusation, denies all that is contained in it, and how her exceptions were put to the test as the said prosecutor in his accusation [illegible], and his depositions were published and accounted all the other that they wanted to say and allege until they concluded, and how after the conclusion done in this trial, the said Juana González was asked by us and confessed certain things under torture, and how she ratified some of them in her confession and others denied. Having overall our accord and deliberation with the *letrados* following their accord and counsel,

WE FIND the accusation attempted by the said prosecutor against the said Juana González not proved nor was proven as according to law (11v) it should be to follow the condemnation asked by the said prosecutor, to the end that we absolve her of the accusation because of the pronouncement made on the part of the prosecutor. This trial redounded to infamy and suspicion against the said Juana González, and also because she confessed that she knew the prayer that begins "of the covering" and others that begin "*cados*" and that this she had shown to Ínez Sánchez: In pain and penitence of all this, wanting no [missing] to have with her benignly, but to follow the [illegible] ordered that shortly she be exiled, and we exile her perpetually from this town and its surrounding countryside to ten leagues, and that within nine days she comply with the said exile and that now nor in any time go against this under penalty of perpetual imprisonment and given our sentence, so we sentence her in these respects and for them [missing].

[signed] Francisco Doctor   Pedro Licenciado

¶ This was read by the said Lord Doctor inquisitor in the presence of the aforementioned, they consented to it and obeyed. Witnesses the said Luis Sánchez [illegible]

INDEX

Alfonso XI, 17, 19, 34.
Alonso de Oropesa, OSH, 46–49, 113–117, 119–120, 124, 141, 204, 218–219, 222.
Alonso the teacher, 105, 183.
Arévalo, fray Nuño de, OSH. *See* Nuño de Arévalo, OSH.
assimilation, 4, 88, 90–91, 94, 97, 99–104, 107, 109, 113, 115, 121, 124, 131, 201, 234, 259.
auto de fe, 28, 60, 85, 123, 157, 166, 168–169, 171, 173–178, 196–197, 217, 261.
ayuntamiento, 127, 129, 137, 243, 245–247.

bailiff (*alguacil*), 35, 43–44, 125, 129, 134, 136, 151, 165.
baptism, 71, 74, 103, 186, 198. *See also* unbaptism.
Berzocana, 31–32.
books, 59–60, 84–85, 173–174, 178, 203, 210, 222, 264, 273–275.
Burgos the Elder, fray Diego de, OSH. *See* Diego de Burgos the Elder.

Cañamero, 13, 17, 33, 239.
Cervantes, Miguel de, 14n.2, 18.
Chancillería, 245–250.
Charles V, 203, 246, 249, 251.
circumcision, 71–73, 81, 115, 191–192, 212–213, 217, 265–271, 275.
civil war, Castilian, 111, 137, 251, 262.
Columbus, Christopher, 2, 225.
confessors, 36, 206, 215, 220–221, 235, 237.
confraternities, 3, 81–84, 226.
conversos, 37–38, 46, 48–49, 54, 60–61, 63–64, 68–72, 77, 80, 83, 86, 88, 90–92, 182–184, 188, 226, 238; attacks against, 48, 109; diverse religious practices of, 194; economic role of, 121, 170, 220, 237; hostility toward by Old Christians, 112, 115, 122, 125–127, 131–132; inquisitorial accusations

against, 50–52; political role of, 226; population of, 3, 38–39; relations of Jeronymites with, 111, 114–116, 124, 126, 128, 140, 170, 219–221, 236, 261; relations of Old Christians with, 46–49, 94–99, 111, 116, 119, 174, 260; servants of, 54, 56, 69–70, 98, 160, 162, 186, 189–190, 234. *See also* Jeronymites.
Córdoba, Alonso de, 123, 133, 136–137, 140–141, 155, 221, 240.

defense attorney (*letrado*), 150, 157–159, 161, 163, 165, 168, 178, 185–187, 190, 193, 195, 265, 273.
devotio moderna, 20, 202.
Diego de Burgos the Elder, OSH, 201, 209–210, 213–215, 217, 219, 236.
Diego de Ecija, OSH, 145, 198, 207–208, 221, 234, 236.
Diego de Marchena, OSH, 67, 85, 106–107, 118–120, 178, 198–199, 201, 209, 211–217, 220, 236.
Diego de París, OSH, 77, 103, 107, 121–124, 127–128, 130–132, 135–136, 139–140, 142, 225, 250.

Ecija, fray Diego de, OSH. *See* Diego de Ecija, OSH.
Enrique II Trastámara, 19.
Enrique III, 39.
Enrique IV, 48, 114–117, 204, 251.
Escorial, 29, 203, 228.
Espina, Alonso de, OFM, 114.
exile, 108, 157, 169–172, 178, 183, 196, 233–235, 237–239, 275.

fasts, 66–67, 86–87, 100, 105.
Fernando of Aragon, king, 23, 98, 111, 112, 131, 142–143, 173, 225, 235, 237, 241, 246, 248, 251–254, 256, 261–262.
Fernando de Ubeda, OSH, 131–142, 185, 216, 219, 221, 236, 250, 261.